The Shape of Scrip

M000248977

Publication of this book and the SAR seminar from which it resulted were made possible with the generous support of the Paloheimo Foundation and The Brown Foundation, Inc., of Houston, Texas.

**School for Advanced Research
Advanced Seminar Series**

James F. Brooks
General Editor

The Shape of Script

Contributors

John Baines
The Oriental Institute, Oxford University

John Bodel
Department of Classics, Brown University

Stephen Chrisomalis
Department of Anthropology, Wayne State University

Beatrice Gruendler
Department of Near Eastern Languages and Civilizations, Yale University

Stephen D. Houston
Department of Anthropology, Brown University

David B. Lurie
Department of East Asian Languages and Literatures, Columbia University

John Monaghan
Department of Anthropology, University of Illinois at Chicago

Richard Salomon
Department of Asian Languages and Literature, University of Washington

Kyle Steinke
Department of Art and Archaeology, Princeton University

Niek Veldhuis
Department of Near Eastern Studies, University of California, Berkeley

The Shape of Script
How and Why Writing Systems Change

Edited by Stephen D. Houston

SAR
PRESS

School for Advanced Research Press
Santa Fe

School for Advanced Research Press
Post Office Box 2188
Santa Fe, New Mexico 87504-2188
www.sarpress.sarweb.org

Managing Editor: Lisa Pacheco
Editorial Assistant: Ellen Goldberg
Designer and Production Manager: Cynthia Dyer
Manuscript Editor: Catherine Cocks
Proofreader: Kate Whelan
Indexer: Margaret Moore Booker
Printer: Versa Press, Inc.

Library of Congress Cataloging-in-Publication Data

The shape of script : how and why writing systems change / edited
by Stephen D. Houston. — 1st ed. 2012.
    p. cm. — (Advanced seminar series)
  Includes bibliographical references and index.
  ISBN 978-1-934691-42-7 (alk. paper)
  1. Paleography. 2. Writing—History. I. Houston, Stephen D.
  Z105.S257 2012
  411'.7—dc22

                          2010052607

♻ This book was printed on paper containing 30% PCW. FSC certified.

Cover illustration: *Top left: Xiaozi X you,* inscription in the lid. Photo courtesy Kyle Steinke.
Bottom left: Top section of the painted wooden coffin of Sebekaa, Berlin, Ägyptisches Museum
45. Twelfth Dynasty, Egypt. Paler signs in the copy are inscribed in red. (After Lepsius
1867:Plate 41.) *Right:* Latin inscription with cursive Roman numeral for 556, seen at the
end of line 5. (Mallon 1948:Plate I.)

For Carol Salomon (1948–2009),

cherished explorer of language

Contents

Figures

Tables

Preface

The Shape of Script—Views from the Middle

Stephen D. Houston

> The middle is not discordant with the beginning, nor the end
> with the middle.
>
> *Horace,* Ars Poetica, *lines 147–148 (trans. H. R. Fairclough)*

One of the main misconceptions about writing is that a particular system of script comes into existence, remains the same, and then "dies." A student learns Maya writing or Chinese script, a scholar researches the nature of cuneiform, and it is presumed that systems of writing retain an integrity throughout their existence. Pedagogically, this approach works. It allows the student to navigate around interpretive complexities best left for specialists. But at the same time, it dehistoricizes systems of writing and sets them apart from human input and intention. We know now that scripts exist as fluid sets of practices, shifting in response to changing historical circumstances, conditions of learning, and arenas of patronage and use. To think otherwise is to fall into the "synoptic fallacy," in which a system, though continuous through time, comes also to be seen as synchronically fixed (see Houston, chapter 8, this volume). This act of temporal leveling and analytical erasure leads to the mistaken perception of script "as homogeneous, its internal variation disregarded" (Irvine and Gal 2000:38, writing with respect to language). The stakes are elevated by the centrality of writing to most complex forms of human organization. Script—defined here as linked intrinsically to records of language—is, for some, a focal expression and disseminator of zeitgeist; it accords with the formation and consolidation of ethnic or group identity and operates, along with memory and strands of oral transmission, as a central tool of information storage.

This volume, resulting from an advanced seminar generously hosted by the School for Advanced Research, addresses how and why writing systems change. It builds on two projects that I supervised and edited (or coedited) on the origins and extinction of script traditions (Baines et al. 2008; Houston, ed. 2004; see also Houston et al. 2003). The impetus for the book arises in part, too, from a summary statement about the "archaeology of communication technologies" commissioned by the *Annual Review* series (Houston 2004c). For me, the SAR seminar and its ensuing publication represent a capstone to a long-term study of past writing systems. This project has been possible only because of necessary collaboration with specialists from related, scripturally focused disciplines (see below).

As a guiding framework, the book adopts what Brian Street has called the "ideological model of literacy" (1993:4; also Basso 1989), an approach that sees writing less as a technology than as a mode of communication, socially learned and culturally shaped or transmitted. To be sure, as a word, "ideological" conveys a certain blunt, driven desire for social control. Michael Silverstein (1979:193) and Judith Irvine's (1989:255) views of ideology are more consistent with those of this volume, in that their formulations funnel down to the beliefs about what language and script are and what they do, according to those who use or perceive them—the proviso here being, naturally, that antiquity and loss make direct elicitation of such beliefs difficult for most of the contributors to this volume. Our access comes largely through cautious inference, excepting fully fleshed-out cases such as Arabic script or Japanese (in this volume, Beatrice Gruendler, chapter 4, and David Lurie, chapter 7). Street was well on target, however, in stressing that scripts flourish or wither in social settings, with meanings and performative activations that extend beyond the contents of writing (e.g., Monaghan 1990). His approach has been doubly helpful in that it frames changes in script as historically unique conjunctures and as exemplifications of shared human processes. Neither achieves intelligibility without the other.

Street and his colleagues have been less attentive to the detail that scripts are objects or materializations that intersect with systems of aesthetics and craft production. Scripts may also accord with local theories of reified, sacred meaning, as in Egypt and Mesoamerica (e.g., Assmann 1994). Nor have Street and his associates addressed the conditions of language change and diglossia (e.g., Hudson 1992), the condition in which several languages are used at one time, some with higher levels of prestige

(Houston et al. 2000b). A final, unavoidable difficulty stems from the task of discerning the multiple varieties of script ideology at any one time, that is, the variant views that seem to splinter according to sectional groups in society (Kroskrity 2000:12). These dimensions of belief and attitude involve subtleties beyond the range of much ancient evidence.

Scholars are close to conceptualizing how scripts emerge and pass into obsolescence. In the case of the former, we have found that the initial functions tend to be limited and fuller linguistic articulation often comes after a long initial period of development. In the case of the latter, demographic collapse or the withering of "complex cultural systems" and attenuation of their functions sign the death warrant for weakening script traditions; nonetheless, writing can show remarkable resilience, especially in its bonds to language (Baines 2008:354, 357–359; Houston 2004d:350–352). But we are still far from explaining how scripts maintain themselves over time or how and why scripts change when they do, during their "middle years." My opening epigram, a quotation from a poem about historical exposition, asserts that the middle may not be discordant with the beginning or end. By an old adage, the child is father to the man, mother to the woman. Within an elderly human nestles the relict infant. Yet, these states and stages are not the same. In scholarship, there is rough monitoring of paleographical modifications but little attempt comparatively to understand the selective processes behind such transformations. This is a gap that needs to be filled. Writing is one of the central cultural productions in human history, yet its many modulations and shifts seem often to be taken for granted, as if they do not need explanation. This book enables anthropologists, philologists, and archaeologists to revisit a key form of communication that channels and conditions most discourse in complex societies. The study of writing needs to be brought back into the fold of anthropology, not as a marginal or recondite specialty but because it is an indispensable tool by which knowledge is transmitted.

THE MOTIVATION FOR THE SEMINAR

The guidelines for applications to the SAR advanced seminar program ask, "Why a seminar, why now?" As suggested above, prior experience suggests that the depth and richness of information about scripts are such that no one person can master the evidence. Comparative studies need regional experts to succeed, provided that a similar vocabulary and set of questions can be found and shared. For the seminar, these terms and concepts were laid out in advance through circulated memoranda and were reinforced or reworked in subsequent communications among the participants. Most approaches to writing have been piecemeal, with brief encyclopedic sketches, as in Peter Daniels and William Bright's *The World's Writing Systems* (1996) or Florian Coulmas' varied work (e.g., Coulmas 1989). In my view, further summations of this sort are not needed, no matter how wide-ranging. Instead, we should isolate and evaluate the individual settings and meanings of script change as a joint effort to encourage debate. Fresh evidence is available from much of the ancient world; many scholars have become intrigued, across disciplines, by the general nature of graphic notations of language. We are ready to talk.

QUESTIONS TO BE ADDRESSED

The book seeks to understand the social (interactional), cultural (semantic), and historical (sequential) forces that influence the course of writing systems. It focuses broadly on issues of transmission from one generation to another or the conscious decisions by which changes occur, along with the kinds of people implicated in a script's use or reception. More specifically, it asks the following questions:

- What processes affect the formal change of script?
- What influences the use of script over time?
- What agents or actors are involved in such shifts, either actively or passively?
- How is literacy achieved, furthered, or deliberately restricted?
- How do script use and aesthetics shape each other?
- What influence do technologies have on script form?
- What relation, archaizing or contrastive, do scripts have with precursors and alternative systems at hand?
- What do formal, paleographic approaches tell us about more general developments at work in script?
- What are the links between images and script?

Some questions draw more interest than others, as became clear during the seminar and in later reworking of the papers.

WRITING > TALK > WRITING

For five and half days, from April 15 through April 19, 2007, the technology of script production led to a specific set of manipulations within a "cursive" tradition that prized rapidity of writing. The theme of change through production resonated with some other participants, as witnessed by recurrent discussion in Santa Fe about the lack of cursivization (ligatured signs whose shape is propelled by rapid, efficient execution) that seemed to obtain in certain scripts, Mesoamerican ones in particular. As McCarter pointed out, inertial tendencies in early Hebrew seem to have disallowed some of this cursivization.

In chapter 4, Beatrice Gruendler looks closely at the effects of language and local concepts of language on Arabic script. She shows that an emphasis on vowels existed from the outset, that the prestige and abundance of Arabic language affected use of the script for writing other languages, and that oral performance continued to play a strong role. However, the script sometimes failed to exhibit close familiarity with linguistic elements of Arabic, especially in the matter of case endings. The script was flexible enough to conceal those "shortcomings" in a way that would bolster rather than fragment a community of faith. More than the other chapters in this volume, Gruendler's discloses the degrees to which users of script fretted about these matters, about the "right and wrong of linguistic usage" (chapter 4, this volume) and the problem of confronting the disengagement between sacred word and colloquial expression— between, in her words, "oral performance and increasing written text."

In an essay of generalizing intent (chapter 5, this volume), Richard Salomon examines script change from two vantages, that of formal change and a systemic, deeper level of such change. The wide cross-citation of this analytical distinction in other chapters indicates that it resonated with our working group. Salomon argues that formal changes—in stylus, stroke rendering, or degree of "economization"—often occured gradually, in an unconscious or unintended fashion. More sweeping changes required stronger, exceptional (if sporadic) forces, particularly when a script was recruited to record an unrelated language. One such example was the shift in Aramaic script after its adoption by speakers of South Asian languages.

In discussing Chinese, Kyle Steinke focuses on a critique of two theories of script development. The first is that of William Boltz (1994), who invoked a notion of a "Chinese worldview-based ethical order" as a mechanistic explanation for change. The second is that of Qiu Xigui (2000), for whom script change occurs as a scribal response to the need for greater efficiency in writing. Steinke is dissatisfied with Boltz's theory. He supports a perspective that balances Qiu's notion of efficient script change ("short-cuts") with a consideration of script changes motivated by the writing's display function, as when artist-scribes accented aesthetic features without sole regard for efficiency. The chapter echoes Bodel's appeal for greater attention to, in Steinke's words, forms "designed for beauty" (chapter 6, this volume). His other proposal is that such calligraphic products "mattered...to the state."

For David Lurie's part, he stresses both the difficult borrowings that characterized the adaptation of Japanese script from the Chinese system and the continuing emphasis in Japanese on logography or word-signs. Phonography, records of sound alone, had come into existence at a relatively early date. It had some impact in extending the use of writing, permitting, as he puts it, the appearance of "expressive effects" (chapter 7, this volume). Like all participants, Lurie draws attention to internal, mechanistic changes in script production, those resulting from the use of brush or print, but also "metalinguistic discourses" about the perceived role of script and its interpretive dependence on context. These comments sit well with the discourses and "anti-barbarism" treatises that Gruendler discusses. Along with Bodel and Steinke, Lurie insists that "writing goes beyond the transcription of speech sounds."

The two chapters on Mesoamerica (8 and 9) share a predilection for social and contextual explanation. I review prior studies of script change in Maya glyphic writing and target "domains" of change (Houston, chapter 8, this volume) that include execution, transmission through guided participation in multiauthored works, and motivation. To explain episodic, non-gradual shifts, I posit "bottlenecks" or "founders' effects." In these, dramatic changes in society truncate the store of glyphic knowledge and result in major alterations to the signary. The greatest shifts took place at the end of Preclassic civilization, a time of profound demographic relocation and, in places, population decline. By the Late Classic period, beginning about 500 CE, a single polity centered on the city of Calakmul, Mexico, began to exercise a hegemonic sway, triggering the production of new signs and the reinterpretation of old ones. In the same period, a novel attitude towards writing materialized in the form of "pseudo-glyphs." These glyph-like elements fulfilled the same display role as writing yet by definition failed to share in its content. Conceivably, the appearance of pseudo-glyphs came from heightened diglossia, especially the splits between speech and writing, along with the relaxation of sumptuary practices that had hitherto restricted the use of writing. There may even have been a new, more inclusive notion of what script is and was.

In a similar vein, Monaghan presents his work (chapter 9) on the use of Mixtec and central Mexican script within social settings that demanded, over time, differing functions from script. Alphabetic and pictorial registers might coexist, but they conveyed different assertions about identity and links to the past. The backward-looking curiosity in Mesoamerica—in fact, a deeply felt fervor—underscores the need in some script traditions to reabsorb past practices and to highlight them in a marked manner as renovated norms, as the old that is new, the new that is old. Monaghan makes a more general argument that the systemic shifts detected by Salomon may well have taken place in periods of major disruptions, such as state reorganization or the turbulence that accompanies colonization.

In Chrisomalis's study of numbers, he decries the excessively unilineal, evolutionary quality in most claims about change in numerical notation (chapter 10; see also his magisterial synthesis, Chrisomalis 2010). Actual change in such systems appears to have been rare, although with a perceptible increase of positional systems over additive ones during the past 5,500 years. From 1500 BCE on, variant systems declined with the growth of imperial, "globalizing," and overarching economic systems. A general trend from cumulative and additive systems to positional and ciphered ones does not belie his main point, that these shifts take place for "a complex combination of cognitive, sociopolitical, and cultural factors" (chapter 10, this volume). Numeration will never reach an "end of history" or settle into final, perfect form.

In sum, the chapters identify joint themes, some well addressed, others not completely resolved: (1) the need to avoid concepts of telos or inevitability in script change yet to balance this wish against the recognition of the role of precedents in channeling subsequent shifts; (2) the desirability of devising typologies of change that reflect contact between languages and script traditions; (3) the central nature of cursive "technologies" or "fast writing," with consequent simplification and other forms of problem solving; (4) the decisive clues afforded by the rhythm of change and the possibility of random processes, akin to evolutionary "drift," some changes being random, others strongly motivated; (5) the role played by social differentiation of script, with close attention to practitioners and users; (6) the questions of why script change fails or achieves force and acceptance and why some registers affect others; and (7) the influence of aesthetics, display, and other external functions on script change. The themes play out in conversation between the chapters, especially with respect to labels that need further review and definition, as in "simplification," "efficiency," "cursive," legibility," "register." The nature of conservatism and resuscitations of earlier forms commanded interest, too, yet require more delineation.

As Chrisomalis doubts an "end of history" for numeration, it is certain that these conversations and explorations have no end. They will and must continue. Whether they should be molded by semiotic or structural theories of analogy, displacement, oppositional stratagems, or ethnogenesis (Irvine and Gal's "fractal recursivity" [2000:38]) may be questions that are too sweeping or vague for some of the participants. They feel the pull of specific examples conditioned by culture, history, and society. A greater level of abstraction could systematize comparison; it could also disinvite those who belong in this dialogue but see little benefit to theories unmoored from context or historical setting. There do appear to be credible generalizations, however: that the fuller embrace of language and its manifold expressions forms part of the "middle" years of most scripts (the Maya case sees this expansion quite late); that a full range of genres develops slowly, with consequences for the shape of script; that broad institutional and political shifts trigger momentous change in script more often than not; that, conversely, close monopolization of writing and its forms tends to be unsustainable in the long term; that changes in the relationship between spoken and written language occasion the most careful attention to the nuances of writing; and that practice, execution, order, and an attachment to precedent repeal and restrain the more unruly experiments in the history of script. Even this: the "shape" of script has its own levels of analysis, from its minute constituents to its macro-setting on a temple wall or its position within community and cosmos. These levels deserve systematic review in each case of script development. The quantity of texts, users, and makers, or special diffusion of the same, may have affected the shape of script as well, but that is hard to gauge on present evidence. A banal but valid comment: an opaque text, made more recondite by script, is by its nature obscure and accessible to few; a text designed to be accessible, by form and content, will attain broader readership. But above all, a script takes shape because someone feels a need for it to look and read a certain way. The maker and user behind writing hold the keys to understanding formal and substantive change.

This volume has taken shape over a long and productive gestation. For their invitation to create this book, their sustained interest, and, above all, their patience for the eventual result gathered here, there can be only gratitude to the president of SAR, James F. Brooks, Vice President John Kantner, then Director of Scholar Programs Nancy Owen Lewis, Leslie Shipman, hostess and chef extraordinaire, and Catherine Cocks, then executive editor of SAR Press, along with Lynn Thompson Baca, current director of the Press, and Lisa Pacheco, the managing editor. Catherine also did a meticulous job with copyediting, to our great benefit. John Baines, a good friend always, gave suggestions for improved wording. Cassandra Mesick performed her customary miracles with initial copyediting. To them, we raise a collective toast of good vintage, in gratitude for a week of intellectual discovery and fellowship and for an opportunity to examine the middle years of past writing.

The Shape of Script

1

Cuneiform

Changes and Developments

Niek Veldhuis

The cuneiform writing system was invented in the south of present Iraq around 3200 BCE and was used continuously for a period of more than three millennia. Because of its long and well-documented history, cuneiform provides numerous interesting case studies in how and why writing systems change. In this chapter I discuss three such changes, each with its own motivation and historical background. Regular developments of the system include adaptations to different languages or genres, as well as random changes in the form and use of cuneiform signs over the centuries. These kinds of developments are usually well documented and well known to specialists; a few of them are illustrated in the first section of this chapter. The administrative reforms of the king Šu-Su'en (ca. 2035 BCE) indirectly caused a very different type of change through the relocation of individuals who brought with them alternative writing conventions. A very broad change, a revolution in writing, took place around 2000 BCE. In this period, writing lost its almost exclusive link to officialdom, resulting in a broad array of changes in the form, function, and social location of writing.

The changes in cuneiform writing discussed in this chapter involve not only the shape of the symbols, or their logographic and syllabographic values, but also the people who employed this writing system and their needs.

Deterministic theories predicting that a writing system will evolve toward greater efficiency or toward a more phonemic representation of the linguistic message are a bad fit for explaining the kinds of changes that the cuneiform record attests to. Writing partakes of the complex structure of a society; it defines the social place of those who use it as scholars, scribes, readers, or uninitiated bystanders.

REGULAR DEVELOPMENTS

Cuneiform writing was introduced in the south of Babylonia at the end of the Uruk period (around 3200 BCE). The period is characterized by strong urbanization and increased societal complexity. The city of Uruk grew to an unprecedented size of some 100 hectares, dominated by monumental temple buildings and surrounded by a system of smaller settlements. The temples played an important role in the exchange of goods, necessitated by the division of labor that accompanied urbanization. It is in this context that record keeping developed into writing.

The nature of the archaic writing system has been much clarified in the past two decades, in particular through the efforts of Hans Nissen and Robert Englund (see, most importantly, Englund 1998). It is, in essence, an administrative system and does not directly represent a spoken language of any kind. Although some signs depict recognizable animals, body parts, or objects, they are thoroughly conventionalized and do not qualify as "pictograms," strictly speaking. The archaic signs are capable of recording commodities, professional titles, and a variety of metrological systems. The texts do not record administrative events in a narrative fashion but use the layout of the tablet (columns, obverse and reverse) to indicate the relationships among items, totals, and persons involved (see Green 1981). In this respect, archaic cuneiform (at least in the more complex accounts) is more like a modern spreadsheet than a modern writing system. Because the writing system does not encode sentences, identifying which language is represented can be difficult. The individual signs that signify "sheep," "beer," or "administrator" could in theory be read in any language. Most Assyriolo-gists agree that the underlying language was probably Sumerian, the language of Southern Babylonia in the third millennium BCE. It is significant, however, that Robert Englund, widely recognized as the world expert on the archaic corpus, does not share this conviction and holds that Sumerian was probably introduced to Southern Babylonia after the end of the fourth millennium (Englund 1998:73–81). Although this controversy may not be settled anytime soon, it is important to note that the identification of the language of the late Uruk texts does not influence in any way our understanding of the archaic texts or the workings of the early writing system.

Archaic writing was intimately related to the societal and administrative complexity of the late Uruk period. The inventories of signs (enumerated in so-called lexical lists) reflect the kinds of commodities that were recorded and the titles of officials who were known at the time and who were (or might be) involved in transactions that required recording (Veldhuis 2006). Perhaps the most extraordinary aspect of archaic cuneiform is its survival after the collapse of late Uruk society. The system was well documented in the lexical lists and apparently flexible enough to survive drastic societal changes.

We know little about the history of cuneiform in the period between 3200 and 2700 BCE. By this time the system was capable of recording sentences, including verbs, and morphology through syllable signs. On the more formal level, all curved lines had been replaced by straight strokes and all signs had become abstract.

Two structural changes that took place during the course of the third millennium gradually allowed the writing system to represent sentences and connected text. First, the introduction of syllabic signs made it possible to provide lexemes with the morphological elements they need to produce grammatical sentences in Sumerian. It is possible that syllabography of some sort was part of the system from the outset (this is a point still debated). However, its widespread use for representing morphology is certainly a third-millennium innovation. Through most of that period, bound morphemes in Sumerian were written sparingly, even when the system had acquired the capability of writing them all. It is only in the early second millennium that full representation of verbal and nominal morphology becomes the norm. This change may be nicely illustrated by one of the few Sumerian compositions that is known in exemplars dating to different phases in this development. The earliest copies of the Instructions of Šuruppak come from the middle of the third millennium and only rarely represent morphological elements. Old Babylonian copies of the same composition (around 1800 BCE) render the same sayings in a much fuller orthography:

gan$_2$ kaskal na-ĝa$_2$-ĝa$_2$ (Adab, about 2500 BCE)
gan$_2$ kaskal-la nam-bi$_2$-ib-ĝa$_2$-ĝa$_2$ (about 1800 BCE)
"Do not cultivate a field on the road."[1]

The late orthography explicitly indicates the locative /a/ (written -la) on the word for "road" (*kaskal*) and cross-references the object of the verb immediately before the verbal root (this is the element /b/ preceding -ĝa₂-ĝa₂). The morphemes that tie the individual words into a sentence were probably there in the mid-third-millennium version of the saying; the writing system had the capability of expressing them, but it was not deemed necessary to do so. By the Old Babylonian period, however, Sumerian had become a scribal language, one that was nobody's mother tongue, and thus the explicit morphology was needed for comprehension.

Second, the introduction of an obligatory sign order around the middle of the third millennium created a straightforward iconic relationship between the visual text and its aural representation. Early third-millennium texts are written in columns, with each column divided into cases. Each case usually contains a single word, but the placement of the signs within the case is free. Around the middle of the third millennium, the order of signs within a case or line reflects the correct linguistic order of the lexemes and morphemes they represent.

During the third millennium the cuneiform writing system had thus developed into a device that was capable of recording the Sumerian language through a mix of word signs (logograms) and syllable signs (syllabograms). Although the inventory of signs changed over time (mainly through splits and mergers), the number of distinct signs always remained at a modest level (about 600 to 1,000), and almost every sign had various logographic and syllabographic values (see also Krebernik 1998).

Before the middle of the third millennium, scribes in Northern Babylonia started to write Akkadian, a Semitic language, in cuneiform. Initially, the writing system hardly changed—the same logographic signs were simply read in another language. As a result it is occasionally hard to judge whether a text is in Akkadian or Sumerian, even though the two languages are very different in grammatical structure, vocabulary, morphology, and phonemics (Rubio 2006, with earlier literature). Over time, however, Akkadian writing introduced many new syllabic readings and other changes in the use of the cuneiform symbols. The sign SAĜ, for instance, originally a depiction of a head (Sumerian saĝ), was employed in Middle Babylonian and later Akkadian with the syllabic value riš, as in šam-riš, "violently." The value riš is derived from the Akkadian word for "head," rēšu, which may be written with the logograph SAĜ.

The sign inventory for Sumerian and Akkadian was more or less the same at any period of time, although the way these signs were used could be very different. The syllabic value riš (SAĜ), for instance, was never used in Sumerian of any period. Akkadian orthography was much more flexible than Sumerian. Almost any given word could be written logographically, in syllables, or in a combination of both, as the following example demonstrates. The term *šarru* (the nominative form of "king") may be written:

LUGAL   logographic
šar-ru   syllabographic
LUGAL^{ru} combined

These three writings are equivalent and may be found as variants in duplicate manuscripts of the same composition. In the third writing, the syllable *-ru* indicates that the logograph LUGAL represents the nominative form of the word *šarru* (rather than genitive *šarri* or accusative *šarra*). Although these three were probably the most common ways to write *šarru*, there are, in fact, numerous other logographs and syllabographs that were used to write the Akkadian word. In contrast, Sumerian *lugal* (king) was virtually always written with the sign LUGAL.

The flexibility of Akkadian writing and the wide range of choices that it presented led to the development of various chronologically, geographically, and generically defined sets of conventions. Thus, the Old Assyrian letters from Kaniš (a colony of Assyrian traders in present-day Anatolia) in about 1900 BCE used a restricted set of logographs (representing very common words, such as E$_2$ = *bētum* "house") and were otherwise entirely written syllabically, with little room for choice between alternate signs. Applying the same basic system, Old Babylonian texts from about the same period used a wider range of logograms and a different set of syllable signs, with much more choice between homographs.

Over the millennia many other languages were written in cuneiform: Hittite, Elamite, Hurrian, and Urartian. In all cases the adoption of this writing system resulted in a more or less rigorous adaptation of it—often resulting in an orthography that used a mix of Sumerian and Akkadian words as logograms, as well as syllabic writing.

Changes in the cuneiform writing system were often bound to a specific genre or class of texts. Perhaps the most extreme example is the body of divination texts. These texts list ominous appearances and their meaning in a highly technical language. Because of their repetitiveness and high level of predictability, they gradually developed their own set of logograms—often new and esoteric inventions that may be understood only by virtue of the strict rules of the genre. Rather than a technical jargon, as in modern specialized literature, these texts display a technical orthography. Although particularly true for divination, specialized orthographies were in fact a widespread phenomenon in cuneiform.

Finally, changes in the form of cuneiform signs may be attributed to writing surfaces. The overwhelming majority of texts were written on clay. Other surfaces on which cuneiform was inscribed were stone, wax boards, and metal. If papyrus, leather, or wood surfaces were used, they did not survive. Although we know that wax boards existed—some have indeed been found—there is little opportunity to compare wax board paleography with clay paleography, and there is perhaps little reason to suspect an important difference. Writing on stone tends to be archaic and monumental because stone was precious and prestigious. Occasionally, stone monuments preserve sign forms and subtle distinctions between signs that properly belong to a much earlier period (see Veldhuis 2008a).

Unlike alphabetic writing, the mixed logographic/syllabographic system allowed for different uses that were more or less scholarly, advanced, or specialized. The Old Assyrian evidence demonstrates that cuneiform could do with a little more than one hundred signs, but in fact such a reduced system is the exception in the history of cuneiform. More intricate uses of the system presumably carried more prestige, and one may observe conscious attempts to add complexity to the system by introducing new sign values or using little-known or obsolete signs. The cuneiform writing system allowed for different orthographic registers, and this flexibility may have been an important reason for its survival after the introduction of alphabetic systems such as Aramaic.

The developments and changes described above belong to the regular life of the cuneiform writing system, adapting to different linguistic, social, and scholarly challenges. Cuneiform was an open-ended system that allowed the introduction of new signs or sign values and that could adapt to new languages without major changes. Although such changes may make the life of modern-day students exceedingly miserable because one has to learn new orthographic rules for every new genre, period, and geographic area, they are not very remarkable by themselves. More remarkable and puzzling are two changes in the system—one small and one big—that are described in the following section.

ORTHOGRAPHIC CHANGES DURING THE UR III DYNASTY

In the third year of Šu-Su'en, the fourth king of the powerful Ur III dynasty, the royal administration went through a number of reforms, including changes in the calendar and administrative terminology and a few detailed ones in orthography.

The Ur III empire (about 2100–2000 BCE) was founded by Urnamma and established as a true empire by his son, Šulgi. Through most of the third millennium, Babylonia consisted of independent city-states that shared cultural and religious characteristics but competed for power and influence. Šulgi made these city-states into provinces of his kingdom and established his rule far to the east and to the north of the traditional Babylonian heartland. Šu-Su'en inherited the empire from his immediate predecessor, Amar-Su'en.

The Ur III period has left tens of thousands of clay tablets, primarily documenting administrative transactions such as the flow of goods through the empire. The largest numbers of documents come from three sites in the heartland: Puzriš-Dagan, Umma, and Ğirsu. The latter two were provincial capitals that had enough independence to use their own calendars; their archives represent the provincial administration. Puzriš-Dagan was a royal administrative center; its records reflect the interests and activities of the state as a whole.

In addition to administrative records, the Ur III period has left us royal inscriptions, often inscribed on bricks used for prestigious building projects. Moreover, a large body of Sumerian literature that is believed to go back in essence (though not in every detail) to Ur III times has been preserved in copies from the Old Babylonian period (ca. 1800 BCE). This literary corpus includes several dozen hymns in praise of the five kings of the Ur III dynasty.

Notwithstanding the enormous mass of evidence, our grasp of social and political developments during the Ur III period is often very limited. The administrative documents simply do not answer the kinds of questions that we would like to ask. Particularly frustrating, in this respect, is the transition in government from Amar-Su'en to Šu-Su'en. Several pieces of data suggest that Šu-Su'en worked hard to erase the memory of his predecessor. The month name "festival of Amar-Su'en," which had been part of the Umma calendar for several years, was replaced by its old name ("two shrines") in Šu-Su'en's third year. At the same time, a festival for Šu-Su'en was introduced in the Puzriš-Dagan calendar, whereas other local calendars did not include either the new month name or festival at any time (Cohen 1993). Amar-Su'en was skipped in the list of recipients of royal offerings, and a temple named after him in Ğirsu returned to its old name. No hymns to Amar-Su'en have been preserved, and he is hardly mentioned in other literature (see Sallaberger 1999a:167).

There are reasons to suspect that, in addition to the calendar reforms, there were important administrative changes in Šu-Su'en year 3, in particular changes related to taxes received by the state (see Sallaberger 1999a: 170). How extensive these changes were and what realities were hidden

TABLE 1.1

Two paleographic innovations

	Before Šu-Su'en 3	After Šu-Su'en 3
adda = carcass		
	LU$_2$xBAD[1]	UDUxBAD
kur = to enter		
	LIL (KWU no. 147)[2]	ŠE.ŠU (KWU no. 636)

1. LU$_2$xBAD is a conventional sign name that means "the sign BAD inscribed inside the sign LU$_2$." Similarly, UDUxBAD, LIL, and ŠE.ŠU are sign names or sign descriptions conventional in Assyriology.

2. KWU refers to Nikolaus Schneider, *Die Keilschriftzeichen der Wirtschaftsurkunden von Ur III* (1935)—still the standard paleography for the period.

behind simple changes in administrative terminology remain hard to establish (no overall attempt has been made so far). What is interesting for our present purposes is that at least two, perhaps three, orthographic changes took place at the same time, as shown in table 1.1 (de Maaijer and Jagersma 1997–1998:280–281; Veldhuis 2008b).

The evidence for *kur* (to enter) and *adda* (carcass) suggests that the introduction of these new writings was sudden at some places but more gradual at others and might have been related to changes in personnel at critical places in the administration.

The change in the writing for *adda* (carcass) can be linked to a single individual named Lukalla, who regularly received carcasses at Puzriš-Dagan. He entered office around the beginning of the year Šu-Su'en 4 and consistently uses the writing UDUxBAD (the sign for SHEEP inscribed with the sign for DEAD), whereas his predecessor, Nūr-Suen, had used LU$_2$xBAD (the sign for MAN inscribed with the sign for DEAD). The new orthography was adopted at Umma a few years later.

The sudden change in the writing of *kur* (to enter) during Šu-Su'en 3 takes place primarily at Puzriš-Dagan.[2] The evidence suggests that the new writing ŠE.ŠU (the sign for GRAIN followed by the sign for HAND) was not so new at all but was the orthography in use at the royal court at Ur. The introduction of this sign use at Puzriš-Dagan most probably represents the replacement of local clerks by trusted servants recruited from the royal court.

The details of a few signs and their distribution are discussed here to illustrate a potential area of research in which politics, administration, and orthography are closely linked. In the period in question, writing was primarily (though not exclusively) a matter of official administration. At the same time, writing is by necessity bound to individuals and traditions of teaching. Thus, we can tie the change in the writing of *adda* (carcass) to a named individual, Lukalla. The influence of high officials on the writing system and its orthography hardly took the form of edicts prescribing the future form of the sign for the word for "to enter." The power to replace clerks or bureaucrats at one place with loyal servants from another, however, is a time-proven tool of government and one that in this situation may well have influenced orthography. It is no coincidence, then, that the writing for *kur* (enter), introduced at Puzriš-Dagan around Šu-Su'en 3, had a history at the royal court of Ur.

The changes in orthography described in the present section take place on a microlevel and are detectable because administrative texts are usually carefully dated and the period in question has a high density of documentation. Although the underlying causes for such changes may be political (as suggested above), the changes themselves are most likely carried out by individuals.

UR III TO OLD BABYLONIAN: A REVOLUTION IN WRITING

A much more drastic change took place between the Ur III period (ca. 2100–2000 BCE) and the Old Babylonian period (ca. 1900–1600 BCE). The collapse of the Ur III empire resulted in a period of political fragmentation in which local dynasties at Uruk, Isin, Larsa, and other places vied for power. It was not until 1760 BCE that Hammurabi of Babylon succeeded in establishing his rule over Southern Mesopotamia, after defeating Elam, Larsa, Ešnunna, and Mari. In comparison with Ur III practices, the Old Babylonian innovations in the writing system include changes in the style of writing (semi-monumental versus cursive), the language of writing (Sumerian versus Akkadian), the uses of writing (official versus private), the teaching of writing (informal versus formal), and the format of some key text types (linear enumeration versus table). These changes are much harder to grasp because much of the documentation is undated (that is, dating takes place primarily through paleography) and many of the changes that will be described took place in a period for which we have little evidence.

Collectively, these changes may be described as a revolution in writing, one that is related to developments in the linguistic landscape (the demise of Sumerian), politics (the fragmentation of Babylonia), and ideology (Sumerian as a symbol of a golden age). Before discussing this revolution and its historical context, we will discuss each of the various aspects of change that took place in this period.

Writing Style

All through the third millennium, cuneiform writing used highly standardized sign forms that are clearly distinguished from each other—even if the difference between one sign and another may reside in some easily overlooked detail. Old Babylonian writing, on the other hand, tends to be crowded, with little care for details. Although the Ur III period yielded tens of thousands (if not hundreds of thousands) of mostly administrative texts, the quantity factor did not lead to a significant trend towards cursive writing, even though the formulaic character of many text types would certainly have allowed competent clerks to read cursive hands confidently and with ease. Each Ur III document is very carefully executed, with sign forms so standardized that no attempts have been made so far to distinguish between individual hands. This Ur III writing style, which may be labeled semi-monumental, is no doubt related to its being a tool of officialdom, an aspect of government.

Although there is a difference between the paleography of Ur III administrative tablets (fig. 1.1) and that of contemporaneous royal inscriptions (primarily on bricks), this difference is minor compared with the variation between the two forms in Old Babylonian and later periods, when royal inscriptions are usually written in archaizing or very archaizing sign forms. Old Babylonian scribes had the opportunity to choose between more or less cursive forms of writing or, to put it otherwise, between different registers of writing (fig. 1.2). Such options were hardly available to Ur III scribes.

Language

Sumerian and Akkadian had existed side by side for several centuries, and both languages, linguistically unrelated, were written in cuneiform on clay tablets. However, throughout most of the third millennium, Sumerian was the dominant written language. To some extent this dominance may be an artifact of the incident of discovery. Akkadian was more at home in the northern part of Babylonia, and Sumerian dominated the southern regions. Large third-millennium text finds come predominantly from southern regions. However, even in Akkadian-speaking areas Sumerian was often used as the language of prestige and government—the opposite was only very rarely the case.

Writing Akkadian, therefore, was not new to the Old Babylonian period, but the extent to which Akkadian was used was new. Sumerian had died out as a spoken language (Sallaberger 2004, with earlier literature), which may well be one, but hardly the only, explanation.

FIGURE 1.1

Ur III tablet from Drehem (Hearst Museum of Anthropology [HMA] 9-2250). The text deals with the payment of a total of 167 sheep to various individuals. Published by Foxvog (1996:74, Text 1). Photograph published online at http://cdli.ucla.edu/P102630.

FIGURE 1.2

Old Babylonian letter (HMA 9-1848); see http://cdli.ucla.edu/P247940. A translation appears later in the chapter.

Several of the new text types in the Old Babylonian period (see below), such as divination compendia, mathematical problem texts, medical hand-books, and royal edicts, were consistently written in Akkadian. Incanta-tions, legal documents, royal inscriptions, law collections, and literary texts existed in both Sumerian and Akkadian. Ritual laments were almost with-out exception written in Sumerian. Perhaps most tellingly, by this period letters were always written in Akkadian, using a style that is much less for-malized or bureaucratic and more persuasive or rhetorical in nature than their Sumerian equivalents from the Ur III period.

The Uses of Writing

The very extensive Ur III text corpus consists primarily of administrative documents, with smaller groups of legal documents, court proceedings, and letters and very few literary or sub-literary texts. Ur III letters (in Sumerian) are short and formal; they usually contain brief instructions from a superior and hardly ever exceed ten lines. A typical Ur III letter reads as follows: "Tell Ur-Šara that he should give one work basket to the messenger of Lukalla, the overseer. The issue should not come up again."[3] The letter follows standard patterns and phraseology, including the final statement of authority. The tablet bears seals all over, emphasizing this authority.

Old Babylonian letters are in Akkadian and are rhetorical in character. Rather than simple instructions, they contain arguments and attempts to persuade. Even letters by the king to a subordinate do not have the quality of simple orders that one expects in Ur III letters but provide arguments and warnings. Administrators wrote letters, but private persons also did so. These messages were very much instruments of business and government—one very rarely reads anything private in the modern sense of the word—but a much more personal sense of involvement transpires through these texts. The number of Old Babylonian letters is very considerable; a recent estimate counted more than 3,000 (Sallaberger 1999b).[4]

The letter illustrated in figure 1.2 (HMA 9-1848)[5] reads as follows:

> Say to Sîn-[...], thus Sîn-magir. May the Sun god keep you alive for 3600 years! When I received your letter I left Maškanšapir and entered Sabum. Rim-Sîn-atpalam came to inspect the troops and he inspected all of them. Thus he said: the city of Tubqum is your encampment....As for the town that I entered, the enemy destroyed its harvest so that the men are hungry. Send me the silver that you have on hand, send it to me, before the grain at the quay falls short, so that I can buy barley and we will not be hungry. By the Sun, you know my case! Speak to the gentleman so that I may come and may meet the gentleman, and he may investigate the matter. Now I have sent to you PN and Silli-[...]. Do not withhold the silver from them. Seal it with your seal and give it to them so that they can bring it here.

The letter refers to incidents in the war between Rim-Sîn of Larsa and Hammurabi of Babylon that would eventually lead to Hammurabi's dominance over the entire area. Rim-Sîn's troops were being moved to Sabum, which might well have been a border garrison.[6] Although many details remain frustratingly unclear, the letter contains a clear plea to send money so that the harvest destroyed by enemy action could be replaced. The letter contains details about the sender's life and circumstances, supporting his plea, and attempts to establish and reinforce the relationship between sender and recipient. The sense of urgency is heightened by the repetition: "Send me the silver, send it to me!" Such elements are common in Old Babylonian letters (Sallaberger 1999b) but almost entirely absent in third-millennium writing.

Letters are only one example of the extraordinary explosion of writing in the Old Babylonian period. Documents such as loans and house and field sales (that is, legal documents of a private character), rare or absent in the Ur III period, became common. In addition, divination experts started to use texts for a variety of purposes (omen compendia, omen reports, liver models with omens, and divination prayers). There is good evidence that divination was practiced extensively in the Ur III period and before, but the use of writing (always in Akkadian) for this purpose was new. Mathematical problem texts are another such area (see Robson 2007, 2008). Although the corpus is not very large, it is significant because, despite a vocabulary that is heavy with Sumerian loanwords and despite the strong association between Sumerian and high culture, these texts are always written in Akkadian.

Sumerian literature derives almost in its entirety from Old Babylonian scribal schools, and the first sizable corpus of literary texts in Akkadian dates to this period as well. Various other text genres might be mentioned here, medical texts and royal edicts, for instance.

Official use of writing by the administration did not stop in the Old Babylonian period. The period has yielded only one palace archive (Mari), but this one example makes perfectly clear that writing was extensively used for running a state. Uses of writing for private purposes were not entirely new; we encounter such texts (sales, loans) in earlier periods as well. The balance, however, had fundamentally changed. Whereas Ur III writing was primarily official with secondary use by private persons, in the Old Babylonian period there seemed to be no restriction at all.

Scribal Education
The little that is known about Ur III writing education points to an informal setting in which writing was learned "on the job," in an apprentice relationship with an experienced scribe—basically the same way other crafts were taught. For the Old Babylonian period we have abundant

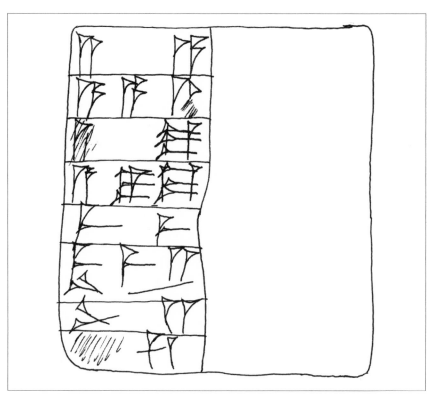

FIGURE 1.3

*Elementary Old Babylonian exercise. Teacher's model with the beginning of a traditional, stan-
dardized list of signs and sign combinations, to be copied to the right by a pupil. N 5147.
University of Pennsylvania Museum. Nippur.*

evidence for formal scribal training in which a student went through a well-
defined curriculum to learn, first, how to write a number of frequent signs
properly, then how to combine them into names and words, and then how
to use these names and words in sentences (Veldhuis 1997).

    After initial exercises in handling clay and styli, students would start
copying the elementary sign list that is now called "Syllable Alphabet B,"
which familiarizes the pupil with a number of common signs by listing
them in mostly meaningless combinations. The tablet in figure 1.3 has the
first few lines of this exercise and may be transliterated as follows:

    A A
    A A A

A KU
A KU KU
ME ME
ME ME A
PAP PAP
PAP A
[MAŠ] MAŠ

This extract introduces five individual signs that are frequently used and consist of a small number of strokes. Every three to five lines, a new sign is added, and earlier ones appear in combination with the newly introduced ones. The full list has several hundred lines, but the only copies we possess are school extracts. In many cases these extracts exhibit oversized signs so that every detail of the design can be properly practiced.

Slightly more advanced exercises introduced Sumerian vocabulary and orthography and the more complex aspects of cuneiform writing. An important set of vocabulary exercises has a thematic organization, including lists of trees and wooden objects, reeds and reed objects, clay vessels, hides and leather objects, and so on. These lists of words are usually in Sumerian only, but in a few cases Akkadian translations are added. We must assume that the pronunciation of the Sumerian words and the Akkadian translations were part of the teaching process and that the students memorized them.

Full Sumerian sentences were introduced by having students copy model contracts and proverbs. The proverbs often use little-known sign values and thus also function to reinforce the pupil's knowledge of the Sumerian writing system. All this training was preparation for copying literary texts of a broad variety, including hymns to gods and rulers, narrative texts that feature gods and mostly legendary kings, and whimsical texts such as the debate between Hoe and Plow.[7]

The textbooks used in Old Babylonian education were loosely standardized. Every teacher seems to have had his own version, but the main elements of the curriculum were more or less the same all over Babylonia. A detailed analysis of the curriculum demonstrates that it was a well thought-out sequence of materials, with plenty of repetition of the same material from slightly different angles. A student who went through this curriculum had a thorough knowledge of the cuneiform writing system, Sumerian, and the Sumerian heritage as preserved in the literary corpus.

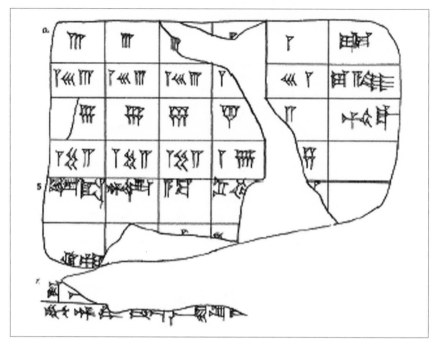

FIGURE 1.4

AUCT 1, 56—the only Ur III administrative table known so far. Published by Sigrist (1984:Text 56).

TABLE 1.2

Ur III administrative text in table form

3	3	3	2	1	Fat-tailed sheep
93	93	93	62	31	*Aslum* sheep
6	6	6	4	2	Billy goats
102	102	102	68	34	
Puzur-	Šul-	Aba-	Sisa	[...]	
From the shepherds [...]					

Although this curriculum did integrate elements that came from the Ur III period, including many royal hymns, in its main outlines it is a creation of the Old Babylonian scribes and a manifestation of the Old Babylonian writing revolution.

Tables

A truly remarkable innovation of the Old Babylonian period is the two-dimensional table (Robson 2003, 2004). Numerous Ur III texts have a data structure for which the table format would have been extremely effective. There is, however, only a single example of an Ur III administrative text in tabular format (fig. 1.4; table 1.2).[8] The table is largely filled with numbers. The rightmost column has animal names. In the fourth row the various kinds of animals are added up. The fifth row contains abbreviated names of the people who received these animals from shepherds. The reverse of the tablet (mostly uninscribed) contains a month (broken) and year name. The preserved section shows that it was written during the reign of Ibbi-Su'en, the successor of Šu-Su'en and the last king of the Ur III dynasty.

To comprehend how remarkable this tablet is, one may compare it with the yearly summary of animals delivered by Abbašaga and received by Utamišaram in the year Amar-Su'en 6 (Erm 14995 = http://cdli.ucla.edu/P212247; Cuneiform Digital Library Initiative), written in the linear style characteristic of the period:

1	gukkal ĝiš-du$_3$ babbar	1 uncastrated fat-tailed white ram
2	3 u$_8$ gukkal babbar	3 white fat-tailed ewes
3	ud 11-kam	day 11
4	1 gukkal ĝiš-du$_3$ babbar niga	1 uncastrated fat-tailed white fattened ram
5	ud 22-kam	day 22
6	1 udu giggi niga	1 black fattened ram
7	ud 25-kam	day 25
8	6 udu	6 sheep
9	iti maš-da$_3$ gu$_7$	month of the eating of the gazelle
10	1 sila$_4$	1 lamb
11	ud 7 kam	day 7
12	1 sila$_4$	1 lamb
13	ud 15-kam	day 15
14	2 udu	2 sheep
15	iti šeš-da gu$_7$	month of the eating of the piglet
16	1 gukkal ĝiš-du$_3$	1 uncastrated fat-tailed ram
17	ud 10-kam	day 10
18	1 udu a-lum	1 *aslum* sheep
19	ud 12-kam	day 12
20	1 gukkal ĝiš-du$_3$	1 uncastrated fat-tailed ram
21	2 u$_8$ gukkal	2 fat-tailed ewes
22	ud 14-kam	day 14
23	2 gukkal ĝiš-du$_3$	2 uncastrated fat-tailed rams
24	2 gukkal ĝiš-du$_3$ babbar	2 uncastrated fat-tailed white rams
25	ud 22-kam	day 22

26	3 u$_8$ gukkal	3 fat-tailed ewes
27	ud 24-kam	day 24
28	1 gukkal babbar niga	1 fattened fat-tailed white ram
29	1 udu a-lum niga	1 fattened *aslum* sheep
30	ud 25-kam	day 25
31	1 gukkal niga	1 fattened fat-tailed ram
32	ud 27-kam	day 27
33	1 gukkal niga	1 fat-tailed fattened ram

Here the first column ends, but the text continues in much the same way for six more columns (covering twelve months). This list is followed by several columns of totals: subtotals for each individual category, grand totals, and a colophon with the date and the names of the officials responsible for these transactions. The large document, a copy of data from daily tablets (some of which have been identified, Veldhuis 2005:118), does not distinguish between different types of data at all. Numbers, commodities, and dates are all entered in a linear fashion. The result is much harder to grasp and to deal with than when presented in a table.

When the tabular format was introduced in the Old Babylonian period, its usefulness was quickly recognized and applied to a variety of documents. The earliest group of administrative tables comes from Nippur and is dated between 1871 and 1795 BCE. The texts record deliveries for regular offerings to various gods and divine objects residing in the temple of Ninurta. Over time, tables became more complex and were used not only for administrative purposes but also for astronomical data, explanations of signs and words (lexical texts), multiplication tables, and so forth.

The use of tables for organizing data does not seem to be a significant achievement. In fact, archaic scribes working shortly after the invention of writing had already done similar things. What is remarkable here is that Ur III scribes chose not to introduce tables, instead continuing to prepare accounts in a linear fashion. Robson (2003) has argued that the absence of tables in the Ur III period may be an indicator of bureaucratic stress or the absence of incentives for innovation.

The Old Babylonian Writing Revolution

The distinctions between writing in the Ur III period and in the Old Babylonian period may well be labeled revolutionary—even though the transformation clearly did not happen overnight. Kraus (1973:18) discussed and described in some detail the problem of the dramatic change in the uses of writing in the Old Babylonian period, but his cautious mode of arguing prevented him from coming to any conclusions. More than thirty years after his contribution, we may see things in a somewhat broader perspective.

The political, social, and cultural changes immediately after the fall of the Ur III empire—a period for which relatively few sources are available—may be summarized under three headings: political fragmentation, ideological nostalgia, and the demise of Sumerian. These three developments contributed to the creation of a new class of scribal professionals, independent, proud of their craft, willing to experiment, and having a strong interest in the history of their discipline.

In the final years of the Ur III empire, the governor of Isin, Išbi-Erra, established himself as an independent monarch (Charpin 2004). The dynasty that was thus established in Isin was important and at times very powerful, but it never succeeded in controlling the entire area. From the outset, other cities, such as Ešnunna in the north, declared independence, and Larsa became a strong competitor for power in the south. Only Hammurabi of Babylon succeeded in the last decades of his reign in controlling all of Babylonia—but that was several centuries later.

The rulers of the Isin dynasty saw themselves as successors to the great Ur III kings and expressed this continuity in various ways. We have dozens of hymns to Isin kings, several of which read as calques of Ur III royal hymns (Klein 1990; Ludwig 1990). Administrative texts of the time look in many ways like Ur III texts, although it has been remarked that several aspects of sentence structure typical of Sumerian seem to have been lost to these later scribes (Sallaberger 2004).

The Isin kings, by identifying themselves as successors to the glory of Ur III, legitimized their attempts to control the entire southern region of Mesopotamia. In the famous Sumerian King List, a list of dynasties that goes back all the way to the mythological past when "kingship descended from heaven," the history of the area is imagined as a rotating kingship.[9] At all times there was a single dynasty, and one city in Sumer functioned as the dynastic seat. Although many of the kings listed are lost in the fog of history or were created in the imagination of the scribes, in several instances we are able to prove that kings listed as belonging to successive dynasties were actually contemporaries competing for power. By imagining themselves as the last in a long succession of dynasties, the Isin kings produced a kind of history that de-emphasized differences between the ancient Babylonian city-states and emphasized their unity. One powerful symbol of this unity was Sumerian, the language of this glorious past, shared by all the city-states. As a symbol of this imagined, unified past, Sumerian was also the symbol of the Isin kings' ambition to dominate all of Babylonia—an ambition they never fulfilled, but one that could easily be adopted by dynasties in other cities.

Walther Sallaberger (2004) has argued that spoken Sumerian did not slowly fade but rather collapsed. The language had already retreated from the northern parts of Babylonia, and with the fall of the Ur III empire it received its final blow. The importance of Sumerian as the language that symbolized the glorious heritage of Sumer, the past to which the future must return, explains the extraordinary amount of energy and time that was spent in preserving this language from oblivion—with the result that Sumerian continued to be used in one way or another for some two millennia.

The development of a new, thoroughly organized curriculum for teaching cuneiform and Sumerian was an answer to the ideological, political, and linguistic developments of the post–Ur III era and created a class of scribes who were truly special—educated in the ancient language, competent in the cultural heritage, aware of their connection to the past. This self-conscious class of scribes, clerks, and scholars was educated to serve the king, but in the fragmented political landscape of the time, the relative political weakness of their patrons left them with more freedom to innovate in their craft, to experiment with new textual genres and formats, and to develop less formal, more cursive hands.

CONCLUSIONS

The cuneiform record offers an almost continuous record of a writing tradition that extended over more than three millennia. For much of this history, writing was a tool of royal and administrative control, and changes in the writing system may thus be understood as changes in how or why this tool was employed.

That writing systems change over time is a common everyday experience. The handwriting of our grandparents differs from that of our own and our contemporaries. It may be more important, however, to note that the role of handwriting has changed fundamentally and that much of its niche has been taken by the telephone, email, and text messaging. Changes in what writing is used for, the place that it occupies in society, and the functions that it fulfills are tied to both social and technological changes. Writing, therefore, is to be studied in a larger context in which its uses become understandable. The cuneiform evidence shows that frequent, daily use of writing for mundane purposes does not necessarily lead to simplification or the introduction of cursive forms. In the Ur III period the connection between officialdom and writing was strong enough to keep in place a semi-monumental type of writing, even for routine trans-actions. The evidence also demonstrates that complexity, under the right circumstances, may be an asset rather than a handicap. Ancient scholars asserted their claims of pre-eminence by listing rare, obscure, or anti-quated words and sign values or by downright inventing new ways to increase the complexity of the system. Such pieces of evidence, rather than exceptions to general rules, demonstrate that writing is a truly social phe-nomenon, to be understood as a tool used by social agents in their daily negotiations of status, power, and control.

Notes

1. This and other examples appear in Civil and Biggs 1966:3. The latest edition of The Instructions of Šuruppak is Alster 2005, chapter 1, in which this saying is line 15.

2. See Sallaberger 1999a:170, with previous literature given in note 170. For the history of the orthography of this word and the paleography of the signs involved, see Krecher 1987.

3. HMA 9-2700, published as http://cdli.ucla.edu/P136076 (Cuneiform Digital Library Initiative); edited by Sollberger (1966:No. 271).

4. This number excludes the several thousand letters from Old Babylonian Mari that belong to a royal archive and therefore do not fall into the category of "Alltagsbriefe" according to Sallaberger's criteria.

5. The letter was studied by Marchant (1990:90). The present translation is based upon Veldhuis 2008c, text no. 7.

6. The exact location of Sabum remains unknown, but it was evidently close to Kisurra in central Babylonia and may well have been right on the border between Larsa and Babylon.

7. For an overview of Sumerian literature, see Michalowski 1995. The great majority of Sumerian literary texts (including proverbs) may be found in translation (with preliminary editing) at the Electronic Text Corpus of Sumerian Literature (http://etcsl.orinst.ox.ac.uk/).

8. A photograph of the tablet is available at http://cdli.ucla.edu/P102902.

9. The Sumerian King List was not an invention of the Isin kings; the earliest copy known today dates to the Ur III period (Steinkeller 2003). The list was adopted by later dynasties to suit their own legitimating needs.

2

Scripts, High Culture, and Administration in Middle Kingdom Egypt

John Baines

Two main motives are widely proposed to have stimulated inventions of writing: prestige (in a broad sense) and administration. These need not be in opposition, and they can be complementary in many ways, as can be seen from the studies gathered by Stephen Houston (2004c). In Egypt, the coexistence of two and then three basic script forms rendered a division in applications of writing explicit because the different forms were used for different purposes on different media in complex, overlapping patterns (triscript principle: Houston et al. 2003:439–440). Prestige forms were privileged over mundane administrative ones; vast resources were expended on them in contexts ranging from large monuments to jewelry and seals. In volume, administrative writing constituted the vast majority, but this is poorly attested, making it difficult to assess connections between prestige and administration. Administrative writing served rulers and elites. There is little evidence of penetration of writing in the wider society, that is, outside archaeologically accessible ceremonial and urban sites and among the peasant mass of the population (Baines 2007:63–94), but surviving materials show that very detailed matters were administered in writing within state-controlled contexts.

In this chapter I describe script forms in Middle Kingdom Egypt (ca.

TABLE 2.1

Chronology of ancient Egypt[1]

Early Dynastic period	
1st–3rd dynasties	ca. 2950–2575
Old Kingdom	
4th–8th dynasties	ca. 2575–2150
First Intermediate period	
9th–10th dynasties	ca. 2150–1980
11th dynasty	ca. 2080–1940
Middle Kingdom	
11th dynasty	ca. 1980–1940
12th dynasty	ca. 1940–1750
Amenemhat I	ca. 1940–1910
Senwosret I	ca. 1920–1875
Amenemhat II	ca. 1880–1840
Senwosret II	ca. 1840–1830
Senwosret III	ca. 1835–1815
Amenemhat III	ca. 1815–1770
Amenemhat IV	ca. 1770–1760
Nefrusobek	ca. 1760–1750
13th dynasty	ca. 1750–1620
Second Intermediate period	
14th–17th dynasties	ca. 1630–1520
New Kingdom	
18th–20th dynasties	ca. 1540–1070
Third Intermediate period	
21st–25th dynasties	ca. 1070–715
Late period	
25th–30th dynasties, Second Persian period	715–332
Greco-Roman period	332 BCE–395 CE

1. Dates have been deliberately rounded and are BCE unless otherwise noted.

1950–1650 BCE). I discuss their functions, demarcations, and social implications, and I model the institutions that set patterns in the use of writing and encouraged or resisted change. I consider high culture before administration not least because the greater prevalence of the former in the surviving record makes it easier to approach, as is also true, for example, of China in the first millennium BCE (Steinke, chapter 6, this volume). In this period, more than a millennium after writing was invented, it was used for a wide range of purposes while continuing to change at a slow pace. The period offers the possibility to study how existing forms were further developed, to ask why specific changes were introduced and, to some extent, to examine their long-term effects (for dates, see table 2.1).

HISTORICAL ANTECEDENTS

Early Development

The Egyptian writing system was invented in the late fourth millennium and developed in stages until it could notate full syntax by the later Early Dynastic period (Baines 2004a, 2007:137–140). Throughout the period termed the Old Kingdom (ca. 2600–2150 BCE), writing remained limited, generally inscribed in relatively large signs that restricted the amount that could be fitted into a given space. Complex content was often conveyed through tables and other features of layout and composition, including pictorial elements on monuments, rather than through script alone; nonsyntactic means of communication through writing remained important. Increases in the range of genres and types of material that could be written came slowly. Such developments were not gradual but appeared mostly in steps corresponding to significant historical changes and were probably initiated and controlled by the ruling group.

The largest known body of third-millennium texts, the Pyramid Texts, was inscribed in royal burial apartments that were inaccessible after their owner's funeral; these are attested within the pyramids from around 2300 onward and in a royal mortuary temple more than a century earlier (Allen 2005; Baines 2004b; Berger-el Naggar et al. 2001). Several lines of reasoning suggest that an archive tradition existed from no later than the time when syntax began to be notated. This tradition would have maintained manuscripts of religious compositions on papyrus or leather so that they could be transmitted in archives and exploited in rituals or carved for the almost purely symbolic or magical purpose of the Pyramid Texts. Other genres, not directly attested, probably included magical spells and medical treatises. All of these continued in use in later periods. Some significant applications, such as personal letters, seem to have been latecomers (perhaps around 2400 BCE), and they were quickly appropriated for elite display alongside their practical use (Eichler 1991). Fictional literary instructions in wisdom and narratives were not written down.

Semipublic inscriptions were important for personal display, notably in biographical self-presentations, which slowly increased in length while remaining constrained in content (Strudwick 2005). Both these and addresses from the dead to the living were sometimes carved on tomb exteriors and thus were visible without the need to observe the rules of purity required to enter the tomb chapels themselves (e.g., Silverman 2000). People also left rock inscriptions of varying degrees of formality on the paths of expeditions and on certain regular routes up the Nile and out into the deserts (e.g., Rothe et al. 2008); some have been found at the site of a frontier town (Seidlmayer 2005). Another significant use of display writing was in legal material that assigned property rights or exemptions (Goedicke 1970). In format these texts derived from the complex layouts of semicursive documents. In monumental usages writing was accompanied by pictorial human figures, without which it seems not to have been complete (exceptions occur in semicursive script; see, e.g., Müller-Wollermann 2005). Pictorial compositions with figures similarly had accompanying captions of varying extent in a wide range of combinations (for this principle, see Fischer 1973b). Overall, third-millennium hieroglyphic writing was not primarily a public display medium but a means of elite expression that was used in restricted contexts.

Script Forms, or Scripts

From the beginning, the Egyptian script existed in a monumental form, normally termed "hieroglyphs," which was inscribed on many different surfaces and objects that were subject to restrictions of decorum (survey and examples: Parkinson 1999; on decorum, see Baines 2007:14–29). Hieroglyphs wrote material that was high cultural or sacred. Significant texts and drafts for inscription on other media could be written in hieroglyphs on papyrus or writing boards, but this practice seems not to have been widespread. Alongside hieroglyphs was the cursive form, written typically in ink on perishable surfaces, especially papyrus. Cursive writing, which was normal for all administrative applications, was not subject to the same symbolically based restrictions as hieroglyphs. When extensive written genres developed, perhaps from the late Early Dynastic period onward, the cursive came to be subdivided, with a more formal "cursive hieroglyphic" (alternatively termed "linear script") being used for sacred and high-value purposes and freer and more fluid styles for administration. The latter script type is a little misleadingly termed "hieratic" following ancient Greek authors, in whose time religious texts were the principal materials written in it. Hieratic script regularly used black ink for the body of a text and red for headings and a few distinct categories of information, such as different types of grain in accounts.

Papyrus, an artificial, paperlike medium that was central to administration from no later than the First Dynasty, was typically inscribed in hieratic. Other media included leather, used for prestigious texts and material that was subject to heavy wear; wooden writing boards faced with gypsum plaster; and clay tablets, which are found at oasis sites, where papyrus was presumably difficult to procure (Pantalacci 1998). Potsherds and limestone flakes, both generally termed "ostraca," and on occasion, pieces of bone (Widmer n.d.) bore ephemeral cursive writing, which was also used for quarry marks and similar purposes, inscribed on the surface of the material to which it related (e.g., Arnold 1990).

The three forms of writing together constituted the script system. All existed in variant styles adapted to specific contexts. In addition to cursive writing's wide usage, it was the primary medium of instruction in writing, which probably began with hieratic, adding cursive hieroglyphic at a later stage. Many people may have known a few hieroglyphs, such as ⸗ reading *ꜥnḫ* "life" (the Egyptian script does not encode vowels), which were significant symbols, some of them used as amulets or derived from everyday material culture. The basic medium of literacy, however, was hieratic. Only a minority among the small literate group could read hieroglyphic inscriptions, which were often set up in places to which few or no people had access.

The signs of all three script forms were pictorial in origin. Carefully executed cursive writing retained some pictorial features, but the reduction of signs to curved outlines and dots, executed in ink with a brush, transformed the distinctions between signs from pictorial differences to differences articulated almost purely in terms of shape, with some ligatures for common groups. Nonetheless, the pictorial analogue to cursive writing remained significant, probably moderating the rate of change in sign forms.

Script and Language

The Egyptian script existed in its two main varieties for some centuries before continuous syntax was notated. There could have been no initial expectation that what was written would correspond with what was spoken. Language was not the original chief focus of writing, so it is anachronistic to posit too close a connection between the two (compare Veldhuis, chapter 1, this volume): language was a system of communication analogous to the script that was in the process of invention, as well as a point of departure for its further development. Moreover, written Egyptian exhibited no dialects and so would have been an alien idiom for those outside the region that supplied the linguistic model (perhaps the area around Memphis). Drift in the spoken language would have moved written and spoken forms apart within a couple of centuries, whatever dialect any particular user might have spoken.

In an extended polity fused from a number of precursor societies, Egyptian—which forms a distinct branch of the Afroasiatic language family—was probably chosen from among several current languages for the elaboration of the writing system. That choice was hegemonic, because the Egyptian script was hardly ever applied to other languages, and when other societies developed their own writing systems out of it, notably the Semitic and Meroitic consonantal alphabets in the second and first millennia BCE, they transformed it almost beyond recognition (for the Semitic alphabet, see below). This isolation of Egyptian is further visible in the development during the Old Kingdom of a special orthography, using many uniconsonantal signs and lacking determinatives/classifiers, for writing non-Egyptian names and conceivably material in a Semitic language (Steiner 2011), unlike the more heavily logographic normal practice. It seems that, for the guardians of script and language, the two went very closely together.

Linguists distinguish two earlier phases of the written language: the Early/Old Egyptian of the Early Dynastic period and Old Kingdom, on the one hand, and the Classical/Middle Egyptian of the Middle Kingdom, on the other (e.g., Loprieno 1995:5–6). Yet, verbal forms present in the earliest known syntactical writing, from around 2700 BCE, are encountered little changed in texts from eight hundred years later, an implausibly long period for spoken language to remain stable (for Old Kingdom language, see Edel 1955–1964). Major sound shifts that occurred during the same period had relatively little effect on orthography. Indeed, the written Egyptian of the late Early Dynastic period and Old Kingdom differs no more from Classical Egyptian than sixteenth- and seventeenth-century written English does from that of the early twenty-first century. (The two phases together are termed "Earlier Egyptian," in contrast with the "Later Egyptian" language current from the mid-second millennium BCE to the extinction of Coptic around 1000 CE, in which verbal syntax, in particular, is very different.)

The main shift toward Classical Egyptian took place during the decentralized First Intermediate period, perhaps in Upper Egypt rather than around Memphis, and was contemporaneous with increased diversity in the content of inscriptions created for individuals (e.g., Lichtheim 1988). Rapid change in a period of decentralization is a reminder that when central authority was powerful, it exercised rigid control over writing, something that is not unique to Egypt. It also shows the stimulus to change given by aspirations from outside the traditional ruling group. Classical Egyptian was perhaps slightly less distant from spoken language than Old Egyptian had been, and this may have made it easier to use in writing, but such advantages would have been minor. Nonstandard forms and vocabulary in captions within Old Kingdom tomb scenes of rustics evoke a range of linguistic registers (Erman 1919), showing that the script could notate different styles on a single monument; their absence elsewhere reminds us that pressures toward central standards affected longer formal texts.

In keeping with the public, often religious character of important texts, most genres written in continuous discourse were composed in a relatively simple meter, the only major change in which seems to have come with the introduction of Classical Egyptian (e.g., Fecht 1982; for its application in the writing process, see Parkinson 2009:92–93, 279–322). This use of a special register of language and rhetoric, which no doubt had a basis in oral practice and institutions, presumably enhanced the distinction between written syntactic forms and everyday speech.

Script and Art

Hieroglyphs were integrated with pictorial usages to make up the central high-cultural mode of aesthetic display. Although hieroglyphic inscriptions are not always present in images and inscriptions are not always accompanied by images, the connection between the two was never lost. Hieroglyphs could relate to pictorial content in complex ways, but they were mostly distinguished from it by some feature, from elements such as a separating line to radical differences in scale (here I differ from Henry George Fischer, e.g., 1986). A basic principle of third-millennium design, often modified in later periods, was that writing was organized in vertical columns, although headings, small captions to figures, and some inscriptions on wide surfaces could be written in horizontal bands. Pictorial representation was laid out horizontally in registers (for its conventions, see Schäfer 1986 [1974]). A crucial feature of hieroglyphic writing was its arrangement not along a baseline but in vertical or horizontal bands delimited on both sides (Gardiner 1957); this organization is more like that of Chinese characters (Steinke, chapter 6, this volume) or Maya glyph blocks (Houston, chapter 8, this volume) than that of an alphabetic script. Vertical bands were more flexible than horizontal because hieroglyphs with awkward shapes could be deployed more fluidly in them. Nonetheless, the long-term tendency was toward horizontal lines, as was true also of hieratic, though not of cursive hieroglyphic. In horizontal writing, a basic principle of organization was to group signs where possible in virtual squares, a little like Maya glyph blocks. Hieroglyphs were generally inscribed and read from right to left, and the direction of reading was signaled by signs that "faced" in a specific direction; these looked to the right. This layout was reversible, and left-facing, left-to-right writing was used for reasons of symmetry, to accompany left-facing human figures, or because the overall context required it, for example, on a stela set up in a location where the viewer would approach it from the left, in accord with principles explored by Henry George Fischer (1977).

It is difficult to say how far scribes understood cursive writing as having a representational character. To us this feature is visible mainly where new signs were introduced. Otherwise, sign forms evolved through processes of simplification, related adaptation of the shape and direction of strokes, and so forth, a development that was laid out paleographically for different periods by Georg Möller (1909–1927; for such tendencies in other scripts, see Steinke, chapter 6, and Salomon, chapter 5, this volume). Within this context of change, in many groups of signs depicting specific domains, such as categories of birds, cursive outlines could retain a generalized similarity to one another. Despite these diverse tendencies and associated tensions in maintenance of the script, for two millennia the link both in usages and in sign repertories between cursive and hieroglyphic modes was not broken. Material drafted in hieratic away from a monument might be executed in hieroglyphs on its surfaces, but probably with an interim draft in ink hieroglyphs or perhaps cursive hieroglyphic (Haring 2010:32–34). When cursive scripts diverged radically from hieroglyphic in the first millennium BCE, inscriptions were always drafted in ink hieroglyphs (e.g., Winter 1967), a form that was rarer in earlier times.

Cursive forms possessed aesthetic qualities, but these were less pronounced than those of hieroglyphs. Important documents were written in larger signs on papyri of larger formats; salient features such as headings or initial dates were composed with a flourish, often at a larger scale than the rest, most clearly in Old Kingdom examples (Posener-Kriéger and de Cenival 1968). This exploitation of calligraphic qualities is visible in the subdivisions of the cursive script into cursive hieroglyphic and hieratic, as well as in differing styles within hieratic. It was less evident in purely routine documents. Aesthetics, however, cannot be separated from practicality, because a well laid out and legible document is easier to use than a badly laid out and written one. What did not develop in cursive writing was an art of calligraphy of the sort known in several civilizations, in which design can override concern for legibility. The only script mode in which such a tendency is apparent in Egypt is in hieroglyphs, whose Greco-Roman-period forms display a virtuosity in choice of signs and extension of their range of readings that enhanced their meaning but rendered texts altogether more difficult to read.

Calligraphic art is normally distinct in character from representational art even when the two are combined in the same artifact (as in Chinese painting and calligraphy), although Arabic-script calligraphy can be used secondarily for pictorial representation. The primary artistic focus of Egyptian writing was in hieroglyphs. Much Egyptian material, like that of many writing traditions, could hardly have been inscribed with the intention that it be read; rather, it was designed to enhance the meaning and beauty of the surfaces on which it was placed. As in other writing systems, nuances of sign forms, which may or may not be the object of focused attention but evoke tradition and make innovations, can be powerful vehicles of meaning and association (McDonald 2007; for Western tradition, see, e.g., Morison 1972; for the importance of arrangement and nonverbal elements, see Bodel, chapter 3, this volume).

TRANSITION: THE FIRST INTERMEDIATE PERIOD

The First Intermediate period (ca. 2150–1975 BCE), characterized in older treatments as a time of collapse and famine, is now seen as one of sociopolitical change, emergence of strong regional forms (Robins 1990), and significant cultural development (Seidlmayer 1987, 2000). Wealth was less unequally distributed than before, and many more people set up inscribed monuments than in the Old Kingdom (e.g., Dunham 1937). So far as can be seen from the very sparse evidence, the textual genres and traditions of the earlier period, such as the Pyramid Texts, were maintained and may have been further developed.

Some First Intermediate period monuments bear extensive, boldly formulated biographical inscriptions (notably Ankhtify of Moʻalla; for an excerpt, see Lichtheim 1973:85–87). As noted, the written language became very close to Classical Egyptian (Franke 1987). Later periods viewed some of these texts as model compositions. Biographical inscriptions in tombs at Asyut were transmitted into Roman times, when copies on papyrus formed part of temple libraries in the Fayyum, hundreds of kilometers to the north (Osing and Rosati 1998:55–100); this did not happen to Old Kingdom biographies. The prestige of Asyut seems to have owed something to an archive or a library that was maintained there, providing evidence for the curation of written tradition across major historical changes (Kahl 1999:283–355).

Many inscribed artifacts of the First Intermediate period are of diminished scale and aesthetic quality—as measured imperfectly by fineness of execution and compositional balance—but textual and linguistic competence was generally maintained. Restrictions on the diffusion of hieroglyphic writing lessened, but not to the point that central symbols might be used anywhere (for exceptional occurrences of the ʿnḫ sign, see Fischer 1973a). The relatively prosperous local cemeteries, far more elaborate than those of the Old Kingdom, included increased numbers of grave goods, but although a few forms of amuletic objects and designs on them derived from earlier high culture, most remained outside the range of forms used for hieroglyphs (Brunton 1928:Plates xciii–civ; Dubiel 2008). Demarcations that were reinforced by considerations of decorum seem to have been maintained.

New styles of hieroglyphic writing that were codified at the beginning of the Middle Kingdom (ca. 1975 BCE), when the country was reunified in the Eleventh Dynasty, descended mainly from local developments of the First Intermediate period, especially around Thebes, the new royal residence. However, they differ only in detail from standard forms and do not constitute a radical departure (Robins 1990).

THE MIDDLE KINGDOM: REFORM, DEVELOPMENT, AND STANDARDIZATION

Early Twelfth-Dynasty Reforms

The Eleventh-Dynasty reunification focused on Thebes was short-lived. Amenemhat I, first king of the Twelfth Dynasty, moved the administrative and cultural center near the ancient capital of Memphis (Arnold 1991). Traditional decorative forms were revived, and the rather ornate but distinctly provincial style of Eleventh-Dynasty monuments, which was of high aesthetic quality (e.g., Bisson de la Roque 1937:Plates xviii–xxviii), was gradually abandoned in favor of ones with a Memphite pedigree (fig. 2.1). At the same time, script styles were reformed and standardized, and orthography became much more regular. The scale of signs in writing was reduced in many contexts, making the inscription of long texts more manageable in both hieratic and hieroglyphs. These developments are well attested in hieroglyphs, whereas for the early Twelfth Dynasty hardly any papyri survive from around the capital. Belles lettres were composed in writing, probably for the first time (Parkinson 2002).

This normalization and change must have been driven by the center, but it is difficult to pursue the process in detail or to identify patrons or significant groups of executants because few monuments of the Memphite area survive (see below for the vizier Mentuhotep; Simpson 1991). The intent was evidently to spread the new forms throughout the country. Written and aesthetic culture was transformed. As in many civilizations, the reforms consisted partly in a return to the past. A premium was placed on controlled, detailed, and "realistic" pictorial elements, whether of images or hieroglyphic signs, that required elaborate and painstaking execution. This focus was in the interest of the political and cultural center: there was

FIGURE 2.1

Limestone relief of Senwosret I seated before an offering table, from his mortuary temple complex at el-Lisht (Arnold 1992:80, Plate 49). Cairo, Egyptian Museum JE 63942. Reproduced with the permission of the author.

no aesthetic of spontaneity and idiosyncrasy. Works that were costly in labor and resources were also those that were highly valued.

Scholars tend to see early Twelfth-Dynasty changes as being driven by practical needs. Administrative and social structures developed strongly for more than a century (Franke 1991), creating a more centralized and bureaucratic society with a sizeable lower elite or "middle class" (Parkinson 1996; Richards 2005). However, most of those who commissioned monuments or created significant documents were probably affected by cultural aspects of the new forms. The reformed written culture was a package—not a number of separate domains—that continued to evolve through the Twelfth Dynasty, expanding on the initial stimulus rather than moving in new directions.

A vital part of the new forms was the standardization of Classical Egyptian, the language of all major compositions of the Middle Kingdom, inscriptional and cursive, religious and literary, royal and nonroyal. Only the language of temple decoration escapes classification by modern scholars, because its small repertory of largely fossilized syntactic forms is not linguistically distinctive. Perhaps people did not ask themselves what stage of the language it represented, but it is superficially closer to Old than to Classical Egyptian, as might be appropriate for one of the most sacred uses of written language (this issue has not been studied in detail).

Classical Egyptian went together with an increase in the writing of continuous discourse in contexts where graphic and tabular arrangement had previously been favored (Helck 1974). Practice of the Twelfth Dynasty was perhaps the earliest that focused primarily on language rather than convey meaning in visual and oral forms by a mixture of graphic and linguistic methods. The development of nonsacred texts such as belles lettres fits with such a focus, although this does not explain it entirely. Like most other genres, belles lettres were intended to be pronounced aloud, not to mention performed (Parkinson 2009), and were by no means imprisoned in the script.

Seals and Sealings

Seals had been used in Egypt since predynastic times (fourth millennium BCE). Throughout the third millennium the normal seal form was the cylinder, originally introduced from the Near East. The use of seals was generally restricted to officeholders, and the seals were inscribed with strings of official titles but not names; it seems that notionally they signified delegated authority rather than belonged to individuals. In the late third millennium stamp seals were introduced. The scarab beetle form for such objects became the norm by the Middle Kingdom, when scarab seals were perhaps the only domain in which writing was disseminated at all widely among social groups. Especially in the late Twelfth and Thirteenth Dynasties, many scarabs bore the names and titles of officials ranging from the high-ranking to those with minor offices (Martin 1971), whereas others bear patterns and designs, often including hieroglyphs used with amuletic significance, not notating language (Ward and Tufnell 1978); a third common type combines a design around the edge with a hieroglyphic inscription in the middle. A rare luxury scarab, in silver with gold inlay, has fully executed hieroglyphs with name and title on the body, which is normally uninscribed, and a pattern and emblematic hieroglyphs on the back, showing that the inscription was not important for sealing (Martin 1971:35, No. 390, Plate 47A, 4–6). This piece, however, was probably a gift from a high-ranking official to his assistant and so may tell us little about administrative scarabs in general.

Thousands of name and pattern scarabs survive, as well as vast numbers of seal impressions, notably from administrative institutions in the traditional frontier town of Elephantine (Pilgrim 1996:234–274), the fortress of Uronarti on the expanded Egyptian frontier in the Second Cataract region, now within northern Sudan (Reisner 1955; Smith 1990), and the mortuary temple of Senwosret III at Abydos (Wegner 2007: 299–361). I know of no estimate of the relative frequency of the two basic modes of design for scarab seals, but among sealings the patterned type is altogether more common than the inscribed (Wegner 2007:303, Figure 136). If patterned seals were more effective for the nonliterate (Smith 2001), and if most of those who possessed inscribed seals were literate, the inscribed scarabs carried a message of social exclusion and furthered the elevation of the literate group over others. Their use was nonetheless pervasive enough to suggest that the "middle-class" literate were more numerous in the later Middle Kingdom than in many other periods, as Richard Parkinson (1996) and Janet Richards (2005), for example, have proposed.

Hieroglyphs on scarabs are at a miniature scale—objects typically 1.5 cm high bear five or more sign groups in a vertical column—and their forms are almost purely linear; more imposing stamp seals of institutions, roughly square and up to 4 cm high, are little different in this respect (fig. 2.2a). The designs aim at elegance and display aesthetic values. The sign forms are not the stylized, curved strokes of hieratic but full hieroglyphs drawn in outline so that they belong with monumental culture. Since millions of sealings must have been stamped and discarded every year, this was the most widespread use of hieroglyphs. As centralized rule dissolved toward the end of the Middle Kingdom and the north of the country came to be ruled by the Fifteenth or "Hyksos" Dynasty (e.g., Quirke 2007), designs ultimately became more schematic. Some formulas derived from sets of hieroglyphs were reduced essentially to patterns, presumably with amuletic meaning (Richards 2001). At the same time, scarabs became increasingly common in Palestine and Syria. Many examples of both patterned and inscribed forms have been found there (mostly not in controlled contexts), demonstrating that the type could travel beyond regions where anyone would understand the inscription. In that context the presence of hieroglyphs seems to have been experienced as a little contradictory, because the designs gradually eliminated anything with a clear verbal reading (cryptographic writing, which is another mode of play with hieroglyphs, became common on scarabs in the New Kingdom).

The use of hieroglyphs on seals shows that restrictions of decorum were flexible, or perhaps rather that "monuments" were available to all members of the elite, however far down the administrative hierarchy they might be and even if they belonged outside that hierarchy, as almost all

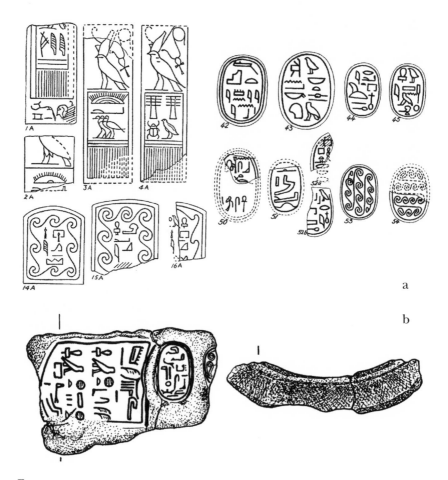

FIGURE 2.2

(a) *Seals from Uronarti. After Reisner 1955:53, 56. Twelfth and Thirteenth Dynasties.* (b) *Jar sealing from Elephantine with imprints of three seals: a larger institutional stamp, and two scarabs, one with the titles and name of an official and the other (fragmentary) of the patterned type. After Pilgrim 1996:235, Figure 93e. Twelfth Dynasty.*

women did (Wegner 2004). From early on, seals could function as amulets, a role that they shared with a few hieroglyphs that could be made into independent objects (Andrews 1994:9–11). Those hieroglyphs are also found in the decoration of patterned scarabs, where they were not meant to be read, while the scarab beetle itself was a sign writing the important root 𓆣 *ḫpr* "to come into being." This intertwining of hieroglyph bearer, hieroglyph, mean-ing, and amuletic function no doubt contributed to the great promi-nence of the scarab as a symbol, but scarabs were disseminated outside

Egypt across the Mediterranean without taking the script—or presumably the verbal association of *ḥpr*—with them. Similarly, in much later periods Egyptianizing art and architecture that bore hieroglyphic writing spread to the West, although knowledge of the script did not.

A revealing exception to this pattern in a different medium is the earliest Semitic alphabet, which is first attested from the Western Desert of Egypt and at Serabit el-Khadim in Sinai, perhaps in the nineteenth and early eighteenth centuries BCE. This script uses forms probably derived from hieroglyphs, as well as perhaps hieratic. It is found incised alongside and among Egyptian inscriptions on stelae and rocks and on at least one presumably Egyptian statue of a sphinx (Gardiner et al. 1952–55:Plate lxxxii). The usage of the new script has a partial parallel in images of nomads whose leader is riding on a donkey that were added to Egyptian monuments at Serabit el-Khadim: Egyptians otherwise almost never depicted donkey riding, even though it was practiced (Gardiner et al. 1952–55:Plates xxxix, lxxxii, lxxxv, Nos. 115, 345, 405; Marchand and Soukiassian 2010:239, No. 1781; Parkinson 2009:118, Figure 5.4; Valbelle and Bonnet 1996:34, Figure 45). It is uncertain whether nomads invented the alphabet as a display script on the model of Egyptian hieroglyphic monuments. Although the occurrence of the two side by side is remarkable (Darnell et al. 2005; Goldwasser 2006), at least equally plausible is that the script originated in Palestine (Hamilton 2006), where survival conditions for inscribed artifacts are altogether worse and rock surfaces are scarce.

Usage of Hieroglyphs in the Twelfth Dynasty

The majority of hieroglyphic inscriptions occur together with pictorial or other graphic decorative elements. Still more than in the Maya world (Houston, chapter 8, this volume), elements in writing and pictorial representation were comparable in appearance. This integration tended to constrain change in the most elaborate sign forms, which were minipictures but not visual information: they generally followed the rules of pictorial images, although their function in context was to convey linguistic and paralinguistic information. Writing and pictorial representation can almost always be distinguished except in deliberately playful usages, most of which are later than the Middle Kingdom.

Many of the most elaborately detailed hieroglyphs are found in temple reliefs and in some tomb decoration. These are typically in captions to scenes, where the scale of the pictorial figures is altogether larger than that of the writing. Remarkably detailed signs and figures carved in the "White Chapel" of Senwosret I at Karnak owe something to the style of the

Eleventh Dynasty while exhibiting influence from the Memphite area (fig. 2.3; Lacau and Chevrier 1956–1969; for photographs, see, e.g., Lange and Hirmer 1968:Plates 90–91). Reliefs of the same reign from the king's mortuary complex at el-Lisht near Memphis have sign forms that are less complex and more directly inspired by those of Old Kingdom Memphis, as are the human figures that they accompany (for an example, see figure 2.1).

In other cases oversize signs were used to create meaningful inscriptions that were also emblematic compositions celebrating in part the aesthetic power of writing. A late Twelfth-Dynasty door lintel from the Fayyum is a classic example (fig. 2.4). The text of this composition states in symmetrical sets of columns that the king is beloved of the gods Sobek and Horus of Shedet (modern Medinet el-Fayyum). The central three columns contain the king's first cartouche flanked by two oversize "signs." These represent Sobek as a crocodile effigy on a standard that rises from an enclosure bounded by pairs of shrines topped with the horned crania of what may be antelopes. The oversize signs are captioned *sbk* "Sobek" by three hieroglyphs behind the crocodiles'crowns, but the full reading is probably *sbk šdtj* "Sobek of Shedet," with the *šdtj*, which is homophonous with the grammatical dual, indicated by the pair of shrines, so that the crocodile-on-base group in effect constitutes two signs. The effigies have human arms offering emblems of life and power that are also mini-hieroglyphs to the cartouche in the center, and the flanking columns of inscription run: "Speech: I have given you all life and power like Re [the sun god]." The central, right-facing column is completed by the three signs beneath the effigy on each side (the signs beneath the cartouches, which are not to be read, are in part supports for them and probably also signify the king's power). Together the central column and the two groups of three signs at the bottoms of the columns read: "Dual King Nimaatre [Amenemhat III—spelled out in the cartouches at far right and left], beloved of Sobek of Shedet," the god's name accompanied by the hieroglyphs *sbk* being the effigy. The emblems held by the effigies integrate the flanking columns into the whole. The three central columns would be decipherable without the flanking speeches, and the captions naming the god would mean nothing different. The effigies, which break normal conventions of scale, show that the composition is ultimately an emblematic transposition of scene forms with pictorial figures of deity and king, such as that in figure 2.3, that has been compressed into a single band of relief. Heinrich Schäfer (1986 [1974]:352–355) discussed details of the execution of the signs in the left and right sides of the relief, which show that two different hands did the carving, but this is more an attributional than a

FIGURE 2.3

Scene on a pillar in the way-station of Senwosret I at Karnak: Atum leads the king into the presence of Amun. Courtesy Hirmer-Fotoarchiv München.

FIGURE 2.4
Limestone lintel relief of Amenemhat III from a temple in the Fayyum; Berlin, Ägyptisches Museum 16953 (severely damaged in World War II). Archival photograph courtesy of the Ägyptisches Museum.

paleographical point: the two sides do not exhibit meaningful variation in sign forms.

Styles of hieroglyphs on nonroyal monuments vary enormously. The two basic media of drawing in ink and carving favored different graphic solutions. Nonetheless, because the ideal complete pictorial work, whether royal or nonroyal, was a painted relief, the two also came together. The media both influenced each other and diverged, notably when the painting of signs that had been carved in raised relief created different effects from those achieved by the sculptor. As it happens, relatively few examples of painted relief survive from the Middle Kingdom.

A range of painted realizations of hieroglyphs, with virtuoso execution of pictorial details, is found in Twelfth-Dynasty decorated tombs at Beni Hassan (early sources include Griffith 1896 and 1898a, with excellent photographs, and Newberry 1893; more recently, see Shedid 1994, also with excellent photographs; for comparable signs from the New Kingdom, see Davies 1958). The artistic strategy of these forms is to create minipictures within the standard outlines of hieroglyphs. Different tombs and areas of decoration do this in different ways. Living beings tend to receive most attention, and the plumage of birds is very detailed, though its color is not necessarily "realistic" (compare the owls, which write the consonant *m*, in Shedid 1994:Figures 70, 73, 145). Many hieroglyphs are not instantly identifiable as depicting beings or artifacts, even though most ultimately derive from something in the natural or manufactured world, as is shown in detail in the sign list of Alan H. Gardiner (1957:438–548). A tabular offering list in the tomb of Amenemhat is an instance of highly realistic treatment (Shedid 1994:Figures 83–85). Particularly striking is a bundle of salad onions that are colored after nature (fig. 2.5a, bottom left sign). The onions may have been executed in a naturalistic way because the word being written means "onions," which are the offering in this column. In terms of the script's workings, the onion bundle sign is a determinative/classifier. Many such signs have a generic relation to the meaning of the word they determine; in this case the relation is made concrete and specific by the execution. A scene showing a visit by eastern nomads offers a different type of treatment: inventories of these people and their animals held up for display on writing boards are inscribed in clear cursive hieroglyphic (figs. 2.5b, 2.5c). This script would not have been used in reality for such a purpose, but it evokes the cursive while remaining within the symbolic register of hieroglyphic forms. For Egyptologists it is easier to read than normal hieratic, but the opposite would have been the case for most literate people in antiquity.

FIGURE 2.5a

Detail of two sign groups in an offering list in the tomb of the high official Amenemhat at Beni Hassan. After Shedid 1994:49, Figure 84. Reproduced with kind permission of the author.

Polychrome hieroglyphs obeyed flexible color conventions. These brought together some signs of similar graphic form that represented quite different things, reinforcing the sense of the script as a system and contributing to a distancing from naturalistic depiction (for a detailed analysis of a New Kingdom monument, see Staehelin 1990). Examples include the blue half-circle ⌒ of the consonant *t*, thought to have originally depicted a loaf of bread. Geometric shapes, such as the house plans ⊏⊐ (*pr*) and ⊓ (*h*), had arbitrary colors, often black but also blue. Blue derived prestige from its association with lapis lazuli, and it seems gradually to have acquired a broader symbolic value that led to its being favored. Where hieroglyphs were incised in outline, they could be picked out in black. They were also often painted in monochrome, for which the normal prestige color was green, with blue becoming more widespread in later periods. Because so much paint has been lost, it is impossible to estimate how common polychrome hieroglyphs were, but black and monochrome ones were the large majority; polychromy was a luxury.

Incised hieroglyphs are the commonest surviving form, occurring in many contexts, including monuments decorated with raised relief figures

FIGURE 2.5b

Detail from painted scene of Amenemhat receiving the products of hunting and a visit of nomads in his tomb at Beni Hassan. Photograph by Margaret Maitland, reproduced with kind permission.

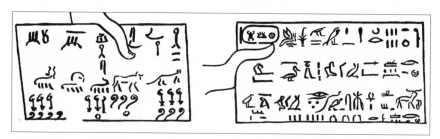

FIGURE 2.5c

Detail of two inventory tablets held out to Amenemhat by the figures facing him (see key to tablets below). After Newberry 1893:Plates xxx, xxxviii. Mid-Twelfth Dynasty.

Left tablet:

oryx	3,300
wild cattle	300/310
gazelle	3,000/3,010
ibex (probably grouped with next)	
addax	3,400

Right tablet:

1 Year 6, under the Person of Horus, Leader of the Two Lands, Dual King Khakheperre:
2 Number of the Asiatics whom the Count
3 Khnumhotep brought for galena: Asiatics of Shu (name of a region),
4 Number thereof: 37.

and scenes (sunk relief figures too are common, but they were seen as second best in this period). Some have internal relief detail—for example, evoking the rounding of human body parts—but their outlines are what identify them. Forms are often strongly simplified, notably in categories such as birds, but outlines are not particularly close to those of cursive scripts, even though some merging would have been possible. This separation is part of the integration of hieroglyphs with pictorial forms and their association with monumental contexts and meanings. Written and pictorial forms could be distinguished by different techniques, for example, where the hieroglyphic inscription is incised directly into the dressed surface of the stone, whereas the pictorial part is in raised relief whose background is carved a millimeter or two deeper (e.g., fig. 2.6). Captions among raised figures might also be raised, incised into the lowered background, or sometimes incised in small patches level with the main inscribed area, a practice found occasionally in many periods. Where hieroglyphs are in raised relief, they have a different character from the incised signs and are often more fully pictorial, sometimes being very finely executed and at a relatively large scale.

An example of multiple forms of incised hieroglyphs is the monumental, double-sided stela of the vizier Mentuhotep from the reign of Senwosret I, which is nearly half a meter thick and has a decorated area nearly two meters high. This stela influenced that of Sehetepibre from some generations later, which is dated by the name of King Amenemhat III and by artistic style (Lange and Schäfer 1902–1925:II:145–150, Plate xl; Leprohon [2009] reads the sides in the opposite order). The stela of Mentuhotep has an emblematic scene with an oversize hieroglyph functioning as a figure of the god Osiris, a prominent royal titulary at an intermediate scale filling the first line of continuous writing, and a highly developed, partly compartmented biographical inscription with figures of the owner in the corners. Some elements of its layout may have derived from Old Kingdom models, as part of the wider phenomenon of a Middle Kingdom "renaissance" (Franke 1995). Mentuhotep is known from other sources as an artistic patron (Simpson 1991). His cultural preferences probably derived from the Memphite area. He was also esteemed in Thebes seven hundred years later (Romano 1979:No. 31). The stela, which was a display piece using the best Memphite models, is very much of its time, mixing old and new so that any one feature could be difficult to date in isolation (studies by Allen [2009], Leprohon [2009], and Simpson [2009] demonstrate the intricate interweaving of old and new in the work of Mentuhotep in particular but do not address sign form and artistic style).

FIGURE 2.6

Limestone stela of Key from Abydos, BM EA 558. Courtesy British Museum. Early Twelfth Dynasty.

FIGURE 2.7

Small limestone stela of Hornakht, inscribed in ink, from the commemorative chapel area at North Abydos. After O'Connor 1969:33. Reproduced with kind permission of the author. Twelfth or early Thirteenth Dynasty.

At the opposite end of the social scale for stelae, some very modest pieces that are functionally equivalent to grand examples have been found in context in mortuary chapels (fig. 2.7). These are inscribed in ink in simple hieroglyphs rather than hieratic, but the signs are similar in appearance to cursive hieroglyphs and thus maintain the basic differentiation of scripts and contexts reviewed here.

Hieroglyphs were prominent on small-scale furniture and jewelry. A group of openwork inlaid gold pectorals exploits the integration of hieroglyphs with images (e.g., Aldred 1971:Plates 33, 37–38, 41–42; Lange and Hirmer 1968:Plate xiv; Wilkinson 1971:Plates ii, xv–xxii). Some are very intricate in composition, evidently in part to make reinforcing junctures for the constituent elements. One group consists solely of hieroglyphs

FIGURE 2.8

Scene in black line on the drawer of an ebony and ivory box of the reign of Amenemhat IV, from a tomb at Thebes. New York, Metropolitan Museum of Art 26.7.1438. After Carnarvon and Carter 1912:Plate xlix.

forming the word for "joy" and "all protection and life" (Aldred 1971:Plate 44). The coloring of the signs in red and blue minerals is determined by considerations of pattern and is unlike that found in most other uses of color for hieroglyphs.

From the end of the Twelfth Dynasty comes a small box for unguent jars inlaid on the front with sheet ivory on which a scene is incised in outline with added black pigment (fig. 2.8; Fischer 1986:178, Plate 55). Here, the signs and figures are quickly executed; the form of the owl hieroglyph 🦉 (*m*) is influenced by cursive hieroglyphic or hieratic, even though it was carved rather than written with a brush. This style was appropriate to the white ground, on which the scene resembles a vignette on papyrus.

49

Cursive Scripts in the Middle Kingdom

For Egyptian cursive scripts in particular, it is difficult to trace gradual, to some extent unintentional change, which is otherwise a prime focus of paleographical study and dating, because of both uneven attestation and the material's diversity. In this section I review groups of papyri that were found together in order to exemplify this diversity, which is not random but expresses cultural values and distinctions, difficult though it is to establish their precise nature.

Documents can belong to more than one category of use and can acquire different functions during their existence. Administrative pieces whose subjects appear pragmatic are sometimes found in contexts that suggest otherwise. The content of four papyri from Nag' el-Deir is administrative, relating notably to a building project and the work of a dockyard in the reign of Senwosret I, yet the group was found intact lying on the lid of one of three coffins in an undisturbed tomb (Simpson 1963:frontispiece; for a summary of the contents, see Simpson 1986:7). The papyri appear to be consolidated accounts, not daily notes. As such, they are fair copies of what may first have been written on another type of surface. Presumably, they had earlier fulfilled a more or less practical administrative function, but their ultimate application was different. Perhaps they were a gift to the deceased from one or more well-wishers; the group could have been assembled from several sources. They could have been written by the deceased, the donor, or third parties. Whoever wrote them, they were perfectly executed on papyrus that had previously borne only ruled lines (except for P Reisner IV, which was palimpsest). Perhaps they had been kept as displays of their writers' skill before deposit on the coffin, making them in a sense aesthetic objects.

The largest body of Middle Kingdom papyri derives from a number of finds in the mortuary temple of Senwosret II at Illahun, adjacent to the Fayyum, and the nearby town (Collier and Quirke 2002, 2004, 2006). The major part came from the antiquities market and includes material that seems to derive from a temple (now in the Ägyptisches Museum, Berlin: e.g., Luft 1992, 2006). The papyri span a period of nearly a century and include many administrative pieces, from both institutions and individuals, as well as significant numbers of literary and religious texts. The accounts are particularly poorly preserved. As in those from Nag' el-Deir, many have a clear display component; hardly any are scribally incompetent. Layout is exploited both for meaning and for aesthetic quality. Even a piece of "hate mail" (perhaps never sent) that reverses normal greeting formulas is beautifully written and exploits symbolic associations of red ink (Parkinson

1991b:93; see also Horváth 2007). Other examples include the will of a man called Wah, which incorporated the will of his deceased brother Ankhren and ends with a set of witnesses' names (fig. 2.9; Collier 2009:208–210, Figures 1 and 2, with related document, 210–211, Figure 3). A cycle of songs in praise of Senwosret III starts with a text that is organized around the king's titulary, written in vertical columns in bold, almost hieroglyphic sign forms, the first three of his titles being especially large (Collier and Quirke 2004:No. UC32157 [photographs on CD]; Griffith 1898b:Plates i–ii). The later songs, which are in horizontal lines, have refrains that are written only once and offset from the remaining verses, a rare practice (partial translation: Lichtheim 1973:198–201; in full: Quirke 2004:203–205). Each is also written in signs of a different scale from the next. The purpose of this papyrus is uncertain, but its royal content surely influenced its design and its mixing of script forms.

The best-defined body of Middle Kingdom material comes from an early Thirteenth-Dynasty tomb at Thebes that contained a chest of papyri, normally termed the Ramesseum papyri, and other artifacts, including a large bunch of reed pens (Gardiner 1955a; Parkinson 1991a:xi–xiii, 2009: 138–172). They are fragmentary, but the genres of the texts and the script forms in which they are written can be established (table 2.2). The owner may have been a ritual practitioner whose activities included magic. The texts range from major literary compositions to collections of magical spells. As often with high-cultural materials, the majority of the papyri were palimpsest administrative documents, some retaining legible words from their earlier use, including frontier surveillance reports from the Second Cataract in Nubia (Parkinson 1991b:91–93; Smither 1945). Robert Ritner (1993:232n1077) has suggested that the papyri might have been removed from a temple library because they had become damaged, but their state of preservation, among other arguments, does not favor that explanation (Parkinson 2009:148n26). Although some of the texts are very specialized, it seems best to see the whole as a collection belonging to someone with high-cultural interests who acquired as many papyri as he could. They are inscribed in a number of different hands. (On the concept of tomb as "library," see Amenta 2002.)

Like the Illahun songs, the Ramesseum group exploits the mixing of vertical and horizontal writing. This style of layout is, however, more clearly exemplified by a find of slightly earlier papyri also from Thebes, now known as the Berlin Library (the primary source is Vogelsang and Gardiner 1908; see also Gardiner 1909; Parkinson 2009:76–89). Sign forms in vertical columns are more elaborate and at first sight might appear to be older.

TABLE 2.2
Script usage and text genre in the Ramesseum papyri find

Papyrus	Script direction	Recto text	Verso text
Manuscripts in cursive hieroglyphic script			
P Ram B (EA 10610)	Vertical with horizontal captions	Dramatic festival ritual	Later plan of building
P Ram E (EA 10753)	Vertical with horizontal title	Funerary liturgy for ceremonies at a mastaba	Accounts with remains of ruled lines
P Ram 5 (EA 10758)	Vertical with horizontal title	Medical prescriptions to do with "vessels," perhaps against stiffness	Very short jottings
P Ram 6 (EA 10759)	Vertical with horizontal title	Hymns to Sobek	None
P Ram 7 (EA 10760)	Vertical	Spells for gaining respect from men(?)	Later accounts
Manuscripts in hieratic script (arranged in chronological phases)			
P Ram 1 (EA 10754)	Vertical with one horizontal title	*The Discourse of Sasobek*	Later accounts
P Ram 2 (EA 10755)	Horizontal	*Maxims*	Continuation of text
EA 10754.D	Vertical	A wisdom text	None
P Ram A (P. Berlin 10499)	Horizontal with some vertical	*The Eloquent Peasant*	*Sinuhe* (over ruled lines, with erased text?)
P Ram C (EA 10752) + P Ram 18 (EA 10771)	Horizontal	Dispatches from Nubian fortresses	Magical texts, including incantation against ghosts; strengthening strip with accounts

P Ram D (P. Berlin 10495)	Horizontal	An onomasticon	Accounts
P Ram 3 (EA 10756)	Vertical	Magico-medical text for mother and child, also eyes	Dated accounts with ruled lines
P Ram 4 (EA 10757)	Vertical	Magico-medical text to do with pregnancy and birth, mother and child	Accounts with ruled lines
P Ram 9 (EA 10762)	Horizontal	Rituals to protect a house from magic, ghosts, and serpents	None
P Ram 10 (EA 10763)	Horizontal	Spell for protecting the limbs against any male and female serpent	Continuation of text(?)
P Ram 11 (EA 10764)	Horizontal	Love-spells(?)	None
P Ram 15 (EA 10768)	Horizontal	Spells to protect the body	Continuation of text
P Ram 19 (EA 10772)	Horizontal	Ritual/magical texts	Continuation of text
P Ram 8 (EA 10761)	Horizontal with some vertical	*The Banquet of Hedjhotep* (against headache)	None
P Ram 13 (EA 10766)	Horizontal	Healing texts(?)	Diary of an embalming with ruled lines
P Ram 14 (EA 10767)	Horizontal	Healing texts(?)	Continuation of text
P Ram 17 (EA 10770)	Horizontal	Protection for days at the turn of the year and other matters	Some continuation of text
P Ram 12 (EA 10765)	Horizontal	Invocations to demons against fever	Later jottings(?)
P Ram 16 (EA 10769)	Horizontal with some vertical	Spells for protection, including ones against evil dreams	Continuation of text

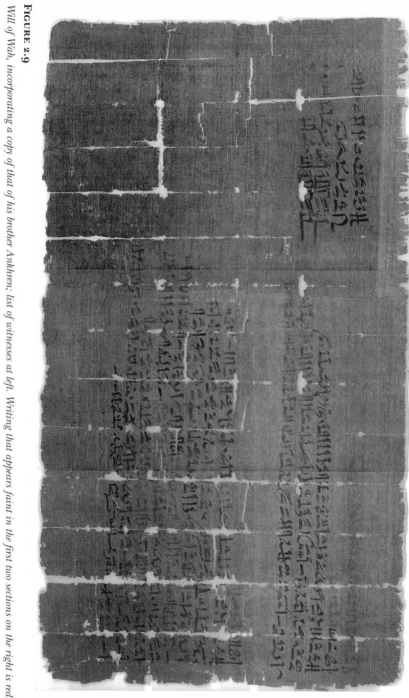

Figure 2-9

Will of Wah, incorporating a copy of that of his brother Ankhren; list of witnesses at left. Writing that appears faint in the first two sections on the right is red in the original. Papyrus. Petrie Museum, University College London, 32058; merged from three photographs of sections. Courtesy Petrie Museum of Egyptian Archaeology. Reign of Amenemhat IV.

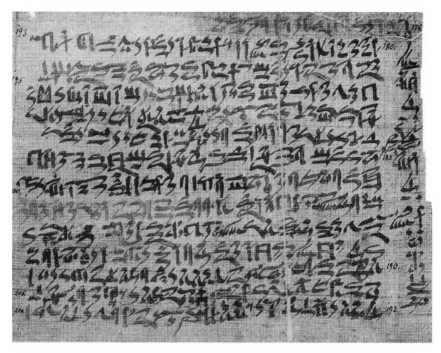

FIGURE 2.10

Tale of Sinuhe, Papyrus Berlin 3022, lines 178–194. Photograph by Lisa Baylis, British Museum. Courtesy Staatliche Museen Preussischer Kulturbesitz, Berlin. Late Twelfth Dynasty.

The horizontal writing within the same texts is more closely packed, with more abbreviated forms that are nearer to those of administrative documents. In the Tale of Sinuhe, the transition between the vertical and horizontal has a "representational" significance: the king sends a letter to the exiled protagonist, the initial titulary of which forms the last vertical column; the text of the letter then follows in horizontal lines (fig. 2.10). A short line, which is written in red at the top, spans both the vertical column and the first half of the horizontal "page" and reads: "Copy of the decree brought to this servant concerning his being brought back to Egypt" (Koch 1990:59, Line B178). At this point the layout of the papyrus resembles a letter ("decree" when sent by a king) and thus evokes the inclusion of a copy of one document in another, as in the will of Wah.

Five of the Ramesseum papyri are inscribed in cursive hieroglyphic (see table 2.2). Many religious texts in cursive hieroglyphic exploit its lack of fused groups and are to be read retrograde, that is, in columns from left to right, against the direction in which the signs face (fig. 2.11). The reasons for this style of inscription and reading are not well understood (the

FIGURE 2.11

Hymns to Sobek from the Ramesseum papyrus find. Papyrus BM EA 10759, 10760.2,5,7.
Courtesy British Museum. Early Thirteenth Dynasty.

explanation of Fischer [1986:119–121] is unconvincing). Three of these
papyri have ritual content; another may be magical. The remaining text is
medical and can be compared to one from Illahun, again inscribed retrograde in cursive hieroglyphic, that bears veterinary prescriptions (Collier
and Quirke 2004:54–57 [images on CD]). Although this range of content
shows that cursive hieroglyphic was not used only to write core religious
texts, the script seems to have been favored for specialized ancient rituals,
represented in the Ramesseum find by a composition giving settings and
speeches for a dramatic festival (Quack 2006; Schneider 2008; Sethe 1928),
as well as an elaborate funeral ritual with a cast of hundreds or more
(Gardiner 1955a:Plate xxviii, 1955b).

A final example, perhaps a little older, is a single sheet consisting of
two papyri glued back to back (Berger-el Naggar 2004). This object was
found in the mortuary temple complex of the Sixth-Dynasty king Pepy I
and derives from a Twelfth-Dynasty revival of his cult. The first, older side
bears spells from the Pyramid Texts, some of which formed part of a royal
mortuary cult. It has ruled vertical columns with horizontal lines at top and
bottom and occupies the full height of the papyrus. It is rather untidily
inscribed in cursive hieroglyphic with sign forms quite close to hieratic.

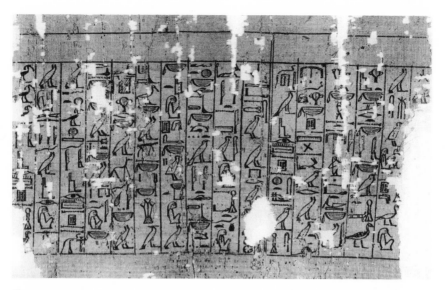

FIGURE 2.12

Papyrus with Pyramid Texts from the mortuary temple complex of Pepy I at Saqqara; side in full hieroglyphs. Berger-el Naggar 2004:Figure 2. Courtesy Institut Français d'Archéologie Orientale, Cairo. Perhaps late Twelfth Dynasty.

This side might derive from a working papyrus for use in ritual or perhaps a routine archival copy. The other side too is inscribed with parts of spells from the Pyramid Texts (fig. 2.12). These are written in full hieroglyphs inscribed in ruled columns framed by horizontal lines, with a full-height double vertical line between one spell and the next. An uninscribed band above the horizontal lines could have borne titles centered over individual spells (not enough is preserved to decide this point). The top and bottom of the papyrus are blank. The text in hieroglyphs is a ceremonial object that had been reinforced by the less neatly written, discarded sheet to which it was stuck. Its sign forms are almost timeless, but its orthography is that of the Twelfth Dynasty and entirely different from that of the Old Kingdom, from which the texts had been inherited. If the papyrus was used in the cult, it would have been cumbersome because the signs are so big that a large area would have had to be rolled out to consult spells of any length. Another possibility is that it was intended for advanced scribal practice and perhaps strengthened for repeated use.

The diversity of practice just outlined, most of it in literary and religious texts and some within single manuscripts, complicates analysis of change. Ancient scribes were knowledgeable, able to execute diverse sign forms and writing styles and at the same time to exploit such differences to enhance the meaning, prestige, and cultural associations of the compositions they were inscribing. Comparable usages might extend to diverting fine examples of accounting for ceremonial purposes. Among papyri bearing literary texts, a manuscript of the Instruction of Ptahhotep, which is ascribed to an Old Kingdom sage, is written in an unusual style of hieratic that may have been designed to fit with its fictional setting (Jéquier 1911), rather as was done with the layout of the king's letter in the Tale of Sinuhe. In this case the whole papyrus is written in horizontal lines, but in "pages" of very irregular extent that are much too wide for comfortable reading. Richard Parkinson (2009:120n13) suggests that the appearance and sign forms of the papyrus are a consequence of transcribing a text originally written in vertical columns, with generally less abbreviated outlines and an older appearance, into horizontal lines. The papyrus is very close-packed; perhaps space was at a premium.

Within different textual and linguistic registers and contexts, this range of strategies in inscribing papyrus and exploitating variations in writing style is comparable to the diversity of usage found with hieroglyphs. As in most written cultures, styles of writing were carefully considered, varying according to content, and integral to the message of the inscribed artifact.

Hieratic signs owe their character to the media of pen—held above the sheet like a brush—and ink. Some Middle Kingdom developments accentuated this dependence. A few common signs exist in distinct variants. The quail chick ⟨ (*w*) has one form comparable to other bird signs and another that is a simple spiral. In the Middle Kingdom the latter form was confined to hieratic, but in the New Kingdom it began to be used also in hieroglyphic (ℓ). The owl ⟨ (*m*) has one form with a clear bird profile and another resembling a calligraphic arabic digit 3. (Along the same lines as *w*, hieratic forms of *m* spawned several hieroglyphic variants, in this case in the Greco-Roman period.) When the common pintail duck ⟨ was used for the word for "son (*s3*)," it could be abbreviated to little more than a tick, which was then reinterpreted in hieroglyphic as an egg outline, ⟨. Thus, a form that originated as a cursive abbreviation came to exploit the association of egg and offspring, presumably in both scripts. Other specifically hieratic features include some extreme simplifications and ligatured groups, but in general, signs remained separate. The interconnections and transpositions among hieratic, cursive hieroglyphic, and full hieroglyphs almost certainly acted as a brake on the pace of paleographical change. By the late New Kingdom, five hundred years after the period considered here, the different styles of hieratic had drifted much further apart, as had the arrangements along the line used for documents and for literary and religious texts. The relationships among these script variants were reconfigured in the following Third Intermediate period (from ca. 1075 BCE).

This slow rate of change, together with moves to reform usage rather than accept drift, exemplifies the symbolic and cultural importance of the different script types and the desire to maintain demarcations between them. The ancient reforms have obvious parallels in reforms of orthography in the modern world. Modern reformers are always motivated by the wish to promote literacy and ease of use. The resistance they encounter shows that far more is at stake in script and orthography than simple usability. Ancient Egyptian reformers had a clearer understanding of the cultural capital invested in their script and its different forms.

Mixing of Scripts

In all periods, different styles of writing were mixed, saliently when headings or opening lines were distinguished from other materials by being written larger and in a more formal style, as in the songs of praise to Senwosret III. These distinctions were often made within a single script mode, typically hieroglyphic or hieratic. Middle Kingdom instances include cursive hieroglyphic on single artifacts alongside one or more other modes. The painted wooden coffins of the period supply striking examples. These are among the most elaborately designed and inscribed objects known and were highly prestigious (Willems 1988, 2008), although much less restricted in distribution than monumental tombs.

Many coffin interiors bear hieroglyphic inscriptions on their upper sections, often painted in several colors, and cursive hieroglyphic texts for the hereafter below, in black ink with some rubrics in red. The upper inscriptions are large in scale, consist mostly of offering formulas, and are often set above depictions of mortuary paraphernalia (Jéquier 1921). The finest pictorial coffins include small offering scenes that are treated as pictures within pictures (Terrace 1968; for further examples, see Lacau 1904). In one scene, a caption identifying the ritual action being performed is written in large pictorial hieroglyphs. Another caption at the top identifying the owner is in small black outline signs, as are the band of inscription around a vase depicted at relatively colossal scale immediately to the left and a set of columns in a square above (Terrace 1968:Plates i–iii, viii). The hieroglyphs in the offering formulas are as elaborate and beautifully executed as the most detailed ones painted in tombs. The coffin, of which this is a necessarily simplified description, thus bears two styles of full hieroglyphs, as well as running texts in cursive hieroglyphic.

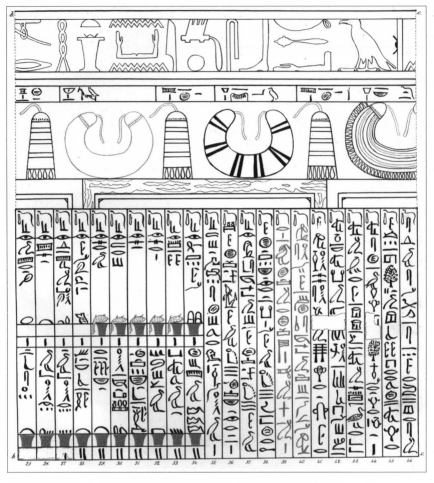

FIGURE 2.13

Section of the painted wooden coffin of Sebekaa, Berlin, Ägyptisches Museum 45. Paler signs in the copy are inscribed in red. After Lepsius 1867:Plate 41. Twelfth Dynasty.

Some coffins that use a comparable threefold division of script types have cursive hieroglyphs in horizontal captions written from left to right, a very rare treatment (fig. 2.13). The "quotation" signs beginning the columns of religious texts beneath also face left, against the direction of the signs they introduce. The captions and the columns beneath are separated by a band of pictorial motifs. The sign forms in both contexts differ relatively little, but the underlying intent was clearly to use two script varieties in addition to the full hieroglyphs in the top band.

The coffins probably adapted modes borrowed from less highly charged contexts. The Coffin Texts, the extensive mortuary compositions inscribed on the lower areas, were written in cursive hieroglyphic, not hieratic. The absence of hieratic required a further, slightly artificial distinction to be drawn between the columns of running texts and the two distinct uses of hieroglyphs above. In relief or large painted compositions, it was possible to signal such distinctions in several ways, but it was more difficult to do this at the smaller scale of the coffin. Here as elsewhere, it was evidently important to retain the hierarchy of three script types.

CONCLUSION

The styles of script and ways of using them described in this chapter were reformed, together with artistic styles in relief and painting, in the early Twelfth Dynasty, a phase that had classical status in the eyes of later periods. The move of the capital back to the Memphite area from Thebes intensified the revival of Old Kingdom forms; as in many cultures, innovation went together with legitimation through the past (Silverman et al. 2009). Throughout the life of the script, the associations between script forms and specific contexts and genres of content reinforced the integrity of the system. In the Middle Kingdom the new configuration endured without major change for a couple of centuries. During the gradual dissolution of the centralized state in the Thirteenth Dynasty (ca. 1750–1620 BCE), production of monuments decreased greatly, and objects like extravagant coffins ceased to be made. In Thebes during the Second Intermediate period (ca. 1630–1520 BCE), a different pattern began to emerge in deliberate contrast to the perhaps less elaborate administrative and cultural modes of the ethnically Palestinian Hyksos rulers of the Fifteenth Dynasty in the Delta. The new pattern was consolidated into the characteristic high culture of the early New Kingdom (ca. 1520–1450 BCE), a period that initially looked back to the Middle Kingdom Theban reunifiers of the late Eleventh and early Twelfth Dynasties, who had begun by reviving visual practice from a couple of centuries earlier. Subsequent expansion in the New Kingdom built upon Middle Kingdom traditions in comparable fashion and developed styles of its own, though without extending significantly the range of applications of writing.

All this engagement with script forms might be seen as a high-cultural overlay to administration. Administration no doubt created most of what was written, albeit in ephemeral forms and media that are almost entirely lost but leave a residue of sealings in administrative contexts, as well as seals as both working possessions and amulets. Large-scale administrative documents must have existed but are hardly attested. The virtual absence of incompetent manuscripts or carved monuments—examples of which are known from the preceding First Intermediate period—emphasizes the importance of writing and cautions us not to overestimate its spread through society. An institution that was so central was worth a vast investment of resources in creativity, training, and maintenance. Literary tradition presents the king and central elite as literate people participating fully in written culture and hence able to monitor administrative uses of writing. They were the ultimate guarantors of the complex of administrative and high-cultural uses of writing, both of which spread to the subordinate professional group of scribes, but they themselves did not normally write (Baines 2007:49–53, 78–83).

The integration of the script modes probably slowed change. For handwriting, change is unavoidable, but reforms and use of past models can alter the path it takes. The sign-by-sign equivalence of hieratic and hieroglyphic was maintained in part through the intermediate position of cursive hieroglyphic, which seems to have been practiced by executants more educated than the average literate person (though New Kingdom Book of the Dead manuscripts often show little understanding of the text being written). The use of more than one style by a single person, whether administrator or scribe, also favored stability. Change might be minimal during a single career or lifespan, but in a very long-term perspective it was self-evident: Egyptian writing of the Greco-Roman period was almost entirely different from that of the Early Dynastic period nearly three millennia earlier. In between, the complex system changed very slowly during stable periods, the main stimulus coming not from drift but from reforms in the aftermath of historical turning points.

The early Twelfth-Dynasty reform explored in this chapter was crucially important. It expanded the range of application of writing and the genres of written high-cultural materials. Going far beyond the usages of the Old Kingdom, it incorporated, regularized, and built upon changes of the First Intermediate period and added new types of text. The Twelfth Dynasty defined a classical style that remained normative thereafter, influencing written practice into the Roman period, through the distinct factors of the enduring Classical Egyptian language and the distribution of textual types and usages over the three script forms of hieroglyphs, cursive hieroglyphic, and hieratic. The most nearly comparable episode was the establishment of the new cursive script of Demotic in the seventh century BCE, which brought with it a reconfiguration of genres and practice across all the forms then in use. By that time the Twelfth-Dynasty configuration had endured in essence for 1,300 years, and the pattern created for Demotic replicated the older one with new script forms. Thus, in more than one way the language and script of the Twelfth Dynasty were essential to later developments. In all of this, cultural considerations contributed at least as much as those of utility and administrative practice. The complexity of script types and wide variation in levels of attestation render paleographical study of change often very difficult, but the material as a whole brings home how much is at stake for a culture in the forms and applications of its writing and—as with examples presented in other chapters of this book—how changes in scripts are not neutral but relate to changes in social institutions that are repeatedly subject to reform, often in the name of maintaining tradition.

Acknowledgments

I am very grateful to Stephen Houston for the invitation to participate in the wonderful SAR seminar and to everyone at the School for the marvelous environment they create. I owe a great debt to Richard Parkinson, Margaret Maitland, and especially Robert Bagley for their help with finding materials and for criticizing drafts, sparing readers of the final version from many imperfections.

3

Paragrams, Punctuation, and System in Ancient Roman Script

John Bodel

PARAFORMATIONS, "ELABORATION," AND WRITING SYSTEMS: PROBLEMS OF DEFINITION

In the 1987 book *Seuils,* French literary theorist Gérard Genette coined the term "paratexts" to define those "liminal devices and conventions, both within and outside the book, that form part of the complex mediation between book, author, publisher, and reader: titles, forewords, epigraphs, publishers' jacket copy," and the like (Genette 1997:back cover). In the history of the book and the sociology of reading, the role of such peripheral materials has come to be recognized as an important aspect of the subject (e.g., Chow 2004). So too in historiography the parallel scholarly instrument, the footnote, has been subjected to learned treatment (Grafton 1997). In the study of writing systems, however, the corresponding phenomena in the field that Gelb (1963) dubbed grammatology do not yet seem to have found a place in the discussion. Such features, when noticed, have generally been classified as "elaboration" in a tripartite functional analysis that distinguishes the category from "spelling" and "script" proper (Mountford 1996:630) and conceives of it as encompassing all aspects of shape differentiation and spatial disposition, as well as the full range of nonalphabetic symbols and graphs (Vachek 1989).

But if writing is defined as "a system of more or less permanent marks used to represent an utterance in such a way that it can be recovered more or less exactly without the intervention of the utterer" (Daniels 1996:3) and grammatology (or "graphonomy" [Daniels 2006:22]) is the study of this practice, then one might think that it should include the sorts of marks and signs that do not simply represent phonemes or morphemes but serve to articulate them into meaningful units (words), as pauses and inflection do in utterance. Methods of word division in verbal languages fall into this category. In written English we distinguish "therapist" from "the rapist" visually in a fashion distinct from but reflective of the way we distinguish the two in spoken language by pronunciation. Other verbal languages convey this distinction in writing with different signs. Some are marks; others are purely spatial and give semantic weight to arrangement and the absence of marks. Many such conventions serve a function at some point in their use, but some lose functionality over time or evolve in ways independent of it whereas others originate as decorative devices or incidentally and acquire a specific function only at a particular stage of their development. Whatever form they assume, such notations seem properly to belong to the system of a written language and thus deserve to be considered integral elements of its script rather than separate elaborations of it.

Following Gelb, many grammatologists "exclude from the category of writing systems those graphic expressions that do not reflect the sounds of the language" (Daniels 1996:8). From a linguistic perspective such a characterization has certain advantages, but as an approach to a writing system it is unduly restrictive because it excludes from consideration any aspect of writing's development that does not reflect an aural origin, even though writing is essentially a visual medium. Even if we accepted the premise and focused only on the sounds of language and their graphic representation, how, from an aural standpoint, would we explain the difference between written sentences such as "You were there." and "You were there?" other than by observing that the question mark (or, for that matter, the period) is a graphic expression that reflects a mode (interrogatory) that, when articulated orally, is conveyed by a change in sound (a rise in intonation). By extending the sound of a language to complete syntactic units, we may seem to push grammatology into grammar, from which it is usefully distinguished, just as the issue of spatial arrangement, if taken too far, approaches the entirety of the visual presentation of the text that epigraphists call "ordination" and paleographers refer to as "impagination." But punctuation, the broadest and most obvious category of devices included under the heading of elaboration of a script, can reflect the oral intonation or articulation of units both large and small, and the conventions of the way a text is disposed within its field, which have their own parallel and at times related development, would seem also to form an essential element of a writing system.

Not all graphic expressions with semantic value in a writing system reflect the sound of the language. Some, indeed, arise of necessity or convenience because of the restrictions of the medium of writing. The various conventions of capitalization in English, for example, reflect different influences at different stages of the development of the written language. The practice of distinguishing the first-person-singular pronoun in the nominative case by capitalization arose from an aural development (an opening in pronunciation of the unstressed form of the Old English [OE] *ic* to *i*) that led to a problem in the written transmission of the language (the tendency by printers transcribing handwritten manuscripts to misconstrue or to overlook the single short vertical stroke), which ultimately acquired a graphic solution: I. The progress of its advance can be directly linked to developments in the spoken language: because the phonetic shift occurred early in the northern and midland dialects, the convention began appearing in print first in northern England around 1250 CE, whereas in the southlands, where the pronunciation of OE *ic* shifted early in the opposite direction by palatization to *ich*, it did not catch on regularly until the 1700s. The capitalization of proper names, however (in English and in other European scripts), seems to have arisen first during the fifteenth century in manuscripts written in humanist hands in Italy purely as a stylistic device and found its way into the printed tradition from there (Knight 1998:72).

Other written markers are developed as metatextual signs that attempt to represent graphically the same clues to attitude that are conveyed in direct oral communication by such visual signs as gesture and facial expression. The ever-evolving conventions of text-messaging and internet chatting (direct, nearly instantaneous textual communication with one or more interlocutors) have already produced a standardized set of combinations of existing graphs in the basic ISO character set to convey such metatextual information as humor or pleasure [:)], unhappiness or sympathy [:( ], and irony [;)], and a term has been coined to describe them: emoticons. Some of these new metalanguages take full advantage of the representational capabilities of hypertext markup language (HTML) by generating both logograms and pictograms from a combination of encoded verbal information and punctuation glyphs, thus creating a new kind of hybrid writing system.[1]

It is for graphic phenomena of this sort that I propose the term "paragram," on the model of Genette's "paratext," since the more obvious and logical "paragraph" (so-called after the mark used to distinguish such units in ancient Greek manuscripts) is already taken by a particular specimen of the genus. Another possibility might be "metagraph," since the category aims to embrace precisely those graphic elements that are not letters (in Greek *grammata*) and that often stand "beyond" (*meta-*) rather than literally "beside" (*para-*) the text, but "paragram" has the double advantage of having Genette's well-known formulation as precedent and avoiding the imprecision inherent in the vast conceptual territory nowadays evoked by the prefix "meta-". If such a miscellaneous category of scriptural information cannot be more succinctly characterized by an existing designation, a novel term with a somewhat open definition may prove useful. However defined, such phenomena must be considered worthy objects of study as part of a writing system.

A related, if distinct, element of a writing system is order. "System" implies a group of functionally interrelated elements forming a collective unity. Although orderliness need not be intrinsic to a system, it seems that, just as the irregularities in a spoken language tend to flatten out and normalize over time, so too do orderliness in the orientation of writing and a regular sequence of the script, if they are not present at the outset, come with time to virtually all verbal writing systems. In that sense, order and regularity of script presentation (as opposed to the more frequently remarked regularity of grapheme formation) can be regarded as one of the common script developments that require explanation generically, as well as specifically for individual scripts. Two newly published Greek *abecedaria*, for example—one from a cache of inscriptions (including Semitic texts) found in Eretria (Kenzelmann Pfyffer et al. 2005:60, no. 3; Wachter 2005), the other a rock-cut specimen from Attica (Langdon 2005)—show that the early Greek alphabet remained fluid not only in its graphic forms but also in its sequence and structure for much longer than was previously thought and acquired both order and a fixed system of graphs only after it had been transmitted to Italy (Benelli 2008:26). Whether that pattern was common or unusual remains for now unclear, but the question of the parallel or independent development of scriptural order and grapheme formation deserves further consideration. Whenever arrived, once a form of order is imposed in a writing system, upsetting its conventions enables a writer to convey graphically a message that departs from language and embarks on symbolic and performative functions independent of any particular semantic value (Tambiah 1968). So, for instance, an inscribed Greek curse tablet of the fourth century aiming to induce confusion and turmoil in its targets deliberately scrambles several words and names in the imprecation, reversing and inverting the order of the script and skewing the orientation of the individual lines of text (Gager 1992:201–202, no. 104; Wünsch 1897:102).

In what follows I illustrate the significance of two of these three elements—punctuation and order—in the development of the Latin script in antiquity, and I indicate briefly some categories of semantically significant scriptural elements that a fuller investigation of paragrams might incorporate. First, however, it is useful to consider the basic building blocks of the alphabetic languages of ancient Italy—the character set of letters—since the history of their reception and evolution provides an essential orientation to the linguistic currents that shaped the scriptural system. Except where otherwise indicated, all dates are BCE.

SIGHT AND SOUND: PHONETIC AND GRAPHIC INFLUENCES ON THE FORMATION OF THE LATIN ALPHABET

With the exception of the Greek alphabets brought by colonists to Sicily and the coastal regions of southern Italy beginning around 800 BCE, all of the scripts we know of from the ancient peninsula were derived from the alphabet in use at about that same date by the late Iron Age people of central Italy (whether indigenous or immigrants from the east) known to the Romans as Etruscans.[2] The alphabet that the Greeks acquired from the Phoenicians had divided early along geographical lines into two branches, an eastern (Ionic) type and a western (Chalcidian) type. The Etruscans adapted their script from a particular form of the western variety (Euboean), which differed in distinctive features from the Ionic type more familiar to us from its use in classical Attica. But the Etruscan character set evidently went back to an earlier stage before the division, since it includes all three Phoenician sibilants (*samekh, sade,* and *shin*), whereas both the western and the eastern varieties employed only a single one, represented consistently as either *sigma* or *san*. To these three sibilants the Etruscans added a fourth, using the symbol (X) employed in eastern Greek for *chi* (Bonfante and Bonfante 1983:45; Cristofani 1978:403–410).

Apart from the writers of Sicel in Sicily, who adopted the Chalcidian form of the western Greek alphabet directly from the Chalcidian colonies planted there (some on earlier Sicel sites), and the Messapians, who employed the Laconian Greek alphabet in use around Tarentum, all of the more than half-dozen languages attested in the Italian peninsula by the end of the fifth century were written (or would be written) in versions of this old Etruscan script. One of the least diffused of those dialects was that spoken by a group of tribes known as Latini that had settled by the late Iron Age in the central western coastal plain of Latium. When around the start of the fifth century warriors from the most bellicose of the Latin city-states (Rome) began the process of conquest and territorial expansion that would ultimately extend across the Mediterranean world and Europe, they spread both the Latin language and the Roman alphabet throughout the peninsula. The diffusion of the Latin script, however, was by no means a straightforward process, nor did it advance in lockstep with the language. Where the evidence allows us to judge, the alphabet seems to have led the way and won acceptance earlier than the language in areas where both were new. The two most important Italic documents we have, for example—a list of municipal regulations for the Lucanian town of Bantia in southern Italy, datable to ca. 150–100 BCE (our longest Oscan text; see Vetter 1953: 13–28, no. 2), and a set of seven (originally nine) bronze tablets found at Gubbio (ancient Iguvium) in north-central Italy in 1444 recording instructions for the religious ceremonies of a group of local priests (our primary source of Umbrian: Prosdocimi 1984; see below)— were both written, the first entirely, the second partly, in the Latin alphabet. Nor was the phenomenon of discontinuity between language and script restricted to Umbrian and Oscan and the Latin alphabet. Inscriptions in Latin characters have been found also in Raetic, Messapic, Lepontic, and Etruscan; texts in Messapic, Venetic, and Latin were occasionally written also in the Greek and Etruscan alphabets; Oscan inscriptions in the south are regularly inscribed in Greek characters; and so on (Bonfante 1996:301–303; Vetter 1953; Wallace 2004:814–817; Whatmough 1933:539; cf. Adams 2003:40–67).

This alphabetic and linguistic promiscuity implies that, in considering the evolution of Latin script and the influences that may have shaped it from its origins in the mid-seventh century until the Roman alphabet and the Latin language became predominant throughout Italy in the middle of the first century, fully disambiguating phonemic, graphic, and cultural (or sociohistorical) influences may be not only impossible but also unhelpful for understanding their collective impact on its development (Benelli 2008:26n1; Rix 2005). With half a dozen sibling languages in the Indo-European family written in as many different scripts that were themselves directly descended from that of a non-Indo-European language (Etruscan) that had borrowed its alphabet from an elder aunt (western Greek) and a great-grandfather (the original Greek alphabet, before the eastern and western divide) of several of them, the opportunities for scriptural and linguistic inbreeding were not only likely but also inevitable.

Classical linguists have come to recognize that the conventional conception of diglossia as distinguishing primarily high and low forms of speech is inadequate to characterize the various linguistic interactions among (particularly but not only) Greek and Latin in both high and low usage during the Roman empire. For determining the social function of bilingual expression, a more promising approach seems to lie in the concept of code-switching, a process distinct from borrowing or interference, whereby bilingual speakers or writers manipulate linguistic registers for sometimes purely local effect, as, for example, when a native speaker of English raises or lowers the tone of an utterance by inserting a single word or phrase in a foreign language (Adams 2003). The same phenomenon is perhaps worth investigating at the graphic level of script as well. Here we can trace only briefly, by way of example, the evolution of a single letter, the Greek *gamma*, in its Italian contexts, to illustrate the processes that might affect the fate of a single graph subjected to the variable currents of a fluid environment.

We owe to Jeffery (1990) the ingenious and, for our purposes, significant observation that when the Greeks borrowed the alphabet of the Phoenecians, they copied the four sibilant signs in their correct places in a sequence but transposed their sounds in pairs. This suggests that the Greeks acquired their alphabet primarily by visual means, copying letters in a row, rather than aurally from repeated oral recitation. In support of this plausible hypothesis, Jeffery noted that whereas in the Semitic languages the word for the character set was *higgayon*, "the muttering," which accords with an aural reception of the *abjad*, in Greek the words for the alphabet were *grammata* (literally "drawings," commonly "letters") or *stoicheia* ("units in a row" or "lines"), implying that the more important feature for the Greeks was the written sign (Jeffery 1990:25–27; cf. the Poinikastas website). Jeffery goes on to suggest that the Latin term *abecedarium* places the Romans with the Phoenecians in favoring an aural conception of the alphabet, but *abecedarium* did not come into Latin usage until the end of antiquity and only became common in the medieval period. In classical times the Romans, like the Greeks, conceived of the alphabet graphically, as a system of signs, which they called *litteratura*, literally "lettering" (probably from *lino*, "to smear").

The earliest inscribed *abecedarium* we have (an ivory and wood tablet from Marsiliana d'Albegna in Etruria, datable to the middle of the seventh century) shows that when the Etruscans copied the Greek alphabet, they copied all of it, even preserving the three non-Euboean characters *xi, san,* and *qoppa* in their correct positions in the sequence of letters (rather than tacked on at the end; fig. 3.1).

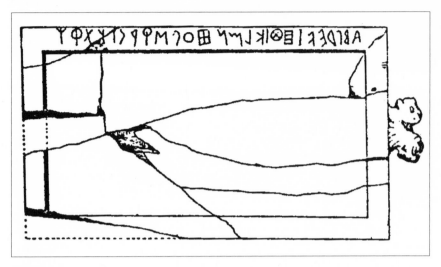

FIGURE 3.1

Ivory tablet from Marsiliana d'Albegna (Etruria) with model alphabet, ca. 700–650 BCE. After Bonfante and Bonfante 1983:Figure 11.

For writing their own language, however, they did not need *delta* (δ), *beta* (β), and *omicron* (o), so they dropped them (β and δ never appear in Etruscan texts), and no more than two of the four sibilants (*sade, samech, sigma,* and *X*) were ever in use in the same place at the same time (Bonfante and Bonfante 1983:65–66; Cristofani 1978; Jeffery 1990:236). This suggests that the alphabet was received as a set of written signs that was subsequently both reduced and augmented through the common practices of inventory expansion and inventory reduction (Daniels 2006:11–12) by the abandonment of unnecessary graphs and the addition of characters needed to distinguish new sounds. This model alphabet (fig. 3.1), which deployed the full range of signs, served primarily a decorative function and, for the latter half of the seventh century, enjoyed a life independent of the spoken language (Bonfante and Bonfante 1983:106; cf. Hartmann 2005:232–236).

Signs of a separate development of the written and the spoken language may be found in the preservation of superfluous signs in written texts, when voiced pronunciation no longer served to distinguish one from the other. For the hard *k* sound, for example, the Etruscans used three different signs, which they differentiated according to the following vowel—*k* before *a* (*ka*), *q* before *u* (*qu*), and, since they had no need for voiced stops, the voiced *gamma* inherited from the Greeks (written as *G* in the eastern scripts, < or *C* in the western varieties) before *e* and *i*. In other words, they observed a representational (phonetic) distinction rather than an aural or semantic (phonemic) one, which they represented through a system of digraphs (cf. Daniels 1990:730). The Latins adopted this system wholesale, preserving the *k* only in a few loan words from old Etruscan (notably *kalendae* for "first day of the month," whence "calendar") and pronouncing the third Greek letter (*gamma*) as the Etruscans did, unvoiced, as *k* (fig. 3.2).

Since the Latins, unlike the Etruscans, also used a voiced *g*, they needed a graph to distinguish it from *c*. The introduction of a new letter, *G*, is thus accordingly credited to a freedman, Sp. Carvilius, reportedly the first to open an elementary school at Rome around the middle of the third century, who created it by slightly adjusting graphically the shape of *C* (Plutarch, *Roman Questions* 54, 59). At the same time, the Romans had inherited a superfluity of characters to express the single hard *k* sound in their own language. *K* itself fell out of use, as it did in southern Etruria, and *c* became the standard unvoiced velar in Latin. But the orthographic distinction in usage of *q* (only before *u*) was preserved by the Romans (and has been passed down to the Romance languages and English), and the original Etruscan phonetic distinction was reflected in the Latin names for the letters, *ce* (pronounced "kay"), *ka* ("kah"), and *qu* ("ku") (Gordon 1973:59–60).

Since we do not know what the Etruscans called their letters, it cannot be claimed that the Romans adopted their letter names directly along with the graphs themselves, but the Latin names do show that the consonantal graphs were acquired with their vocalic delimiters, which served as mnemonic devices for usage. A comparable type of syllabic notation, in which a consonant letter represents both the consonant and a following vowel, usually the letter's name, is characteristic of the Latin written at Praeneste, some twenty miles east of Rome. The superabundance of *k* sounds in the Latin alphabet did not go unremarked by the Romans themselves: during the middle years of the first century, a prominent orator refused to write the letter *q*, and a contemporary grammarian went so far as to try to abolish *q*, *k*, and *x* from the language altogether (Keil 1859: VII:8–9; Ullman 1932:37). Neither initiative took hold, but the notices merit attention for the rare glimpse they provide of a contemporary response to a perceived superfluity of symbols; neither the master of oratory nor the teacher of elementary reading and writing had any use for a graph not needed to represent a distinctive sound.

We remark here on two phenomena, one common, the other more unusual. In the creation of *g* we find a typical example of one of the standard

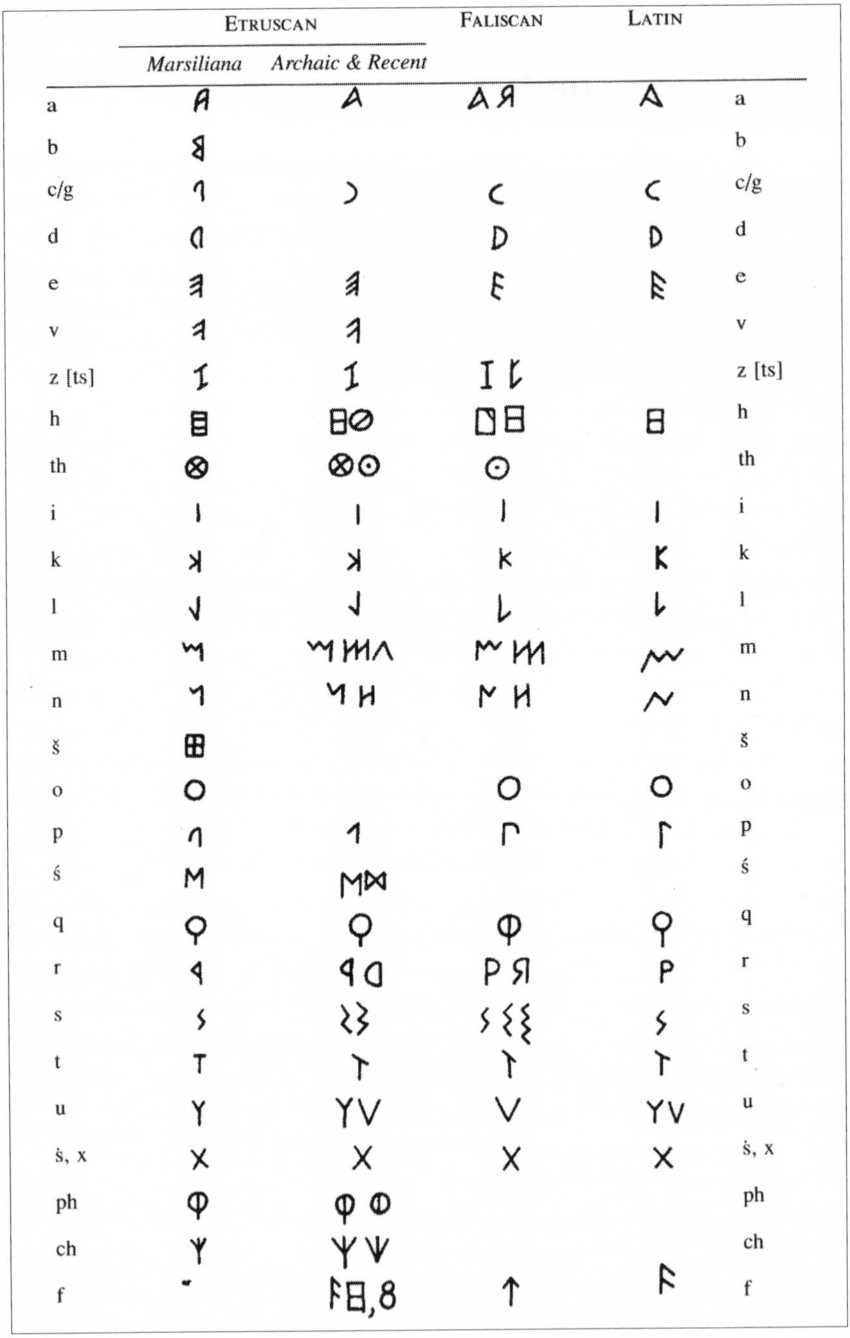

	ETRUSCAN		FALISCAN	LATIN	
	Marsiliana	*Archaic & Recent*			
a	𝖠	𝖠	𝖠 𝖱	𝖠	a
b	𝟪				b
c/g	⌐	⟩	C	C	c/g
d	◁		D	D	d
e	∃	∃	E	E	e
v	⅂	⅂			v
z [ts]	I	I	I Ɫ		z [ts]
h	⊟	⊟⊘	⊓⊟	⊟	h
th	⊗	⊗⊙	⊙		th
i	I	I	I	I	i
k	K	K	k	K	k
l	⅃	⅃	L	Ⅼ	l
m	M	M Mꟿ Λ	M ꟿ	N	m
n	⅄	⅄ H	N H	N	n
š	⊞				š
o	O	O	O	O	o
p	⌐	⅂	Γ	Γ	p
ś	M	Mꟼꟼꟼ			ś
q	Q	Q	Φ	Q	q
r	⅂	⅂◁	P Я	P	r
s	Ϟ	⟩⟨	Ϟ ⟨⟩	Ϟ	s
t	T	⊤	⊤	T	t
u	Y	YV	V	YV	u
ś, x	X	X	X	X	ś, x
ph	Φ	Φ Φ			ph
ch	Ψ	ΨV			ch
f	·	Ⅎ⊟,𝟪	↑	Ⅎ	f

FIGURE 3.2

Model alphabets of central Italy, ca. 650–600 BCE. After Morandi 1982:29.

processes of alphabet change, "character alteration." The only unusual feature in the Roman story (which perhaps adds to its plausibility) is the attribution of the innovation to a private person of low status whose position carried no authority but whose profession brought much practical experience in teaching the rudiments of reading and writing. In the retention of *q*—and with it the preservation of a phonetic distinction irrelevant to the spoken language (more lack of process than process)—we see something possibly more rare and certainly less often observed, the fossilization of a character set that prolongs the use of a graph long after its phonemic utility is lost. Lack of change, it seems, may be as significant a phenomenon as change for understanding the development of a script. Inertia, linguistic conservatism, and a human fondness for matters learned young perhaps explain why stagnation rather than dynamism seems to characterize certain periods in the history of a script, but without wider investigation of the phenomenon in other linguistic systems, generalization is impossible.

That the process of adding new characters to the alphabet because of their phonetic utility seems to have been easier than eliminating characters of no phonemic value suggests, again, that the evolution of the Roman alphabet was related to but not limited by the sounds of the language—so long as the basic character set retained a certain fluidity, at any rate. By the middle of the first century CE, when the Roman emperor Claudius tried to introduce into the alphabet three new letters—an inverted *digamma* (Ⅎ) for consonantal *v*, to distinguish it from vocalic *u*; the left vertical and horizontal stroke of the aspirate *H* (Ⱶ), to represent an intermediate vocalic sound (possibly between short *e* and *i*); and a reversed *C* (antisigma Ɔ) to represent *ps* or *bs*—on the grounds of their phonetic advantages, the basic character set had become more stable, and a phonetically justifiable approach to altering it, even one originating from the highest authority, could no longer effect lasting change: only the first two letters are ever found in inscriptions, almost all in official public documents, and none, apparently, after the death of Claudius in 54 CE (Oliver 1949).[3]

As for *gamma*, by the time it was "invented" (or perhaps more accurately, came into use) around the middle of the third century, the sixth place in the alphabet occupied by the Greek letter *zeta* inherited from the Etruscans had been vacated by the letter's falling out of use, since its Etruscan pronunciation (as a voiceless alveolar fricative, like English *ts*) came to be represented in Latin at first by *s* and then by *ss*. In order to preserve to the extent possible the internal order and possibly the numerical sequence of the alphabet, the new letter was inserted into the place of *zeta*. When later, around the middle of the first century, closer linguistic contact with the Greeks made clear the need for a grapheme to represent the Greek sound of z (voiced, as in English "buzz"), the Romans reintroduced the character for *zeta* (z), but, having lost its place in the sequence, it was tacked on to the end of the series, now already extended by the addition of the non-native letters *x* and *y*. This was the more normal practice with the addition of new alphabetic characters to a set (Daniels 2006:12). The installation of *g* in its current position is more striking and shows, again, the independent operation of phonetic and purely graphic influences on the development of the Roman script.

An epilogue, or footnote, to the story raises the specter of another common influence on the development of a writing system, one occasionally recognized but not yet sufficiently categorized and analyzed: the miscellaneous group of extralinguistic influences that might be defined broadly as cultural or more narrowly, perhaps, as sociolinguistic. In the case of *gamma*, the Roman onomastic system provides an illustration of such influences at work. The name of a Roman male citizen comprised three basic elements, of which the first (*praenomen*) was practically limited during the historical period to a dozen possibilities, all of which were conventionally written in abbreviated form, usually a single initial letter, when preceding other elements of the name, as for example, *M.* (= Marcus) Tullius Cicero. That this development in Roman onomastic practice occurred before the introduction of *g* into the alphabet, at a time when Etruscan *gamma* still had the value of both *c* and *g*, may be inferred from the fact that the Roman *praenomina* Gaius and Gnaeus, both pronounced with an initial hard *g* and spelled with that character when standing alone, are invariably represented by the initials *C.* and *Cn.* (never *G.* or *Gn.*) when abbreviated in Roman names. In one culturally determined linguistic context (nomenclature), in other words, one graph (*C*) took the place phonetically of another (*G*) and thus functioned more as a symbol than as an abbreviation; expanding the symbol properly required decoding the graph within its peculiarly defined context. Half a century after the emperor Claudius' failed effort to introduce new characters into the Latin alphabet, the official Professor of Rhetoric Quintilian urged a similar employment of the inherited letter *k*, which he recommended be used only as a single letter abbreviation to represent particular words in context (e.g., the *praenomen* Kaeso) (Quintilian, *Institutio Oratoria* 1.7.10). His efforts and authority, like those of the emperor Claudius, availed naught, and the practice never caught on. In Roman culture, at least, such developments seem to have endured only when they arose organically from common practice.

ORDER AND THE EPIGRAPHIC SCRIPT

With the exception of a very few examples of Latin figure labels in tomb frescoes at Rome and an Etruscan religious text of the second half of the second century originally painted on a linen scroll, then torn into strips and wrapped around an Egyptian mummy now in Zagreb, all the specimens of writing we have from the Italian peninsula before the middle of the first century were carved or scratched in hard surfaces, usually stone or bronze; they therefore provide direct evidence of only one form of the script. With some dialects and alphabets, inscriptions may have been the only or the main medium of writing, but in others, notably Latin, we know something of the handwritten types, even if we cannot see or describe them. A slave character in an early comedy of Plautus (late third century), for example, describes the cursive script etched into the waxed tablets used for business documents and private correspondence as resembling chicken scratches (*Pseudolus* 21–30). To one accustomed only to the capital letters of monumental inscriptions, characters scraped with a stylus in old Roman cursive might well seem more like random lines than an organized script (Camodeca 1999). From about the middle of the first century, we begin to have handwritten documents on papyrus and parchment and painted campaign posters from Pompeii, but before that time, when we speak about the development of Latin script, we are effectively talking about the epigraphic script, and more particularly about that form of it known as *capitalis*, because it was carved in stone or etched onto pottery after firing. What is more, the number of specimens of it that have more than a few letters and are datable to before the third century is fewer than a dozen. We have only that slender foundation on which to base our estimation of the nature of the Latin script for the first three hundred fifty years of its development.

One thing, at least, is clear. In our earliest Latin writing, as in our earliest (contemporaneous) Etruscan texts, words were not separated from one another but were written continuously, and the text ran in a variety of directions—left to right, right to left, boustrophedon ("as the ox plows," first in one direction, then in its opposite), or following the contours of the surface of the object. By the end of the fifth century, words were regularly divided in the scripts of both languages, and lines of text were written consistently and systematically in a single direction: Etruscan (like Umbrian and Oscan) right to left, Latin left to right. In Etruscan inscriptions of the third century and later, the writing often runs from left to right under Roman influence—a clear indication that script orientation, like the alphabet, was a distinctive but independent element within the Italic writing systems. Unfortunately, since most of our earliest specimens of the Latin script belong to the sixth century and none can be precisely dated, establishing a firm chronology or even a clear sequence of the earliest developments is impossible (Hartmann 2005:426–434). The oldest alphabetic writing yet found in Italy, etched on a vase found in a grave datable to the early eighth century at Osteria dell Osa (also known as Gabii), eleven miles east of Rome (Ampolo 1997), has recently been interpreted as a Latin formula written left to right in characters drawn right to left, thus further confounding the relative priority of Etruscan and Latin influences in the orientation of the earliest Italic scripts (Colonna 2004). A *bucchero* (black pottery) cup recently recovered from a trench grave datable to the middle of the sixth century at Magliano Sabina, thirty miles north of Rome, and inscribed with a text in Faliscan written in Sabine script suggests that the entire array of paleo-italic alphabetic and graphic systems needs reconsideration (Poccetti 2008:40). Under the circumstances, we can only observe the variety of modes of writing and try to deduce from them how and perhaps why, if not when, order emerged in the Italic scripts. A brief review of some of our earliest specimens of the Latin script will thus illustrate the range rather than the evolution of practices in script disposition, character formation and orientation, and punctuation before the fifth century.[4]

Perhaps our earliest specimen, dated by some scholars to as early as the mid-seventh century, is the famous "Duenos" vase found in Rome in 1880 (*CIL* 1^2 4), which bears a text generally agreed to consist of three units written retrograde in a script that follows the contours of a tripartite clay receptacle (fig. 3.3). The first unit of text, inscribed nearest the lip of the vessel (thus appearing as the inner string of the bird's-eye-view transcription in the upper right of figure 3.3), begins with the word IOVE at the point where it overlaps the end of the second, solitary unit.

Where the exterior string of text is to be divided is uncertain, but the initial sequence (beginning at the top of figure 3.3) reveals it to be one of the "speaking" inscriptions commonly found on portable objects of the archaic and later ages, which purport to represent the voice of the object itself in declaring authorship, as (in this case) "Duenos [either 'a good man' or 'Good'] made me" (*Duenos med feced*). Of four corrected letters, two *C*s, in PACARI (unit 2) and FECED (unit 3), seem to have arisen out of uncertainty whether to write *C* or *K*. A separator line divides the first word of the text, IOVE, from what follows (as in the Phaistos disk, a clay disk datable to around 1700 BCE, found at the Minoan palace site of Phaistos in southern Crete, and inscribed with an undeciphered pictographic writing [Morritt 2010]); otherwise, the articulation of the units is perhaps based on the syntax of the text.

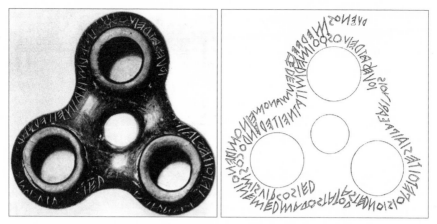

FIGURE 3.3

Inscribed triform bucchero *vessel, Rome ("Duenos" vase), ca. 650–450?* BCE. *After Hartmann 2005:111–112, Figures 82, 84. Text:*

> IOVEISATDEIVOSQOIMEDMITATNEITEDENDOCOSMISVIRCOSIED
> ASTEDNOISIOPETOITESIAIPACARIVOIS
> DVENOSMEDFECŒDENMANOMEINOMDZENOINEMEDMAOSTATOD

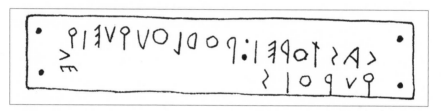

FIGURE 3.4

*Dedication to Castor and Pollux (*CIL *1² 2833), Madonetta (Pratica di Mare, Latium), ca. 550–500? After Bloch 1960:187. Text:* Castorei Podlouqueiq~ue~ / qurois.

A thin bronze plate found in 1958 at an archaic sanctuary outside Pratica di Mare (Lavinio, ancient Lavinium), some eighteen miles south of Rome, bears a dedication to the divine twins Castor and Pollux written right to left. The names in their Latin form are glossed with a transliterated Greek word, *kurois* ("the boys"), that reveals the influence of the Etrusco-Latin environment in employing the old Italic *Q* (Ϙ) for the Greek *kappa* before *u* (fig. 3.4).

Although the text is disposed horizontally along the length of the plate, the last two letters of the first line are carved down the left side, with the tops of the letters toward the edge of the bronze, as if the reader's viewpoint were imagined from the center of the field or the object or the viewer

79

were thought to be mobile. A single interpunct after the first word (the lower, larger dot in figure 3.4 represents a nail hole in the plate, as do those at the four corners) perhaps indicates the development of a graphic notation, in addition to line division, to distinguish words or units of text.

Probably the best known and certainly the most studied early Latin text was carved on a truncated obeliskoid tufa block found in situ beside an altar in the Roman Forum, where it was partially preserved and marked in antiquity when the area in which it was located was paved over by a series of volcanic black slabs (hence the name Lapis Niger [Black Stone], commonly misattributed to the block itself; fig. 3.5).

Though displayed vertically when set in place, the text was evidently carved horizontally along the four main sides of the block (lines 1–15) and along a fifth face made by shaving off the southwest corner (line 16). Two features of the text's disposition suggest that the carver was unfamiliar with his medium. Though generally boustrophedon, line 12 (line 1 of the south face) reverses the sequence, evidently because the carver changed position when he reached the edge of the stone and lost track of his place. Similarly, lines 8–9 (lines 1–2 of the east face) and 16 (the southwest edge) are inverted with respect to the other lines, either because the carver carved the letters upside down or, more probably, because he changed positions and carved the lines in pairs: thus, lines 7–8 would have been carved right to left, lines 15–16 left to right.

Among notable palaeographic features, *M* is regularly written with five rather than four strokes and *U* is carved in the shape of *Y* (lines 7, 10, 13). The more familiar *V* shape known from inscriptions incised in hard surfaces did not become established before the fourth century, when it first emerges in both the Latin and the Etruscan script, possibly under the influence of a neighboring dialect, Faliscan. *Y* returns to the Latin character set only during the first century, when it is borrowed to represent the Greek *upsilon*. The complex early history of the hard *k* sound (see above) in Latin is illustrated by the use of *C* for *G* in RECEI (line 5) and *K* before *A* in KALATOR (line 8) and KAPIA (line 11). The second term (*kalator*), a loanword from Etruscan that names an Etruscan religious office, retains its traditional orthography (as indeed did all loanwords from Etruscan with initial *ka-*) and thus skirts the boundary between translation and transliteration. If the third (*kapia*) is correctly understood to represent the classical Latin *capita* ("heads"), then we might conclude from its "Etruscan" orthography that scriptural consistency here trumps linguistic origin in the graphic representation of the early language. Most strikingly, perhaps, *S* is carved consistently with the same orientation, regardless of which way

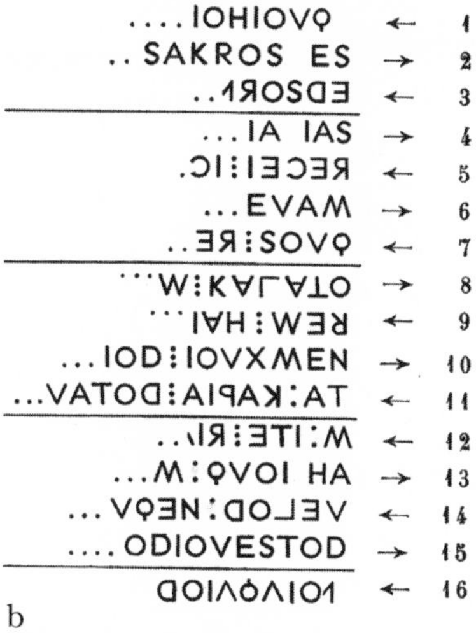

a

b

.... IOHIOVϘ	← 1
.. SAKROS ES	→ 2
..Ǝ�8OᴚH..	← 3
... IA IAS	→ 4
.ƆI:IƎƆƎᴚ.	← 5
... EVAW	→ 6
..Ǝᴚ:SOVϘ	← 7
⋯W: KⱯ⅃ⱯⵏO	→ 8
⋯IⱯH:WƎᴚ	← 9
...IOᗡ:IOVXWEN	→ 10
...VATOᗡ:AIᗡAᴋ:AT	← 11
..ⵏIᴚ:ƎTI:W	← 12
...W:ϘVOI HA	→ 13
... VϘƎN:ᗡO⅃ƎV	← 14
.... ODIOVESTOD	→ 15
ᗡOIΛόΛIOᴣ	← 16

FIGURE 3.5

(a) *Forum Romanum* cippus *(CIL I² 1),
Rome, ca. 550–500? BCE. Plaster casts
of the five inscribed faces of the block
arranged horizontally in the sequence of
the text. (b) Transcription of* (a) *showing
the direction and orientation of the lines
of text. After* CIL *I² 1.*

the text runs (thus, "correctly" in lines 2, 4, and 15, "incorrectly" [unre-
versed] in lines 3 and 7). Perhaps the orientation of the character
was not yet fixed, and the carver, confused by his familiarity with both the
Etruscan *Z* and the Latin and Faliscan *S* (found also in the Marsiliana
alphabet), settled on a visually regular orientation rather than a scripturally
consistent formation of the graph. The text is inconsistently punctuated
throughout by the use of dots, either three (the standard form in Etruscan
texts) or two (the form later predominant in Latium) disposed vertically as
word-dividers.

FIGURE 3.6

Statue base with dedication to Publius Valerius (Lapis Satricanus) *(CIL I² 2832a), Satricum (Latium), ca. 500? BCE. After CIL I² 2832a. Text:* [- - -]uiei steterai Popliosio Valesiosio / suodales Mamertei.

To the end of the archaic age of Rome, around the year 500 BCE, belongs what may be the latest of the early texts here surveyed, the dedication by members of a Brotherhood of Mars of a statue to one Publius Valerius, probably the semi-legendary figure recorded as consul during the first year of the Republic, following the expulsion of the kings (traditionally 509 BCE; fig. 3.6).

A yellow limestone base found in 1977 at Satricum (near present-day Consa), about thirty miles southeast of Rome, bears on its front face a brief, two-line dedicatory text with letters upright and oriented in their conventional positions, lines centered, and text running orthograde left to right. *M* is carved in its standard four-stroke form, and *V* (rather than *Y*) is used interchangeably for both vowels (*suodales*) and consonants (*Valesiosio*). There is no punctuation or word division other than by lines. Here we have, in every respect other than interpunctuation and individual character formation, a model of a standard scriptural form of honorific dedication common throughout the rest of antiquity.

To sum up, our earliest Latin texts, deriving from a variety of private and public contexts—civic, domestic, and religious—exhibit much inconsistency in orientation and disposition of the text, as well as in the formation of individual graphs. By the end of the fifth century, Latin texts regularly ran left to right, Etruscan texts right to left, and greater regularity had come to both scripts. Why? Two hypotheses may briefly be entertained; neither excludes the other, but neither, in the present state of our knowledge, can be proved correct. As models for the ways that order might come to a script, they usefully represent two fundamental aspects that are generally regarded as determinative. One focuses on the physicality of the earliest preserved writing and concerns itself mainly with the monuments that carried texts (the medium); the other privileges authorial intent and the communicative functions of language, however conveyed (the message).

One possibility is that order came to Latin script when monumental writing became more common. When writing was largely confined to portable objects, this theory holds, the various (irregular) shapes of the text-bearing objects and the fact that they could be manipulated manually discouraged systematic arrangement and encouraged ad hoc design. The "Duenos" vase (see fig. 3.3) and the dedication to Castor and Pollux (see fig. 3.4) provide good examples of both. When inscribed writing began to be used to label larger monuments, however, the fixed position of (generally) rectilinear objects necessitated accommodating a more limited range of viewing perspectives. The less than successful experiment of the boustrophedon mode in the *cippus* (pillar) from the Forum (see fig. 3.5) shows the disadvantages of displaying vertically text inscribed to be read horizontally and employing a character set in which graphic orientation remained mutable, a practice that led to errors in both representation (carving) and interpretation (reading). A teleological linear progression could thus be imagined from retrograde texts that followed the contours of objects ("Duenos" vase, Castor and Pollux dedication) to boustrophedon writing with a vertical orientation (Forum *cippus*) to orthograde lines of text written with fixed graphs and running in a set direction (the inscription on the limestone base found at Satricum). But recent discoveries in central Italy, particularly Latium, suggest that variability and experimentation characterize the development of the Italic scripts more accurately than the tidy picture of linear progress from randomness to order that current scholarship favors (Santoro 2008).

A second possibility is that Roman script ran left to right as a pointed statement, in order to mark itself distinctively as un-Etruscan. Whether by inheritance (a famous stele from Lemnos written in a language like old Etruscan in an archaic alphabet with words divided by two-dot interpuncts has long been taken to provide a clue to the origin of Etruscan) or by indigenous development on the Italian peninsula, the Etruscan script seems always to have run right to left, as did those of the other Italic dialects (Umbrian and Oscan) predominant in central Italy. To the Etruscans, as to the Greeks, the Romans acknowledged a strong cultural debt that both inspired and challenged their own claim to an independent identity. The ambivalence of attitude that resulted from this conflicted view of their own heritage at times bordered on outright contradiction but generally aimed to reinforce both the autonomy and the superiority of the Roman version over the presumed mother traditions. With the Greeks, a full confrontation with Hellenism came only after Roman conquests in Greece during the third century. With the Etruscans, geographical proximity on both borders may have prompted from early on the development of a scriptural system that, though manifestly related to those of its older neighbors in central Italy, stood out as distinctly different from—even opposed to—them. As Roman military power and ambition grew in the centuries following the establishment of Etruscan kings at Rome toward the end of the seventh century, a desire to project Roman civic, as well as military, authority in public contexts might thus have led to the custom of inscribing honorific dedications in a distinctively Roman scriptural fashion. Support for this hypothesis may perhaps be found in the Roman numeric system, specifically in the formation of Roman numerals.

The Roman whole-number numeral system is generally and rightly recognized as a modified version of the Etruscan tally-mark system, wherein I (a single tally mark) stands for one; X, a second-rank symbol (two crossed tally marks), stands for ten; and $*$, a third-rank symbol (three crossed tally marks), represents one hundred (Keyser 1988). In order to represent the numerals five and fifty, the Etruscans used the lower half of each succeeding decade sign, thus Λ for five and $\uparrow$ for fifty. The Romans, it seems, distinguished their corresponding numerals by adopting the opposite halves of the same signs. In order to represent five and fifty, in other words, they employed what appears as the upper, rather than the lower, half of the following decade signs in the Etruscan system, thus V for five and $\downarrow$ for fifty. When combined with the conventional sequence of the script, the effect was to make Etruscan numerals Roman by inverting them and reversing their direction: I Λ X $\uparrow$ in Etruscan and $\downarrow$ X V I in Latin represent the same number, sixty-six. Whether orthograde sequence came earlier to the Roman numbering system or to the Latin script is difficult to say (and whichever came first undoubtedly influenced the other), but each bears signs, in addition to a left-to-right orientation, of both derivation from and systematic variance from an earlier Etruscan system of graphs.

PUNCTUATION AND PARAGRAMS

Somewhat lost in the penumbra of grammatology studies, along with the issues of order and sequence in the development of a script, are the marks, or absence of marks, that serve to guide readers or viewers of a text in ways not tied to the inflection of individual phonemes (diacritical marks). Most widely recognized in this category are the signs that serve the functions of punctuation, but conceptually and functionally there is often little difference between recognized marks of punctuation and other signs or spatial arrangements that serve similar purposes but do not normally come into discussion and therefore tend to be overlooked. Brief consideration of three such examples of variable and ambivalent markers in the Latin script—the medial interpunct, the supralinear diagonal stroke sometimes known as an *apex* (´), and the *S* bracket—may suggest how little territory separates punctuation from paragrams and how certain signs may move back and forth between the two categories over time, acquiring or shedding semantic significance as they come and go.

The medial interpunct

In the earliest preserved examples of both the Etruscan and the Latin scripts, the writing was continuous, without word division. In Etruscan texts from the end of the seventh century, words often and syllables occasionally were separated by one or more dots placed vertically above one another. Around the middle of the sixth century, syllabic punctuation marking closed syllables began to be used in southern Etruria and Campania, but the practice evidently died out toward the end of the fifth century, when word division by spatial separation became the norm (Peruzzi 1980:137–149). A similar system of punctuation, wherein a short vertical line or dot in the center of the line on either side of the last letter of a syllable marked it as bearing an accent, was introduced into use in Venetic texts early in the fifth century (possibly through a scribal tradition originating at the southern Etruscan sanctuary of Apollo at Veii, just north of Rome) and remained standard until the end of the second century (Conway 1933:191–197; Wachter 1986). Traces of both practices can be observed occasionally in Latin script well into the second century CE, but it was the habit of verbal interpunctuation that the Romans principally took from the Etruscans. In the earliest Etruscan texts, the oldest form of interpunct, a single vertical line (as in the Phaistos disk and the "Duenos" vase; see fig. 3.3), is broken into three vertical dashes or dots, possibly in order to avoid confusion with the letter *I*. This is the form in which it appears also in the *cippus* from the Roman Forum (see fig. 3.5), where the two-dot version is also found. Around the end of the sixth century, however, the single medial dot that would later become standard begins to appear in monumental inscriptions such as the dedication at Satricum (see fig. 3.6). Later it is found regularly also in private texts and, from the end of the first century if not before, in handwritten manuscripts, on wax tablets, and in graffiti scrawled on walls at Pompeii (*CIL* IV 1893, 1894).

That the single medial dot as a word-divider was regarded as an integral part of the Roman script can be seen from the Umbrian tablets found at Gubbio (see above). The first four tablets (and the obverse and first half of the reverse of the fifth), datable to the first half of the third century, are inscribed on both sides in the Umbrian alphabet (thus right to left) and show words separated by the double dot; the last part of the fifth tablet and the last two tablets, belonging to the end of the second century, are likewise opisthograph but are inscribed in the Latin alphabet (left to right) and exhibit only the single medial dot (Prosdocimi 1984). Similarly, a papyrus fragment of the first or second century CE (*PSI* 1912:743) bearing a Greek text written in Latin characters duly includes interpuncts between words, whereas contemporary Greek texts were normally written without word break (Oliver 1951:241–243) and Oscan texts written in the Greek alphabet rarely used interpuncts to divide words (Wallace 2004:817). The philosopher Seneca, in contrasting the Greek and Roman temperaments, observed that whereas the Greeks ran their words together, Romans had "grown accustomed to interpunctuating" (*interpungere adsuevimus*) (*Epistulae Morales* 40.11). Whether he alluded to any forms of notation other than word-dividers is uncertain, but the use of a medial dot to divide words was evidently regarded by Romans and other Italian peoples as an integral part of Latin script.

Elaborations of the medial dot during the period from the third through first centuries—square holes, crosses, triangles—seem to have been purely decorative, as originally was also the interpunct in the shape of an ivy leaf (*hedera distinguens*) that first appeared during the first decades of the first century CE (Gordon and Gordon 1957:183). Later, the *hedera* began to be used to mark off lines of verse, at times in conjunction with and thus distinguishing itself from the interpunct word-divider (Wingo 1972:149–153). A practical device (the interpunct used to divide words) elaborated for decorative effect (the *hedera*) thus came to acquire a functional purpose in distinguishing different types of punctuation in the articulation of a text. The single dot word-divider was used regularly in written texts of all sorts until the second century CE, at which time it began to fall out of use. It never fully disappeared (a papyrus of the fourth or fifth century CE written in a good book hand shows the medial interpunct used regularly), but by the third century it seems already to have been regarded as an archaism and was used mainly for special effect. The question naturally arises, why did such an apparently useful device fall out of use after having been established so securely for so long (Oliver 1951:242)? The relation between such metatextual marks and their apparent functionality is by no means direct, nor is it stable over time.

The *apex*

Apart from the medial interpunct, Roman punctuation was characterized by a wide variety of signs that were used irregularly but systematically within individual documents. Although the set of graphs remained open and wide latitude was granted to stylistic innovation in the formation of individual marks, a few basic symbols established themselves as common. Their usage, however, varied, and although context often made clear what significance each sign carried in any particular instance, their very malleability and mutability inevitably gave rise to confusion. The mark known as the *apex* provides a revealing example. The professor of Latin rhetoric Quintilian, writing at the end of the first century CE, remarks on the utility of the *apex* as a phonetic sign to mark long vowels that would otherwise remain ambivalent, but he characterizes as wholly inept the practice (widely attested in inscriptions) of so marking all long vowels, since the quantity of most was made clear by usage or position (Quintilian, *Institutio Oratoria* 1.7.2–3). The context of his remarks (a discussion of sandhi phenomena) suggests that Quintilian saw the *apex* as serving a phonetic purpose and proper usage as variable by aural context, but he lamented that phonetic utility had ceased to form a reliable guide to the use of the mark in written texts.

No doubt contributing to the confusion was the contemporary use of a virtually identical but proportionally longer sign, an acute accent, as a mark of punctuation, most commonly to indicate the end of a syntactic unit. Sometimes this extended *apex* was supplemented within a single inscription by a slightly longer mark called a *virgula*, which in turn could be amplified by being repeated (*virgula geminata*). The system worked on the principle of a flexible hierarchy in which each document provided its own blueprint for interpreting the significance of the individual marks used within it, which were (in theory) deployed systematically according to a discernible hierarchy of levels—syllable, word, grammatical or syntactic unit, sentence, paragraph, and so on. A similarly methodical evolutionary scheme of progressive graphic elaboration might be hypothesized for the remaining half-dozen signs of punctuation regularly employed, but what evidence we have suggests that the coherent system that ultimately survived into the Middle Ages is unlikely to have evolved so neatly (Wingo

1972:94–95). As Quintilian's complaint about the *apex* reveals, inconsistent usage might lead to ambiguity of meaning, especially when the same sign served multiple functions; irregular or unskilled use of the conventions was thus at times difficult to discern from creative experimentation. The standard method of representing the Roman *praenomen* Manius in inscribed texts provides a case in point.

When the Romans developed their system of abbreviated *praenomina* (see above), they needed a way to distinguish Marcus from Manius and Caius from Cnaeus. With the latter, they adopted a phonological guide in indicating the first with the simple initial *C* and the second by the initial consonant cluster *Cn*. With Marcus and Manius they followed an ostensibly similar procedure in assigning the initial *M* to stand for Marcus and marking Manius by its initial consonant cluster, *Mn*, conveniently and conventionally represented, since the four-stroke *M* had by then become established, with the older five-stroke form, now fallen out of use, which to all appearances resembled a ligature of the two letters. Over time the convention developed, probably in order to save labor, of representing the fifth stroke of the abbreviation cursorily with an elongated mark like an *apex*, placed high to the right of the initial *M* (thus *M'*. in modern typographic conventions). Occasionally during the first and second centuries CE, when one convention had not yet fully replaced the other, one can see confusion develop about the nature of the sign, as, for example, in an epitaph of the middle years of the second century, in which the carver apparently tried to "correct" a pseudo-*apex* into a fifth stroke by extending it with a second elongated *apex* (or *virgula*)—a practice more normally used to mark secondary levels of punctuation (fig. 3.7).

The *S* bracket

The history of the graphic representation of the *praenomen* Manius illustrates well the complex interplay among character formation, punctuation, and paragrams in the evolution of the Roman script. A similar complexity seems to characterize the development in the Latin script of an *S*-shaped bracket to mark items to be read together with or supplemented by another text. Perhaps our earliest clear use of it occurs in the longest and most authoritative Latin text to exhibit the use of punctuation for sense, the monumental inscription recording the accomplishments of the first emperor Augustus inscribed (in Greek and Latin) on the retaining wall of the Temple of Rome and Augustus at Ankara. This famous "queen of inscriptions" (*regina inscriptionum*), as Theodor Mommsen (1873:769) called it, the so-called *Monumentum Ancyranum*, itself was a copy of the

FIGURE 3.7

Representations of the abbreviated praenomen Manius, *ca. 50 BCE–150 CE:* (a) AE *1974,*
257 (MI.AA.UM.KM.L.1049), ca. 50 BCE; (b) CIL *VI 38623 (KY.Lou.SAM.L.1929.17.448),*
ca. 25–75 CE; (c) AE *1984, 410 (MA.Camb.HU.Sack.L.1932.56.129b), ca. 150 CE. Image*
references are to the cataloging system of the U.S. Epigraphy Project; see http://usepigraphy.brown
.edu/numbers.html.

document inscribed on bronze tablets and erected in front of Augustus'
mausoleum at Rome shortly after his death in 14 CE. Whether the punctuation preserved in the Latin inscription at Ankara was present in the same
form in the original text or was produced locally remains uncertain, but
the surviving inscription exhibits at least five different types of marks, as
well as blank spaces, that served to articulate the text; none serves a definitive function, but each is used variously (and interchangeably) according
to whatever other marks are employed in the vicinity (Wingo 1972:29–49).
The overall impression is of fluidity and variability: the apices that appear
irregularly over long vowels, for example, are found in some eight different forms (Marcillet-Jaubert 1959:140).

The most commonly employed sign is an elongated *S*-shaped bracket,
deployed vertically but oriented in either direction, to mark off units of
text. The origin of the mark is uncertain, but a similar use can be seen to
be developing around the same time out of the expansion of the initial *S*
of the abbreviation *SVF* (for *suf*[*fecti*], "substitutes") to bracket and group
together the names of replacement consuls in a list of the annual magistrates set up at Rome in 7 CE (fig. 3.8; Degrassi 1947:279–290).

When the sign is reduced to a single graph in the shape of *S*, as it is in
the next to last entry at the bottom of the last full column to the right of

89

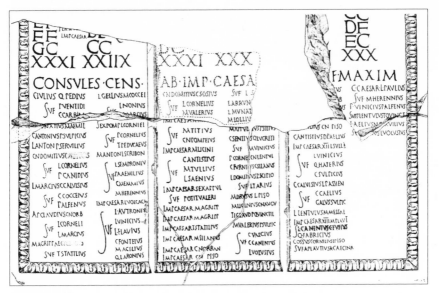

FIGURE 3.8

Section of a list of the names of annual magistrates (consuls) at Rome, with the names of substitutes for each year marked with an initial S *of variable size in the abbreviation* suf(fecti), *meaning "substitutes" (*Fasti magistrorum vici, *ca. 5 CE). Detail of Degrassi 1963:Tabula XXV.*

the stone, the semantic difference between an enlarged initial capital and an expandable mark of punctuation is difficult to determine. Mutual influence of each upon the other may be supposed, and both may be seen to underlie the later development of the Roman caret mark in the form of an expandable hooked brace, which combines the functions of grouping items graphically and indicating where to supplement them in the text.

In functional scriptural devices such as the expandable *S* bracket, which shares features in common with both a letter of the alphabet and a mark of punctuation but is not fully comparable to either, or the variable *apex*, which is normally separable and mutable in significance but when combined with *M* to represent Manius is integral to the formation of a distinctive glyph, we encounter the sorts of marks that serve to articulate and differentiate texts but that are not normally included in discussions of punctuation or character sets (alphabets, *abjads*, *abugidas*, syllabaries, and the like) and for which I propose the term "paragram." Along with spacing and impagination, such devices served to guide readers through the interpretation of a text and were thus integral to its reception. It is unclear how far one might usefully extend the concept—whether, for example, in the

Roman script the paragram should embrace such code-switching phenomena as the monogram formed of the two Greek letters *chi* and *rho*. This is found in Christian Latin texts after Constantine and appeared variably, apparently without semantic distinction, in two forms (with upright cross ☧ and with diagonal cross ☧). It was used at times as a symbol (for Christ) and at times as a simple ligature representing the consonant cluster (*chr*). Another, the Greek *theta* (θ), was prefixed to the names of the deceased in group epitaphs listing persons both living and dead. Further exploration of the characteristics and limits of the category may help us to refine our still rudimentary understanding of the nature of early scripts and how they developed. If the preceding discussion of a few particular aspects of the use of paratextual signs, spacing, and order in the early writing of the Romans has succeeded in demonstrating the relevance of such considerations for understanding the formation and evolution of a script, it will have fulfilled its purpose.

Notes

1. For emoticons, see the Language Log website: http://itre.cis.upenn.edu/~myl/languagelog/archives/004935.html. The Unicode consortium now includes characters for "smile" (U+2323 ☺) and "frown" (U+2322 ☹), reflecting their passage from symbol to standardized glyph.

2. The theory that the Latins and Etruscans received the Greek alphabet independently and more or less simultaneously from the Euboean colony at Cumae (Cristofani 1978:408–409) hangs mainly upon the oldest presumed example of the Latin script, which appears on a clothing pin found at Palestrina (*fibula Praenestina*), some twenty miles east of Rome, whose authenticity has been vigorously disputed for the last quarter century (e.g., Formigli 1992; Guarducci 1981, 1984–1986; Hartmann 2005:67–106) and has been complicated by recent discoveries of early texts near Rome (Benelli 2008). I exclude a few Phoenecian, western Semitic, and Iberian inscriptions found in Sicily and Sardinia, as well as isolated pockets of non-native scripts used locally in Italy, such as a set of bilingual gold leaf tablets in Phoenician and Etruscan found at Pyrgi on the Tuscan coast north of Rome (ca. 500 BCE) or Nabataean business records at the port city of Puteoli (*CIS* II.i.2.157–159). It is perhaps worth noting that the oldest Greek alphabetic writing is not found in Greece but in Italy and is attested outside Rome (at Gabii, twelve miles away) as early as ca. 770 BCE (Peruzzi 1992).

3. For the ancient testimony, see Quintilian, *Institutio Oratoria* 1.7.26; cf. 1.4.8; Tacitus, *Annals* 11.14.3; Suetonius, *Life of Claudius* 41.3. It is perhaps not coincidental that the three processes of character alteration adopted by Claudius, a specialist in Etruscan learning, in creating new graphs—inversion, reversal, and truncation of

an existing graph—correspond to the three basic types of transformation that the Etruscan alphabet underwent in Roman hands.

4. On all of these, see Hartmann (2005), who discusses also the handful of other, shorter texts that make up the corpus of archaic Latin inscriptions, all of which were found in Latium (modern Lazio), the region of central western Italy to the south and east of Rome. They include a surname (possibly Etruscan), Vetusia, scratched retrograde beneath the lip of a terracotta bowl found at Palestrina in an archaeological context datable to the seventh century; the *fibula Praenestina* mentioned above (note 2); a votive dedication carved either boustrophedon or spirally around the face of a squat tufa base found at Tivoli (*CIL* I^2 2658); a dedication declaring ownership by Trivia scratched in a circle around the bottom of a bowl found at Minturnae (Garigliano bowl); three inscribed fragments of a *peperino* (or tufa) altar found in 1975 near Corcolle (*CIL* I^2 2833a); and three fragmentary *bucchero* vessels etched with brief declarations of ownership ("I am of [i.e., belong to] X") found in a grave at Ardea (*CIL* I^2 474), near the Regia in the Roman Forum (*CIL* I^2 2830), and at an unknown location (*CIL* I^2 479).

4

Stability and Change in Arabic Script

Beatrice Gruendler

During Arabic script's long history from the fourth century CE until today, it has undergone the two types of change outlined by Richard Salomon (chapter 5) in this volume: adaptations of the entire system and phases of minor external adjustments mostly designed to denote what had been left out or become ambiguous in the consonant-based alphabet (*abjad*). The usage of the minor, phonetic optimizations was in premodern times fully at the discretion of the writers, who could opt to demonstrate their correct performance of the language or hide potential errors by leaving the writing unmarked. The standardization of modern typeface has substantially reduced these choices.

In contrast to the Indian example that Salomon offers, language change does not necessarily bring along systemic changes in the Arabic case. The only systemic alterations occurred in the initial shift from late Aramaic to Arabic writing and the recent trend to typing, in electronic media, the (usually spoken) Arabic Colloquial in Latin letters; the adoption of the Arabic script after its initial formation to write the diverse languages of Islamic polities led solely to small external adjustments. The cause for the script's stability lies in its unifying role in Islamic scripture and the shared Arabic lexicon. Arabic script enjoyed a far greater dissemination worldwide than Arabic language.

ADOPTION OF THE ARAMAIC *ABJAD*: A SYSTEMIC CHANGE

The first systemic change is the formation of the Arabic script itself. Like all other Semitic alphabets, Arabic script ultimately derived from the Old Canaanite inventory of twenty-two consonants.[1] Here, "alphabet" designates what Peter Daniels (1990) has defined as an *abjad* (i.e., a script consisting of consonants, including the semiconsonants, which served in a secondary role to denote long vowels). Throughout this chapter, I use the term "alphabet" in its broader idiomatic sense, subsuming the *abjad*.

Various scholars (Grohmann 1971; Gruendler 1993; Healey 1990; Nehmé 2010) have established that Arabic script descended from Nabatean, a late Aramaic script, rather than Syriac (proposed by Jean Starcky 1966), though Syriac affected the style of Arabic script once it was constituted. The adaptation occurred in the interstice between the prevalence of Aramaic as a lingua franca and the rise of Arabic in the same role, notably after the Roman conquest of the Nabatean city-state in 106 CE. During an era lacking any government control of scribes, experimentation that led ultimately to the new Arabic script could occur. While the epigraphic variant of Nabatean script slowly deteriorated and vanished by the mid-fourth century, the cursive variant was acquired by speakers of Arabic, city dwellers and nomads alike (as shown in the Jabal Ramm graffito; see Gruendler 1993:13, 153, Figure A1), so as to write their own language; by the sixth century the script essentially emerged in its present form. In the process, existing trends in late Aramaic, such as the execution of final letters with longer tails or other enlarged elements and the Nabatean use of a continuous line to connect letters at their base, were generalized.

The facts that the speakers were bilingual in Nabatean and Arabic and that both languages were Semitic allowed for a systematic denotation of sounds lost in the donor language with letters used in etymological cognates of the receptor language. Letters that came to serve more than one sound (through graphic and sound mergers) were distinguished by auxiliary supralinear signs (dots or strokes), inspired by such signs in Syriac.

The consonantal nature of the *abjad*, fixing only about 85 percent of a given text, suited the structure of Semitic languages; the omitted information, short vowels and grammatical endings, could be reconstructed by the speakers. Simultaneously, the abbreviated nature of the writing made the etymological roots of words more visible, creating a secondary logographic legibility. All in all, the *abjad* proved an efficient tool for recording the Arabic language. Although a consonant thus stood for itself and any added vowel (or no vowel), it did not specify this vowel (which required an additional sign for *a, i, u,* or *ø*), and references to Arabic script or its Phoenician ancestor as a "syllabary," such as by Ignace Gelb (1963:147–153), are mis-leading and driven by ideological bias, seeking to credit the alphabet to the West (Coulmas 1996:1:1383; Strohmaier 2003:7–11).

The salient characteristic of the *abjad* is that the script divides the lan-guage into two kinds of sounds and that it privileges one group to be fixed in writing. Different theories have been brought forward to explain this selective denotation. One hypothesis is that in Semitic languages conso-nants are simply more significant than vowels, for they make up the mainly triconsonantal roots that supply the basic semantic range of a word, which is then further specified by a morphological pattern and affixes. Hans-Jürgen Sasse states that "the most characteristic trait of Semitic morphology is the relationship of consonant and vowel" (Sasse 1981:233; cf. Coulmas 1989:110–111, 2003:177).[2]

According to another hypothesis, the alphabet's precursors, the Proto-Sinaitic and Proto-Canaanite letters (dating back to the early Twelfth Dynasty of the Egyptian Middle Kingdom, 1850–1700 BCE) were derived from a mix of hieroglyphic and hieratic word signs (pictographs), such as ⊏⊐ for *pr* (house) and ⊶ for *jrt* (eye), which were relabeled by the Semitic writers with their cognate words for "house" and "eye," *bêt* and *'ayin* respec-tively, and used as alphabetic signs to denote the first letter of the word associated with the sign (Darnell et al. 2005; Gardiner 1916; Hamilton 2006:21–22, 282–295; Sasse 1988). The *bêt* sign thus denoted the sound *b* and the *'ayin* sign the sound ' (an emphatic laryngeal spirant). This proce-dure is called the acrophonic principle. It follows logically that only such sounds that begin a word can become letters. In Semitic languages a vowel cannot do so, as any initial vowel would always be preceded by a glottal stop, which is a written consonant (') in Semitic scripts.

The latter is a more plausible explanation for the absence of vowels in the Old Canaanite alphabet, and it most likely triggered the privileging of consonants over vowels initially. Later the root-and-pattern structure of Semitic, with its functional distinction between the two kinds of sounds, made such *abjads* thrive into the present.

One example may illustrate the usefulness for the *abjad* system not merely for regular communication but also for the science of linguistics, which counts among the earliest disciplines to emerge in Arabic-Islamic civ-ilization. Using a combination of the *abjad* and the lexical roots, the first major Arab lexicographer, al-Khalīl b. Aḥmad (d. 791 CE), in collaboration with his student al-Layth (d. ca. 805 CE), was able to capture the totality of the Arabic lexicon with all its etyma (al-Khalīl 1980; Schoeler 2002: 93–94; Wild 1965:35–36). He simply recombined all consonants (minus the semiconsonants) of the alphabet three times in phonetic order (26 × 25 × 26, to groups of C^1-C^2-C^2 and C^1-C^2-C^3, excluding C^1-C^1-C^2, which does not occur in Arabic) and therewith exhausted all root combinations (each section on a sound root preceding another with semiconsonants as second or third radical, followed by sections containing additional consonants). Then al-Khalīl permuted the letters of the consonant groups in all existing sequences (maximally six), eliminating combinations that did not produce lexemes. Thus he arrived at a list of *every single root* that occurred in the Arabic language. Subsequent lexicographers might well add further meanings to a given root and its derivations, but for the number of entries, al-Khalīl's system could not be improved.

Semitic Vowel Writing Preceding the Arabic Auxiliary Signs

A word must be said about the writing of vowels. The previous statement that mainly consonants were written down in the Semitic scripts requires qualification. Leaving aside cuneiform writing, which was a syllabary, some Semitic alphabetic scripts, such as ancient South Arabian, used no vowels at all. Others, however, resorted variously to auxiliary vowels (Aramaic), vowels inherent to consonantal letters (Old Ethiopic), or independently written vowels (Mandaic and Punic; I am using Florian Coulmas' [2003:111] classification of vowel denotation). The general rule of Semitic alphabets being consonantaries is thus attenuated. By the fourteenth century BCE, in Ugaritic three versions of the initial glottal stop combined with the short vowels '*a*, '*i*, '*u* (as well as a further sibilant) were invented and added to the alphabet. This being the formative stage of the alphabet, its still fluid state allowed an openness to invention, with a long and a short version (of twenty-one and thirty letters each)[3] and two different sequences beginning with '*bgd* and *hlḥm* used side by side in the Ugaritic script. The latter order survives in Ethiopic and in the etymology of the Latin word *elementa*, "letters, alphabet; beginnings" (Dietrich and Loretz 1988:102, 172–173, 263, 270; Müller 1994–1996:1:309). Given this variety in denoting consonants, it is not surprising that vowels were recorded in a few instances.

The Semitic scripts that would add vowels to the consonantary were Mandaic, Punic, and Old Ethiopic. In Canaanite and Aramaic the semiconsonants (also called semivowels) *w* and *y* were retooled for the second function of denoting the long vowels *ū* and *ī* (called *matres lectionis*). In Mandaic, the script of a gnostic sect in south Mesopotamia, these *matres lectionis* were extended to record short *u* and *i*, and the loss of the sounds ', ', and *ḥ* freed up the graph ' to denote *a* and the graph ' to denote the infrequent *e*, as well as initial *i* and *u*. All of these were represented on the baseline of the script as independent letters (Daniels and Bright 1996: 511–514). In Punic, a Phoenician derivative, the sounds ', *h*, and *ḥ* had fallen out of the phonological system, and their graphs became likewise available to serve as independent vowel signs, following here the Latin model (Coulmas 1989:147; Février 1984:223–224). Old Ethiopic (Ge'ez) went a different route toward the same end; in the fourth century CE, Ge'ez displayed a full syllabary combining each consonant with six different added symbols for vowels and vowellessness (*a*, *ū*, *ī*, *ā*, *ē*, *schwa*, and *ō*) but leaving both elements graphically distinct, so the script reads simultaneously as an alphabet and a syllabary. This system preserved the legibility of the words' roots as logographs, which was lost in the cases of Punic and Mandaic, whose vowels are denoted as separate segments. Semitic consonantaries, or *abjads*, thus evince numerous variations in the extent and manner in which they incorporate vowels into the body of the script.

Adaption to the Internet: A Systemic Change

A second systemic change was the writing of Arabic Colloquials, spoken variants, by the process of Latinization. Here numbers are used for the Arabic sounds missing in the alphabet, such as *3* for the sound '. Internet Arabic turns a usually oral idiom into writing. Official websites, however, retain the written language of Modern Standard Arabic in Arabic script (Gonzales-Quijano 1999). It remains to be seen how the written colloquials will affect the balance of the Arabic multiglossic situation (Schallenberg 2006). In the following, I focus on changes in the formal written variant in premodern times.

OPTIMIZATION OF SCRIPT: AN EXTERNAL CHANGE

As stated above, the *abjad* suited the Semitic structure of Arabic. The consonants' remaining immediately visible in the script conveyed a word's basic semantic range. To be read aloud, the abbreviated recording required the reader to complete the sounds by adding vowels, but this posed no problem in the earliest phase, when writing was often still an aide-mémoire for readers who memorized the text (fig. 4.1).[4] However, from the eighth century onward, proliferating practical applications for writing and the influx of non-Arab converts required the script to include more phonetic detail.

The twenty-two Nabatean graphs did not suffice to represent the twenty-eight extant sounds of the Arabic language. The resulting homographs, or letters serving several duties, were already distinguished in the earliest preserved texts of the Islamic period (beginning in 622 CE). One graph's

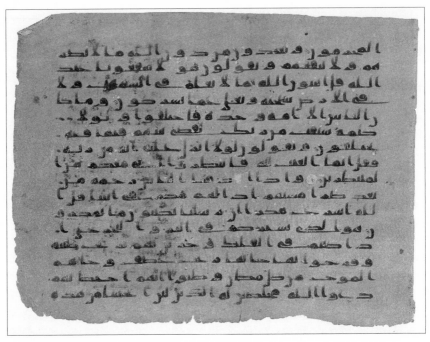

FIGURE 4.1

Folio of eighth-century dyed parchment Qur'ān in Abbasid script with few diacritical dots (Déroche 1992:58).

different functions were marked by auxiliary signs (diacritical dots or small strokes) placed with the variant of a letter that expressed a different sound, resulting in punctuation of letter pairs or triplets, such as *s* ﺱ receiving three supralinear dots to denote *sh* ﺵ, *t* ﺕ receiving an extra dot to denote *th* ﺙ and a dot underneath to denote *b* ﺏ. A miniature replica of the letter *k* ﻙ placed inside it distinguished it from *l* ﻝ. The markers were inspired by Syriac (cf. Salomon, chapter 5, this volume), and they kept fluctuating during the earliest phase. Minimal variations still remain between the Islamic East and West: *f* and *q* are distinguished by a dot below and above in manuscripts of the Maghreb but by one versus two dots above in the East. Some of these ambiguities had resulted from sound mergers, for *th* had been lost in Nabatean, and others from graphic mergers, such as the letter pair *b* and *t*, or *k* and *l*, still distinct in Nabatean, that had come to look alike in early Arabic script. Complementary *muhmal* (undotted) signs were further devised to indicate unmarked consonants. This marking of ambiguous letters was optional and became an open space that common language users, literati, and scholars inhabited in various ways. Usage of diacritics varied widely between different types of texts and social contexts and even within a single text until modern print regularized their application. Typeface instated diacritics as permanent parts of letters and discarded the *muhmal* signs that had therewith become redundant.

As to vowels, one way to clarify them, namely by *matres lectionis*, had been inherited via Nabatean from the Canaanite alphabet. As early as the tenth century BCE (in the "calendar" of Gezer), final *h* serves as long final *ā* and other final vowels, and the semiconsonants *w* and *y* as long medial and final *ū* and *ī*. In pre-Islamic Arabic inscriptions from the fourth to the sixth centuries CE and the Qur'ān, whose first fragments date to the seventh century CE, the use of the semiconsonants *w* and *y* for the long vowels *ū* and *ī* survives as part of the Aramaic orthography (Diem 1979:§§7–9). This usage allowed the denotation of long vowels but also created a new source of ambiguity, for semiconsonants now served a double duty as long vowels and consonants.

In Arabic, there came to be a third long vowel, the long *ā*, also read as the case ending *an*, which fulfilled important grammatical functions (e.g., accusative case, adverbial circumstance, and the vocative). Sound change in the Ḥijāzī dialect, which provided the basis for the oldest layer of Arabic orthography, led to the loss of the glottal stop (called *hamza* in Arabic phonetics), which had originally been expressed by the letter *alif*. The orthography remained historical in keeping the graph of the now unused *alif*. Its presence offered the opportunity to reinterpret it in the way it now sounded, such as in *rās* رأس (head) from the original pronunciation **ra's*, so it came to be understood as long *ā*. The usage spread by analogy to similar-sounding words, such as *nās* ناس, where no *alif* had been lost. Gradually, this lengthening *alif* expanded throughout the entire script, as can be seen in the different orthographic stages still visible in the Qur'ānic text. As a sacred scripture, its seventh-century orthography has been carefully pre-served and can therefore be analyzed for its historical layers, as Werner Diem (1976a, 1976b, 1979:§§61–68) has done. *Alif* for long *ā* was eventu-ally generalized except in the ubiquitous name of god, *allāh* الله, and several frequent particles (*hādhā* هذا, *lākin* لكن).

Alif was further utilized to distinguish common, similar-looking words, to wit, the particle *an* أن (that) from *ana* انا (I), the second receiving a final *alif* even though its final *a* vowel was short. Past tense verbs in the plural received a final *alif* to distinguish them from past tense verbs in the singu-lar followed by the conjunction *wa-* and from present tense verbs ending with the radical *w* (al-Ṣūlī 1341:246). Arabic thus used two semiconsonants and the *alif* to denote the three long vowels *ā*, *ī*, and *ū*.

But these modifications did not yet suffice to record Classical Arabic (*ʿarabiyya*). This form of the language had been instituted by the Umayyad caliph Abdalmalik (r. 685–705 CE) as the official language when he converted the government bureau (*dīwān*) in his capital of Damascus from Greek into Arabic in 700 CE (Duri et al. 1965; Puin 1970; al-Ṣūlī 1341: 192–193). Classical Arabic was a learned idiom confined to formal oral and written purposes and used by people with different levels of competence. Some texts and situations necessitated the denotation of the short vowels (*a*, *i*, and *u*). These written vowels represent the last phase of optimization, and they took the shape of supralinear signs (strokes or dots) inspired, like the diacritics, by Syriac.

Another type of change occurred with the case endings (*iʿrāb* إعراب), which were not written in Nabatean because the case system had been lost, as in the Arabic Ḥijāzī dialect, the first variant of Arabic committed to writing. However, once the formal variant of Classical Arabic, which still preserved the case system, was recorded, this lacuna in the orthography needed to be addressed. The short vowel signs and the *alif* would then be used to express the grammatical functions of word endings and the final *n* signifying indeterminacy. This notation (and its oral realization) required a writer to understand the grammatical function of each word, and its optional, supplementary status in the script was one of the driving forces for codifying Arabic syntax so as to enable a correct performance by its users.

The loss of the glottal stop in the Ḥijāzī dialect caused further problems for writing the classical language, which had retained the glottal stop as a regular sound. Because it had been mostly lost in the script except at the beginnings of words, it had to be reintroduced as a supralinear sign resting on an extant letter (أ إ ؤ ئ), called its "chair" (كرسي), and if it had been dropped in postvocalic position, it was placed upon the line (ء). Supplemental signs indicated, in addition to short vowels and case markers, initial vowel elision (*waṣla*), initial long *ā* (*madda*), and the doubling of consonants (*shadda*). Like the diacritics, these signs appeared with varying density (full, intermittent, rare, or absent) within a single text, with different implications for the reader. Their use predominated in difficult texts (e.g., the Qurʾān, poetry, and linguistic manuals) to safeguard their correct reading (fig. 4.2). Within the first two centuries of Islam and its emerging book culture, the basic Arabic script (*rasm* رسم) had thus been optimized with a large inventory of supralinear signs (*tashkīl, ḥarakāt*) to become more fully phonetic.

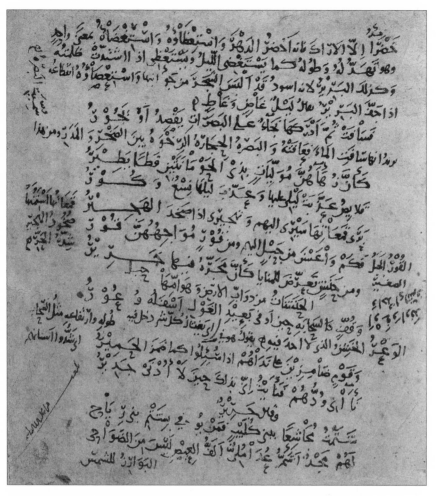

FIGURE 4.2

Page from a tenth- or eleventh-century paper codex of the Collected Poems (Dīwān) *of Jarīr (d. 728) with full diacritics and vowel markers (Pétrosyan 1994:99).*

ADAPTATIONS OF ARABIC SCRIPT: PLIABILITY OF A STABLE SYSTEM

With the spread of Islam and Arabic-Islamic civilization in Western Europe, Asia, and Africa, the predominant Islamic script, Arabic, came to be adopted by languages within its realm that had many more vowels to express. These non-Semitic tongues were as diverse as Indo-European, Indo-Aryan, Berber, Turkic, Austronesian, and Dravidian. Nonetheless, the script did not undergo systematic alterations; instead, its extant supralinear signs (such as diacritical dots and miniature letters) were put to new purposes and a few new ones were invented, such as a small circle in Pashto and Kashmiri. Only Kurdish changed to rendering all vowels with separate letters. Those languages that continue to use the Arabic script today are Berber, Kurdish, Persian, Urdu, Pashto, Sindhi, Kashmiri, and Uighur (Kaye 1996; Naim 1971).

To express sounds not inherent in the Arabic alphabet, existing graphemes were modified; for example, the Persian *p*, *č*, *ž*, *g*, and *w* adapted the Arabic letters closest in sound, *b*, *j*, *z*, *k*, and *v*, with three added dots or a stroke. This mode of adaptation fully conformed to the principle of supralinear signs used in the donor alphabet. Because of a built-in capacity to generate new consonants through diacritics, the Arabic script retained its stability in drastically different linguistic environments.

The most ingenious new auxiliary signs for vowels were developed in Arabic-Afrikaans. This pidginized form of Dutch, spoken by the Malay slaves of Dutch settlers in South Africa, represents a particular case. In the nineteenth century, its literate Muslim writers created the most sophisticated system of supralinear signs for Arabic in an adaptation that aimed to reflect the full inventory of vowels and diphthongs in the evolving Afrikaans language (e.g., combined *fatḥa* and *kasra* denoting the short vowel *e*, or *y* with an *alif* beneath the line denoting the dipthong *ei*; Davids 1991:8). Later, the Christian Afrikaaners changed their official language from Dutch to Afrikaans and used the Latin alphabet instead. But the earlier documents in Arabic script make it possible today to reconstruct the historical pronunciation of evolving Afrikaans.

Other languages converted to Latin script for ideological or practical reasons. For instance, Arabic script was singularly unsuited to Ottoman Turkish, which contained a rich vowel repertoire, and in 1931 it was replaced by an adapted Latin alphabet. Here the script change cut the language off from its Arabic-Islamic heritage. But this was precisely the motive for the shift, which was part of a policy of creating an ethnic-national Turkish identity that could be divorced from the Ottoman past. During the same reform the ratio of Arabic words used in Turkish was reduced from 50 percent to 26 percent. Further languages that converted to Latin script were Medieval Spanish, Azeri, and Serbo-Croatian in Europe; Malay (from the Arabic-based *jawi* script) in the Malay archipelago; and Sulu, Malgasy (from the Arabic-based *sorabe* script), Swahili, Hausa, and Fulani in Africa. Maltese, the only case of an Arabic Colloquial becoming a written language, used the Latin alphabet from the beginning (Vanhove 1993).

Most Indo-Aryan languages have retained the Arabic alphabet. This retention may largely be due to the vast quantity of Arabic words in these languages, notably in Persian, though many letters distinct in the script are pronounced alike, such as ذ, ز, ض, and ظ, all rendered as z.

But otiose Arabic letters cannot be discarded without changing the historical orthography of the imported Arabic lexicon. To abandon Arabic script would in fact entail the loss of a cultural heritage that informs Persian literature, scholarship, and religion to this day and that evolved in close dialogue with Arabic literary models, including numerous bilingual works.

Unlike Mayan script (see Houston, chapter 8, this volume), the system of the Arabic script thus exhibits a remarkable stability since its first official instatement in minting and local bureaucracies during the Umayyad period (ca. 695–705 CE), supplanting Middle Persian and Greek. The script was safeguarded in Islamic countries by the Qur'ān, which was by doctrine untranslatable, and throughout premodern times the *kuttāb* schools taught writing via the Qur'ān, side by side with its memorization. Arabic script's status today as the second most frequent segmental writing system in the world is owed to its flexibility, and its spread far exceeds that of the Arabic language. Multiple adaptations to other languages occasioned no substantial alteration, for the mechanics of the script system were variable enough to accommodate a vast range of new sounds. As such, Arabic writing can be compared to Japanese as "simultaneously changing and staying the same" (Lurie, chapter 7, this volume).

PROBLEMS AND SOLUTIONS

An area of less obvious change, and not visible in the writing system, was in the orthographic response to problems that arose in the course of the script's use. The spread of Arabic-Islamic civilization was bound up with the technology of a paper-based communication system that, in the ninth century, facilitated a radical expansion of private and public writing in a veritable "revolution of the book" (Déroche 2004:44). This revolution included the codification of oral heritage, the formulation of the linguistic sciences, the development of codicological conventions, and the emergence of a literary canon and a reading public.

Within a century of its first formation, the script diversified according to the function of a particular text (Gruendler 1993): different hands came to characterize Qur'ān codices, chancellery letters, and scholarly writing (fig. 4.3). In papyri, a chronological shift is observable from an earlier angular to a more looped writing, exhibiting a simplification of strokes and cursivization comparable to that which occurred in the Indian scripts

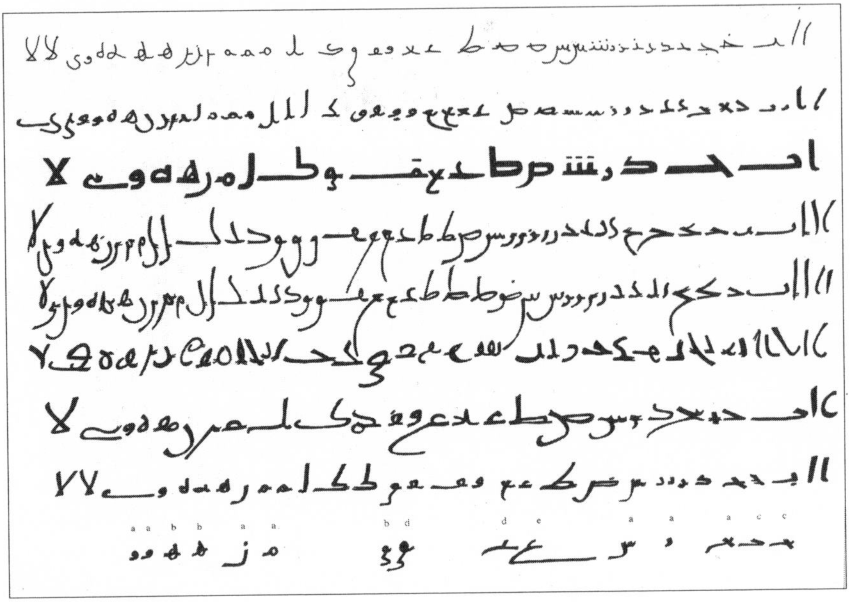

FIGURE 4.3

The different function-based script styles of the first Islamic century. Lines 1–2: early cursive; line 3: epigraphic script; line 4: chancellery cursive; line 5: entagia (tax note) cursive; line 6: protocol cursive; line 7: cursive of a voucher; lines 8–9: Ḥijāzī script of early Qur'āns (Gruendler 1993:141).

(Salomon, chapter 5, this volume) and increased connections between separate words (Khan 1992:40). Script sizes varied between tiny pigeon-post missives and gigantic display Qur'āns. Space constraints, such as in tort redress verdicts that were recorded directly on petitions submitted on small scrap notes, led to an elliptic style (Gruendler 2009a). Conversely, official correspondence used a widely spaced script, deliberately wasteful of the costly papyrus produced under government monopoly. Texts proliferated through mass dictation to amateurs and the new professional copyists. These latter "venture publishers" sold copied dictations whose intellectual property status, divorced from the author's oral control, was not yet firmly established (Zayyāt 1992). In Qur'āns, private albums, official correspondence, and architecture, the script evolved into a prestigious art form whose practitioners were highly esteemed. With this proliferation of writing came a wealth of material formats; for instance, the western Qur'ān was written on square parchment pages, whereas in the east it appeared on high oblong paper pages. Codicological conventions developed for the multiple ways of glossing and commenting text on one same page: as *scholia*, folded within the same text; *in margine*, in the margins and connected by reference marker; or as parallel running marginal text (Déroche 2000; Gacek 2001, 2008). The possibilities of correcting, glossing, and affiliating texts in manuscripts far exceeded those of subsequent printed books—which may be one of the factors for book print's slow acceptance—and the interactive nature of the manuscript tradition bears a considerable resemblance to today's linkage of hypertext.

Since the late eighth century CE, script offered an alternative to those oral mnemotechnics that had heretofore vouchsafed the integrity of prose, including the Qur'ān (by the rhythmic structure of the prose rhyme, or *saj*) and that of poetry (by combined rhyme and meter, or *'arūḍ*). It was precisely the disputes about the correct recitation of Qur'ān passages that eased the acceptance of supralinear signs in the scripture; according to historical lore, they even spearheaded the very codification of grammar (al-'Askarī 1982:II:115–116; Gruendler 2006b; al-Zubaydī 1984:21–22).

However, writing did not replace oral transmission in a teleological fashion. Instead, both continued to coexist in changing combinations, all the way to a stylized orality used in literary prose. Until the ninth century the transmission of texts—notably poetry, the Qur'ān, prophetic traditions, and historical records—had been entrusted to the reliable and professionally trained human memory in the persons of the *rāwī*, *ḥāfiẓ*, *muḥaddith*, and *akhbārī*, thought to be more dependable than writing. There was also an initial reticence towards writing. For instance, transcribing the legally important prophetic traditions would have challenged the scripture's unique status by placing a second book side by side with it. The oral knowledge of those traditions also remained malleable under the control of scholars, and it took the coaxing of a caliph who commissioned a book on *ḥadīth* to make one scholar relinquish oral control (Schoeler 2006: 111–141, esp. 121–124). In the teaching tradition, the reading of a text aloud for correction (*qirā'a*), listening to such a reading (*samā'*), and dictation (*imlā'*) were deemed more valid than written modes of communication lacking an oral interface, such as correspondence (*murāsala*), the handing over of a text (*munāwala*), or reading on one's own (*wijāda*) (al-Sam'ānī 1952). An individual who solely relied on written sheets (*ṣuḥuf*) or notebooks (*dafātīr*, *karārīs*), in use since the eighth century, received the derogatory label of amateur (*ṣuḥufī*), literally, someone who mispronounces words in a text because he has not heard their correct vocalization from a teacher (Gruendler 2004).

This being said, the oral teaching process did not imply that such knowledge could not *also* be written down as personal lecture notes. Even at the peak of its prestige, people were not free of mistrust in the human memory, and writing served as a complementary and secondary way of recording knowledge in unredacted notebooks used by scholars in private or circulated among their students and colleagues. Text thus alternated between being stored in writing and performed and corrected orally. This complementarity of the two modes, first described by Gregor Schoeler (2002:23–26, 2006:40–42), offers an alternative to the evolutionary models of Marshall McLuhan, Walter Ong, and Jack Goody, who assume a linear and unidirectional progression from spoken to written media, and is similar to recent alternative views (cf. Clanchy 1979; Coleman 1996; Finnegan 1988; Street 1984). But only gradually were real books (with title, preface, table of contents, and cross-references) published at large, and those often by demand of the government, such as the earliest poetic anthology of the *Mufaḍḍaliyyāt,* collected by its eponymous author, al-Mufaḍḍal (d. 780 or 786), for the education of a prince (Schoeler 2002:65, 2006:71).

The shifting fault line between oral performance and increasing written text generated a host of normative writings about the right and wrong of linguistic usage. The Classical Arabic language was systematized and codified by fieldworking philologists on the basis of the Qur'ān and oral poetry, which they collected and edited (Versteegh 1997a, 1997b). Writing made knowledge ready for use in the newly emerged, vast bureaucracy and the flourishing, heavily patronized literary and scholarly realms. Problems arising in reading and writing spurred genres devoted to remedying them, to wit, secretarial manuals on orthography, spelling, and (the mostly unwritten) grammatical endings. In this context the optimization of the script described above took shape.

Here efficiency and easy legibility were not universal principles (as proposed by Salomon, chapter 5, this volume). Writers chose among various options for denoting equivocal vowels, depending on a text's more or less pragmatic purpose, linguistic difficulty, and the competence of the addressee. Professional guilds' self-protection and the display of learning played an equally large role and occasionally led to intricate literary artifice. Especially in the ornate prose arising in the tenth century, authors luxuriated in the ambiguity of the script and created double entendres (*tawriya*) with lexical homonyms (Bonebakker 2000). Others toyed with the diacritics, like the prose stylist al-Ḥarīrī (d. 1122), who composed in his *Stances* (*Maqāmāt*) sermons using only letters without diacritics (1969:3: Nos. 28 and 29, 337–353, 392–400; see also Rosenthal 1971) (fig. 4.4).

Specifically, the gap between unwritten vowel and written consonant created an area of problem solving and potential social differentiation.

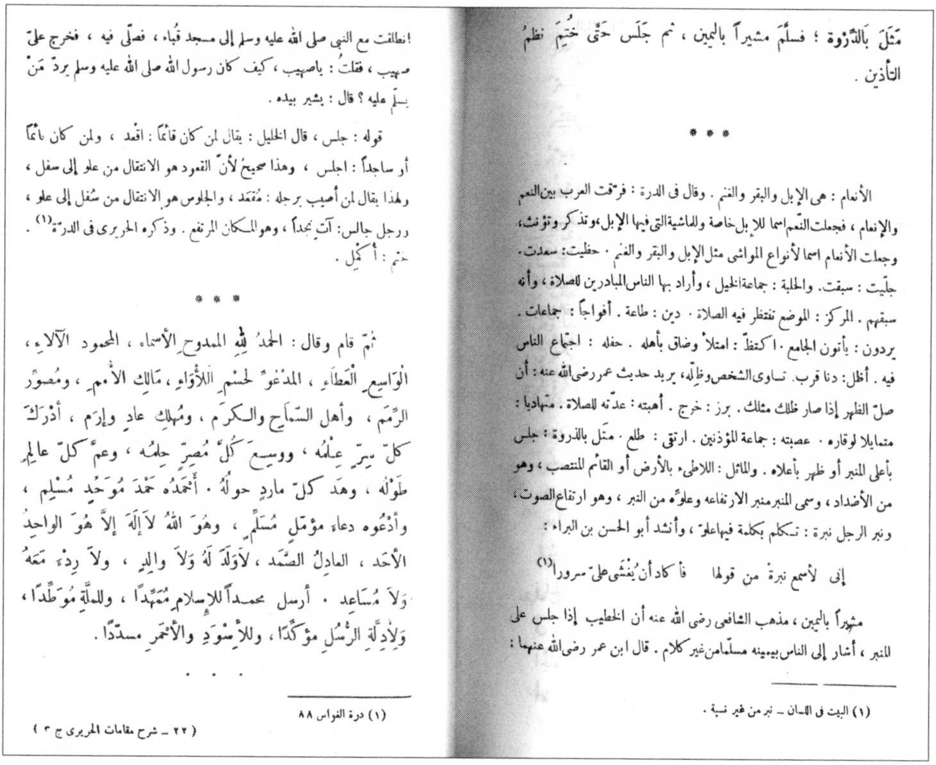

مَثَلَ بِالذَّرْوَةِ ؛ فَسَلَّمَ مُشِيرًا بِالْيَمِينِ ، ثم جَلَسَ حَتَّى خُتِّمَ نَظْمُ التَّأْذِينِ .

* * *

الأنعام : هي الإبل والبقر والغنم . وقال في الدرة : فرّقت العرب بين النعم والأنعام ، فجعلت النعم اسما للإبل خاصة والماشية التي فيها الإبل ، وقد وتوفنث ، وجمعت الأنعام اسما لأنواع المواشي مثل الإبل والبقر والغنم . حظيت ، خلّيت : سبقت . والخلية : جماعة الخيل ، وأراد بها الناس المبادرين للصلاة ، وأي سبقهم . المركز : الموضع تنتظر فيه الصلاة . دين : طاعة . أفواجًا : جماعات . يردون : يأتون الجامع . اكتظّ : امتلأ وضاق بأهله . حفله : اجتماع الناس فيه . أظلّ : دنا وقرب . تساوى الشخص وظلّه ، يريد حديث عمر رضي الله عنه : أن صلّ الظهر إذا صار ظلّك مثلك . برز : خرج . أهبته : عدّته للصلاة . متهاديا : متمايلا لوقاره . عصبة : جماعة المؤذنين . ارتقى : طلع . مثل بالذروة : جلس بأعلى المنبر أو ظهر بأعلاه . والماثل : اللاطي بالأرض أو القائم المنتصب ، وهو من الأضداد ، وسمى المنبر منبرا لارتفاعه وعلوّه من النبر ، وهو ارتفاع الصوت ، ونبر الرجل نبرة : تكلّم بكلمة فيها علوّ ، وأنشد أبو الحسن بن البراء :

إلى لا أسمع نبرة من قولها   فأ كاد أن يُغْشى علي سرورًا (١)

مشيرا باليمين ، مذهب الشافعي رضي الله عنه أن الخطيب إذا جلس على المنبر ، أشار إلى الناس بيمينه مسلّما من غير كلام . قال ابن عمر رضي الله عنهما :

(١) البيت في اللسان ، نبرمن غير نبرة .

انطلقت مع النبي صلى الله عليه وسلم إلى مسجد قباء ، فصلّى فيه ، فخرج على صهيب ، فقلت : باصهيب ، كيف كان رسول الله صلى الله عليه وسلم يردّ من بسلّم عليه أ؟ قال : بشير بيده .

قوله : جلس ، قال الخليل : يقال لمن كان قائمًا : اقعد ، ولمن كان نائمًا أو ساجدًا : اجلس ، وهذا صحيح لأنّ القعود هو الانتقال من علوٍ إلى سفلٍ ، ولهذا يقال لمن أصيب برجله : مُقعَد ، والجلوس هو الانتقال من سُفلٍ إلى علوٍ ، ورجل جالس : آتٍ نجدًا ، وهو المكان المرتفع . وذكره الحريري في الدرة (١) . ثمّ : أكّل .

* * *

ثمّ قام وقال : الحمدُ لله الممدوح الأسماء ، المحمود الآلاء ، الواسع العطاء ، المدعوّ لحسم اللأواء ، مَالك الأُمم ، ومُصوّر الرّمم ، وأهل السّماح والكرم ، ومُملك عادٍ وإرَمَ ، أدرَكَ كلّ سِرٍّ عِلمُه ، ووسّعَ كلّ مُصرٍّ حلمُه ، وعمّ كلّ عالمٍ طَولُه ، وهدَ كلّ مارِدٍ حولَه . أحمَدُه حمَد مُوحِّدٍ مُسلِمٍ ، وأدعوه دعاء مؤمّلٍ مُسلِمٍ ، وهو اللهُ لا إله إلا هو الواحدُ الأحَدُ ، العادلُ الصّمَد ، لا ولَدَ لَهُ ولا والِدٍ ، ولا ردَّ مَعَهُ ولا مُساعِد ، أرسل محمدا للإسلام مُمَهّدًا ، وللملّة مُوَطّدًا ، ولأدلّة الرُّسلِ مؤكّدًا ، وللأسودِ والأحمرِ مسدّدًا .

(٢٢ ـ شرح مقامات الحريري ج ٣)   درة النواص ٨٨ (١)

FIGURE 4.4

The beginning of a sermon in Stance no. 28, composed only of letters without diacritics, in al-Ḥarīrī's Maqāmāt *(1969:III:337), with commentary by al-Sharīshī in smaller font.*

Reading aloud required an understanding of sentence and context and the performance of correct grammar; as a result, inflectional word endings became ideologically charged. Educated readers might well regard diacritics and vowel markers as an insult to their intelligence, but those less firm in their grasp of the language needed lists of difficult words and frequently committed errors, which proliferated from the late eighth century in the form of treatises on barbarisms and scribal handbooks (examples include Ibn Qutayba 1963:238–332; al-Ṣūlī 1341:57-61; al-Zubaydī 1981; see also ʿAbd al-Tawwāb 1967; Ayoub 2007; Pellat 1986). In the following I illustrate with two examples how the selective and reductive code of the Arabic *abjad* triggered compensations on technical and literary levels.

Inflectional Endings

The script's Aramaic and Ḥijāzī history had bequeathed it the largely unwritten desinential inflections (*i'rāb*) that became a prime focus in grammar books. To aggravate the problem, the case and mood system was not only ignored in the inherited orthography but also had fallen out of use in many of the spoken urban dialects and at least some Bedouin dialects (Versteegh 1997b:93–113; for a different view, see Owens 2006:85–101, 114–118). Both Arabic orthography and Arabic colloquials thus contributed to morphologically isolating this intrinsic element of the language as part of a separable and prestigious expertise. Moreover, the innumerable Iranian, Aramean, Jewish, Byzantine, and Berber converts (*mawālī*) to Islam, who constituted the larger part of the conquered cities' populations, acquired the *i'rāb*-less spoken Arabic (or Neo-Arabic) and passed it on to their descendants—according to some premodern philologists (al-Zubaydī 1981:34), these converts were ostensibly the reason for the general corruption of language. The knowledge of inflection was thus necessary for two groups of people. The converts who joined the young Muslim community had to acquire the *'arabiyya* from scratch, and the Arabs of the cities (*muwalladūn*) who had not, like Bedouins, grown up with the literary practice of the *'arabiyya* needed to learn it as well. Conversely, the incorrect performance of *i'rāb* in speaking, reciting, and reading a text aloud revealed an educational deficit.

In informal writing, *i'rāb* was often misplaced. Simon Hopkins (1984), in his study of early Arabic papyri replete with Middle Arabic features (relaxed grammar, reduced grammatical inventory, and pseudo-corrections), shows that even those writers who were at sea when it came to marking case and mood inflection sprinkled their writings with occasional accusatives (*tanwīn alif*, one of the most frequent case endings and visible as a separate letter). Thus writers showed an awareness of desinential inflection, even if they misplaced it. One early medieval writer explains with unintended humor, "For I am in needing of it" (فإني إليه محتاجًا, *fa-innī ilayhi muḥtājan*, instead of the correct محتاج *muḥtājun*; Hopkins 1984:168). In early papyri the word "father," belonging to this category, changes between accusative and genitive (ابا/ابي, *abā* or *aban/abī*) with nothing but statistical regularity (Hopkins 1984:158–159). This is the situation of Middle Arabic literature, and it unfortunately covers up much of what we would like to know. Scholars need to resort to the rare cases of transcription into other languages, such as Greek.

Most liable to master *i'rāb* were members of the scholarly elite, and Ibn Fāris (d. 1004) severely chastises their ignorance and laxity regarding it (1963:66). To give an example, in one (lopsidedly reported) dispute between a logician and a grammarian, the latter silenced the logician because of his insufficient linguistic skill (which had no bearing upon the subject of the dispute) and won the argument (al-Tawḥīdī 1953:107–117). For all practical purposes, *i'rāb* came to signify whether a person understood Arabic syntax (*naḥw*) as a whole, which itself constituted half of grammar, the other half being morphology (*taṣrīf*).[5] Both together became a shorthand for a person's basic education.

The topic, then, with which most early grammars begin, from the founding work of the Iranian Sībawayh (d. 793) to the late epitome of the *Ājurrumiyya*, titled after its Moroccan Berber author, Ibn Ājurrum (d. 1323), is the inflection of nouns and secondarily of verbs (*marfū'āt, manṣūbāt, majrūrāt, majzūmāt*), whose case and mood designations are subsumed under the verbal noun *i'rāb*. The related verb *a'raba* (and *'arraba*) means "to express oneself clearly" and, in its technical sense, "to pronounce the inflection of a word" (Bohas et al. 1990:149–172; Dévényi 2007; Versteegh 1997a:45). The lexicographer Ibn Manẓūr (d. 1311) explained, "*I'rāb* is so called precisely because of its making [language] plain and clear" (1955–1956:I:588b). Adding the linguistic context, 'Abdalqāhir al-Jurjānī (d. 1058) defined it as "the change of word endings literally or virtually [by short vowel or letter] due to the change of grammatical agents (*huwa hkhtilāfu ākhiri l-kalimati bi-khtilāfi l-'awāmili lafẓan wa-taqdīran [bi-ḥarakatin aw ḥarfin]*)" (*Ta'rīfāt*, and, based upon him, al-Zamakhsharī [d. 1144], *Mufaṣṣal*, both cited after Fleisch 1971:1249). The founding father of Arabic philology in France, Sylvestre de Sacy (d. 1838) abbreviated this to "terminational syntax" (Corriente 1971; Dévényi 2007; Fleisch 1971).

I'rāb thus served to disambiguate the script, being "that which distinguishes between competing meanings in words (*huwā l-fāriqu bayna l-ma'ānī l-mutakāfi'ati fī l-lafẓ*)" (Ibn Fāris 1963:66, 77). The variable meanings were of syntactic order, as al-Zajjājī (d. 949) elaborated: "*I'rāb* enters speech in order to distinguish difficult meanings, by which one indicates the subject, the object, the first and second term of a genitive annexation, and other meanings that interchange in nouns" (1973:77; see also al-Zajjājī 1995). *I'rāb* could also define the meaning of an entire sentence as a question or an exclamation. Taking a cue from the *i'rāb*'s absence from the script, al-Zajjājī and the subsequent representatives of the system-building Basran-Baghdadian school of grammarians defined the inflection of a word as separate from and secondary to a word's lexical and morphological dimensions. With him and his teachers, the separation of *i'rāb* thus received a theoretical foundation, namely, a word had to be completed first before its inflectional information could be added at the end (al-Zajjājī 1973:67).

The gap between graphemes and phonemes with this theoretical underpinning made visible a shortcoming in the script and its users' expertise, but by the same token it created the potential to gain social prestige through the demonstration of mastery in the *'arabiyya* (Fück 1955; Gruendler 2006a; Suleiman 2007; Versteegh 1997b:53–73). But in some situations when the educated orally addressed less-educated people, too perfect a performance of case endings could appear pedantic. Ibn Qutayba (d. 889) wrote, "The rule of writing in this regard is different from that of speech, because no part of *i'rāb* is found ugly or heavy in writing" (1963:13–14; cf. Sanni 2008; Ullmann 1979:18–19). The occasional slip of an educated person was found charming, and scholars even used this as an intentional act of intellectual understatement, as Abū Bakr al-Ṣūlī (d. 946) opined: "Most scholars commit errors in their speech in order not to be deemed pedantic or irksome, but in writing and reciting poetry this is very ugly and not permitted" (1341:130–132). There was, moreover, a sociodidactic benefit in addressing commoners in language that included errors (Ibn Fāris 1963:66).

This separate life of *i'rāb*, to be studied and performed as standing in for Arabic linguistic knowledge, was triggered by the writing system—even though spoken uninflected Arabic and the esprit de corps of linguistic experts were contributing factors. From there *i'rāb* became both a scholarly pursuit for its own sake and a cultural symbol. Only its absence in the script had made this possible. Its appraisal was brought to a peak by Ibn Fāris, who considered it a cultural monument on a par with Arabic prosody and genealogy: according to him, *i'rāb* made Arabic surpass all other languages and Greek in particular (1963:77).

Vocalization of Simple Nouns
The described diglossia between written Classical and Colloquial Arabic and the massive influx of foreign vocabulary created another problem—the vocalization of simple nouns, personal names, and foreign terms, none of which could be deduced from the morphological pattern. The short vowels of such words received treatment in books on linguistic barbarisms and manuscript corruption and in scribal manuals.

The first genre of works on "barbarisms of the commoners" (*laḥn al-'āmma*) was misnamed. It was directed not at "common" people but members of the elite and the educated middle class who lapsed into the commoners' register (Ayoub 2007:630b–631a; Pellat 1986:606a; al-Zubaydī 1981:37). It began with the earliest grammarians, those who systematized and codified Classical Arabic, such as al-Kisā'ī (d. 805), al-Farrā' (d. 822), Abū 'Ubayda (d. 825), al-Aṣma'ī (d. 831), and Ibn al-Sikkīt (d. 858; but only the works of the first and last [Ibn al-Sikkīt 1965] have come down to us). A century later Thaʻlab's (d. 904) much commented work entitled *al-Faṣīḥ* (literally, "The Articulate") became a model for the genre. A later classic was the *Durrat al-ghawāṣṣ fī awhām al-khawāṣṣ* ("The Pearl of the Diver about Fancies of the Educated") by the above-mentioned prose stylist al-Ḥarīrī. Like other subjects in Arabic grammar, barbarisms became a pursuit in themselves, with authors of the Mamluk and Ottoman periods (twelfth to early twentieth centuries) rehabilitating some of the alleged corruptions because they actually followed ancient precedent (e.g., Ibn Hishām, d. 1182) or compiling earlier works into one (e.g., al-Ṣafadī, d. 1348, and Raḍī al-Dīn al-Ḥalabī, d. 1563). The genre has persisted to modern times with Ibrahim al-Yāzijī (d. 1906), Ṣalāḥ al-Dīn al-Zaʻbalāwī (d. after 1939), and Maʻrūf al-Ruṣāfī (d. 1945). The Egyptian scholar Ramaḍān ʻAbd al-Tawwāb lists a total of fifty-two titles spanning eleven centuries, which leads Georgine Ayoub to conclude that error collecting became more of a puristic exercise than an attempt to protect actual usage (ʻAbd al-Tawwāb 1967:97–100; Ayoub 2007:631; Pellat 1986).

Beyond enumerating faulty vocalizations, the barbarism genre comprises incorrect realizations of sounds, wrongly derived morphological patterns, some syntax (such as omitting or misplacing the letter *alif* marking the accusative), some etiologies of idioms, and, most copiously, mispronounced foreign terms that had made their way into common usage but fitted no Arabic morphological pattern that might guide their pronunciation. The mode of presentation was a simple list of correct entries or groups of morphological types (and occasionally their incorrect realizations) as lexical items to be learned by rote. There was no investigation into the underlying linguistic changes that had caused the errors.

The second genre addressed the corruption of written text by faulty diacritics (*taṣḥīf, taṣaḥḥuf*). This was treated by Abū Aḥmad al-ʻAskarī (d. 993) in several works that concerned less common vocabulary and proper names prone to cause scribal mistakes. Responding to public demand, he dedicated two different compendia to theologians and literati respectively, showing again that the target audience for anti-barbarism tracts was professional users of the language, not the uneducated (Gruendler 2009c).

Professional concern also applied to the third genre, secretarial handbooks (*adab al-kātib, adab al-kuttāb*), which partially served the same remedial functions. These handbooks routinely contained the history and conventions of administrative correspondence and basic information on matters of taxation, land surveying, weights, currencies, and accounting.

A major portion treated script, enjoining the use of diacritics and short vowels in official letters to forestall the miscarriage of orders and elucidating difficulties in the orthography of the retooled letters (*w, y, alif;* see al-Ṣūlī 1341:58–59, 243–255). The second longest chapter of Ibn Qutayba's *Adab al-kātib* ("Handbook of the Scribe"), running almost one hundred pages, lists precisely those types of error that the consonantal script invited: misplacement of the nondenoted and unpredictable short vowels in nouns, errors in theme vowels of verbs, and mistakes in the often omitted supralinear signs for the glottal stop (*hamza*) and doubled consonants (*shadda*).

In all these writings, the simple noun figured largely. The vocalization and meaning of a verb form can often be predicted from the root and its morphological pattern. For the derived noun, affixes and morphological pattern likewise guide the vocalization and meaning to a varying extent. But nouns consisting of simple roots show a great diversity in both the (unwritten) vocalization and the meaning. According to Edward Lipiński (2001:213), simple roots are "free morphemes"—they can stand alone—and "full morphemes"—they possess a more or less independent meaning. In consonantal writing, the meanings of such nouns are ambiguous because they lack affixes displaying cues about their vocalization and the meanings are also harder to derive from the context. In the simple noun, the script becomes utterly ambiguous; three completely different meanings can be served by one written form, distinguishable only in pronunciation. If pairs of simple nouns distinguished only by short vowels have either adjacent or opposite meanings, the context offers no help, for different readings change the sense of the whole sentence. For instance, قدر can be read either as *qadr* ([human] ability, quantity) or *qadar* (divine decree); a third possibility, *qidr* (kettle), could probably be excluded in such a context. To give another example, كبر can be read as *kibr* (pride), *kubr* (greatness, authority), or *kibar* (old age), which meanings may be hard to weigh against one another in any given context. It took lexical expertise and a grasp of the whole argument to identify the meaning and reading of a word.

To establish the short vowels, philologists did not use supralinear signs, which would rely on future copyists' fully and correctly placing them; instead, they devised a paraphrastic way to denote the vowels. This method is not considered in Coulmas' classification of vowel notation but is comparable to the principle of Japanese phonographs inserted into logographic *kundoku* writing (Lurie, chapter 7, this volume). Thus a word's vocalization in a text was supplied either by added glosses specifying the single short vowels through technical terms (*maftūḥ, maksūr, maḍmūm, sākin* for *a, i, u,* and ∅ respectively) or by analogous words used as examples. For instance, a past tense verb of the type *fa'ila* فعل (as opposed to *fa'ala* or *fa'ula*) was explained to be "like *shariba*" (كشرب *ka-shariba*). Many terms were created for final *alif* orthography (*mahmūz maqṣūr, mahmūz mamdūd,* and so on). However, no shared terminology for short and long vowels developed. Rather, they were referred to by the respective ways of writing them down, the short auxiliary vowels being called "vowel marks" (*tashkīl,* literally, "shaping, fettering," or *ḥarakāt,* literally, "movements") and the long, re-tooled semiconsonants being called "quiescent" or "defective" consonants (*ḥurūf sākina* or *ḥurūf al-'illa*). Such lengthy but precise paraphrase suited linguistic treatises, dictionaries, and encyclopedias because it safely survived the manuscript copying process. But because the paraphrastic way consumed much space, it was restricted to these reference works.

The large lexical category of the simple noun gave rise to its own subgenre, the vocalization triplet (*muthallath*), a word that could be read in three different ways. It was pioneered by the early lexicographer Muḥammad b. al-Mustanīr (d. 821), nicknamed Quṭrub (Werewolf) for his habit of pestering his teacher early in the morning with questions. Even though the original version of his work can no longer be disentangled from its later commentaries, his role as an inventor is attested by the biographer Ibn Khallikān (d. 1282; 1968–1972:IV:312–313 and, following him, al-Ṣafadī 1962–1997:V:19–20).

As with other lexicographical subjects, later scholars down to the nineteenth century strove to improve upon earlier models and expand their material, and they thrived on highlighting the seemingly inexhaustible polyvalence of the Arabic language, a topic that had originated in the literary-cultural debate about whether Persians and Arabs were superior (*shu'ūbiyya*).

The genre hit true fame with the triplets' versification by 'Abdalwahhāb b. al-Ḥasan al-Warrāq al-Bahnasī (d. ca. 1286; Quṭrub 1315 AH; MS Yale Landberg 489; Sezgin 1982:61–67). He utilized Quṭrub's list of twenty-nine words (Quṭrub's unpublished 103-item list, tabulated by Ṣalāḥ al-Farṭūsī, received no such treatment) for an ode in quatrains (*dūbayt*) in *rajaz* meter, each quatrain placing the variants of a triplet in the order of *fa'l, fi'l* and *fu'l* at the end of a hemistich, producing a threefold internal rhyme.

Rajaz poems, more often occurring in rhyming couplets (*muzdawij*), were a common teaching tool, most famously in the case of the thousand-verse grammar (*Alfiyya*) of Ibn Mālik (d. 1274), still a staple of the Islamic college curriculum (*madrasa*). But al-Bahnasī transcended the usual doggerel

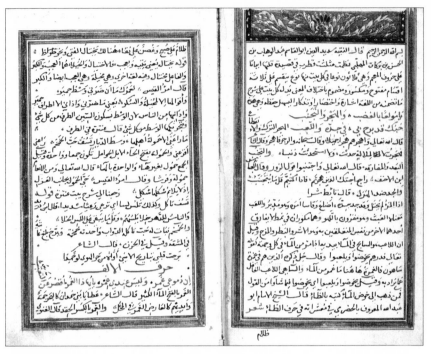

FIGURE 4.5

Al-Bahnasī's versification of Quṭrub's triplets with prose super-commentary by Ibrāhīm b.
Hibatallāh al-Maḥallī al-Lakhmī (d. 1321), including poetic proof texts and some paraphrases
of ambiguous orthography. MS Yale Landberg 489, Nemoy no. 189, fols. 1b–2a, eighteenth cen-
tury. Beinecke Rare Book and Manuscript Library, Yale University.

to write a truly literary composition, and he cast it as love lyric (*ghazal*), the
most popular genre of Arabic poetry. By means of this highly conventionalized genre, he evoked a rich repertoire of themes and motifs in a succinct
way in the educated reader's mind as a background for the lemma to be
explained. In his preface he boasts about accomplishing the tour de force
of providing a minimal context for each shade of meaning within the short
space of a hemistich: "Each verse indicates the explanation of the lemma
it includes, in a suggestive, concise, and memorable manner to be easily
learnt by heart" (Quṭrub, *Sharḥ qaṣīdat Muthallathāt Quṭrub*, MS Yale
Landberg 489, folio 1b) (fig. 4.5).

It is interesting to see how the rendition in *rajaz* quatrains brings the dis-
parate meanings into a poetically sensible ensemble. The poem reunites
familiar *topoi* of the love lyric (cf. Bauer 1998): it proceeds from a scene of a
morning of separation between the poet and his male beloved to the poet's

physical departure, journeying through the desert (triplets 1–8), followed by a drinking scene (*khamriyya*) with the beloved and his companions. The versification's hard-earned literary quality is best exemplified by the second and sixth couplets (the triplets are marked by italics in the translation)[6]:

و ليس عندي غمر	إنّ دموعي غمرُ
أقصِرْ عن التعتّبِ...	يا أيّها ذا الغُمرُ
وما بقىلي حلمُ	جدّ الأديمَ خَلمُ
مذْ غِبتَ يا مُعذّبي	وما هنا لي حُلمُ

inna dumū'ī ghamru   *wa-laysa 'indī ghimru*
yā ayyuhā dhā l-ghumru   *aqṣir 'ani l-ta'attubi...*

jadda l-adīma ḥalmu   *wa-mā baqā (var. baqiya) lī ḥilmu*
wa-mā hanā lī ḥulmu   *mudh ghibta yā mu'adhdhibī*

My tears are a *sea*   though I hide no *grudge* [toward my beloved]
O you *foolish* [one] there,   cut short your blame!...

Decay wore out my skin,   *Composure* has left me,
No *dream* [of the beloved] delights me, since you, my torturer (var. who beats me), are gone.

The poetic structure of the *dūbayt* clarifies the vocalization and ingeniously stands in for any (potentially omitted) supralinear signs. Attesting to its widespread use, Quṭrub's *Muthallath* (1315) figures among other propaedeutic classics in the catalog of books studied by the Andalusian Ibn Khayr (d. 1179; 1963:361–362), who received it through several lines of transmission, two of them traced back all the way to Quṭrub himself. Al-Bahnasī's quatrains proliferated in numerous manuscripts, and they generated thirteen super-commentaries in prose and poetry (cf. preface by al-Farṭūsī in Ibn al-Sīd al-Baṭalyawsī 1981:I:53–56; Sezgin 1982:61–67). They were even included in the tabulation of sciences by Ibn al-Muqri' (d. 1433; 1996)[7] in which each page can be read in five ways, depending on the discipline desired (fig. 4.6)—this in addition to the transmission of the prose list and its commentaries (for a full listing, see the preface by al-Farṭūsī in Ibn al-Sīd

FIGURE 4.6

The scientific compendium by Ismāʿīl b. Abī Bakr Ibn al-Muqriʾ (d. 1433), ʿUnwān al-sharaf al-wāfī fī ʿilm al-fiqh wa-l-taʾrīkh wa-l-naḥw wa-l-ʿarūḍ wa-l-qawāfī ("The Dependable Badge of Honor in the Sciences of Jurisprudence, History, Grammar, Prosody and Rhyme Theory"), including the versification of Quṭrub's triplets within the top arches.

al-Baṭalyawsī 1981:I:51–62, 97; Sezgin 1982:62–64; preface by al-Tamīmī in Fīrūzābādī 1988:41–47).

CONCLUSION

In sum, the optimized Arabic *abjad* could distinguish vowels in three ways: by reinterpreting consonants and semiconsonants, supplementing letters with auxiliary signs, or adding glosses. The first method had been adopted from the Aramaic orthography and extended in Arabic, whereas the second and third developed internally but were applied only selectively, depending on the difficulty, type, and prestige of a text and the presence of a context. Though never making vowels a fully segmental component of the basic Arabic *abjad*, the multiple ways of including them shows that vowels were vital elements and their correct understanding mattered.

In connection with desinential inflection (*i'rāb*), I have shown that the reductive script revealed an incomplete grasp of Arabic in its oral performance and created the need for literati and professionals to prepare themselves appropriately. But the reverse is also true: by not requiring writers to specify the case endings, people who did not master them could conceal many of their shortcomings. Compared to full segmental writing, the *abjad* significantly limited chances for error. Only where case or mood needed to be marked by a letter did less competent writers betray their incomprehension of them.

The wealth of grammar manuals and antibarbarism treatises highlights the significance of these problems and their solutions and, what is more, the zeal of scholars and writers in remedying or manipulating the unfettered and inviting phonetic indeterminacy of the Arabic script.

Acknowledgments

I gladly acknowledge the helpful comments made by my colleagues at the SAR seminar and the Harvard Semitic Studies Seminar and the two anonymous reviewers on an earlier version of this chapter.

Notes

1. Even though Old Aramaic, written with this alphabet, had twenty-six sounds, four of these were not distinguished.

2. All translations are the author's unless otherwise noted.

3. The twenty-one-letter version, however, depended on the double use of four signs to record twenty-five sounds; Dietrich and Loretz 1988:271.

4. One should keep in mind that no alphabet is fully phonetic (Hyman 2006).

5. Phonology plays a minor role in the Arabic linguistic tradition.

6. Cited after Quṭrub AH 1315. The phrase *jadda fa-l-adīmu*, which violates the meter, is emended after Quṭrub 1908 (see also Quṭrub 1914). The verb *baqiya* is used in the Middle Arabic form *baqā metri causa* (as also *laqiya* > *laqā* in quatrain 23). The 1908 edition corrects it to *baqiya*, disregarding the meter.

7. I am indebted to Muhammad Aziz for this reference. The work consists of a précis of jurisprudence if read horizontally and four further treatises on prosody, history, grammar, and the theory of rhymes if read along the vertical columns of the same text. The first and last columns are repeated in two arches on top of each page, between which a poetic commentary on al-Bahnasī's versification of the *Muthallathāt* is inserted. This may be, however, a later addition, since it appears only in some early editions (Aleppo AH 1294 and Cairo AH 1309) but not in others (Cairo AH 1318 [1900] and Karachi AH 1304); see Ibn al-Muqri' 1996:203.

5

Some Principles and Patterns of Script Change

Richard Salomon

INTRODUCTORY COMMENTS: TWO TYPES OF SCRIPT CHANGE

In Stephen Houston's original proposal for the seminar whose proceedings are published in this volume, he pointed out, with regard to the processes and factors that underlie script change, that "there is rough monitoring of paleographical modifications but little attempt comparatively to understand the selective processes behind such transformations" (n.d.a:2–3). Peter Daniels has made essentially the same point: "The study of writing systems...has been almost exclusively from the formal point of view.... Such comprehensive works as those of Hans Jensen...and David Diringer...deal exclusively with the shapes of characters and their changes over time and space. Works dealing with the relation of script to language...are written by area specialists and are marred by errors" (2006:8–9).

In light of these remarks, I propose in this chapter a fundamental distinction with regard to script change, between formal or superficial changes in "the shape of script" on the one hand and deeper systemic changes on the other. The discussion focuses on my own area of specialization, namely, the scripts of India and South Asia, but I cite examples from other areas in support of my general argument, which is that these two types of script development operate on different levels and in different historical circumstances. In short, I argue that external changes in the shape of script in the literal, visual sense are the inevitable product of a constant natural process of evolution, whereas systemic changes are typically conditioned by exceptional and sporadic forces, most often connected with language change. By "language change," I mean, in the present context, the adoption or adaptation of a pre-existing script for one language to represent a different, often unrelated language.

EXTERNAL SCRIPT CHANGE: THE SHAPES OF SCRIPTS

Within a given script, changes in the shapes of individual letters and often even in the overall ductus of the script as a whole normally develop in a gradual, continuous, and evolutionary process. Several factors determine this universal pattern. First of all, there is the innate human fondness for variety, novelty, and change for its own sake. Human beings are a curious, fickle, and whimsical lot who love to fiddle with their playthings and amuse themselves by changing these, even when the innovations may have no practical advantage. In this regard, script change is comparable to the endless ebb and flow of all cultural styles, be they hairdos, skirt length, necktie width, or—to mention a less ephemeral phenomenon—gravestone motifs.[1]

To begin with a trivial but apposite example, when I was in high school, it was fashionable among the girls to write a circle instead of a dot above their *i*s. Some of them took this style a little further and drew a tiny heart instead of a circle. These are purely aesthetically—as opposed to linguistically—motivated innovations of a sort that are widespread in scripts and constantly arise and, in most cases, fall away again in short order. This example is trivial in that it is ephemeral and had no lasting effect on the standard form of the script in question. But similar aesthetic or arbitrary modifications that are developed by persons in positions of authority or influence, such as (in a premodern setting) professional scribes, may have lasting effects in establishing new standard forms for particular letters.

Besides such intentional, aesthetically motivated or merely whimsical innovations, changes in the external forms of scripts can also arise as the result, conscious or unconscious, of technological changes and exigencies. For example, among the medieval and modern Indian scripts, one finds a striking contrast between the ductus of the northern scripts, such as Bengali, in which straight lines and sharp angles predominate (e.g., ক *ka*,

थ *tha*, and य *ya*), and the southern scripts, such as Kannada (e.g., ಕ *ka*, ಥ *tha*, and ಯ *ya*), which are generally characterized by curved lines and rounded forms. This contrast is usually explained as the consequence of the different writing materials most common in the regions in question: birch bark or paper in the north and palm leaf in the south. Straight horizontal lines and sharp angles cut into palm leaf with a metal stylus are prone to cause splitting, and the resulting avoidance of such shapes is believed to have motivated the rounded forms that predominate in most of the south Indian scripts.

For a second example of technologically conditioned script change, I turn momentarily to the contemporary world. Here, new letter forms are developing in response to the requirements for entering data into personal digital assistants (PDAs) by the "graffiti input system," in which each letter must be formed as a single stroke without lifting the stylus. For example, the letter *A* must be written not in the traditional form but with a simplified shape without crossbar, like a Greek *lambda* (Λ). It will be interesting for script scholars to observe the fate of this new form of *A*. In theory, it could come to be perceived as the standard form of the letter and replace the current one; for example, it has already been adopted in the logo of Kia automobiles (KIΛ). But it is more likely that the new *A* will continue to be restricted to its current specialized purpose or similar ones. Or it may turn out to be an ephemeral innovation, especially if the technology that has motivated it turns out to be ephemeral, so the single-stroke *A* will fall out of use before it comes to be established as standard.

However that may be—and only time will tell—this recent development of a new form of the letter *A* is simply one more manifestation of an ancient principle of script change, namely, stroke reduction and reordering. There is, however, an important difference: although the result, a distinct change in the graphic shape and visual impression of a graph, is similar, the motivation underlying the development of the new single-stroke *A* differs from that which provoked stroke reductions in premodern scripts. In the contemporary case, the motivation for stroke reduction is the fact that the graffiti input system has been programmed to perceive a separation between characters whenever the stylus is lifted from the screen. In contrast, the development of simplified forms of graphs in traditional forms of writing—by which I mean those forms of writing in which a concrete, as opposed to an electronic or "virtual," document is the outcome—results from a natural inclination to maximize speed and economy in writing. After all, in most circumstances writing is or quickly enough becomes a tedious chore, and the scribe inevitably develops an urge to finish his job as quickly and painlessly as possible.

Thereby arises the principle of economy, which is one of the most potent forces driving external script change. In writing, as in all industries, there is an inherent motivation to maximize the output and minimize the time and effort required for it. This principle affects the history of writing at various levels, but at the moment, I refer to the paleographic level, that is to say, to changes in the forms of individual graphs. Here, the desire to increase the speed of production leads naturally to the development of simpler forms, particularly graphs with fewer individual strokes. Thus, for example, in the Kharoṣṭhī script that was current in northwestern India between approximately the third century BCE and the third century CE, the original form of the consonant *s*, ౯, required two separate strokes, the first forming the curved upper portion and the second the vertical stem. Around the beginning of the Christian era, this letter developed into a more economical form made with a single complex stroke ౯. This new form was constructed essentially like the older form, but with the end of the first stroke connected directly to the beginning of the second, without lifting the pen. Thus, by the phenomenon of "pen drag," the two-character stroke developed into a form requiring only a single stroke, thereby reducing, if infinitesimally, the time and effort required to write it.[2]

But this was not the end of the story. At a slightly later period, this second form of the Kharoṣṭhī *s* developed into a further streamlined form, ౯. Here, the angle that in the second stage of development had represented the remnant of the juncture between the two originally separate strokes has been eliminated, so the stem of the letter becomes a wavy line in which a small bend toward the left at the middle of the stem is the only trace of the older form. At this stage, the maximum desirable degree of simplification had presumably been reached, and this third form of *s* remained more or less stable through the rest of the period in which Kharoṣṭhī script was in use.

By "maximum desirable degree of simplification," I refer to the inevitable balance in any writing system between economy and ambiguity. The Kharoṣṭhī *s*, or for that matter virtually any character in this or any other script, could in theory have been further reduced to a simpler and faster shape. But excessive simplification carries with it the danger of reducing the visual distinctiveness of a character to the point that it cannot be distinguished readily, if at all, from other similarly reduced characters. This is no mere theoretical problem. There are cases in the history of scripts in which two or more characters have become practically or even completely indistinguishable, the classic instance being the Pahlavi script of Iran, in which as many as four basic characters became virtually identical (Skjærvø 1996:524–525, Table 48.5).

In such cases, secondary disambiguating devices, such as diacritical dots, are sometimes introduced to distinguish the otherwise identical or nearly identical characters, although in the case of Pahlavi "little effort was made to develop diacritical marks to distinguish them" (Skjærvø 1996:524). The classic example of disambiguation through diacritics is the Arabic script and its many derivatives. In Arabic, as in Pahlavi, the same basic shape can represent as many as four different sounds, but in contrast to Pahlavi, the intended reading is indicated through the addition of dots or other diacritical marks (e.g., ب *b*, ت *t*, and ث *t*). Thus, the principle of economization can lead to a cyclical process whereby additional strokes must be introduced to counterbalance the ambiguity caused by excessive simplification. This process is analogous to linguistic developments whereby morphological changes such as the decay of inflections lead to ambiguities that are then rectified by the introduction of new inflections or other grammatical elements.

Another common type of paleographic change is related to stroke reduction but involves more complex motivations and results: stroke reordering. Here, the total number of strokes in a given character remains the same, but the order of their application or their individual formation produces changes, small or large, in the form of the character as a whole. For an example, I turn once again to Kharoṣṭhī, in which the standard early form of the consonant *k* was ﾌ, written with two strokes, the first comprising the horizontal head and the diagonal stem and the second the hook added to the right side of the stem. In some late forms of the script, however, this normal form was supplanted by an alternative one, ﾌ, in which the first stroke was reconfigured to comprise the head of the letter and the hook at the right, whereas the diagonal stem of the letter was written separately as the second stroke.

In this instance, as usual in such situations, the motivation for the reordering of strokes was presumably simplification or speed of writing, since the new form avoids the sharp angle at the upper right corner of the old first stroke and replaces it with a broad curve. But the cost of the simplification was, as is so often the case, a higher degree of ambiguity, for the resulting new form of *k* is sometimes virtually indistinguishable from the normal form of the letter ṣ (ﾌ), so in some documents written by scribes who used the later form of *k* the two letters can be distinguished only by the context, that is, by their position in a word. In such cases, we can assume that the writers and readers of such documents were able to intuitively gather, on the basis of their native sprachgefühl, which letter was intended. Presumably, this principle applied even in extreme cases such as Pahlavi, and the development of extremely ambiguous scripts such as these must have arisen in circumstances in which the primary users were professional scribes who could deal with such high degrees of ambiguity on the basis of their extensive experience and consequent intuition.

Many other instances of stroke reordering and reduction in various scripts could be cited, but I will mention only one more example, again from Kharoṣṭhī. The character in Kharoṣṭhī for the consonant *bh*, originally written as ⟨, has developed no fewer than ten attested varieties, most of which result from reorderings or reductions of the three strokes that composed the original form (see Glass 2000:86–90, especially 87, Figure 4). Although some of these restructurings are apparently idiosyncratic, that is to say, determined by the personal preferences of individual scribes rather than by any obvious economization of effort, some may also have been influenced by practical factors such as different writing materials and implements, for which certain types or orientations of strokes may have been easier to write than others.

So far, I have been discussing processes of economization like stroke reduction or restructuring that affect the natural development of scripts. But there are, of course, also counterbalancing factors that can *increase* the number of strokes and thereby the complexity of graphs. A typical development conducive to this contrary trend is the incorporation into the standard form of a character of what were originally incidental marks, in other words, portions of the graph that resulted from purely technical factors, as opposed to intentional manipulations on the part of the scribe. Such incidental elements most often result from onset and offset marks caused by the momentary pause and pen drag, respectively, that a scribe tends to make when beginning and ending an individual character.

In the case of scripts that are normally written in pen and ink, the onset mark typically takes the form of a short horizontal line at the top of the character, where the ink spreads out as the scribe momentarily sets the pen on the writing surface in preparation for writing the letter. In some scripts, this originally incidental onset mark eventually came to be perceived as an intrinsic part of the graph itself and therefore began to be written with a separate stroke. The result was the addition of an extra stroke or extra strokes to each character; thus, we have stroke *augmentation*, operating in counterpoint to the forces conducive to stroke reduction.

The results of the incorporation of originally incidental lines into the standard form of a graph are well attested in familiar scripts. For example, the serifs that are present in most printed forms of the "Latin" script and its various European derivatives (including, for example, the font used in this chapter) are in origin nothing but such onset marks. But in the Indic scripts, the effect of this phenomenon is even more pronounced, for the top line that is the most striking feature of the ductus of the Devanāgarī (e.g., क *ka*, च *ca*, and र *ra*) was initially simply a drastic extension of the onset line. At an early period in the history of Brāhmī script, the ancestor of all the modern Indic scripts, the onset line was incorporated into the standard form of the letters as a short horizontal serif written as a separate stroke. This serif stroke was gradually extended to the point that, in Devanāgarī and some other north Indian scripts, it came to extend across the entire width of each graph, and in rapid or informal writing it is often rendered as a single stroke drawn across the top of an entire word. In other Indic scripts, particularly in south India, the old onset line developed into various curved or angular forms rather than the straight horizontal line of Devanāgarī, in keeping with the preference discussed above for curved and rounded shapes among the southern scripts. Thus, the extension of the onset head-mark produced the characteristic "umbrella" that encloses many of the graphs of Oriya script (e.g., ଲ *ka*, ଚ *ca*, and ର *ra*) and the equally distinctive "check mark" of Telugu (e.g., క *ka*, చ *ca*, and ర *ra*).

Up to this point, I have been discussing the development of variant forms of graphs as if they were operating in a totally free environment, without any restraints on idiosyncratic innovations. But this, of course, is by no means always the case. In certain historical and cultural circumstances, a writing system may indeed be left free to develop more or less naturally, but in other situations scripts are more strictly regulated by educational, professional, or political authorities. In the case of Kharoṣṭhī, from which I have drawn several of my examples, the script does appear to have developed freely and without much external interference, and this freedom is more or less typical of the situation in the Indian world, where writing systems have not usually been subjected to regularization and standardization by external forces. But in other parts of the ancient and modern worlds, the case may be quite different. For example, in ancient Greece and China at various points in history, officially approved script forms were set in stone, as it were, by bureaucratic authorities, with the effect of largely—though, of course, not completely—freezing a particular script form deemed to be "correct" and rendering it a stable and more or less permanent system.

By way of conclusion to this section, I would characterize the forces that govern script change on the graphic or visual level as operating in a dynamic balance or tension between several pairs of factors, including the desire for speed and convenience versus the requirements of clarity and legibility; forces conducive to simplification of graphs versus those that produce complications; and free natural development and personal creativity versus externally imposed regulation and standardization. The result is that, depending on the balance between these forces, script change on the superficial level may be relatively rapid and continuous, as in the case of Kharoṣṭhī and many other premodern Indic scripts, or it may be incremental and gradual, even to the point of virtual stasis, as in the case of Chinese in the post-archaic period.

SYSTEMIC SCRIPT CHANGE: THE SHAPE OF SCRIPT

As discussed in the first part of this article, script change can be conceived of as operating on two distinct levels: that of changes in the outward form of individual graphs and that of changes in the underlying system, that is, in the strategy of mapping linguistic elements (whether words, syllables, morae, or phonemes) to graphic elements. As the result of an admittedly somewhat cursory survey of the question, I have come to the conclusion that these two types of change are prone to operate under different historical circumstances. As I have tried to show above, changes in the shapes of scripts involve natural processes that are constant and continuous unless checked or retarded by some external force that imposes standardization and freezes the system. Such incremental changes typically operate within an established system, that is, a particular script used to represent a particular language over an extended period. Substantial changes[3] in the underlying principles of a writing system, in contrast, occur rarely in the course of the continuous use of a script to represent the same language. Rather, fundamental systemic alterations are typically provoked by the adaptation of a pre-existing script for a different language, especially a genetically unrelated language whose phonological or morphological systems are substantially different from those of the donor language.

Such instances in which the underlying system of a script is altered in the course, and presumably as a consequence, of its adaptation to a new language are not at all hard to find among world scripts. I begin by mentioning the best-known case: the transformation of the old northwest Semitic consonant syllabary into an alphabet in the course of its adaptation to represent Greek. In this case, certain characters in the Phoenician consonantal syllabary that represented consonants absent in Greek and therefore dispensable were adapted to represent Greek vowels. Thus, the Phoenician consonant *alif* (glottal stop) became the symbol for the Greek vowel α (alpha), Phoenician *he* became ε (eta), and so on. The end result was that Greek script came to be an entirely different type of writing system, namely, an alphabet, a script in which all vowels and consonants are explicitly and separately represented, such that in theory one graph corresponds to one phoneme of the spoken language.

Of course, in reality the matter is hardly as clear and simple as I have sketched it here, where I follow the conventional formulation in order to make my general point. For example, on the one hand, at the time of Phoenician's adaptation for Greek, Phoenician and related northwest Semitic syllabaries had already developed partial systems of vowel notation by the *matres lectionis* system, so the adaptation of the Phoenician syllabary to Greek was perhaps more of a stimulus to an already incipient development than a revolutionary innovation. On the other hand, the representation of the vowels in the Greek alphabet remained incomplete in that, for instance, vowel length was distinguished for some vowels, such as *e* (ε = ĕ vs. η = ē), but not for others, such as *a* (α = ă or ā), this inconsistency being apparently an accidental result of the available graphic repertoire of the donor script. Moreover, the complete details of the adaptation—its date, location, and especially the motivations and cognitive awareness of its agents —remain very much a matter of controversy. Nevertheless, this case can serve as a classic example of my main point that language adaptation acts as the prime stimulus to the development of new types of writing systems.

But behind this most famous instance of the systemic remodeling of script type lies one that, though less widely known and less well understood, was of equal or even greater moment for the history of writing in the Western world. This was the formulation of the ancestor of Phoenician script in the script group variously known as Proto-Sinaitic, Proto-Canaanite, or simply "linear alphabetic writing." Unfortunately, our understanding of the precise nature of this script group, its linguistic associations, and the circumstances of its origin is still very limited and controversial. But recent discoveries have significantly advanced our knowledge, and there now appears to be something of a consensus that the linear alphabet arose in or around the early second millennium BCE as an adaptation of Egyptian writing (hieroglyphic or hieratic) for the representation of some as yet unidentified Semitic language.[4] According to this scenario, Egyptian logographs (mono-, bi-, or triliteral) were reapplied to represent Semitic consonants according to the acrophonic principle; thus, for example, the Egyptian logograph for "house," *pr* (⌐), was employed to represent the consonant *b*, which was the initial sound of the corresponding Semitic word (*bêt*). Hereby, an entirely new type of script was created. The logosyllabic Egyptian writing was transformed into a pure consonant syllabary in which each graph represented a single consonant, and that in turn would eventually develop into an alphabet. And the stimulus for the systemic change was, as usual, the adaptation of a pre-existing writing to a new language.

Looking to other areas of the ancient world and a considerably later historical period, another prominent example of systemic change involves the adaptation of Chinese characters for the representation of the genetically unrelated Japanese language. In the course of the history of Japanese writing, several systems gradually developed whereby a specified set of originally logographic Chinese characters were recycled, so to speak, as syllabic characters representing the phonetic but not the lexical value of the underlying Chinese characters. These characters were graphically simplified and eventually (though only quite recently) came to be codified in the two syllabic character sets, *hiragana* and *katakana*, that are nowadays used primarily to represent inflections, grammatical markers, and loan words and that function in conjunction with an extensive repertoire of Chinese characters (*kanji*) that have continued to be used with logographic value. As a result, the originally logographic system of Chinese has, in effect, been transformed into a combined logographic-syllabic system in Japanese. As usual, the stimulus for this systemic restructuring was the adaptation of the parent script for the representation of a different language.

But there are at least two important differences between this case and the paradigmatic Greek example. The first concerns the nature of the linguistic characteristics that conditioned the systemic change in each case. In Greek, it was the difference between the phonetic structures of the two languages concerned, Phoenician and Greek, that underlay the alphabetization process. In Japanese, it was evidently not so much the phonetic as the grammatical structure of the borrower—an agglutinating, polysyllabic language in contrast to the isolating monosyllabic donor Chinese—that promoted the development of a set of syllabic characters useful for the representation of grammatical affixes. The second contrast between the Greek and Japanese examples involves the chronological dimension of the adaptation process. In the case of Greek, the change from a primarily consonant-syllabic Semitic system to the alphabetic Greek seems to have happened early on in the process of adaptation, apparently even more or less simultaneously with it. The development of the Japanese syllabaries, in contrast, was a gradual and complex process that continued over many centuries, during which the donor and borrower languages remained in close contact. Nonetheless, the general principle remains the same: the adaptation to a new language conditioned a systemic restructuring, albeit only partial in this instance, in the receiving system.

Returning to the South Asian zone, similar processes can be traced in at least two major developments in Indic script history. The first case involves the initial development of the distinctive Indic script type, variously known as alphasyllabary, abugida, neosyllabary, *akṣara* writing, and so on.[5] Although the date and historical circumstances of the origin of this distinctive Indic graphic system script type are poorly understood and controversial, it is now generally agreed that this first arose in connection with the Kharoṣṭhī script, rather than with the historically more productive and thus better-known Brāhmī script. Although we lack (and are not likely to ever find) specimens of Kharoṣṭhī script in its formative phase,[6] it is reasonably clear that this originally arose as an adaptation of Aramaic script in the northwestern corner of the Indian subcontinent at some time in or around the fourth century BCE, at which time the region in question was still under the control of the Achaemenid Empire of Iran, where Aramaic was in wide use.

In this case, the adaptation of the underlying Semitic consonant-syllabic script for Indian languages had a result that is partially analogous to the case of Greek, insofar as the resulting script developed a way to indicate vowels more consistently than did the donor. But the specific Indic mechanism for the expression of vowels was systemically different from that of Greek. Whereas in Greek the alphabetic system represented all vowels explicitly by means of separate characters on a par with consonantal graphs, Kharoṣṭhī and thence, apparently, nearly all later Indian scripts developed a system whereby all vowels were specified, some explicitly and some implicitly, but in most cases not as independent characters. Instead, post-consonantal vowels within a word (which constitute the great majority of all vowels in the system) were represented by diacritic additions to the preceding consonant, except for the "neutral" or "inherent" vowel *a*, which was understood to be present by default whenever a consonant remained unmarked.

There is no obvious linguistic motivation for the development of this particular systemic modification, such as there was in the case of Greek, in which some superfluous Semitic consonants could conveniently be used to represent vowels.[7] Perhaps the Indic development was conditioned less by linguistic and more by cultural factors, such as a pre-existing tradition of analyzing spoken language in terms of syllabic units or *akṣara*, which may have been conducive to the construction of a system in which the graphic unit was the syllable of the types C, CV, CCV, and so on. But this is, admittedly, little more than a guess.

However it may be, this distinctively Indian system has been extraordinarily stable throughout the history of Indian scripts, although it was not, as we shall see shortly, totally immune to change. It seems that the alphasyllabic or *akṣara* system that was originally developed for Kharoṣṭhī was subsequently adapted into the other major early Indian script, Brāhmī (Salomon 1995:272), which would in turn become the parent of all the Indic scripts. The vast majority of these scripts preserved the basic *akṣara* system with only minor modifications, despite the fact that they were used to represent many different languages.

This latter fact, which at first glance might seem to contradict my main thesis, can be readily explained on the grounds that most of the languages involved, namely, the various Prakrit dialects and Sanskrit in the earlier phases and the several modern Indo-Aryan languages in later times, belong to the Indo-Aryan language family and are very similar in phonetic structure. This situation also applies to most of the Dravidian literary languages of south India, notably Kannada, Telugu, and Malayalam, whose phonetic repertoire and vocabulary are strongly influenced by Sanskrit and whose Brāhmī-derived scripts retain the standard *akṣara* system.

The exception that proves the rule, however, is Tamil. This language, spoken in the far southern tip of the Indian subcontinent, is the only literary Dravidian language that has preserved the original phonological structure of the Dravidian family, lacking, for instance, the phonemic voicing and aspiration distinctions characteristic of the Indo-Aryan group. Tamil also most effectively resisted the influence of the lexicon of the Indo-Aryan family to the north. So it is hardly surprising, in light of the patterns that I have been discussing, that in Tamil, and in Tamil alone,[8] we find the only significant systemic modifications of the *akṣara* script system within the Indian subcontinent. This point applies, moreover, both to the "Tamil-Brāhmī" script of the early Tamil inscriptions, used from about the first century BCE until the fifth century CE (Mahadevan 2003:232), and to the later and modern forms of Tamil script that arose separately from other Brāhmī-derived scripts.

The systemic innovations in the two Tamil scripts are, to be sure, not drastic ones, constituting modifications to rather than complete reformations of the standard *akṣara* system. In the case of the old Tamil-Brāhmī script, the principle of the inherent vowel, that is, the default indication of post-consonantal *a* by an unmarked consonant, which is everywhere else a fundamental and consistent component of the *akṣara* scripts, was subjected to various modifications, as authoritatively formulated by Mahadevan (2003:225–236; summarized in Salomon 2004). In the most drastically modified variety of the several systems used in the early Tamil inscriptions, Mahadevan's TB-1 system, "the Brāhmī principle of the 'inherent' *–a* was given up and the consonantal symbol was regarded as basic (mute)" (Mahadevan 2003:227); that is to say, the unmarked consonant could stand for the consonant alone, without a following vowel.

In the later and modern varieties of Tamil script, the standard Indic system of vowel notation was reinstated, but another anomalous technique for marking vowelless consonants was developed. In nearly all other Indic scripts, these are normally indicated by a system of ligatures in which the vowelless consonant is joined to or combined with the following consonant or consonants to form a graphic syllabic unit (*akṣara*) of the type CCV or CCCV, and so on. In the later Tamil scripts, this somewhat cumbersome system was done away with by the use of a simple dot above the first consonant of a cluster to indicate the cancellation of its otherwise inherent vowel *a*. This was a seemingly obvious step toward simplification, obviating the need for a large number of sometimes complex consonantal ligatures, but one that was nonetheless never taken in any Indic script other than Tamil.

Thus, even though the systemic innovations of the Tamil scripts are not nearly as radical or far-reaching as the other non-Indic examples discussed above, they remain striking in comparison with the systemic stability of all the other Indian scripts. In view of this contrast, it is reasonable to suppose that the distinct phonetic structure and cultural independence of Tamil among Indian languages underlay the parallel innovations that arose independently in both its earlier and later script forms.

This pattern, moreover, also applies with regard to numerous cases of borrowing Indic scripts and adapting them to non-Indian languages. For example, the adaptation of the Brāhmī-derived script of medieval northern India, the so-called "Siddhamārtkā," to the Tibetan language entailed a major systemic remodeling whereby the basic graphic unit was restructured to suit the mono-syllabic character of the borrowing language. In Southeast Asia, Indic archetype scripts have been modified in various ways to suit the very different phonetic structures of the several languages concerned, for example, in developing various techniques for indicating tones through modifications of the vowel notation systems.

CONCLUSIONS

Any number of further examples could be invoked in support of the patterns and principles I propose above,[9] but I trust that the few I have cited suffice to establish my main point, that what is casually referred to as "script change" can best be understood as two distinct phenomena. The first type of script change involves the gradual, incremental, and often unconscious or unintended changes in the physical form of graphs that inevitably occur within a particular script as it remains in continuous use for representing a particular language. The second kind of script change involves major systematic shifts in graphic representation, which seem to occur rarely if at all within the history of a single script-language complex but instead typically arise in the course and presumably as the result of the application or transfer of an existing writing system to a new language. These systemic reconfigurations, in contrast to gradual, formal modifications of graphs, presumably involve more or less conscious efforts on the part of the inventors or developers of the adapted script forms.

Notes

1. I mention this last example because it has been carefully documented by, among others, Deetz (1996:89–124 [chapter 4, "Remember me as you pass by"]), who traced and documented the patterns and influences that governed the designs of gravestones in colonial New England, such as urban and rural styles, cultural values and identities, and technological innovations. These factors, mutatis mutandis, are not very different from those that govern the ever-changing forms and fashions of scripts.

2. Any number of similar examples could be cited from Indic or other scripts. I will note only one more, a relatively recent innovation involving Devanāgarī, the pre-dominant modern script of north India. The now-archaic form of the consonant ṇ (ण) in this script required four separate strokes. This rather cumbersome form has within the past century been gradually replaced by a new shape, ण, in which the first and second strokes (from left to right) have been joined by a pen drag connecting their bottoms, resulting in a simpler three-stroke form.

3. Here, I do not address the issues discussed in Daniels 2006 regarding the adjustments made to the set of graphs of a parent script when it is adapted to a new language by mechanisms such as reduction of inventory, additions of letters, combinations of letters, alternations of letters, and so forth. Rather, I restrict my discussion to deeper levels of systemic change, which Daniels treats only briefly in the article in question, in the section "The history of writing" (2006:10–11).

4. Note, for example, the following comments by Darnell and others regarding the newly discovered inscriptions from Wadi el-Ḥôl: "The Wadi el-Ḥôl inscriptions, as two of the earliest known alphabetic inscriptions, thus provide the crucial link that conclusively proves the derivation of early alphabetic signs from both hieratic and hieroglyphic Egyptian writing" (2005:91).

5. For descriptions of this script type and discussion of the terminological issues, see Salomon 1996:376–377, 1998:14–17, 2003:70–72.

6. The earliest extant specimens of Kharoṣṭhī are the rock edicts of King Aśoka, dating from the mid-third century BCE.

7. The Indo-Aryan languages in question have a large consonantal repertoire, typically some thirty phonemes, so the Indic adaptation of Aramaic script probably used all or nearly all of the Semitic consonantal characters to represent Indic consonants. For example, Semitic *qof* and *ṭet* were apparently adapted to represent the Indic voiceless aspirated occlusives *kh* and *th*, respectively (Salomon 1998:30).

8. A partial exception to this statement is a small anomalous set of early inscriptions in Prakrit from Bhaṭṭiproḷu in south India (Andhra Pradesh) that show modifications of the vowel notation similar to those observed in the early Tamil-Brāhmī inscriptions (as described below). But this unique modification of the *akṣara* system in connection with an Indo-Aryan language being used in south India probably arose under the influence of the Tamil system (Salomon 1998:34–37).

9. Some other examples of script reformation resulting from adaptation to a new language are noted in Salomon 2000, especially page 94. Still further instances that could be cited in this connection include the Ugaritic cuneiform syllabary and various other adaptations of Sumerian-Akkadian cuneiform with drastically reduced graph inventories, such as Elamite, Hurrian, and Urartian (Gragg 1996:58–65).

6

Script Change in Bronze Age China

Kyle Steinke

In this chapter I look at script change over the first millennium or so of the (known) history of the Chinese script, from the earliest substantial body of inscriptions down to the early imperial period, in other words, from the Shang oracle bones (ca. 1200–1050 BCE) down to the Han dynasty (206 BCE–220 CE). Although I try to give a general impression of the multitude of changes happening during this period, my main concern is to show how our ideas about script change are influenced by our ideas about the functions of writing. In order to make this point as concretely as possible, I devote the first half of my chapter to a close reading and comparison of the two main accounts in English of the early history of the script, *The Origin and Early Development of the Chinese Writing System*, by William Boltz, and *Chinese Writing*, by Qiu Xigui. Boltz, a philologist by training, looks at script change as a response to writing's function as a representation of language. Qiu, a palaeographer, focuses on changes that arise from writing's role as an everyday tool of communication. Examining the ideas of these two authors side by side suggests not only that it can be difficult to explain the changes we observe but also that it can be difficult even to observe a process of change if its cause lies outside the range of explanations we are in the habit of considering. In the latter part of my chapter, I suggest that the Chinese script has been shaped in important ways by a display function that neither Boltz nor Qiu pays much attention to.

In the introduction to Boltz's monograph, he tells us that his account of the Chinese writing system is an internal linguistic history. This he defines as "an account of the origin and evolution of a script seen in terms of its relation to language, i.e., how the script is structured and operates in its primary function as a graphic representation of speech" (1994:10). Boltz (1994:9–10) contrasts this linguistic approach with what he calls an external material history, which covers things not directly concerned with how writing represents spoken language—the physical aspects of scripts and the societal contexts for writing. The only script changes that concern him are changes that affect the techniques for representing speech.

In the first half of the monograph, Boltz (1994:73) describes the invention of writing as the creation of a lexicon by means of a set of sign formation processes. The motive he sees driving the invention is a wish to represent the spoken language. In his view only three sign formation processes were required for the purpose. The first was the invention of zodiographs, noncomposite signs with pictographic origins that represent words. The second was the multivalent use of those zodiographs for either their semantic or phonetic value. The third was the addition to them of phonetic or semantic components to fix the readings of multivalent graphs and relieve the ambiguity introduced by multivalent usage.

Since the only function of writing that Boltz (1994:38) considers is the representation of speech, for him the formation of the writing system had to be a sudden leap to full writing capable of recording extended discourse. Deeming the first two sign formation processes insufficient for notating the complete lexicon, he believes that they had no function independent of the third. It follows that all three processes had to be thought up at the same time or in near simultaneity. The set of formation processes Boltz envisions is a toolkit that had to be created overnight by an inventor who had already seen the possibility of full writing.[1]

How did the inventor accomplish this? Boltz believes that in one form or another zodiographs may often be invented but only users of monosyllabic languages with large numbers of homophones will think of using them in rebus fashion. He therefore hypothesizes that in the centuries before 1300 BCE a once polysyllabic Chinese language was evolving toward monosyllabicity and that writing was invented when the language became sufficiently monosyllabic to enable recognition of the rebus principle. Because Boltz is looking at script change, including script invention, as an internal linguistic process insulated from society and culture, script change has no reason to occur at one moment rather than another unless in response to a change in the spoken language. Since he believes that the Chinese script was invented suddenly around 1300 BCE, he proposes that the Chinese language arrived at monosyllabicity around that time.[2]

In concluding his section on the formation of the writing system, Boltz (1994:125–126) tells us that once the toolkit for inventing characters was operational, the technology for representing speech did not change. In other words, the essentially logographic Chinese script that emerged fully formed sometime before 1000 BCE stayed a logographic script. The main thing Boltz has to tell us about script change is that the kind he is interested in did not occur.

This absence of internal change is a puzzle that he feels a need to explain. In the second half of his monograph, he (1994:160–167) examines manuscripts excavated from a Han tomb of the second century BCE at Mawangdui in Hunan province and notices that the scribes use many rebus graphs. Boltz calls these graphs paronomastic, and their use intrigues him because he sees in them an opportunity for just the kind of change he would expect to see in the history of a logographic script. If graphs are being used as rebuses without the addition of determinatives, this opens up the possibility that the Chinese script could desemanticize. Instead of being a script in which every graph is tied not only to a syllable but also to a distinct word or word part, the script would represent syllabic sounds divorced from meaning. It would become a syllabary.

Boltz sees syllabaries as more efficient than logographies because they allow a script to go about its business of representing speech with a vastly reduced inventory of signs. For him, therefore, the rebus variants he notices in the Mawangdui manuscripts are disorganized and unsystematic first steps in the direction of an exclusively phonetic writing system. Though he does not say so explicitly, he seems to view them as simplifications driven by the same need or instinct for efficiency that eventually leads, or should lead, to a syllabary. In the second century BCE, Boltz (1994:170) believes, Han scribes were suddenly on the verge of replacing their logographic writing system with a more efficient one.

The corpus of excavated manuscripts now goes back to the fifth century BCE, and rebus variants of the kind Boltz noticed at Mawangdui in the second century BCE go back as far as we have manuscripts.[3] But the Mawangdui manuscripts were discovered in 1973, a time when few excavated manuscripts were known, and they had special interest for Boltz because they contained versions of a famous text in the received tradition (the Daoist classic, the *Laozi*). Perhaps impressed by the appearance of rebus variants in excavated texts related to the received tradition, Boltz took the Mawangdui finds to signal that the moment for the invention of a syllabary arrived in the second century BCE.[4] It was at this moment, he believes, that the scribes' unsystematic shortcuts had generated enough rebus variants to put the idea of a syllabary within reach.

He also has a source to suggest for the idea of desemanticization. Boltz (1994:171) hypothesizes that, just as an evolution toward monosyllabicity triggered the invention of the script, a process of bisyllabification just prior to the Han paved the way for a syllabary by adding a number of rhyming binomes with disyllabic morphemes to the language.[5] He (1994:172) suggests, in other words, that an influx of asemantic syllables taught scribes that rebus graphs could be stripped of their determinatives and used to represent sound alone.

But this is an explanation for a change that did not happen. Boltz hypothesizes that rebus variants and language change had together brought early Han scribes to the brink of a syllabary but the scribes did not take the plunge. Why not? Since in his view a syllabary was the logical next step, failure to take it requires explanation. For this, Boltz (1994:173–177) invokes an essentialist notion of a Chinese worldview favoring ethical order. It is an ad hoc answer to a problem created by his assumption that syllabaries are more efficient at representing speech than logographic scripts. What he has assumed, in fact, is I. J. Gelb's theory of the evolution of writing systems.[6] The only moment in the early history of the Chinese script at which Boltz finds it necessary to invoke nonlinguistic factors is the moment when the script fails to take the path Gelb prescribed for it.

If we turn now to Qiu Xigui's *Chinese Writing*, we find that, unlike Boltz, Qiu has much to say about external change. He also gives an account of internal change that is different from Boltz's. Since Boltz (1994:71–72, 148–149) maintains that all composite graphs were created by combining a phonetic element with a semantic element, he denies the existence of composite graphs formed in any other way. But his insistence that all composite graphs have the same structure is only a postulate; it is not something he can demonstrate. Thus, when Qiu offers us another plausible analysis of a graph—and he offers us a wealth of shrewd analyses—Boltz gives us no a priori reason for rejecting it.

Qiu in fact sees a variety of sign formation processes operating throughout the history of the script. One of them generates graphs from components that all function as semantics; he calls these 會意字 *huìyìzì*, for which his translator coins the term "syssemantographs" (2000:185–186). Among the more than a hundred examples Qiu (2000:202) analyzes is the graph 𝕄, which means "cut off a person's nose (as a punishment)." He tells us that this graph is found in the Shang oracle-bone inscriptions and is composed of the elements ∫ "knife" and 𝕄 "nose," each of which is pictographic in origin and appears as a component in numerous graphs. The oracle-bone script includes many such semantic composites (cf. Bottéro 2004:252–253).[7]

However, very few syssemantographs were created in later times. Qiu (2000:58) believes that semantic-only sign formation processes fell into disuse because of a loss of iconicity in the script, a loss driven by the need to write more quickly and easily.[8] At a stage when graphs were highly depictive, creating or combining semantic elements was an obvious way to form new graphs, but it ceased to be easy or natural when the pictorial content of the signs had become less apparent. Thus, Qiu sees a change that Boltz would classify as external—loss of iconicity—as causing a change that Boltz would classify as internal—a change in the type of graph used to represent a word. In Qiu's view it was only as iconicity receded that the creation of new graphs came to be dominated by phonetic sign formation processes. Boltz, of course, does not see a change here at all, since for him all composite graphs were semantic + phonetic combinations from the moment of the script's invention; he does not admit the existence of syssemantographs or any of Qiu's other composite sign formation processes. Since Boltz (1994:54) sees no function for iconicity after the moment when the idea of writing occurred to the inventor, its loss has no impact on the script.

Another phenomenon Qiu (2000:130) notices is that when elements within a graph were abbreviated or contracted, for instance by combining several elements into a single form, the end product might look like the result of a formation process different from the one that generated the original graph. For example, consider the following Han simplifications of Warring States forms:

奉 → 奉 "offer"

泰 → 泰 "peaceful"

春 → 春 "spring"

In the first example, the early form's two hands 𝅷𝅷 have merged with the phonetic ¥ "beautiful" to give the element 夫 ; below, a semantic element for "hand" 𝅷 remains distinct (干) (Qiu 2000:232). In the second example, 𝅷𝅷 two hands have merged with the phonetic element 大 "large" to give the same element 夫, again leaving the semantic element at the bottom, in this case "water," distinct (2000:254). In the third example, the semantic for "grass" ₩₩ and the phonetic ⅄ "hill" combine to give the element 夫, the semantic for "sun" ❂ remaining distinct (2000:20). A user of the new graphs would see each of them as formed from two components. One component, the one at the bottom, is and always was a semantic element. But the other component has several different histories, none of which is now visible to the user.

Changes like these meant that users of the script were often unaware of the original structures of particular graphs. This observation leads Qiu (2000:57–58) to suggest that many phonetic and semantic elements and hence many whole graphs came to be seen only as arbitrary signs by most members of the script community, as indeed they are by the vast majority of users of the Chinese script today.

Qiu catalogs all sorts of changes in the outward forms of graphs. He notes that early in the script's history there was much variation in the way the parts of a graph were put together but that over time these variations tended to disappear. For example, the oracle-bone graph 男 (a title; later, "male"), composed of the components 田 "field" and ⅃ "strength," is also found written 田⅃ and ⅃田 (2000:102–103). He also suggests that when we find certain graphs rotated ninety degrees from their natural orientations, it is because the practice of writing in vertical columns has brought about a sacrifice of iconicity. In the oracle-bone graph 豕 "pig," the feet are "stranded in midair." Similarly, in the syssemantograph 疒 "illness," the semantic elements representing 亻 "person" and 爿 "bed" are turned upright (Qiu 2000:42). Notice, however, that these rotated graphs do not represent a change in the script unless Qiu is correct in assuming that in some lost earlier stage of its history they were written in their natural orientations.

In Qiu's history of the script, both simplification and complication of graphic forms have roles to play. He (2000:48) explains the complication of graphs as resulting sometimes from caprice, sometimes from the need to reduce ambiguity. But he sees it as a minor phenomenon by comparison with simplification. In his view the need for simplification was the driving force behind all progressive developments in the Chinese script.

Two early developments, Qiu says, reduced the pictographic qualities of graphs. The first combined linearization and streamlining. "Linearization refers to the phenomenon of changing thick strokes to fine and replacing squared or rounded solid elements with lines" (2000:70). By linearization Qiu means the sort of change that converted the graph 山 for "fire" into 火. "Streamlining of graphic forms refers to the phenomenon of changing curvilinear lines to even lines and joining disconnected lines into one" (2000:70). Thus, the graph 馬 for "horse" was streamlined

TABLE 6.1

Development of the graphs "horse" and "fish"[1]

Ancient script				Clerical	Standard
Identificational	Bone	Zhou bronze	Small seal		

1. After Qiu 2000:45.

to produce 馬. Linearization and streamlining were followed by a second change, the segmentation of graphs into a smaller number of strokes. Segmentation intensified in the Qin and Han dynasties and continued to the fourth century CE, resulting in the 隸書 *lìshū* (Clerical) and 楷書 *kǎishū* (Standard) scripts. Qiu summarizes this whole sequence using the graphs "horse" and "fish" as illustrations (table 6.1).[9] In Qiu's view what these changes have in common is that they all made the physical act of writing easier and more convenient. The script lost its iconicity because graphic forms had to be simplified in the interest of easier execution.

In a sense both Boltz and Qiu are interested in simplification; they just see the problem differently. For Boltz with his linguistic interests, the shapes of the signs do not matter much. For him the only kind of simplification that is important is simplification that affects how speech is represented structurally in the writing system, and the evolution of logographies to syllabaries and thence to alphabets is the obvious path to simplification because it vastly reduces the number of distinct signs. Qiu never considers this kind of change. Instead, he looks for simplification in the physical process of writing characters. Coming from outside the script tradition, Boltz finds it natural to assume that scribes would wish for a writing system that would be easier to learn because it has a smaller sign inventory. For Qiu, who learned the system as a child and does his own daily writing in it, progress is being able to write characters faster.

In Qiu's history, therefore, the simplification of graphic forms in the interest of efficient writing is the main catalyst of script change—or the main catalyst of the changes he considers important. Efficiency drives the creation of what he (2000:66) calls 通俗文字 *tōngsú wénzì*, or popular scripts. Qiu's concept of popular script is important to his account of script change, but it is also difficult to pin down. He divides scripts into formal and informal. Formal scripts are shielded from the pressures towards efficiency found in everyday writing. No script that faithfully repeats graphic forms inherited from earlier periods, for instance because of government mandate, or that creates new forms for applications such as monumental inscriptions, in which speed of writing is not a factor, will lead to simplification. Popular scripts, in contrast, are practical, everyday scripts that are always throwing off useful shorthand variants—variants that may in time be drawn into formal scripts (2000:404).

Qiu's earliest example of popular script is the Shang oracle-bone script. Noticing that the graphs in Shang bronze inscriptions usually display stylistic features consistent with brush writing but that the oracle inscriptions carved on bone seldom do, he reasons that the oracle script is a simplification of contemporary brush-written forms. Since the intractable nature of bone made the carving of inscriptions an arduous task, the engravers altered the usual forms of many graphs for the sake of efficiency. For example, the oracle-bone inscriptions often use the graph 孑 in place of 孓. This simplification serves Qiu's (2000:63) argument because it reappears later in the script.

But the oracle inscriptions are not popular texts at all; they are royal texts that served a ritual purpose. Qiu calls them popular writing only because many of their graphs have been modified for easier execution. Thus, although he uses the word "popular" and tends to think of all his popular scripts as being produced by common people, in practice the scripts he identifies as popular are the ones that have been simplified in the interest of efficiency, regardless of who actually did the writing or for whom it was done.

Qiu's book gives a thorough history of the script from the late second millennium BCE to the fourth century CE. It is a complicated story, too complicated to sketch here, but we should notice where he finishes it and why. Qiu ends in the fourth century CE because by then a script called *kǎishū* (Standard Script) had supplanted all others as the official script of Imperial China. In his view *kǎishū* strikes an optimal balance between ease of execution and the distinctiveness required for legibility (2000:58). His history of the script is an account of progress toward this optimum, and in this progress, popular scripts are what contributed the essential innovations (2000:66). Qiu does not ignore the existence of other, very diverse scripts in the period he covers, but to his way of thinking, scripts designed for art or monumental purposes, however important in their own time, had no long-term historical importance. He describes the scripts of later Chinese history as arising from efficient simplifications that cropped up in the writing of humble scribes and were from time to time adopted into the standards set by official script reforms. That Qiu sees popular scripts and the common man as the agents of progress is perhaps only natural considering the time in Chinese history in which he has lived.

In the remainder of my chapter I look at a source of script change that Qiu does not consider. I suggest that some important and lasting changes in the script were brought about not by scribes pursuing efficiency but by something very close to the opposite—scribes designing for looks. To do so, I examine two of the same inscription types that Qiu discusses—inscriptions on bronze and writing in brush and ink—but with an eye to some features that he neglected (figs. 6.1–6.7). The two types do not actually occur together in the archaeological record until the fifth century BCE, when we find them abundantly represented in the tomb of Marquis Yi (d. 433 BCE), ruler of the state of Zeng. I take two of my examples from this remarkable tomb. The first is a bronze inscription, one of many on a spectacular set of sixty-five bells (see fig. 6.5). The audience privileged to view Marquis Yi's bells saw an array of almost three thousand characters, most inlaid with gold. This is a display inscription written in characters more than 5 centimeters high, as far from everyday writing as it is possible to get. The second is a document written with brush and ink on bamboo slips, a list of funerary gifts (see fig. 6.6). Marquis Yi's bamboo slips are the earliest yet unearthed: they give us our first opportunity to see actual examples of the work of the scribe in an everyday medium.

These slips are a reminder that documents of the kind in which Qiu expects important script changes to occur, documents written with brush and ink on everyday writing surfaces, do not survive in the archaeological record before the fifth century. Most of what he tells us about the script of earlier periods is inferred from monumental inscriptions either carved or cast into durable surfaces, inscriptions that were not everyday documents at all. For the first millennium in the history of the script, we can study everyday writing only indirectly. Hence, when Qiu (2000:72) looks in bronze inscriptions for clues to script change, he looks above all at the inscriptions that were written the most perfunctorily, because they are the ones that he feels might come closest to popular script: perfunctory writing is efficient writing. Nevertheless, in the Shang and Western Zhou periods even a finely executed bronze inscription, the tenth-century one in figure 6.2c, for example, will interest him if it looks as though it might faithfully imitate a

Figure 6.1

Xiaozi X you. (a) *Vessel. Height 27.8 cm. Eleventh century* BCE. *Hakutsuru Fine Art Museum. After Umehara 1934:No. 12.* (b) *Inscription in the lid. Diameter at mouth 13.6 cm (long axis), 10.3 cm (short axis). Author's photograph.* (c) *Rubbing of inscription in the lid (approx. actual size). After Zhongguo shehui kexue yanjiusuo 1984:No. 5417-2.*

144

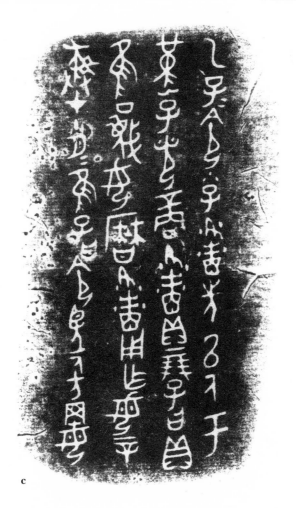

c

model done with brush and ink. By the fifth century, however, bronze inscriptions look nothing like contemporary brush writing—compare the two inscriptions from Marquis Yi's tomb—and as Qiu approaches the fifth century, he loses interest in bronzes. Inscriptions like those on the Zeng bells he (2000:71–72) dismisses as artful embellishments of the everyday script.

Yet, the tenth-century inscription, no less than the one on the bell, was written for display. Instead of viewing bronze inscriptions only as substitutes, sometimes poor substitutes, for the perishable documents we have lost, we should ask how their display function shaped their script. With this thought in mind I want to look at four bronze inscriptions from Shang and Western Zhou.

FIGURE 6.2

Xing Hou gui. (a) *Vessel. Height 18.5 cm. Tenth century BCE. British Museum. After Rawson 1987:No. 25.* (b) *Overhead view. Diameter at brim 27.8 cm. After Yetts 1929:Plate14–A17.* (c) *Inscription (approx. actual size). Author's photograph.*

146

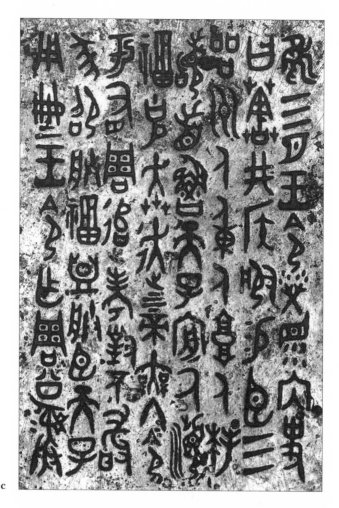

c

The first is cast in the lid of the *Xiaozi X you* in the Hakutsuru Fine Art Museum, a vessel made toward the end of the Shang period, probably in the eleventh century BCE (see fig. 6.1a).[10] The inscription of more than forty graphs is laid out in four columns (see figs. 6.1b and 6.1c). Shang inscriptions of more than a few graphs are rare and apparently confined to the reigns of the last two kings. The inscription of the Hakutsuru *you* seems to be the longest that survives.

My second inscription appears inside the *Xing Hou gui*, the *gui* of the Marquis of Xing, a large four-handled bowl in the British Museum (see fig. 6.2a).[11] This dates from early in the Zhou period, perhaps the beginning of the tenth century BCE. The inscription is a crowded rectangle of sixty-eight graphs in eight columns (see figs. 6.2b and 6.2c).

a

b

FIGURE 6.3

Yu ding. (a) *Vessel. Height 102.1 cm. Diameter at brim 78.4 cm. Tenth century* BCE. *National Museum of China. After Shanghai bowuguan 1959:Plate 1.* (b) *Inscription rubbing (reduced). After Zhongguo shehui kexue yanjiusuo 1984:No. 2837.* (c) *Detail of inscription (approx. actual size). After Zhongguo shehui kexue yanjiusuo 1984:No. 2837.*

c

My third inscription is on the inside wall of the *Yu ding*, a massive tri-pod bowl now in the collection of the National Museum of China in Beijing (see fig. 6.3a). This vessel stands a meter high and weighs more than 150 kilograms. It is roughly contemporary with the *Xing Hou gui* but much larger, and at nearly three hundred graphs its inscription is easily the longest known from its time. Figure 6.3b shows a greatly reduced rubbing of the entire inscription, and figure 6.3c a detail at actual size.

My final inscription is cast inside the neck of the *Shi Wang hu*, a large

a   b

c

FIGURE 6.4

Shi Wang hu. (a) *Vessel. Height 45.5 cm. Ninth century BCE. British Museum. After Rawson 1987:No. 29.* (b) *Overhead view. Diameter at brim 16.8 cm. Author's photograph.*
(c) *Inscription rubbing (approx. actual size). After Rawson 1987:No. 11.*

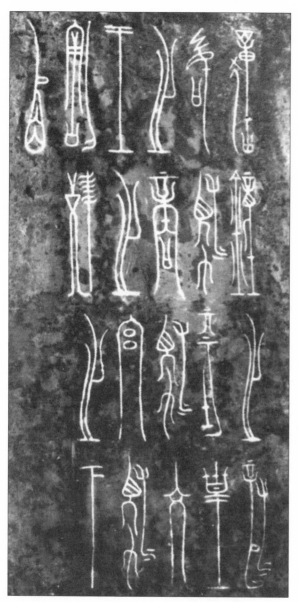

FIGURE 6.5

Inscription from first bell of lower tier (2/3 actual size). Tomb of Marquis Yi. Fifth century BCE. After Rao and Zeng (1985: Plate 8. The inscriptions of all but two of the large bells are inlaid with gold. Here I illustrate one of the inscriptions without inlay because it is more legible in a black-and-white illustration.

FIGURE 6.6

Inscribed bamboo slip (2/3 actual size), photographed in three sections running from left to right. Tomb of Marquis Yi. Fifth century BCE. After Hubei sheng bowuguan and Zhongguo shehui kexue yan-jiusuo 1989:Plate 222.

FIGURE 6.7

Inscribed wooden tablet from Juyan. 51 BCE. (a) *Tablet (reduced).*
(b) *Detail (two and a half times actual size). After Gansu sheng
kaogu yanjiusuo et al. 1994:No. EPT53.186.*

vase made sometime in the ninth century BCE (see fig. 6.4a). Consisting of sixteen graphs written in four columns, this is a very typical, very ordinary late Western Zhou inscription (see figs. 6.4b and 6.4c).

In my first two examples the graphs vary enormously in size. On the *Xiaozi X you* (see fig. 6.1c) the graphs second from bottom in the middle two columns, 畧 and ꃔ, are of radically different sizes. On the *Xing Hou gui* (see fig. 6.2c) the last graph 🦅 (lower left corner) is three times the size of the one that precedes it ꃔ. The graphs in these two inscriptions have sizes and proportions that were determined by their internal structure and by the medium in which they were normally written. They belong to a script that was written mainly on vertical slips of bamboo, and writing on bamboo slips favored uniform width but put no constraint on height. Graph height varies either because of the number of components a particular graph required or because of the space needed to draw the iconic referents of those components. In other words, graphs had natural proportions. They could, of course, be adjusted a little: in the *Xing Hou gui* inscription the graph ꃔ near the bottom of the second column from the right and the same graph ꃔ in the second column from the left have been written to fit different spaces. However, the graph 🦅 at the end of the inscription is taller than the graph ꃔ next to it, not because of stretching or compressing but because ꃔ depicts a child whereas 🦅 must depict two hands holding a bird by the legs. Similarly, on the *Xiaozi X you* 畧 depicts a woman, whereas ꃔ depicts "speech coming from a mouth" (Qiu 2000:191).

Let us turn our attention now to the layouts of the four inscriptions. In the first two the graphs are similar, but the layouts are quite different. The forty-odd graphs of the *Xiaozi X you* inscription (see fig. 6.1c) are arranged in four columns of equal width. The columns are about the same height, so the inscription fills roughly the dimensions of a rectangle. The spacing between columns is generous. We could imagine squeezing six columns into the area occupied by these four. If we were thinking about this inscription as Shang-period word processing, we would probably say that this is 1.5 line spacing, if not quite double. On the other hand, the graphs within a column are packed together rather tightly, more like the font used in this chapter than one like Courier, which gives each character equal space.

Horizontally loose but vertically tight, the *Xiaozi X you* inscription (see fig. 6.1c) looks not at all like the next (see fig. 6.2c). Why? Perhaps this was the first time the caster had executed so long an inscription in bronze. The inscription was no doubt supplied to him in the form of a fair copy written on slips, and he prepared it for casting in the bronze in the same way that he would have written it in his everyday medium. We seem to be looking at four bamboo slips laid side by side.

The designer of the *Xing Hou gui* inscription (see fig. 6.2c) thought very differently. Conscious of the vessel's continuous surface in a way that his predecessor was not, he gave as much thought to horizontal as to vertical spacing, and he produced an inscription that is composed for a rectangle. When he received the text from the marquis, he first had to think about the space that would be available inside the bowl and decide roughly on the size and proportions of the rectangle he would place there. As we see in figure 6.2b, he chose to restrict himself to an area much smaller than the space available. Perhaps he preferred writing graphs of a certain size, or perhaps he did not want to crowd the inscription up against the circular frame. Next he had to decide on the number of columns and allot graphs to columns (the number of graphs per column varies from eight to ten). This might have taken some experimenting, but once it was done, he could begin the process of shaping individual graphs and fitting them together. The shaping and fitting probably required several drafts. Certainly it called for a kind of visual thinking very different from anything we see in the *Xiaozi X you* inscription (see fig. 6.1c). The scribe who wrote the inscription on the *you* made sure that his columns were of equal height but otherwise treated them as independent of one another and just packed graphs into them. The designer of the *Xing Hou gui* inscription (see fig. 6.2c) made his columns disappear into an expanse of densely arranged graphs.

My third inscription, that of the *Yu ding*, presents an artistic problem of a different order (see fig. 6.3b). To lay out the *Xing Hou gui*'s sixty-eight graphs as a unified composition must have been difficult and time consuming, as well as requiring much artistry. To compose a significantly longer inscription in the same way would seem hardly possible. Faced with the task of distributing nearly three hundred graphs over an area approximately a tenth of a square meter, the *Yu ding*'s designer imposed a less subtle order on his text by starting with a rectangular grid.[12] The grid was a completely new organizing principle, and it is a good deal less obvious and more remarkable than it might seem. It gave the designer an attractive layout, but at a price. On the *gui* the design problem was to arrange sixty-eight graphs within a rectangle. The *Yu ding*'s writer faced instead the problem of redesigning individual graphs: using a grid required redesigning every graph in the text to fit a standard rectangular module. Compare two successive graphs from the *Xing Hou gui*, 𓎛 and ㄗ, (see fig. 6.2c) with their counterparts on the *Yu ding*, 𓏤 and ㄩ (see fig. 6.3b). The designer of the

Yu ding inscription managed to compose graphs that seem equally well suited to the rectangle they occupy, regardless of how many or how few strokes a graph contains.

The designer cannot have been quite unconscious of the momentousness of the step he was taking, because it involved not only the decision to design graphs uniform in size but also a decision about their proportions. At the outset he had to choose the proportions of his grid, in other words, the shape of the rectangle within which every graph, simple or complicated, would be redesigned. Interestingly, he chose not a square grid but a rectangular module about 1.4 times as high as it is wide.[13] Choosing this ratio meant choosing the look of the script, as he no doubt realized.

My fourth inscription, that of the *Shi Wang hu* (see fig. 6.4c), was made more than a century after the *Yu ding*. Neatly written but hardly inspired, it is typical for its period. Layouts as dense as the *Xing Hou gui*'s are found only in the early Western Zhou; later Western Zhou inscriptions are laid out with liberal spacing between graphs, both vertically and horizontally, resulting in compositions of greatly diminished intensity. The inscription on the *Shi Wang hu* is short and its designer did not follow a grid in laying it out.[14] Nor did he make his characters exactly the same size. Yet, if we compare his work with the *Xiaozi X you* (see fig. 6.1c) and the *Xing Hou gui* (see fig. 6.2c), we will not see the *Yu ding* as anything less than a watershed. In his mind the script was a collection of graphs designed to the same dimensions. But the script was not conceived that way until someone built into it the idea that graphs could be thought of as all the same size. The graphic modularity that every user of the Chinese script today takes for granted—generations of schoolchildren have learned to write by tracing over model graphs in grids—had to be invented, and it was the designer who first used a grid to lay out a long bronze inscription, on present evidence the creator of the *Yu ding* inscription, who invented it.

Characters of equal size were certainly in the mind of the fifth-century calligraphers who supplied the inscriptions for Marquis Yi's bells. The calligrapher who inscribed the bell in figure 6.5 chose to stimulate his imagination by adopting a grid of truly extravagant proportions, not the *Yu ding*'s 1 to 1.4 but something nearer 1 to 3.3. His success in making each graph command this fantastically tall and narrow module gives his design fascinating visual power. Compare the graph from the Marquis' bamboo slips (see fig. 6.6) with its counterpart—composed of the same four strokes but fully 5.5 centimeters high—in one of the bell inscriptions . In appearance, at least, the designer has invented an entirely new script.

The scribe who wrote the Marquis' bamboo slips (see fig. 6.6) was not asked for anything so ostentatious, but he was certainly asked for something more than the scribal efficiency Qiu would credit him with. The graph 辶 was faster to write than the version created for the bell inscription, but ease of writing alone does not explain the way it looks. Modulated line is probably an inevitable product of brush writing, but lines of this quality are not. Like the professional designers of bronze inscriptions, the scribes who worked in brush and ink wrote for an audience that demanded fine writing.

Let me close with a Han official memorandum from the middle of the first century BCE discovered at Juyan in Gansu Province (see figs. 6.7a and 6.7b). In this document we see not only scribal artistry but also state intervention. The module here is wider than it is high. Heavy, bladelike, rightward strokes give weight and, unexpectedly, buoyancy too, combining power with elegance. This is writing in an official script of the most formal kind, a script whose stylistic features were selected by Han bureaucrats and strictly required of the scribes they employed. The only thing efficient about it is the clarity with which it delivers a message of bureaucratic control.

In trying to understand script change in China, we must remember always that the script was continually influenced by aesthetic decisions, decisions made by those who produced and selected the models for proper writing. No government-sanctioned script was ever established without finely written exemplars, nor did anybody learn the script without also receiving instruction in proper penmanship. Whatever scribal shortcuts may have arisen through the instinct for efficiency, there were always master scribes working to redesign those shortcuts for adoption into standard scripts.

Qiu Xigui is right that everyday scribes permanently shaped the script by contributing efficient shortcuts. But those same scribes also contributed embellishments native to their brush-and-ink medium. Modulated line, something we think of as an intrinsic feature of the Chinese script, something that is even incorporated into type fonts for printing, originated with scribes writing in brush and ink. If it is hard to conceive of the script without its shaped lines, this is owing entirely to the artistry of scribes doing everyday writing. Finally, the script owes a debt also to the professional artists whose job it was to design display inscriptions. It was in the work of court professionals, not that of journeyman scribes, that the idea of equal-size characters arose. Throughout its history the Chinese script has had features that were designed for beauty rather than efficiency, features that mattered not just to the private calligrapher but also to the state. If we overlook them, it is only because we take them for granted. Not even the most earnest seeker of efficiency would consider giving them up.

Acknowledgments

My warmest thanks to Stephen Houston for organizing the SAR seminar and inviting me to join it. For valuable comments on drafts I am grateful to Robin McNeal, Susan Naquin, and Wang Haicheng. My arguments were much improved by Robert Bagley's sharp eye for essentials. I would like also to thank Osamu Yamanaka of the Hakutsuru Fine Art Museum, Carol Michaelson of the British Museum, and Zhang Changping of the Hubei Provincial Archaeological Bureau for making it possible for me to examine objects in their institutions' collections.

Notes

1. Boltz 1994:38–39, 69; cf. Bagley 2004:248n88.

2. This is an addition to his original account, made not in his monograph but in a later paper (2000:15). Cf. Bagley 2004:247n84. Qiu (2000:26–27) also cites the preponderance of monosyllabic morphemes, but only to explain why characters eventually came mostly to represent single syllables.

3. Galambos (2005:124–125) cites rebus variants from fifth century BCE covenant texts found at Houma in Shanxi province.

4. Boltz (1994:13–14) dismisses the variant forms found in a Warring States silk manuscript from the state of Chu discovered in 1942 as a localized, nonstandard variety of pre-Han Chinese writing. The text, a kind of ancient almanac, is introduced briefly in Harper 1999:845–847.

5. The monosyllabic origin of rhymed binomes was first hypothesized by Boodberg (1937). Boodberg, however, did not assign a date to the process of bisyllabification, nor did he attempt to explain all disyllabic morphemes in the language as arising from a process of bisyllabification. Many of the polysyllabic words in existence by the Han arose from compounding monosyllabic morphemes, a process distinct from the one Boltz discusses.

6. Gelb 1963:198–205. See Boltz 2001:1–4 for a summary of Gelb's theory.

7. Qiu (2000:170) also describes graphs composed exclusively of phonetics.

8. In fact, since Qiu (2000:2–4) believes that the script originated as nonlinguistic picture writing, in his view loss of iconicity played a role even at the stage of invention.

9. Qiu's chart is meant to be read chronologically from left to right, but his first stage is hypothetical. The "identificational" graphs in his first column are bronze inscriptions contemporary with the oracle-bone graphs in the second column. Qiu takes them to represent a lost earlier stage because he believes that the oracle-bone graphs must have been preceded by a stage in which graphs were more pictorial. Cf. Bagley 2004:227–228, 246n73.

10. By modern convention, inscribed bronze vessels are named after the person who had the vessel made, in this case one Xiaozi X (the X stands for a graph that has

no clear modern reading). A shorter inscription in the body of the vessel dedicates it to one of Xiaozi X's ancestors.

11. Cf. Shirakawa (2004:605), who refers to the vessel as the *Rong gui*, interpreting the inscription to mean that the vessel was cast not by the Marquis of Xing but by Rong, another individual mentioned in the inscription.

12. It is not clear whether the division of the text into two blocks a short distance apart, a feature known from other lengthy inscriptions as well, had something to do with casting technique or is instead a sort of paragraphing of the text.

13. Cf. Qiu (2000:26), who cites a square module (*fānggé*) composition rule to explain why the same character components are often placed in different positions within characters but who does not address the problem of the origin of the script's modular design or note the frequent use of rectangular rather than square modules.

14. A faint grid visible in the area of the inscription has to do not with the laying out of the inscription, I believe, but with the preparations for casting inscriptions on curved surfaces.

7

The Development of Writing in Japan

David B. Lurie

Writing in Japan has been continuously remade, from the earliest appearance of artifacts inscribed with Chinese characters around the first century BCE to the present era of postwar script reforms and digital communications. But the pace and consequences of change have not been always the same: the seventh through twelfth centuries CE were the critical period in which the fundamental set of technical innovations for writing and reading in Japanese developed. Furthermore, even within those six-hundred-odd years, the core developments took place early, during the seventh and eighth centuries. One of the keys to this history is that it begins in medias res. Inscribed artifacts first appear in Japan well over a millennium into the recorded development of writing in China, and the core period of innovation there takes place long after Chinese writing had begun to be adapted to the non-Sinitic languages of the Korean peninsula. In surveying the development of writing in the linguistic environment of the Japanese archipelago, this chapter deals with transformations of transformations, and an underlying question is to what extent the authority of an "original" system persists.[1]

HISTORICAL AND LINGUISTIC PARAMETERS

The earliest inscribed artifacts in the Japanese archaeological record appear in what scholars now refer to as the Yayoi period (early or mid-first millennium BCE to ca. 250 CE). Almost all of these objects are bronze coins and mirrors with cast inscriptions imported from China, and there are no signs that the characters on them were systematically associated with particular linguistic forms in the archipelago. The inscriptions seem rather to have been significant patterns, valuable for magical effects or perhaps merely for their association with rare prestige goods from overseas. As the small chiefdoms of the early centuries CE gave way to more extensive polities, much of the archipelago (from Kyushu to northern Honshu) came under the control of a league of local rulers associated with paramount kings in the Yamato region (the area around the modern cities of Osaka and Nara). The huge mounded tombs that emerged at this time have commonalities in design that are thought to reflect these associations and that provide the name of the Kofun (Old Tomb) period (ca. 250–600 CE) (Barnes 2007; Piggott 1997). Several of these mounds have yielded fifth-century swords with inlaid inscriptions that show that the Yamato kings employed scribes from the Korean peninsula (and probably their descendants), but there is little to suggest much use of writing for administration or extensive language-based communication in these centuries (Lurie 2011; Seeley 1991:9–25).

This situation changed dramatically over the course of the seventh century, especially in its latter half. As China, newly unified under the Sui (581–618 CE) and then Tang (618–907) dynasties, put diplomatic and military pressure on its eastern periphery, a long period of strife among three kingdoms on the Korean peninsula ended with its unification by the state of Silla. The Yamato rulers on the Japanese archipelago had intervened in this conflict on the losing side, and in the last decades of the seventh century, they were greatly concerned about further hostilities. This anxiety and related domestic developments that spurred the growth of a more powerful central government triggered a rapid expansion of the scope and variety of written communication.[2] The resulting interdependent process of state formation and development of writing culminated in the emergence of an elaborate world of legal codes, histories, belletristic writings, local administrative documents, sacred scriptures, personal letters, and so on. As might be expected from the varied Chinese and Korean influences, this world involved a palette of different techniques of reading and writing shaped by complex interactions among multiple languages. Contrasting styles of inscription functioned in parallel: there was some replacement of the old by the new, but the tendency was for multiple practices to coexist as those with earlier origins continued to develop alongside newer counterparts.

The classical state that formed in the late seventh century, centered on the emperors and their court and elaborately regulated by written laws and amendments, remained in place (as an ideal, at least) for nearly a millennium, but from the tenth century there was considerable growth in local autonomy, leading ultimately to diarchic rule in which the court was paralleled by increasingly independent military authorities.[3] This institutional complexity generated many new contexts for written communication as land titles and records of service by military vassals became central to the fates of new and old elites alike. The same period also saw the emergence of popular literary forms, involving the circulation of itinerant oral performers but also production of written works that drew on and influenced spoken (and sung) genres. In the tumultuous years of what has come to be seen as a medieval era (roughly the thirteenth through sixteenth centuries), increases in population and productivity were accompanied by further expansions in the scope and variety of writing (Amino n.d.; Conlan 2009; Fröhlich 2007). Endemic warfare caused the loss of large numbers of early manuscripts and records (especially in the fifteenth century), but it also spurred the spread of court culture and associated literary practices into the provinces.

This was a largely manuscript culture, with all manner of texts brushed by hand onto paper (wooden slips were also used extensively in the seventh through early ninth centuries and thereafter primarily in limited forms like luggage tags). Printing was known, however, from as early as the mid-eighth century, and great temples in the cities of Nara and Kyoto produced extensive woodblock editions of both Buddhist and secular works. From the end of the sixteenth century, there was a transformative change in the technology of writing as printing expanded out of these niche areas (though copying by hand persisted in various contexts). The rise of printing accompanied the development of the central regime of the Tokugawa shoguns, who sponsored the industry in its earliest stages. The Tokugawa ruled over the newly (though by no means completely) unified country from the early seventeenth through the mid-nineteenth centuries.

These decades saw the formation of new cultures of literacy as new types of education (government-sponsored schools on various levels but also private academies) and new printed genres came to include widening sectors of the population, which itself increased markedly through the early eighteenth century (Berry 2006; Kornicki 1998; Rubinger 2007). Development of urban communities, expansion of commerce, and rising numbers of people who could read and write all contributed to a massive increase in the production of documents and records across the archipelago, a less familiar counterpart to the oft discussed burgeoning of popular genres, annotated classics, and practical guides in woodblock print editions during this period.

The pre-existing variety of scripts, genres, and styles developed further in the new niches for writing created over these centuries. With the rise of commercial printing, there were changes in the content, layout, and, of course, quantity of circulating texts, but woodblocks allow for remarkable continuity between handwritten and printed texts and there was no fundamental change in the technical bases of Japanese inscription. Some standardization came with the increased integration of the country and circulation of both people and printed materials, but considerable variety continued.

Much of this culture of publishing and education continued unchanged for decades after 1868, when the Tokugawa Shogunate fell and was replaced by a government of oligarchs ruling in the name of the emperor, but two developments of the late nineteenth century had a transformative effect on Japanese writing (Twine 1991; Ueda 2008). Movable-type printing brought about a considerable degree of script standardization, and direct government involvement in schooling changed the ways that literacy was imparted to increasing portions of the population. A third development, whose influence was more gradual, not becoming decisive until the mid-twentieth century, was the engineering of new prose styles closer to the standard language (which was itself partly a product of the newly emergent nation-state). More visibly influential on the nature of the writing system have been postwar script reforms, which are responsible for the specific form taken by Japanese in the vast majority of contemporary publications, from newspapers to novels to websites.

Despite considerable ferment in the styles and functions of written Japanese between the seventh century and the present, the fundamental building blocks of the system exhibited remarkable continuity. With the exception of Sanskrit (used in limited Buddhist contexts) and the Roman alphabet (first encountered in the sixteenth century and important, though in a decidedly subsidiary way, since the nineteenth), the raw material for all forms of writing employed in Japan has been the Chinese writing system. As discussed below, the nature of that system is controversial, but for the time being it will suffice to stipulate that, taken as units—that is, not analyzed into modular graphic subcomponents—Chinese characters correspond to morphemes of literary Chinese.[4] These morphemes are monosyllabic and the majority of words in the literary language are monomorphemic, so characters also correspond to syllables and in many cases to words.[5] Syllables consist of an initial consonant (in earlier times, often a cluster of consonants), a vowel nucleus, and an optional final consonant. (The tones that are such a distinctive feature of the language from at least the period following the fall of the Han dynasty in mid-third century CE may have developed as the consonant repertory was reduced.) Though it appears not to have been the case for earlier stages of the *spoken* language, in literary Chinese there is little sign of inflection or affixing (hence the traditional designation of Chinese as an "isolating" language). In general, relations between words are expressed through grammatical particles and word order, the fundamental patterning of which is Verb Object (VO), as in English.

If one were to set up a laboratory experiment in script adaptation for a radically different language, it would be difficult to find a more vivid case of linguistic contrast than that provided by Japanese as it comes into contact with the Chinese script. Japanese morphemes are generally polysyllabic, especially before the absorption of Sinitic loanwords; verbs and adjectives are highly inflected; and plentiful affixing creates complex conglomerations of free and bound morphemes (hence its traditional designation as an "agglutinative" language). Syllables, comprising a vowel nucleus and an optional initial consonant, are open and far simpler than those of Chinese, and there are fewer distinct consonants and vowels as well. Grammatical relations are indicated by inflections and postpositioned particles, as well as word order, which, though amenable to a degree of inversion, is fundamentally Object Verb (OV).

In using the Chinese script to inscribe this very different Japanese language, one strategy is to take the syllabic values of the Chinese graphs and use them as phonographs for similar Japanese syllables.[6] In part because this process fits deep-seated prejudices about how writing should function and hence how it evolves over time and across languages, the development along these lines of sets of phonographs is by far the best-known aspect of the history of Japanese inscription. By virtue of its familiarity and its undeniable importance, it is the focus of the first of the following sections. But the central point of this chapter is that phonography is neither the sole nor the most important strategy for the adaptation of Chinese writing in Japan: the subsequent section takes up the comparatively neglected story of *logographic* adaptation and the related issue of the importance of reading practices for the history of writing.

PHONOGRAPHY: THE *KANA* SYSTEMS

There is a long history of phonographic use of characters for their syllabic values in Chinese-language environments. Indeed, part of the controversy over the "original" nature of the Chinese writing system is the prevalence in early texts of sound-based substitution and glossing of characters. Characters used phonographically, with little or no attention to the semantic associations of the morphemes with which they were otherwise associated, were also widely employed in the transcription of special terms and proper names from non-Sinitic languages. In Chinese translations of Buddhist sutras, such characters were even used to record entire incantations (*dharani*) in Indic languages, providing a precedent for phonographic transcription beyond the realm of individual foreign words.

Early Chinese treatises on the culture and society of surrounding "barbarians" transcribe terms and names in this manner, and those devoted to the *Wō* 倭, the Chinese ethnonym for the inhabitants of the archipelago, contain what are commonly believed to be the first recorded forms of pre–Old Japanese. In particular, the history of the Wei dynasty (220–265 CE) in the third-century *Sanguozhi* 三國志 contains a famous account of these inhabitants with numerous words spelled out phonographically, although there is insufficient evidence for firm identification of their later forms. It is, in fact, not even certain that they are from earlier stages of what became Old Japanese (Miyake 2003:6–7). Regardless, it is clear that the Chinese practice of using characters as phonographs for non-Sinitic languages underlay the first transcriptions of pre–Old Japanese terms undertaken within the Japanese archipelago. The fifth-century sword inscriptions produced by scribes from the Korean peninsula or their descendants contain numerous personal and place names, spelled out character by character. The best known of these, that found in the Sakitama-Inariyama burial mound (north of Tokyo), contains a genealogy of service to a "great king" (大王) that spells out nine personal names and one place. There are clear signs that the large number of Chinese graphs available for particular syllables had already been reduced to a smaller set of characters. Furthermore, there are parallels between this set and the characters used for phonographic transcription of names and terms from Korean languages in sources quoted in later Japanese histories.

As writing in Japan expanded out of the narrow niche it had occupied in the fifth and sixth centuries, multiple sets of phonograph characters emerged, distinguished by the historical and geographical changes in the Chinese (and Korean) pronunciations on which they were based. Some of these sets appear earlier or later than others, but there are also cases of simultaneous use in different contexts. Within the sets as well, the norm was for multiple characters to be employed for given syllables, a practice that meant a large reserve of homophonic alternatives. In some cases, it seems that differing levels of formality were involved in selection among these alternatives, but the sociolinguistic implications of graphic variation are not always apparent. (And, as the following section makes clear, multiple phonographs for given syllables were only the beginning of the potential variation.)

Regardless, all of these phonographs were derived by ignoring the meaning of the Chinese morpheme or word originally linked to the character and using it solely as an indication of an Old Japanese syllable phonetically similar to that morpheme. Formally, these graphs were indistinguishable from the Chinese characters on which they were based, but retrospective scholarship has dubbed them *man'yōgana* 萬葉假名.[7] Metalinguistic discussion of writing is rare in early sources, but the preface to the 712 *Kojiki* 古事記 (Record of Ancient Matters) describes writing based on these phonograph characters as "stringing out [words] using sounds [of characters]" 以音連.[8]

In seventh- and eighth-century sources, phonograph characters are used in various contexts. Substantial prose texts written out entirely phonographically were rare, but vernacular poems—often incorporated into longer works but also freestanding as graffiti or writing practice—were frequently inscribed this way. Tantalizingly, two eighth-century business letters written out phonographically survive in the Shōsōin storehouse of Tōdaiji, the great eighth-century temple in the then capital of Nara; it is unclear whether they represent flukes or chance survivals of a widespread practice. As in earlier periods, phonographs were also employed to write proper names and special terms, but another important function was glosses in notes and lexicons, as well as the related role of auxiliary specification of grammatical elements.

Phonographic use of graphically unmodified Chinese characters continued after the eighth century in particularly formal contexts, lexicography, and antiquarian or archaizing writing. The use of such characters for proper nouns never ended, and they were also often used for common grammatical elements and honorifics in conventionalized paronomastic spellings known in subsequent ages as *ateji* (宛字 or 當字). However, the trend from around the early ninth century onward was toward formal simplification, which eventually yielded loosely organized sets of phonographs that were visually distinct from their original Chinese characters.[9] There were two main pathways of graphic simplification: cursivization and abbreviation.

Formally, Chinese characters had already evolved through several stages before the beginning of widespread writing in the Japanese archipelago. The clerical script (*lìshū* 隷書) of the Han Dynasty (202 BCE–220 CE) eventually gave rise to three broad stylistic categories that dominated artistic and everyday calligraphy from the Six Dynasties (317–589 CE) onward. Standard script (*kǎishū* 楷書), later the basis of printed fonts, was the fundamental style in seventh- and eighth-century Japan. The remaining two formalized styles, semicursive (*xíngshū* 行書) and cursive (*cǎoshū* 草書), were produced by running together and simplifying the separate strokes of the clerical style. Varying degrees of cursivization were already apparent in Japanese writing before the ninth century. The line of graphic simplification that continued from these practices was an extension of cursivization processes already codified in Chinese calligraphic styles (and, more importantly, embodied in everyday writing in China, Korea, and elsewhere). The written form of phonograph characters was gradually simplified to the point where they took on a visual identity distinct from cursive-style Chinese graphs: 安 > あ or 以 > い. Significantly, numerous intermediate forms coexisted, in some cases as stylistic registers explicitly distinguished by Japanese readers and writers (fig. 7.1).

The other line of graphic simplification, abbreviation, also drew on Chinese precedents. The characters' modular structure (Ledderose 2000:16–18), at least in their noncursivized manifestations, meant that components could easily be alienated and made to stand in for absent wholes, as in the Buddhist abbreviation of "bodhisattva" (*púsà* 菩薩) as 〹 (Tsukishima 1981). Existing phonograph characters were similarly abbreviated, yielding simpler graphs: 加 > カ *ka* or 伊 > イ *i* (fig. 7.2).

These two pathways loosely correspond to sets of graphically distinct phonographs (*kana*) that were used for different purposes and in different contexts and that emerged over the initial century or so of the Heian period (794–1185 CE). The modern term for the set stemming largely from cursivization, *hiragana* 平假名, emerged relatively late, but there are Heian references to the term for the set largely derived through abbreviation, *katakana* 片假名. Because the terms *hiragana* and *katakana* are likely to summon anachronistic images of simple sets of forty-eight discrete moraic signs, in this chapter I refer to their pre-modern manifestations as "cursive phonographs" and "abbreviated phonographs," respectively. (It is important to keep in mind, however, that there was some mixing of graphs produced by the two principles—or, indeed, both, as abbreviation could be followed by cursivization, or vice versa.)

To some extent, the emergence of these sets of *kana* meant an increase in the variety of available phonographs because the earlier, graphically undifferentiated variety persisted in some contexts and there were now contrasts in degrees of cursivization or abbreviation. These influences were

FIGURE 7.1

Variant forms of cursive phonographs used in premodern manuscripts of vernacular literary works. The heading columns indicate the syllables with modern standard hiragana *(from the right, e [え], te [て], and a [あ]) and provide the noncursive phonograph base characters underneath (these are formally identical to standard printed Chinese characters). The two columns following to the left of the headings collect examples of cursive phonographs for the syllable in question (with one-character indications of the calligraphers to whom the original manuscripts are attributed). From an appendix to a widely used guide to variant character forms,* Hōshōkai henshūbu 1916.

counterbalanced by a tendency toward reduction and standardization of the number of base characters, as well as their final simplified forms, but even so a great deal of variety persisted, between (of course) but also within the sets of cursive and abbreviated phonographs. This graphic diversity persisted long after the twelfth century. Early attempts at movable-type printing of cursive phonograph texts in the late sixteenth and early seventeenth centuries maintained that homophonous variety, as well as accommodating

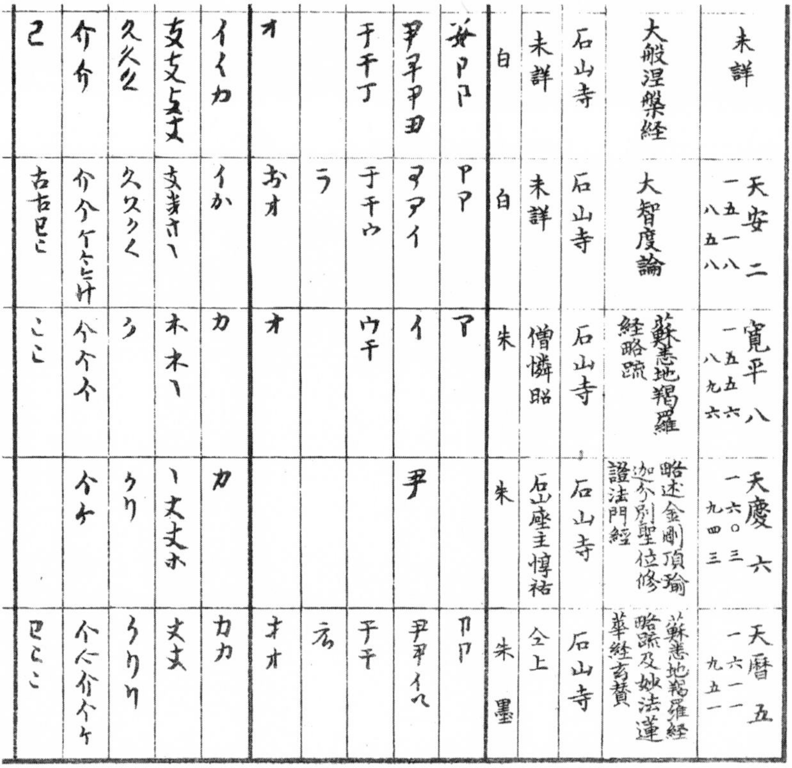

FIGURE 7.2

A chart of abbreviated phonographs employed in glosses on Buddhist manuscripts from the ninth and tenth centuries. From the right, the first five columns indicate the dates, titles, locations, annotators, and colors of ink employed in the glosses. The next ten columns show variant graphs for the following syllables: a (modern standard katakana *form:* ア*), i (*イ*), u (*ウ*), e (*エ*), o (*オ*), ka (*カ*), ki (*キ*), ku (*ク*), ke (*ケ*), and ko (*コ*). From Ōya 1909, a report on a survey performed under the auspices of the official National Language Research Council (Kokugo shingikai), which was involved in script and dialect reform efforts in the early twentieth century (see Gottlieb 1995:54–66).*

the calligraphic ligatures that were central to the aesthetics of this mode of writing. Subsequent woodblock printing, to say nothing of the thriving manuscript production of the same period, also continued to employ multiple homophonous phonographs. It was not until the late nineteenth-century adoption of Western moveable-type printing that the decisive steps were taken toward the modern one-to-one correspondence between *kana* graphs and syllables (technically, morae).

As an overview of the history of writing in Japan, the preceding may seem familiar. It might appear that, with the addition of an account of Chinese characters used as is to inscribe Sinitic loanwords, the story would be more or less complete. But actually the foregoing discussion tells only half—perhaps even less than half—of the story. Not only is it impossible to comprehend the development of Japanese writing in general without sustained attention to the role of logography, but such attention is also essential to understanding the appearance of the phonographic systems themselves. For complex reasons, both internal and external to Japanese linguistic thought, histories of writing have tended to overemphasize the importance of both phonography in general and the graphically distinct *kana* in particular. But there is much about Japanese inscription that does not make sense without tracing the immense role played by logographic writing during the early formative period and thereafter.

LOGOGRAPHY AND THE *KUNDOKU* METHOD OF READING AND WRITING

Thus far, this chapter approaches the problem of how writing developed in Japan as a matter of finding graphic signs for the transcription of the phonetic shape of the Japanese language. This is an undeniably important issue, but a very different picture emerges if the same history is approached through the question of how pre-existing graphic signs were rendered into that language: that is, the nature of reading in early Japan. The central phenomenon here is *kundoku* 訓讀, literally, "reading by gloss." This technique involves linking Chinese characters to Japanese words and then rearranging their syntax so that the reading accords with Japanese rather than Chinese word order.

The following is the opening of the Confucian *Analects* (*Lùnyǔ* 論語), glossed with its standard reading in modern Mandarin:

<blockquote>
xué ér shí xí zhī
學 而 時 習 之   "To learn and at due times to repeat what one has learned" (Waley 1938:83).[10]
</blockquote>

The traditional Japanese vocalization of these characters is entirely unrelated to their Chinese reading: *manabite toki ni kore wo narafu.* This is a translation of the Chinese reading into literary Japanese, but in practice it is not derived from the phrase *xué ér shí xí zhī* (or any of its premodern equivalents) but directly from the five characters themselves. For example, the initial character, 學, is associated with Chinese words meaning "learning" or "study" and by interlingual extension with the equivalent Japanese verb, *manabu.* The second character, 而, is associated with a Chinese particle that connects verbs in series: in *kundoku*, this grammatical relationship is indicated by conjugating *manabu* in the continuative form (*manabi*) and following it with the conjunctive particle *te*.[11] Similar equivalences link the fourth and fifth characters to the verb *narafu* (to practice) and the demonstrative pronoun *kore*, but to render an acceptable literary Japanese phrase, their order is reversed (from VO to OV) and the direct object marker *wo* is added: *kore* [this] *wo* [ACCUS] *narafu* [practice].[12]

Broadly, *kundoku* involves a lexicon of equivalences between characters and Japanese words and a set of transformations for rearranging syntax and adding grammatical elements that have no Chinese counterpart. In a sense, this is a form of translation, not least because in practice it involves complex interactions between an emerging sense of the whole and specific decisions about how to treat particular characters or patterns of characters. And many aspects of the history of *kundoku* parallel that of more familiar forms of translation; for example, from the fifteenth century until the early twentieth, the opposing positions in a Japanese scholarly debate about how closely the language of *kundoku* should hew to the patterns of Chinese resemble in many respects the contrasting German/foreignizing and French/domesticating approaches to translation in the European tradition (Venuti 2004:16–20).[13]

But the ways *kundoku* differs from interlingual acts of translation, at least as they are commonly conceived, are at least as significant. Literary translation replaces—or at least displaces—one text with another (even in the case of parallel-text translations, the two texts do not occupy the same space), but *kundoku* (at least in the abstract, idealized sense in which it has been treated thus far in this chapter) does not involve the production of a separate text. (In some respects, *kundoku* parallels oral interpretation but with the crucial difference that the "original" is not an oral utterance.)

The crux here is the nature of reading, which at the most fundamental level, we conceptualize as the generation of an utterance from graphic signs that, through their presentation of linguistic information sufficient for that generation, are inherently linked to the language in which the utterance takes place.[14] There are problems with these notions of "generation" and "presentation," but the important point here is that in *kundoku* the graphic signs cannot be said to be inherently linked to a particular language. On the page, the "original Chinese text" and the graphs that are read as the Japanese translation of the original are literally identical: in a step beyond Pierre Menard's *Quixote*, the text of the translation *is* the text of the original.

For these and other reasons, *kundoku* has serious implications for the history of writing in general, but I will postpone addressing those until I have considered its more local significance for the development of Japanese scripts. A crucial point in this connection is that *kundoku* is a method not only of reading but also of writing. The equivalences and transformations that make it possible to read, in Japanese, texts originally written "in Chinese" can be reversed, so a Japanese speaker in a Japanese-language environment can produce a text that is legible "in Chinese." (Certainly, this operation requires considerable training and experience, but then so does the production of correctly spelled, formal written English.) From the seventh century until the twentieth, a principal method of writing was *kundoku*-mediated production of character texts legible as literary Chinese. In practice, of course, writers aiming at a formal style in keeping with Chinese norms often fell short, such that there are admonitory catalogues of Japanese usages (*washū* 和習 [or, more pejoratively, writing that stinks of Japanese: 和臭]). But in principle and often in actuality, it was possible for correct literary Chinese prose and even poetry to be produced by people who did not speak Chinese—indeed, who did not read it, at least in our conventional sense of reading in a given language.

The historian of Japanese writing is thus faced with what might be called invisible vernacular texts: one cannot necessarily tell what language was associated with the writing and reading of a text that, on the surface, appears to be in formally correct Chinese.[15] But there are two ways in which the presence of *kundoku* reading practices becomes visible: (1) telltale departures from correct Chinese style and (2) the explicit indication of readings and transpositions in glossaries and dictionaries or annotated alongside characters of the texts themselves. The key to #1 is that in less formal contexts, writers who expected *kundoku* reading would maintain Japanese word order or include collocations that clearly indicate Japanese constructions rather than labor to produce a text that was legible as correct literary Chinese. As mentioned above, some such departures were inadvertent—and undesired—traces of inattention or inability, but some were so dramatic and so simple (most prominently and most commonly, OV rather than VO order) that it is hard to see them as mistakes. Essentially, if texts showing #1 or #2 can be traced to a certain period, then at least the possibility of reading by *kundoku* exists for all texts of that period, even those that on the surface are completely in accordance with literary Chinese norms.[16]

A flood of archaeological discoveries in recent decades and accompanying re-evaluation of transmitted manuscripts and epigraphic material have made it increasingly clear that *kundoku*-based reading and writing were already present at or very near the beginning of widespread writing in the Japanese archipelago (Lurie 2007). For example, wooden tablets bearing fragments of character glosses—category 2 from above—have been excavated from seventh-century sites in the island of Shikoku and in Shiga (near what became the city of Kyoto), whereas stele and statue inscriptions, as well as wooden tablets, show non-Sinitic character arrangements—category 1 above—from the same period. Unsurprisingly, given the Korean origins of so many Japanese writing and literacy practices, it appears that *kundoku* developed first in the Korean states of Koguryŏ, Paekche, and Silla by the sixth and seventh centuries. Surviving Korean materials from this period are comparatively rare, but wooden tablets and stele inscriptions show evidence of #1 whereas manuscripts of later centuries attest to readings and transpositions into Old and Middle Korean (#2).[17]

If *kundoku* developed on the Korean peninsula and was transmitted to the Japanese archipelago at the onset of widespread reading and writing, there are profound implications for the history of writing and literacy. The complex of characters, the rules for their arrangement, and the associated mass of authoritative works (religious, technical, historical, belletristic, and so on) that arrived in Japan did not do so as a written manifestation of the Chinese language per se but as a script that was already multilingual or translingual (even, again, when not visibly so on the surface of the texts). As it developed in Japan, *kundoku* was not produced by incorporating translation into reading for the first time but rather by extending to Japanese already developed links to non-Sinitic Korean languages. It is important to keep in mind that this issue is distinct from the Korean provenance of the earliest strata of phonographs used to write Japanese proper nouns (and eventually employed more extensively). Important though the emergence and development of those phonographs was, in its core functioning the overall system of writing was logographic rather than phonographic. Indeed, the term *kundoku* could be translated as logographic reading and writing of non-Sinitic languages with "Chinese" characters.

From the mid-seventh century emergence of widespread reading and writing in Japan, *kundoku*-mediated logography lay at the center, with phonography a peripheral, auxiliary mode. From everyday communications brushed onto wooden slips by low-ranking clerks to lavish editions of the complete Buddhist canon on fine paper scrolls with brocade covers, from short messages with characters arranged in Japanese word order to extensive histories and treatises almost completely legible as correct literary Chinese, logographic writing was the basic and, in many cases, the only medium of inscription. Phonographs were employed alongside logographs in both informal communications and more elevated contexts to indicate particles and other grammatical elements, to specify particular forms of conjugating words, or to write notes glossing logographic characters. In all of these cases, the phonographs spell out products of the *kundoku* process that could also be derived from logographs by themselves: they are, in essence, optional.[18]

From the earliest appearance on wooden slips (also around the mid-seventh century), written vernacular poetry had strong connections with phonography, and in eighth-century works like the *Kojiki* (712) and *Nihon shoki* (720), poems are consistently spelled out with phonograph characters. But even this association is not absolute: of the twenty books of the *Man'yōshū* (an immense late eighth-century poetry anthology), thirteen (arguably, fourteen) are dominated by logographic inscription. Most of these poems do make use of phonographic adjuncts, but some are even written out entirely in logographs. At any rate, vernacular poetry is only a partial exception to the overall dominance of logographic inscription.

It is important to acknowledge another exception to the prevalence of *kundoku*, which is an alternative mode of reading known as *ondoku* 音讀 (reading by [or for] sound). This mode involved reading characters one by one, approximating their Chinese pronunciations (that is, pronouncing them in Sino-Japanese) and vocalizing them in their original order. The traditional picture of the development of writing in Japan posited *ondoku* as originally the sole method of reading, gradually replaced by *kundoku* after it developed (in Japan) and as Japanese knowledge of spoken Chinese deteriorated (Miller 1967). But the evidence available now is not consistent with such a late emergence. As mentioned above, it is increasingly apparent that Korean models of *kundoku* predated and probably aided the rise of writing as a widespread practice in the seventh century. At this point, it seems likely that from the beginning, *ondoku* reading was used in limited contexts, such as recitation of rhymed Chinese-style poetry or formal intonation of highly valued religious and philosophical works, and was always accompanied by the possibility of *kundoku* reading. A more important aspect of *ondoku* is the rendition in Sino-Japanese pronunciation (*on'yomi* 音讀み) not of entire texts but of particular characters or compounds. Within an overall framework of *kundoku*, piecemeal *on'yomi* readings were often inserted when for stylistic or other reasons, the reader chose to avoid "translating" those terms. This incorporation of Sino-Japanese readings was a major vehicle for the adoption of the Chinese loanwords that by the eighth century had already begun to reshape the Japanese lexicon.

Logography, animated by *kundoku* reading and writing, continued to play a central role after the emergence of visually distinct phonographs (Heian *kana*) from the ninth century on. Moreover, that emergence itself only makes sense within the broader context of continued logographic inscription. This simultaneity is clearest in the case of the abbreviated phonographs (ancestors of modern *katakana*), which developed from phonographic character annotations of *kundoku* glosses. Such annotated texts survive from the turn of the ninth century on (although, as mentioned above, separate glosses of *kundoku* readings appear as early as the seventh century). From the ninth century and increasingly thereafter, plentiful annotated manuscripts of Buddhist and, eventually, secular works attest in detail to the emergence of this lineage of visually distinctive phonographs (Seeley 1991:59–69; see also Kobayashi 1998; Tsukishima 1981).[19] Given the small amount of space available and the limited time for writing (many of these annotations record readings expounded during lectures on the texts), it is natural that simplified forms would rapidly develop, and abbreviation had the advantage of speed and clarity. (Even so, as mentioned earlier, cursivized phonographs did play a limited role in this line of development, and some abbreviated graphs were subsequently further simplified through cursivization.)

The central role played by *kundoku* in the emergence of the abbreviated line of visually distinctive phonographs could not be more clear: such phonographs evolved in order to record *kundoku* readings and only subsequently came to be employed more independently in mixed logograph/phonograph styles and eventually in pure or nearly pure phonographic inscription.[20] It is not as obvious or direct, but nonetheless there is a relationship between *kundoku*-mediated logography and the cursivized line of visually distinct phonographs (ancestors of modern *hiragana*). The two major contexts for their development were mixed (logograph/phonograph) and all-phonograph texts. The mixed style originates, in effect, as an expansion of purely logographic writing, specifying phonographically certain aspects of the *kundoku* reading. All-phonograph texts include vernacular poetry, which seems to have been one of the major venues for the emergence of cursivized phonographs, but the two eighth-century all-phonograph prose letters from the *Shōsōin* archive in Nara were forerunners of similar prose writings from the ninth century onward. (This mode of writing is the origin of the Heian *kana*-based style that was the medium for the *Tale of Genji*, the *Pillow Book*, and other classics of high Heian vernacular prose.) This sort of all-phonograph writing may seem to be outside the realm of *kundoku*'s influence, but syntactical patterns and particular usages—and more broadly, the logical armature of vernacular prose in its earliest stages—show extensive debts to it (Okumura 1978a, 1978b, 1985, 1988, 1999; Tsukishima 1965, 1969).

Indeed, the complex of logographic characters and the *kundoku* practices used to read and write with them had a lasting fecundity, generating new forms of written (and, indirectly, spoken) Japanese throughout its recorded history. This influence is true for the mixture of logographs (*kanji*) and phonographs (*kana*) that is the graphic basis of most forms of written Japanese, but it is also true for its various linguistic styles (involving usage, lexical registers, syntactical patterns, and so on). For example, much attention has been devoted to the late nineteenth-century emergence of a written style more consistent with vernacular speech than the various forms of literary Japanese. This new style, *genbun itchi* 言文一致, eventually became the sole modern prose style in almost all contexts, but at the end of the nineteenth century and the beginning of the twentieth, the term "regular written [style]" (*futsūbun* 普通文) referred to a variety of what would now be termed "literary Japanese" derived not from the language of Heian vernacular prose classics but from *kundoku* as it was practiced in the mid-nineteenth century (Yamada 1935).

From the seventh century until the twentieth, *kundoku*-mediated logography, with or without phonographic adjuncts, remained the privileged—and in many cases the only—mode for legal, historical, religious, scientific, lexicographic, and administrative writing (fig. 7.3). Even in literature, where vernacular prose and poetry have been strongly—and to a large degree misleadingly—associated with visually distinct phonography, *kundoku*-based logography sustained a long-standing tradition of Chinese-style writing and mediated a striking degree of absorption and exchange between that tradition and the intimately related development of vernacular writings (Kurozumi 2000; Wixted 1998). Chinese-style logographic writing was central to the education, aspirations, ideals, and daily lives of male elites into the twentieth century and represented an expressive model and source of quotations, allusions, and catchphrases even for those who were unable to read and write the texts themselves.

CAUSES OF CHANGE AND CONTINUITY

There is, then, ample reason to contend that *kundoku* logography occupied the center of written Japanese until the twentieth century. But not to qualify such an assertion would be to prejudge unacceptably the history of literacies in Japan. Until the twentieth century, purely logographic texts remained common, especially in elite contexts, but logographs were also often accompanied by phonographic adjuncts in one form or another.

FIGURE 7.3

The initial passage of the Analects of Confucius, *from a late nineteenth-century Japanese woodblock edition that incorporates a commentary by the influential Chinese thinker Zhu Xi (1130–1200 CE) and glosses attributed to the prominent Japanese scholar Gotō Shizan (1721–1782). The text of the work itself begins with the second column and is followed in small graphs by Zhu Xi's commentary. Circles on the lower right corners of a number of graphs are punctuation marks indicating pauses or stops, but there are also extensive diacritics specifying the* kundoku *readings of the text. In the initial string of characters, discussed in this chapter, abbreviated phonographs on the lower right of the third, fifth, sixth, and seventh graphs spell out final syllables of words or grammatical particles:* (manabi)te テ, (toki)ni ニ, (nara)fu フ, (kore)wo ヲ. *On the lower left of the sixth character, the L-shaped mark indicates that this graph is to be transposed with the following one.*

Although logography was never supplanted by phonography—even the contemporary simplified orthography is a mixture of the two—it was undeniably supplemented by it in complex and varied ways, with important consequences for the social extent of acts of reading and writing.

This is clearest for the various modes of purely or mostly phonographic writing. In addition to vernacular poetry (written in phonographic characters in many cases in the eighth century and most—eventually, nearly all—cases thereafter) and high Heian belletristic prose (in cursivized phonographs), there are reports, letters, petitions, and other documents relying to varying degrees on cursivized or abbreviated phonographs from the late Heian period onward (Amino 1993: 353–404; Fröhlich 2007). After the rise of extensive woodblock printing, some of the most popular illustrated genres were written almost entirely in cursivized phonographs.[21] Perhaps even more important is the supplementary use of phonographs, which ranges from indication of grammatical elements (modern *okurigana* 送假名) to glosses on logographs. Such glosses appeared as interpolated notes, as interlinear annotations added by readers, or eventually as smaller graphs written alongside the logographs by the author or scribe (*furigana* 振假名 or *tsukegana* 付假名), which were standard in most printed texts from the seventeenth century until the mid-twentieth (Ariga 1989).

The intense and varied *mixture* of writing in Japan has important consequences for the history of literacy, as well as for the question of how and why the shape of script changed—or remained the same—during what I have called the critical period (from the seventh to the twelfth centuries) and thereafter. The parallel use of logographs (arranged in the Chinese style and otherwise) and various sets of phonographs, in different contexts and also within the same texts or genres, meant that a wide range of social groups, separated by class, gender, location, and so on, had access to distinctive, though overlapping, bodies of texts. To become a competent reader and writer of Chinese-style belletristic prose and poetry required many years of concerted effort, but mastering the limited number of logographic characters and patterns of usage needed for basic documentary forms would have been a far simpler matter. Similarly, writing poetry or prose in elegant cursivized phonographs required extensive training, of one's hand and one's eye (that is, taste), but scrawling a rough-and-ready note in simple phonographs would become possible comparatively quickly. In a sense, visually distinct styles of writing (combinations in varying degrees of varying types of phonographs and logographs) instantiate the plural literacies that have been theorized so extensively in recent decades (Collins 1995; Collins and Blot 2003). But the same readers and writers would often have had contact with multiple modes of inscription, so in many cases there is no one-to-one correspondence between particular populations and distinctive styles.

One of the most important aspects of the prevalence of *kundoku* is that this written variety does not map onto linguistic variety, at least in the sense of visually distinctive forms of writing corresponding to writing "in" different languages. At a given time, the vocalizations of the various forms of writing were linguistically contiguous, though there were profound stylistic differences between the Japanese used to read logographic texts in the Chinese style and that used to read phonographically inscribed vernacular poetry or popular fiction. But despite the differences, the contiguity of these styles meant that crossing over was possible. For example, a phonographically written vernacular poem could echo a classical Chinese work (without including any loanwords or characters from it), or a fictional character could make a grand vernacular proclamation that drew on the rhetoric and usage of the Chinese classics. Moreover, the vocalization of those classics through *kundoku* meant that they were orally accessible to and, in a sense, culturally possessed by those who had no ability to "read" them on their own.[22]

These factors make it particularly difficult to speculate about the reasons for or consequences of change in the history of writing in Japan. On the one hand, logographic texts in the Chinese style, read or written primarily through *kundoku*, held a central position from the seventh to the twentieth centuries and were never dislodged by the various phonographic systems that developed over that span of time. Moreover, the phonographic systems themselves and various strategies for using them independently or mixing them with logographs had all developed by the twelfth century. There have been changes in the graphic styles and internal structures of these sets of logographs and phonographs, but up to and including the present age of digitization, the fundamentals of how the syllables and words of the Japanese language are represented in writing have not changed significantly.

On the other hand, the emergence of visually distinct phonographs had profound impacts in many areas. Socially, they expanded access to writing and reading in general (and more narrowly, to glossed or otherwise supplemented logographic texts as well). The coexistence of parallel scripts also provided writers with resources for a range of expressive effects, such as shifts in mode for emphasis (along the lines of italics) or play with tensions between logographs and the phonographic glosses paired with them. In cultural terms, the visually distinctive phonographs were scripts that in particular contexts—and often when discussed by writers with strong ideological investments—came to be conceived of as a "native" mode of inscription (Shinkawa 2002).

But the last of these—the identification of *kana* as native scripts—is a consequence, not a cause, of their development. The tenth- to twelfth-century siniform scripts of Central Asia (Kara 1996; Kychanov 1996; Nakamura 1988) and the fifteenth-century Korean alphabet (Ledyard 1966, 1997; Lee 1997) were officially promulgated with state sponsorship. But the various modifications of "Chinese" writing in Japan—from the initial adaptation of Korean *kundoku* and phonograph characters onward—were driven by expediency and evolved gradually rather than instantiated by fiat. Physically, countless writers formed the same characters under similar conditions, leading to graphic simplification; linguistically, the phonology and morphology of the Japanese language created a kind of "design space" (to use a neo-Darwinian term) within which scripts adapted to selection pressures for speed and clarity. Such factors undoubtedly spurred the considerable changes that did occur, but their influence does not mean that the considerable continuities—most notably, the persistence of logography—were retrograde developments stemming from the stifling of a natural progression. Moreover, if scriptural authority, accordance with past precedent, and social prestige were also selection pressures that slowed or eliminated change in certain aspects of the overall writing system, it is only from an anachronistic, ahistorically "moralizing" perspective that they can be seen as undesirable or extraneous.

Much as was the case in China itself, where the classical written language (*wényán* 文言) maintained a central position long after the development of a written vernacular (*báihuàwén* 白話文), in Japan, logography in the Chinese style was the most authoritative medium and extended its influence into other forms of writing—and even into actual speech as well.[23] The combination of *kundoku* and phonographs (both supplementary and independent) meant that the overall system of writing in Japan maintained a remarkable degree of flexibility, in some areas remaining rooted in ancient authority and in others becoming accessible to lightly trained readers—or even, through vocalization, to "nonreaders." The overall writing system was essentially capable of simultaneously changing and staying the same.

IMPLICATIONS FOR THE HISTORY OF WRITING

In conclusion, I will outline a few comparative consequences of the Japanese experience with script change. The first is not necessarily comparative: the implications of the foregoing for the history of the Chinese writing system, broadly construed. As mentioned above, the nature of that system is a controversial subject (Lurie 2006). Scholars like Peter Boodberg (1940) and John DeFrancis (2002) are quite right to reject the notion that Chinese characters are or ever have been "ideographs"—that is, signs that indicate ideas directly—but there is still room to argue about how logographic or phonographic the script has been in its various "implementations." One of the principal contributions of the history of Japanese writing to this debate is that it illustrates the importance of context and usage, indicating that the outward formal continuity of "Chinese" graphs (and more broadly, any writing system) can be deceptive. The historical origins of the system, its formal structure, and its sundry uses to write earlier forms of Chinese, modern Mandarin, or various stages of Japanese, Korean, and so on, are all distinct issues, and any argument for a fundamental phonographic or logographic essence must consider in detail the historical and linguistic variety of character-based writing and reading. It is appropriate to insist on the priority of phonography in particular contexts—certainly the earliest and most recent uses of the characters to write Chinese are more phonographic than has traditionally been maintained—but the phenomenon of *kundoku* and its central importance to the history of writing and reading in Japan (and Korea) means that logography must also be given its due. The extent to which characters were adapted, both visibly and—especially —invisibly, in non-Sinitic contexts (and here I have alluded merely to Vietnamese and Central Asian writing) also encourages us to rethink the easy identification of this writing system with the Chinese language.

The central and enduring role of logography in the history outlined here also has implications for the study of writing in general, which is still shadowed by the remnants of Gelb's (1963) influential teleology of development towards full phonography, a teleology that was, of course, expressive of fundamental cultural attitudes toward what writing is and should be. I wholeheartedly agree with Bruce Trigger's critique of the notion that logographic writing is "inherently inferior to phonographic and especially alphabetic scripts," but there is room to complicate his stipulation (following Gelb) that "the major shifts towards more phonographic writing occurred when scripts were adopted by foreign peoples" (2003:602–603). In certain cases, that has been true. But in East Asia, one could argue that adoption by foreign peoples actually led to an intensification of logography.[24]

Further comparative insights lie in the recognition that *kundoku* is not as exotic as it initially seems. It is very likely that the large number of graphically discrete individual characters, as well as the metalinguistic and cosmological ideas that shaped their development, contributed to the phenomenon in East Asia, but there are numerous suggestive parallels in other traditions of writing. Perhaps most strikingly, in medieval Europe, Latin texts were glossed with diacritics and other markings that suggest they may have been translated and read, on the fly, into local vernaculars (King 2007). The parallels between Sumerian and Akkadian writing and the mixture of phonographs and logographs in Japanese have been frequently noted, and there is room to speculate about Akkadian readings of Sumerian *texts* (not just individual cuneiforms). Another suggestive example from the same region is the use of whole Aramaic words in the Aramaic alphabet as "heterograms": word-signs for unrelated Parthian and Middle Persian words (Skjærvø 1996).

More broadly, attention to *kundoku* and the persistence of logography in Japanese writing encourages us to take more seriously the many ways in which writing goes beyond the transcription of speech sounds, such as orthography, punctuation, and spacing. In place of anachronistic notions about the integrity of national languages or prescriptive dicta about the absolute superiority of phonography, the complex interactions between writing and language are better approached through emphasis on factors such as the coexistence of (visible and invisible) old and new forms, the influence of metalinguistic discourses like that of lexicography, and the context-dependence of scripts and the literacies that are their lives in society.

Notes

1. This chapter is a condensation of arguments from Lurie 2011, which contains more extensive discussion and references. For a survey of the entire history of writing in Japan, see Seeley 1991; another important anglophone resource is Kornicki 1998, a history of the Japanese book that concentrates on the early modern period (sixteenth through nineteenth centuries) but provides extensive information on earlier developments.

2. A critical factor in the seventh-century expansion of writing was the presence of trained personnel, including refugees and prisoners of war from the conflict on the peninsula and also people from the archipelago (some from lineages of peninsular extraction) who around the turn of the century had begun going to China and the Korean states as secular or Buddhist students.

3. The term "emperor" (*tennō*) is often translated "sovereign," in part because in this period (and until the modern era) Japan had no empire to speak of, unlike China. Here I have opted to employ the more familiar English term.

4. I use the problematic term "literary Chinese" for the written language exemplified by and then modeled on the transmitted classics of the Warring States and Han

periods (accompanied, as written languages are, by a standard—and by no means sta-
tic—vocalization considerably different from the spoken language of later periods and
possibly also the periods in which the written language developed).

5. One of the problems presented by this sort of discussion is the difficulty of
sorting out the role played by the characters themselves in the development of concepts like "word," not to mention their role in less abstract aspects of both metalinguistic ideas and actual functioning of written (and eventually certain registers of spoken)
language.

6. The basic unit of modern Japanese phonographic writing is not the syllable
but the subsyllabic mora (Backhouse 1993:40–41). Syllables like *kō* こう, *tsū* つう, and
man まん are bimoraic, whereas *ko* こ, *tsu* つ, and *ma* ま are monomoraic, as reflected
in both sets by the number of hiragana required to write them. For a summary discussion of the mora versus syllable distinction in modern Japanese, see Tsujimura
1996:64–72.

7. The misleading term *man'yōgana* literally means *kana* (a blanket term for various phonographs derived from Chinese characters) of the *Man'yōshū* 萬葉集 (an
immense late eighth-century anthology of vernacular poetry). Although the *Man'yōshū*
does contain numerous poems written partially or entirely in phonograph characters,
they are not the dominant method of inscription in the anthology as a whole, and conversely, they were widely used in other texts and contexts.

8. This emphasis on *use* of the same characters contrasts with metalinguistic or
metagraphic discussion in works of the Heian period (794–1185 CE), which refer to
distinctive sets of graphs and styles of writing using those sets (Seeley 1991:76–80).

9. The process of graphic simplification that produced visually distinctive phonographs was accompanied by two dramatic changes in the internal structure of the
script. One reflected a shift in Japanese phonology: as three pairs of vowels (possibly
dipthongs, vowels with glides, or other combinations [Miyake 2003]) fell together, the
number of homophonous phonographs increased. The other was a purely graphic
change: although the phonograph sets of the seventh and eighth centuries distinguished, for the most part, between voiced and unvoiced consonants like those in *ga*
and *ka*, the visual simplification of graphs was accompanied by abandonment of this
distinction, so distinguishing between voiced and unvoiced became a contextual matter. (Diacritics indicating voicing eventually developed, but their application was
inconsistent until the twentieth century.)

10. A more pertinent romanization would be one derived from a reconstruction
of Early Middle Chinese, but the specific details of how this passage would have been
vocalized in China at the time *kundoku* arose in Japan are not germane to this discussion, hence the expedient anachronism.

11. Here and below, English equivalents of the traditional Japanese grammar are used (see Shirane 2005; Wixted 2006); for an alternative account more in keeping with modern Western linguistic analysis, see Vovin 2003. On literary Chinese grammar, I rely on Pulleyblank 1995.

12. Lurie 2011 presents a fuller analysis of the *kundoku* process as applied to this phrase from the *Analects*.

13. This is not the place to address the vexing problem of defining translation, whether in an ideal or historical sense. For the time being, I stipulate that it is the production of an utterance or text modeled on, and in some way equivalent to, another pre-existing utterance or text from a different language. Jakobson distinguishes "interlingual translation or *translation proper*" from "intralingual translation or *rewording*" and "intrasemiotic translation or *transmutation*" (1987 [1959]:429); both of these other kinds, but in particular the latter, are relevant for this discussion of the nature of *kundoku*.

14. In a discussion of "reading" that raises fundamental and unexpectedly difficult problems for the study of writing, Wittgenstein opens by stipulating, "I am not counting the understanding of what is being read as part of 'reading' for the purposes of this investigation: reading here is the activity of rendering out loud what is written or printed; and also of writing from dictation, writing out something printed, played from a score, and so on" (1958:61, §156). As is suggested by the subsequent direction of this discussion, the problem of "understanding" in reading haunts the study of the history of literacy.

15. R. A. Miller vividly states that in the early period "people often did not really know what language they were writing in, Chinese or Japanese; and we are often in no better position to make a judgment on the question when we study some of the documents they produced" (1967:131). A better way of putting the former point would be to say that in this period the notion of "writing in" a specific language is not always an appropriate description of what scribes and authors were doing. Seeley quite appropriately adopts "an 'agnostic' approach," using the term "Chinese style" for "a form of writing in which Chinese characters are arranged and used according to the conventions of literary Chinese syntax" (1991:25). But it is necessary to extend this approach to incorporate "agnosticism" toward the *reading* of texts imported from China (such as the *Analects*) as well.

16. Of course, it is quite possible that *kundoku* was an option in certain contexts and excluded in other contemporaneous ones, but as argued below, the overall tendency in sources from the mid-seventh century on suggests that it was the default norm for reading from very early on.

17. A brief overview of writing in early Korea can be found in Lurie 2011; see also

Ledyard 1966, republished as Ledyard 1998; Lee and Ramsey 2000:45–55; Yi 2005. Discussions of Korean *kundoku* include Fujimoto 1988, M. Kim 1988, and Y. Kim 2005.

18. An apparent exception is the use of phonographs to spell out words that are difficult to "translate" into Chinese and thus not susceptible to being represented logographically by the existing stock of characters. This category includes distinctive terms such as local plant and animal species and also, of course, proper nouns. In many, perhaps most contexts, it was often more convenient to spell out such words phonographically than to search for logographic representations. But at least in principle, such representations would have been available. A Japanese word that does not correspond to a single character could be circumlocutorily represented by multiple characters as a kind of composite logograph, or a new logograph could be created from the modular components of "Chinese" characters. Such new logographs, or *kokuji* 國字 (graphs of [our] country), are a minor element of the development of scripts in Japan (in strong contrast to their prominent role in the central Asian scripts of the tenth through the twelfth centuries and Vietnamese *chu nom*), but they are particularly common in hard-to-translate lexical areas like plant and animal names. Significantly, they are usually created by combining semantic determinatives without the phonetic element that is present in the majority of characters created in China (Commons 1998; Sasahara 2006). A good example of terms initially rendered phonographically but then replaced with logographic equivalents is provided by the foodstuffs and other products referred to in wooden slips found at the site of the eighth-century Heijō palace compound in Nara (Kobayashi 1983, 1988:306–318).

19. The primary context for the development of abbreviated phonograph characters is marginal glosses of *kundoku* readings, but the converse is not the case. Glosses can also be found as slightly or extensively cursivized phonographs, as well as in the form of *okoto-ten* 乎古止点, coded marks (dots or lines) whose position on a character indicates what grammatical elements should be added to it. One of the great subfields of Japanese linguistics (*kokugogaku* 國語学) has been the study of the language preserved in such annotated manuscripts, which provide many insights into vocabulary and usage (admittedly, in limited contexts) of the Heian period in particular (see Yoshida et al. 2001).

20. Amino Yoshihiko (1993) argues that these abbreviated phonographs (*katakana*) never lost their association with recording the spoken voice, even as they came to be used in post-Heian documents by surprisingly rural and plebeian writers. (For an introductory treatment of the same ideas in English, see Amino n.d.)

21. For popular literacy after the emergence of widespread printing, see Rubinger 2007.

22. This is a major reason for rejecting the still prevalent distinction between masculine elite Chinese literacy and feminine (or popular) Japanese literacy in the Heian period and thereafter. It is also a key to the enduring enthusiasm at many levels of society for literary Chinese anecdotes, catchphrases, and rhetorical flourishes—all of which circulated in oral form, as well as written (see Maeda 2004 and Sakaki 2000:91–97).

23. A major source of that authority and a likely factor in the persistence of logographic writing in much of East Asia was a set of normative ideas about correspondences between the order of the cosmos and graphic patterns (paradigmatically, the hexagrams of the *Yijing* (the *Classic of Changes*) and thus between words or concepts and graphs (Boltz 1994; Lewis 1999). As embodied in lexicography and commentary (themselves locked in a productive feedback loop), these ideas provide a kind of justification for the development and persistence of *kundoku* itself.

24. Of course, in Japan this intensification of logography was accompanied by the development of graphically simplified phonographs, but this serves as a reminder that contradictory changes can occur simultaneously.

8

Maya Writing

Modified, Transformed

Stephen D. Houston

A writing system has, by definition, form and substance. It also has makers, users, critics, and caretakers, each living within communities that carry, share, or challenge values and meanings. The connection between a thing, in this case the characters or "glyphs" of Maya writing, and the people who produced and employed it elevates its study into something more than an obscure exercise in paleography. The task enlarges to a study of how humans recorded sound, meaning, and indirect memory over time and place. Plainly, as seen in the chapters of this volume, writing is a shifting practice: it lies at the intersection of different interests, motivations, and experiences, conjoining features as distinct as aesthetics, phonic transcription, grammar, and social function. This chapter explores script as an evolving expressive practice of Mayan speakers, a group of peoples who used glyphs in and around the Yucatán peninsula over a span of more than 1,800 years. After sketching a brief background, it reviews prior attempts to understand shifts in Maya script, framing those changes in terms of "domains" that triggered small, incremental modifications and larger, systemic alterations (see Salomon, chapter 5, this volume). The targeted time is what might be called the middle years, when the script was already well along in its career, subject to "transformations of [earlier] transformations" (Lurie, chapter 7, this volume), yet at some remove from its final phases of decay and discontinuance.

STEPHEN D. HOUSTON

BACKGROUND

Maya writing was employed for a period of at least 1,800 years, from before ca. 250 BCE, as dated recently by the San Bartolo finds from Guatemala (Saturno et al. 2006:1281), to a probable time of extinction in the early centuries of the colonial era (fig. 8.1). In all likelihood, full graphic fluency departed fairly quickly after the sixteenth-century conquest by the Spanish (Houston et al. 2003:463–464). The number of scribes was not likely to have been high at any period (Houston 1994), but there must have been a sustained investment in scribal training, underwritten by a discerning public that desired written productions (see below, under "transmission"). A way of understanding the script's use over time is by compiling a series of periods, each characterized by multiple traits that occurred broadly across the Maya world (Houston 2000:Table 1, slightly emended here; most dates approximate):

- Period IA (>250 BCE–150 CE): Glyphs = glyph block; minimal suffixation; lists of head signs; minimal syntactic transparency; general lack of monumentalism; emphasis on portable objects; inception of codification alongside great variety of signs
- Period IB (150–250 CE): Enhanced grammatical transparency; slight increase of monumentalism
- Period IIA (250–500 CE): Full range of use; heightened glyphic monumentalism
- Period IIB (500–550 CE): Innovation of signs; cross-script transfer, possibly from Teotihuacán contact
- Period IIIA (550–650 CE): Inception of heightened epigraphic legibility; advent of pseudo-glyphs
- Period IIIB (650–700 CE): Period of innovation; enhanced complementation; full syllabic substitution for logographs; increased range of content; Calakmul hegemony influential
- Period IIIC (700–800 CE): Greatest number of Maya texts
- Period IIID (800–900 CE): Pronounced regionalisms; localized disintegration and grapholectal innovation; cross-script transfer
- Period IV (900–ca. 1600 CE): Codical and painterly emphasis; near absence of monumentalism
- Period V (1600 CE–?): Script death, sudden or gradual depending on region, as literates died or discontinued glyphic craft

In large part, the script is deciphered. Well-established standards are in place for evaluating proposals about readings of signs, to the extent that

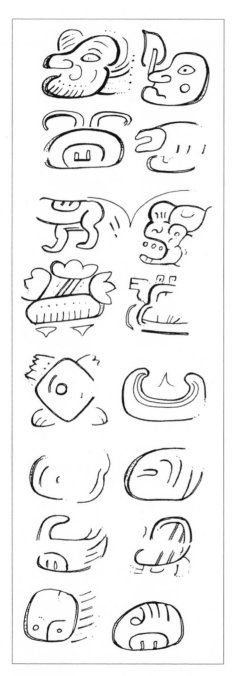

FIGURE 8.1

Preclassic Maya inscription. Peabody Museum Yale University (drawing by author).

the minutiae of grammar and orthography are now under close discussion (see Houston et al. 2001:9–10, for methods and protocols). Yet, for the foreseeable future, Maya script will have some gaps of interpretation and decoding. Insufficient evidence makes it difficult to propose meanings of the rarer signs and test the possible decipherments. Whole strings of esoteric texts in monumental and codical formats resist the boldest attempts to read them. But enough is known—and known well—to understand the content, structure, and graphic display of Maya writing over time.

PRIOR STUDIES

Studies of Maya script risk falling into the synchronic fallacy, the assumption that a writing system remains unchanged from one period to another or, in subtler form, that a script contains similar themes, signary, or principles of composition throughout its varying periods of activity (Houston 2004b:299). By implication, a pattern in one period would operate in others. This fallacy becomes clearest in the various efforts to catalogue Maya glyphs. In essence, each catalogue serves as a balancing act, reconciling the wide variability of such signs and the necessity of establishing a finite, workable list of signs. One early catalog, by Gates, focused on meaning alone, with sputtering scorn for those who troubled themselves with "sound names [which] are of no value whatever" (Gates 1978 [1931]:vii). It avoided the challenge of dealing with chronological shifts by restricting the tabulation to Maya codices, all made within a few centuries of one another during the Late Postclassic period (ca. 1250 CE to the conquest; Gates 1978 [1931]:vii–vii). A catalog by Zimmermann (1956), also of the codices, fell into the same problem of mining an overly restricted sample. Yet, it succeeded in making a case for distinct "hands" or paleographic identities within the manuscripts.

Still the most widely used, Thompson's catalog (1962) included what he perceived at that time to be a full range of signs from the Classic period (ca. 250–850 CE), with due acknowledgment of variant forms. The drawings were done by Avis Tulloch, who worked with Thompson to reduce the pages of drawings and photographs that he had collected into a smaller number of exemplary forms (Thompson 1962:ix); this catalog contains many chapters with fonts, all exemplary forms, but these seldom work well in Maya studies because scholars have learned that idiosyncratic variations reveal almost as much as the sign value itself.[1] Elongated signs, or "affixes," might be shown with as many as seven variants; larger, almost square glyphs—Thompson's "main signs"—were more likely to be shown as a single shape (see, e.g., Thompson 1962:46, 87). Heedless of time period, the catalog identifies the context of signs, a spelling from a codex being recorded next to one from many centuries earlier.

The most recent catalog, by Macri and Looper (2003; see also Macri and Vail 2009), extracts its contents from a much wider sample than Thompson's but presents Maya signs in an idiosyncratic arrangement that is unlikely to gain favor with scholars (Zender 2006). Aside from organizing signs by their perceived origin within categories of "body parts" or "animals," the catalog charts evolving interpretations of glyphs with only a few comments on formal changes over time. The rectilinear quality of glyphs are said to come from their early disposition into "paired columns" (in fact, a relatively late development for Maya signs); "irregular silhouettes" supposedly arise from glyphs with the attributes of human faces; and the shift from variable shapes to "closed outlines and few projecting forms" reflects, it is stated, the "change from incising technique to relief carving," with some continued "slant" from the influence of painted forms by right-handed scribes (Macri and Looper 2003:33–34; and see below).

As compilations of signs, catalogs generate homogeneity. And justly so: their main goal is to sort through a welter of idiosyncrasy and achieve a sense of ordered comparison within a functioning system of script. The variability is all lateral, between distinct signs in concurrent use, and not sequential and vertical over time. This is not to say, however, that specialists have overlooked temporal shifts. As early as 1915, Morley (1975 [1915]: 22–23) commented on the dissimilarity between Classic-era inscriptions and later codical forms, whose differences resulted, he felt, from shifts in material, the former being carved, the latter painted. He stressed the role of individual "hands" but noted, as with all such variation, that they were "unessential" to the more important task of reading glyphs (1975 [1915]:25).

The long-term shift of signs became a systematic concern only with Beyer's reports (1932, 1934, 1937) on the "stylistic history" of Maya signs, a study occasioned by a wish to date texts that did not otherwise yield firm anchors in chronology. By targeting four common Maya signs, Beyer discerned a progression of five periods, beginning with a hypothetical time of origin ("Epoch of Glyph Formation"), followed by a time with "Type A" signs (of the "Great Epoch," or the Classic period), then a time of transition, especially at Beyer's focal site of Chichén Itzá, in Yucatán ("Epoch of Nahua Influence"), leading eventually to "Type B" ("Epoch of Maya Nationalism," or the Postclassic) and from there to glyphs of diminished competence that dated to the postconquest period ("Epoch of Decadent Forms"; Beyer 1932:73–74, 1937:159). The paleography was always of secondary interest to the objective of dating difficult texts, although Beyer (1937:165) seemed also to have found it necessary to discriminate between "good," "fairly good," or "mediocre" inscriptions at Chichén, in part because of his notion of successive decline in glyphic production. In fact, despite the pressures not to make such judgments, it is hard not to see many of the texts from the Terminal Classic period (ca. 800–900 CE), aside from focal areas of excellence, as progressively less competent, perhaps because of reduced preparation, composition, workforce, and, above all, number of discriminating patrons (e.g., Proskouriakoff 1950:Figure 79).

Beyer's scheme soon found its critics. Linton Satterthwaite applied the Beyer "types" to freshly excavated material at Piedras Negras, Guatemala, and discovered their unreliability: glyphs thought to be later often appeared in earlier settings, suggesting that, when applied to other sites, Beyer's notion of sign development oversimplified what would prove to be a complicated body of evidence (Satterthwaite 1938:419). A short time later, Morley (1938: I:8–9) revisited Maya paleography, proposing a series of further refinements of glyphic style during the "Old Empire" (Classic period). His periods involved, in succession, (1) cursive, relatively unembellished shapes (ca. 500 CE) > (2) rigid shapes with high degree of interior decoration, all in high relief (ca. 600 to 800 CE) > (3) rigid shapes with reduced interior decoration (ca. 800 CE and after). By subdividing Beyer's Great Epoch into three subphases, Morley perceived subtler gradations in paleographical style yet placed them within a far broader understanding of shared technique or manner of execution than earlier analysts. Here as with later work grew a tension between scholarly attention to the details that attracted Beyer and Satterthwaite and larger trends that reflected the labor of several generations of scribes working separately at many sites.

An enlarged sample now casts doubts on Morley's sequence: "cursivity," presumably meaning a fluid line, occurs in all of his phases (cursivity in the sense of rapidly ligatured and simplified signs does not seem to have been a directional impulse in Maya script). Depending on preservation, interior decoration can be just as elaborate in earlier texts as later ones. Morley had no immediate successors in this concern, no one to refine his sequence: forty years would pass before epigraphers paid greater attention to the intrinsic shifts of Maya writing. The few specialists in the script detoured to other matters, such as Thompson's (1970, 1972) studies of Maya codices, culture, and colonial history, along with forays into Maya history, place-making, and syllabic content by Berlin (1958, 1977), Kelley (1962, 1976), Knorosov (1958), and Proskouriakoff (1960, 1961, 1963). In such heady research, so mindful of content, so clearly productive, there seemed little need to return to the formal, even pedantic details of shifts in Maya script.

Two developments reawakened interest. First was Zimmermann's discussion of hand-styles in the codices, stimulating Morellian studies of hands on certain kinds of Classic Maya pottery (the so-called "codex style"; Cohodas 1989:202–203; Kerr and Kerr 1988:236; Robicsek and Hales 1981:237–250; see also Wollheim 1974), monuments at Yaxchilan, Mexico (Tate 1992:39–49), and Postclassic codices (Lacadena García-Gallo 2000:56). Second, more sophisticated research on changes in Maya script appeared in the form of two doctoral theses, one from Nikolai Grube (1990, 1994), the other a landmark dissertation on Maya paleography by Alfonso Lacadena García-Gallo (1995). Grube proposed that sign inventory—the absolute presence or absence of a sign—was inconstant, with about three hundred signs in use at any one time (Grube 1994:178), and that there was a highly episodic quality to renovations in the inventory. One period of significant enlargement occurred in the initial years of the Classic period (up until ca. 450 CE), another about 525 CE, and the most dramatic at about 650 CE, with more than eighty new signs in fresh evidence, with creative invention in isolated Terminal Classic communities such as Chichén Itzá (Grube 1994:178). Relatively large numbers of signs were used for short periods of time, and syllables of CV form tended to last longer than word signs or logographs (Grube 1994:179). The heightened commitment to purely phonic or syllabic spellings after about 650 CE suggests to Grube "that Maya scribes became concerned with the unambiguous pronunciation of words" (1994:179–180), along with an impulse to provide alternative spellings. A possible motivation was a process of aesthetic involution: a wish for variety in the form of virtuosic conflict with legible, conventionalized formulae. The thoroughgoing aestheticism of Maya courts, which displayed rulers sniffing bouquets of flowers and enjoying rich food, drink, and amassed treasure, provides a frame for such refined discriminations of quality (Miller and Martin 2004:Plates 6, 14–17).

It may be that the playful alternation of variant forms in later Maya texts simply results from rules or conventions, some peculiar to a scribe, others more general, that we do not yet understand: a text such as the Tablet of the 96 Glyphs at Palenque appears unable to countenance repetition of the same sign for the pronoun *u*, a common grammatical particle in Maya writing (Schele 1982:frontispiece). The role of whim, individual caprice, or preference weighs heavily in certain well-attested examples. For example, the number of sculptors named on some Maya inscriptions goes to eight and beyond (Montgomery 1995; Stuart 1989; Stuart and Graham 2003:63). The quantity that can be inferred from stylistic evidence alone, as at Yaxchilan (Tate 1992:Figure 8) and the Classic stela at the De Young Museum in San Francisco, is two or more. In the latter, one sculptor carved glyphs with a fluid, slanted quality and the ellipsoid facture of a "right-handed" painter, the other a more rigid outline. The proposal by van Stone (2000:4) that as many as eight sculptors worked on a single monument at Palenque, the Temple XIX Platform, suggests a level of collaboration that was not matched by the few calligrapher signatures on pots, which show individual production (Houston 2000:Figure 4). Van Stone (2000:6), a professional calligrapher, felt it probable that the compositor and carver were one and the same, with a "house style" enforced or guided by a master working with many other sculptors, as on the Palace Tablet at Palenque (see below). The exceptions were smaller sculptures the size of, in van Stone's words, "a grown man," which seemed on the whole to issue from one scribe (van Stone 2000:3). Large commissions required sizeable staff.

Grube (1994:185) prefers to see some of these changes against a backdrop of splits in Mayan languages, with consequent need for greater phonic clarity. This argument is belied, however, by more recent evidence for a prestige language in the Maya glyphs, namely, a "high" language written and presumably spoken across the Maya lowlands throughout the Classic period (Houston et al. 2000b:338).[2] Yet, even with this revision, Grube can preserve his argument. The need for greater clarity of pronunciation fits well with a language that was not necessarily used by many people outside royal courts and increasingly less so as noncourtly languages diverged from the conservative and hieratic speech and script of elites: correct pronunciation needed reinforcement when errors were more likely to be made. In a compelling synthesis, Grube, with Martin (Martin and Grube 1995, 2008:20–21, 108–109), later provided evidence that the period around 650 CE expressed a deep, far-ranging turmoil between two major cities, Calakmul and Tikal, with Calakmul taking the upper hand in much of this regional conflict (see Period IIIb above). Within this scrim of alliance and antagonism were, one presumes, many opportunities for dissemination of glyphic knowledge, along with the possibility of less porous boundaries that at smaller scale led to divergence in glyphic style, execution, and content. Nonetheless, Grube's study needs amplification and perhaps revision. The great innovation of new signs correlates with a vastly increased sample of texts in the Late Classic period (post-600 CE, Periods IIIA–C above), and Grube's research takes broad aim at inscriptions across the Maya world, not at regional traditions per se—other patterns may arise at local scales of view. But his study does pave the way for more intensive research.

Another decisive monograph is Alfonso Lacadena García-Gallo's (1995) doctoral dissertation, the most complete yet of Maya paleography. It is systematic and theoretical in its notice of underlying principle. Most important, it insists on linking paleographic patterns to culture and society, particularly to political setting, and distinguishes random from deliberate changes and standardization from idiosyncratic flourish (Lacadena García-Gallo 1995:7, 18, 189, 33n1). Lacadena García-Gallo (1995:55, 59, 120) identifies the widespread existence among epigraphers of an intuitive notion of date and region for particular forms of signs, along with the severe sampling problems that beset Maya paleography. We do not have sufficient samples of text from the earlier periods, a condition that compels overly broad temporal comparisons, of decades rather than the five-year periods allowed by other evidence from the Late Classic period. Eroded texts and photocopied line drawings raise for Lacadena García-Gallo (1995:76, 88) the additional problem of mediation, of seeing texts through a rendering or image that cannot, by definition, capture all attributes of the glyphs it records. As with much of our evidence, the lithic work and nature of surface often disappear behind present-day drafting conventions that eliminate these attributes as unwanted "noise" or analytical distraction. An emphasis on reading texts tends to displace a concern with their production and material presence.

Lacadena García-Gallo's study is analytically lucid, centered on four main approaches: a focus on base elements that compose the minimal features of a legible sign, a tally of supernumerary elements that do not convey meaning or sound, a distinction between constituent elements and their overall combination within a sign (some elements added or substituted, others suppressed through a process of sign development), and a Saussurean contrast between abstract rules and the actual expression on the conditioning media used by the Maya (Lacadena García-Gallo 1995:93, 114, 181, 187, 200–201, Figures 2.51, 2.52). Through maps and case studies—individual reports on all eight hundred or more glyphs would take far more than a single study—Lacadena García-Gallo shows that forms appear to begin at one site and then spread to others (e.g., 1995:Figures 3.17, 3.18). He suggests the operation of almost mechanical pressures on scribes to achieve symmetry of internal elements and reduce brush strokes, both to ease execution through simplification and to improve economy of movement.

His most daring proposal is that glyphic change took place in a quasi-linguistic, analogical process that arose from a subjective perception of regularities between shapes. A design such as dangled circles might migrate through time from one glyph to signs that vaguely resembled it (Lacadena García-Gallo 1995:220–236, Figure 4.17). Such a process appears in Late Classic stuccos from the Caana pyramid at Caracol, Belize (Martin and Grube 2008:95). There, glyphs found close to each other in a single text ([ji] + [ya] and the bottom of a day sign) are made to look virtually the same, despite the clear knowledge of the scribe that the elements possess different values. This process might have led to "errors" in which certain glyphs adopted elements that confused the clarity of reading, only to be rejected by other scribes and sculptors (Lacadena García-Gallo 1995:Figure 4.31). For Lacadena García-Gallo, some changes took place because of prestige accorded to their place of origin, not necessarily because a scribe came from a populous city that dominated another politically. His case in point is a conflated sign ([AJAW-wa]) that began to be reproduced as though it were one element instead of two (epigraphers note the same development, if at an earlier time, in the syllable [xa] inserted into the sign [YAX] so as to distinguish it from a similar sign, read [yi]). The novel form spread from a site, Dos Pilas, to ones that it did not control, such as Ucanal (Lacadena García-Gallo 1995:273). Some sites tended to preserve earlier forms (Palenque, Copán, and Caracol), and even sites in major convulsion, such as those in the Terminal Classic period just prior to the Maya Collapse, continued to receive and transmit glyphic styles (Lacadena García-Gallo 1995:286–287).

A final point concerns the rate of stylistic change, which appears to be gradual in some cases and abrupt in others, especially after a rupture taking place about 550–600 CE (the beginning of Period III above). This may be Lacadena García-Gallo's less persuasive suggestion, for he proposes a fixed rate of change with consequences for dating the Postclassic period (Periods IIID and IV above). For him, if glyphs of that later time resemble those of the Classic period, then the amount of time implicated in any changes cannot be great—and the correlation of European and Maya calendars must be incorrect (Lacadena García-Gallo 1995:411–413). The clear difficulty comes from seeing cultural changes solely in terms of steady drift, not as deliberate choices or changes that obey variable rates of development.

DOMAINS OF CHANGE

With such work in mind, we can examine a number of ways in which glyphs change and why. These might be described as "domains," areas of practice and motivation that contain their own bustling dynamic yet link inevitably to other domains. A selection of such domains follows, including execution, transmission, and motivation.

The most basic is *execution*, the manual practices that lead from an intention (with all the templates and precedents this term implies) through engagement with material (the instrument of execution and the substance on which the shape is made) to the finished form. An obdurate material, such as stone, typically consumes more time than the play of a moist brush on prepared *Ficus* bark or the surface of a wall. The use of brushes, quills, and pigments prepared and diluted to varying degrees is well understood, thanks to the depictions of such activities and instruments in imagery and the excavation of buildings, particularly at Aguateca, Guatemala, given over to scribal production (Coe and Kerr 1998:145–158; Inomata 1995, 2001a, 2001b; Inomata et al. 2002).

Through close study of painted lines on pottery, Coe and Kerr (1998:154–158) have shown that, in the Late Classic period, the main outlines—the border of a subjectively "physical" sign—were limned first, then the interior details, often guided by horizontal lines that kept the text from straying up to the rim and into illegibility against the painted band that tended to circumscribe the pot. Maya glyphs were not placed against edges but needed space around them for maximum legibility. The only violations of this practice occurred within the glyph block itself, which in later periods extended beyond one sign to include four or more, each compressed against the others as though it were a pellet of rising dough, once distinct, now puffing out in delicate pressure against other signs within the glyph block. For the Maya, the underpinnings of glyphs as existentially distinct entities (Houston et al. 2006:76) did not seem to permit the cursive ligatures and rapid execution documented elsewhere in this volume. There is also a strong sense that the Maya did not conceive of sign production as the result of a hand moving fluidly from top to bottom or left to right (cf. Salomon, chapter 5, this volume). Rather, text issued from a set of "stations," brush held in the hand above the writing surface, shifting to another station at fixed intervals.

An unusual panel from near Emiliano Zapata in Tabasco, Mexico, even shows the carving of a *k'an tuun* (a yellow? stone) by a seated figure, who leans over slightly in the mode of all scribes, in a posture that shows dignified but close attention to the matter at hand (Stuart 1990:Figure 1). (By dipping their upper body farther, scribes departed from conventions for royal poses.) He grasps a double-edged chisel, presumably tipped on either end with peccary or rodent tusk; by the Postclassic period, these tools would have been replaced by copper chisels (Karl Taube, noted in Stuart 1990:13, Figure 37). This image suggests that carving, after the blocks were roughed out with a tranchet axe, began with two widths of chisel, perhaps of two levels of hardness, and eventually involved polishing. The larger the text, particularly on stone, the more likely it would have required a chain of separate competences and practices, from quarrymen to final finisher (Beekman 1992:101; Ruíz 1985). The investment in scribal training suggests that such expertise would not be wasted on mere roughing out of stone blanks, although that may have played a role in early apprenticeship. After all, the chef-in-training is enjoined to understand prep work or dishwashing as part of his eventual sphere of responsibility.

But can a script that was often carved or engraved be understood as "handwriting," and the study of ancient forms of it "paleography"? The answer is a qualified yes. The earliest, well-dated Mayan writing, from San Bartolo, Guatemala (ca. 250 BCE and perhaps before), shows a slightly elliptical quality, as though expressing the wrist movement of a right-handed scribe (Saturno et al. 2006:Figure 4). At the same time, a few glyphs follow a more rigid pattern. Outlines resemble a human elbow, with some softening of the outline at the point of bending. The writing at San Bartolo reflects a pattern of execution that yields in part to painterly execution but tautens it with sharp corners. These harder, more pronounced lines may express the influence of carving or incision. The rigidity of carving and the fluidity of brushwork should not be seen as categorically distinct but as aesthetic possibilities from which the scribe can draw variable inspiration. The Preclassic and Early Classic facture (Periods IA–IIB) weighted the square overall outline against the more rounded forms of the Late Classic period. But it clearly was influenced by the fluid expression of paint—the contrast with purely carved script, such as runic in Europe or Isthmian writing in the Isthmus of Tehuantepec, Mexico, is patent (e.g., Moltke 1985:32; Winfield Capitaine 1988). For Maya signs, the carver often followed what is presumed to be a now-effaced version in ink. Transparent examples of this practice are many of the inscriptions from Late Classic Xcalumkin, Campeche, Mexico, where the carvers so attended to painted guidelines that the texts suffered in legibility. Outlines appear not as crisp edges but as mechanical copies of brushstrokes, the negative, recessed surfaces confused with positive, outthrust ones (fig. 8.2; see also Graham and von Euw 1992:168–178, 181–185, 194, 195). An even clearer example is probably the Tablet of the 96 Glyphs at Palenque, Chiapas, Mexico, which builds on a well-attested local proclivity for rendering first in paint, followed by carving or modeling in stucco (Robertson 1977:320–322; Stuart 2005:59). Nonetheless, the process of refiguring a painted line—with its distinct ductus and variable effusion of pigment—into a chiseled, scraped, and polished form must inevitably introduce features that were not in the original: depth, angle of beveling, cross-hatching to show a fill of dark paint or ink. The carved glyphs are not replications but transformations, tracking from relatively spontaneous media to ones that involve multiple movements of the hand and acts of tooling.

For all such evidence of cross-influential media, there is evidence of a marked reorientation in execution during the use-life of Maya script. The earliest writing, beginning about 250 BCE, is small and lightly incised, perhaps to be picked out by cinnabar or other red pigment but resolutely focused on a limited readership at any one time—only a small group gathered around such a piece could make out the characters. (The situation is slightly different with portable objects: the small texts imply both limited readership and an invitation to pass the object to other hands. But the act is intimate, hardly the "propaganda" said to motivate much early writing in Mesoamerica [Houston 2004a:8–10; cf. Marcus 1992:438]. To be sure, Marcus applies the term "propaganda" to any small-scale communication between elites in unequal societies.) The influence of other engraved scripts of the same general time, including Isthmian, remains unclear, but there seems increasing evidence of sign transfer, including cross-ties in

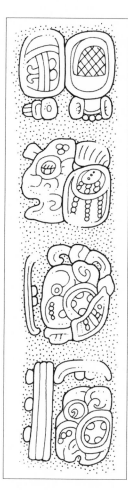

FIGURE 8.2

Portion of Xcalumkin Jamb 6. Photograph by Ian Graham in Graham and von Euw 1992:168 (redrawn by author).

particular signs (cf. Macri and Stark 1993:19–20; Saturno et al. 2006:Figure 4). The direction of that transfer is uncertain in that Isthmian was, on the most secure evidence now available, contemporary with or even later than the earliest Maya signs.[3]

By the Early Classic period, the emphasis on flatness continued, as though scribes and sculptors felt constrained to create, albeit on distinct levels in glyph blocks, the minute scale of a flush, engraved object. In this sense, a mode of presentation suitable for portable texts dominated new, more ambitious modes of presentation on free-standing sculptures that extended beyond the height and width of a human body. (The somatic link between sculpture and the human frame diminished only after about 550 to 600 CE.) By contrast, the Late Classic period showed an evident, growing concern with glyphs that might be seen from varying angles, not flush but erupting in rounded form from the background surface, with some exceptions that retained the engraved quality of line from the Early Classic and before. To an extent not previously obvious, texts invited a larger number of viewers, with a stress on multiple slants of inspection and the capture of shifting light during the day and at night by lambent torch. By the Postclassic period, a renewed emphasis on flatness pervaded the creation of text, building on a severe flatness in many texts of the Terminal Classic period. The motivation may not have been a glyptic concern with incision but an overriding calligraphic sensibility—the few carved texts of Postclassic date are little more than flat surfaces for paint, as at Mayapan, or they occur in the form of sequential day signs that find their closest parallels in manuscripts (Proskouriakoff 1950:Figure 90f; Taube 1988). The dominant mode of expression thus shifted from incised, rectilinear, and flush > volumetric and curving > painted and flush, not because particular instruments of execution were unavailable at any one time but because of a preference for certain favored, focal practices. These probably resulted from a variable concern with the effects of light, the viewing angle, the number of readers and receivers, and, in aesthetic terms, the balance between a flat, painterly surface and an eruptive one that penetrated the existential world of the viewer.

Another domain involves *transmission*. That is, glyphs were made by people who learned to make them. They either accepted models or reacted to them under the pressure of discerning patrons who provided food and other forms of support. As Galenson (2005) has pointed out, Kant identified geniuses who innovated purely from a mysterious, internal calculus; for his part, Galenson divides such intellects into incremental experimenters and conceptual mappers, both traveling on routes unknown to others. These formulations are likely to be a social absurdity for the Maya (and, one suspects, for most of humanity). There can be no presocial or extrasocial human outside Kaspar Hauser and other unfortunates with cognitive challenges. For this reason, the transmission of glyphic knowledge necessarily coalesced from social acts, involving people in a chain of doing and learning, sustained by contact with a set of direct and indirect interlocutors. Where innovation took place, it may have occurred with sanction of a supernatural sort or through oneiric warrant: that is, the instruction to introduce changes may have been perceived to have come from a compelling external source, as channeled by dreams or visions (Monaghan 2008:330–333).

Of the various types of glyphic transmission, the most likely was something akin to the "legitimate peripheral participation" described by Lave and Wenger (1991; Wenger 1998, 1999). This process involves an effective means of learning that does not have a finite beginning and end, a set curriculum, or knowledge that is separate from other aspects of life. It is learning and transmission that is jointly done, integral to identity, and predicated on shared terms, procedures, and understandings that lead to tangible results (Lave and Wenger 1991:98; Wenger 1999:73–84). The question for the Maya is not, did learning occur outside of practice, the actual making of texts? but rather, how were these settings constituted over time? For most Maya practices there were always mythic templates, as elegantly described for Maya scribes by Coe (1977): monkeys of clever if somewhat phlegmatic disposition (particularly in the case of leaf-chewing howler monkeys), perhaps originating in earlier creations of sentient beings by the gods, and then a whole range of other creatures, from rabbits to vultures to the Maize God (Coe and Kerr 1998:101–110). A set of pots shows sculpting, too, as the result of a primordial action in which two scribal deities shape human heads, identified in text as "1 shining, new person" (see independent work by Boot [2006], who nonetheless errs in seeing the object being shaped as the shaper). The act of creating representations and the texts on them probably had magical qualities, a craftsman thus being associated with supernatural capacities (Houston et al. 2006:73; also Kris and Kurz 1979: 73, 79). The lone attested scene of instruction shows older, eagle-eyed scribal gods teaching subservient youths. Only the old gods speak. One group of students focuses on a sequence of numbers, the other on an enigmatic expression that is, as so often in decipherment, readable but not interpretable, *1 K'an 1 Yax u-tuut-il chokoon tatib*—alas, decoded sounds that do not as yet result in transparent meaning (Coe and Kerr 1998:2–3).

The only glimmers of textual evidence for social organization among producers of glyphs comes from the final years of the Late Classic period, particularly at Piedras Negras. A certain sculptor is said literally to be the "head sculptor" ([u-ba-u-?-lu]) of the final known ruler of the site (Houston et al. 2000a:Figure 11). At Piedras Negras, too, data show the concurrent careers of particular sculptors who cluster in time according to the dates of their signed work yet overlap surprisingly little with other such groups at the site (Houston 2000:Figure 5). This suggests clustered entities of masters, associates, and apprentices operating in a system of ateliers with unclear tethers between them. The fact that Piedras Negras is one of the few sites to have vestiges of "student" work indicates a certain formality of instruction and practice at this city (Satterthwaite 1965:11, 15–17); at other courts, the apprentices may have learned solely on the job. The paucity at other places of multiple signatures and arrangements of masters as primus inter pares is difficult to interpret. At some point, the presence or absence of such references to sculptors must have involved royal decisions as to what was decorous and what was not. Piedras Negras shows an unusual degree of royal advertisement of sculptural talent, perhaps on the initiative of certain rulers who gloried in their patronage of not only works but suitable personnel to undertake them. The near invisibility of scribes in the earlier Maya texts reflects the singular frame of reference in such texts, which seldom extend beyond mention of royal personages. But personality will out: in the Madrid Codex, a Postclassic document, Lacadena García-Gallo (2000:81) has found what appear to be conscious gaps or caesurae in which scribes broke with the work of those in preceding sections.

An ingenious attempt to massage statistically the occurrence of variant forms of signs indicates that antagonistic dynasties drew on distinct inventories of signs (Brewer 1998). That this was a subtle advertisement of difference is less likely than the probability that the scribes in such cities did not communicate readily: in other words, they belonged to different "script communities," and scribes and sculptors were less free agents than

servants bound tightly to certain dynasties (Houston 2004b:299). A series
of statements that read *yanabil*, "his [*a*] *anab*" (see Tzotzil Maya, '*an*, "hew,
carve" > *anib*, "thing for carving"; Laughlin 1988b:I:136) occur in several
sculptors' signatures from sites in the upper Usumacinta River and envi-
rons, followed by the name of an overlord. A reward to pliant subordinates
could have been the loan of such specialists. An ostentatious prize of this
sort, perhaps indicating the actual presence of a sculptor at a subordinate
center, underscores a relationship of high trust between polities and hints
of the relatively finite numbers of exceptional sculptors. Several
courtiers—never royalty—in the celebrated Bonampak murals appear to
carry this title, presumably the most esteemed of their accomplishments
(Miller 1986:Figures III.7, III.16).

A curiosity of Maya script—restricted largely to Periods IIIA to IIID—
is the appearance of "pseudo-glyphs" (fig. 8.3). These are attempts by
painters and a few sculptors to show the suggestion of writing but not its
reality: they fool only a casual glance and seem largely to fill a compositional role, marking areas where legible glyphs usually appear, in bands
around the rim, vertical lines, or "captions." Some contain actual signs but
in a repetitive, nonsensical order; others simply hint at writing by focusing
on rounded outlines of varying weight and size, some mimicking larger
signs, others smaller, elliptical ones. The reasons for these are unknown,
but they are clearly a late innovation. They occur at a time when, presumably, writing became more abundant in the Maya world. Their specific reason to exist may have varied. Yet, most scholars suspect that they show a
desire to possess script when such was not widely available. Earlier periods
may have had more rigorous sumptuary codes in place to control such
arrogation and imitation of privileged knowledge (for a comprehensive
review, see Calvin 2006); alternatively, script may have partially lost its
sacred, hermetic character and could now be imitated for aesthetic embell-
ishment alone, a signal departure from the past. The larger point is that
the "shape of script" discussed in this volume also affected ancillary forms
of display. Arguably, for example, the glyphic allergy to sharp corners (but
not sharp edges) existed in tandem with an architectural and formal aesthetics that insisted on rounded corners, perhaps explaining why a form of
containment and definition that could have taken many directions did not
(see Herring 2005; Ricketson 1937; and below).

Yet another domain is *motivation*. Even in the earliest known examples
from the Preclassic period, Maya glyphs highlight areas defined by line, not
line per se. Their perceived physicality causes them to cleave from the

FIGURE 8.3

Pseudo-glyphs: (a) *use of glyph-like elements in "textual" sequence, Uaxactun, ca. 600 CE;* (b) *legible signs in uninterpretable order, Burial 45, Piedras Negras, ca. 600 CE. Photographs courtesy of Inga Calvin.*

surface, to be distinguished from it. The sustained, iconic nature of Maya writing helps it to retain a lasso to the existential world, perhaps resulting in the bold animations that characterized glyphs first at the opening of the Early Classic period, then in fuller form at select Late Classic cities (see, e.g., Fields and Reents-Budet 2005:Plate 97; see also Houston 2004b:291; Houston et al. 2006:35, 76). The presence of quotative expressions, which describe glyphs as speech, slides this sense of materiality into Maya concepts of formal utterance, which can appear as physical wisps in Late Classic imagery, concrete, visible, twisting, as though likened to an expressive quality of line (Grube 1998; Houston et al. 2006:Figures 4.22, 4.23; see Herring 2005:23–26 for a view that painted facture comprehensively ordered Late Classic aesthetics).

With few exceptions, Maya signs preserve evidence of their iconic

STEPHEN D. HOUSTON

origin. Epigraphers have known for some time that scribes created syllabic signs from CVC words in which the final element is a "weak" vowel or semiconsonant (e.g., Houston et al. 2000b:328):

[ba] < CM *b'aah, "pocket gopher"
[hu] < pCh' *huj, "iguana"
[ka] < CM *kay, "fish"
[ko] < GTz *kok, "small turtle" (?)
[k'u] < CM *q'uu', "nest"
[ch'o] < CM *ch'o', "mouse, rat"
[lu] < CM *luk, "hook, to fish" (?) or lu', "catfish"
[mo] < GTz *mo', "macaw"
[ne] < CM *neh, "tail"
[ni] < CM *ñii', "nose"
[no] < CM *nooq', "cloth" (?)
[pu] < GTz *puj, "cattail"
[to] < CM *tyooq, "mist, cloud"
[tzu] < CM *tzu', "gourd"
[wi] < pCh' *wi', "root"

This might be called the "syllabification principle," with a likelihood of relatively rapid introduction once a full range of such sounds was needed (Houston 2004b:299). It is possible that some of the syllables came into existence as a means of indicating vowel length in preceding word-signs (Houston et al. 2004) or for onomatopoeic reasons, as in a marker for a rattle yielding the syllable [xa], perhaps the perceived noise of a rattle. Other signs are simply abbreviated versions of others, as in the syllables ['e] and [cha], each from a body part of an animal that, in fuller, glyphic form, had very different readings. Another set appears to use the most common Maya sign (T501) as a handle for innovations in syllabic spellings (Beliaev and Tunesi 2005), including [t'u], [ma], [yu], and [ja]. An incipient alphabetic tendency stressing pure vowels hints at new levels of phonological analysis in the initial years of the Late Classic period, particularly with phonemes like /e/ and /o/. Phonemic discriminations between [b] and [m] in signs that closely resemble each other point equally to such a sensibility. David Stuart (personal communication 2000) noted a pattern in which later versions of signs, especially of the [WAHY] glyph or a sign for "consumption" (the outlines of a generic youth's head) lose track of their iconic origin, motivating reinterpretations by scribes on the basis of perceived similarities

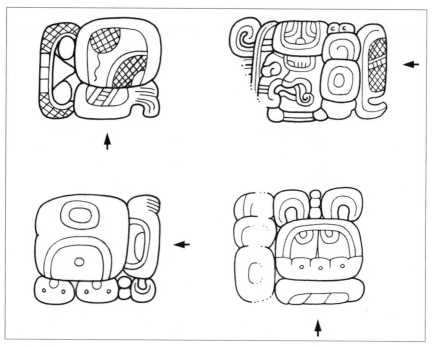

FIGURE 8.4

Comparison of [ji] and [li] signs, Early Classic and Late Classic periods. Upper row, left to right: *Tikal Stela 31:F13 and Tikal Stela 39:pA4;* lower row, left to right: *Tikal Temple 1, Lintel 1:C4, F9 (all redrawn by author).*

(see Lacadena García-Gallo's point about analogy above). These reinterpretations bespeak later bottlenecks in scribal transmission, not just the one that occurred at the end of the Preclassic (Period Ib).

Many otiose or supernumerary features begin to flourish, too, perhaps by analogy, perhaps as space fillers to achieve the compaction beloved of Maya scribes: dotted supports that have no meaning, along with the "doublers" that condense more information into ever-tighter spaces, a doubled syllable transcribed with two dots to the side (Stuart and Houston 1994:Figure 57; Zender 1999:106–127). By a contrasting process, the [ji] and [li] signs, similar in early texts, diverge forcefully by later times, as though scribes felt discomfort in potential blurring between signs with critical morphological meaning (fig. 8.4). Finally, at times, the Maya scribes made important distinctions, as between the [le] and [li] in northern texts, that epigraphers do not always perceive (fig. 8.5). Several scholars have commented on the seeming ubiquity of syllabic signs in Terminal Classic

FIGURE 8.5

Comparison of [li] and [le] in texts from Late Classic to Terminal Classic sites in the Yucatán peninsula (note the direction of curves within the highlighted sign): left, [IXIK-BAAK-'e-le], Xcalumkin Jamb 9:pA1–pA2; right, [wo-jo-li], Xcalumkin Jamb 1:A3. Graham and von Euw 1992:163, 171 (redrawn by author).

sites like Chichén Itzá, perhaps an indication of the need for clarity in the presence of multilingualism (Wichmann 2006:289–290). Perhaps, yet the pattern could simply underscore a local notion that language was the target, not the mediating script, a point made in this volume (chapter 2) by John Baines for certain periods of Egyptian writing.

Some of these changes took place close to the 600–650 CE transition noted by Grube, in which dramatic renovations swept through the Maya signary. Yet, the opportunity for change might have loomed largest when there were ruptures with what came before. Preclassic inscriptions are at best barely legible, with many patterns that diverge from Early Classic texts (Houston 2004b:308, 2008:237–240). Early Classic texts differ tangibly from Late Classic ones. This difference was not a matter of deliberate choice but likely an indirect reflection of an epistemological bottleneck, suggesting that script communities innovated partly because they wished to, so as to satisfy new needs, and partly because they had no choice. In biology, the founder's effect explains why genetic legacies narrow when a subset of a population sets off for a new island or remote valley. The process ensures that the genetic inheritance of the subset will fail to reflect the attributes of the larger original population. The shifts evident in Maya writing hint at new openings and, in the negative, restrictions of glyphic knowledge through "die-offs" in scribal knowledge—probably among scribes themselves—resulting in the failure to transmit their specialized knowledge across generations (Houston 2008:248). Thus, scribes: reduced in number, displaced physically, unsustained socially. Transmission: interrupted, narrowed, or truncated. Our current interpretation of these shifts: necessarily thin.

AN EVOLVING PRACTICE

Much has not been discussed, including shifts in sign inventory and textual substance, along with the changing dispositions of glyphs, as new locations and contexts opened to their display. Continuities abound, especially in the propensity of Maya texts to denote possession through "name-tagging," by which an object records the name of its owner or maker (Houston 2004b:304). Yet, a synchronic approach to Maya script, so essential to treating it as a comprehensible system, falls short as an overall, domain-oriented approach to glyphs over time. Small shifts—modifications—could be both incremental and episodic, but they responded mostly, in all probability, to the incidental change that comes with daily and even cross-media practice, such as the analogical processes that caused signs to blur or share features or the carving of painted texts. In contrast, major systemic changes arise from profound social ruptures and envelopments: a need for renovated syllabaries, for new kinds of phonic and semantic expression, because cross-generation transmission experienced a profound disruption. The earliest Maya signs can scarcely be penetrated because of bottlenecks between later practice and the earliest coalescence of writing; the innovations of the Late Classic hint at a rupture with the Early Classic, perhaps in the very groups of scribes who served to maintain tradition in recorded form. The focal groups who learned and performed the skills of Maya glyph production existed at moments of intense, if politically mediated, communication. They experienced episodes in which craft lost some of its links to established practice. With the Spanish conquest, this loss became irreparable.

What comes forcefully to mind in studies of Maya script as a formal system is how much remains to be done (e.g., Carter 2010; Doyle 2009). Paleographical research seldom has follow-through, because its authors go on to other worthy and enticing projects—the details of script change, although the chapters in this volume assert their crucial importance, may seem esoteric to outsiders, attention to them a harmless if ineffectual pursuit. But how can a major medium for accessing Maya thought be left to the side, with often exclusive focus on its content rather than on the precise means of recording that content? In Maya studies, what stores of material evidence are better dated, more tightly bound to historical setting, more open to examination of cultural process? Few, perhaps none. Maya epigraphy has always been adept at finding wedges into recalcitrant evidence. As decipherment winds down in hopeful expectation of further data to decode rare signs and opaque texts, the shape of Maya glyphs beckons, a subject of promise for considering the rhythms and determinants of social and cultural change.

Acknowledgments

This chapter was made stronger by comments from Simon Martin, Megan O'Neil, and Karl Taube, along with the warm and productive discussions in the meeting room at the seminar building at SAR. A complementary piece, touching on distinct but related themes, appears in Houston n.d.b.

Notes

1. A more daring position is that for Maya script, exemplary forms are intellectually dubious and perhaps unethical. They can be seen as data—a perfect median of available evidence, a standard from which deviations occur—when in fact they arise as creations of a present-day exercise in graphic typology. To avoid this unwitting imposture, the more deliberate step is to illustrate or reproduce glyphs from actual texts.

· 2. For a partial critique of this hypothesis, see Mora-Marín 2009. Its argument is not so much an assault on the prestige language proposal as an attempt to show that Maya glyphs recorded an earlier stage of the language than is recognized. The study is disqualified by its misunderstanding of cognate forms in descendant languages and its inattention to the varying or evolving functions of diagnostic elements in grammar (Robertson et al. n.d.).

3. Isthmian is a controversial script that scholars claimed to have deciphered in the late 1980s and early 1990s (Justeson and Kaufman 1997, 2008; Kaufman and Justeson 2008). A detailed study of these proposals raises grave doubts about the methods, protocols, and results of the supposed decipherment (Houston n.d.b; Houston and Coe 2003). A cautious view—and, in likelihood, the correct one—would require a decipherment based on clear linkages to known scripts (the basis of all earlier decipherments of ancient scripts), a corpus that is more than a handful or two of texts, and clear support from captions that accompany interpretable images, all of which afford controls on decipherment. At present, none of these elements are in place.

9

The Shape of Script in a Colonial Context

*Alphabetic and Pictorial Registers
in Mixtec Texts*

John Monaghan

Richard Salomon makes a distinction between a gradual change in the shape of script as a result of being tinkered with by one generation after another and "systemic changes" in script that are "conditioned by exceptional and sporadic forces, most often connected with language change," which is "the adoption or adaptation of a pre-existing script for one language to represent a different, often unrelated language" (chapter 5, this volume). The alphabet used to write the Mixtec language of central Mexico falls into the latter category. Not long after the Spanish arrived in the sixteenth century, they began to adapt the Latin alphabet to Meso-american languages, beginning with Nahuatl but extending to all the major languages spoken in the region. In the Parra orthography used in highland Guatemala, for example, the Spaniards introduced symbols to represent glottal stops, and for Mixtec, a tonal language, some writers began to mark tone. The context for these changes in script—the "exceptional" force mentioned by Salomon—was, of course, a colonial project. When the Spanish conquered most of Mesoamerica in the sixteenth century, they imposed their version of Christianity on the survivors, and they integrated the region into the Atlantic economy. The spread of literacy was so important for administrative and religious purposes that by the second half of the sixteenth century, every major settlement in Mexico had at least one scribe trained to use a modified alphabet. The Mesoamerican situation is not unique, and there is no doubt that many of the systemic script changes that occurred in the past took place in the context of colonization.

This chapter takes a closer look at a related process, also in a colonial context. This has to do with a situation in which the scripts of both the colonizers and the colonized remained in use. In Mesoamerica, people continued to produce texts using an indigenous graphic system for several generations after the conquest. However, hybrid texts developed that used both the indigenous writing system and alphabetic script. This chapter focuses on the changes that occurred in indigenous texts, with a specific focus on the shifting relationship between the alphabetic writing introduced by the Spanish and writing in the Mixtec script. In keeping with the theme of this volume, attention is on the social transformations that underpinned the shifting relationship (Houston et al. 2003)

SEEING MESOAMERICAN TEXTS

When the Spanish arrived in Mesoamerica in the early years of the sixteenth century, there were at least four writing systems in use. The pre-Columbian-style illuminated screenfold books, or codices, are of special interest because they present a picture of native society that is largely unmediated by Spanish colonialism. These manuscripts recount heroic histories and royal genealogies, record calendrical and divinatory information, and contain accounts of world creation, the origin of humanity, and the actions of the gods. Unfortunately, very few have survived. Of the sixteen surviving examples, half are in the Mixtec tradition, from Oaxaca, Mexico (Smith 1973).

In Elizabeth Boone's recent book on Mesoamerican divinatory codices, she notes that early Spanish chroniclers described the books of central Mexico as being written in "symbols and pictures" (Boone 2007:1). Mixtec writers, in addition to using some signs that had to be read in the Mixtec language, employed the resources of the visual arts in their texts: color, spacing, juxtaposition, human figures painted in stylized costumes using a gestural vocabulary, and a range of conventional symbols. In the past, we would have placed this script in an evolutionary scheme partly based on its ability to replicate speech. The terminology would also have implied an historical sequence—that once an inferior system is confronted with a superior system, it would eventually be replaced. But as Boone points out, we are now so well aware that different graphic systems can be used simultaneously and, it might be added, that alphabetic writing itself has a complex relationship to speech, there is little need to review why Mesoamerican people persisted with their own system after exposure to an alphabetic script. At the same time, the connection between Mesoamerican texts and legitimate, performed knowledge has given them a remarkable resiliency.

It is important in understanding any writing system to consider how the expectations, practices, and conventions associated with reading shape the form and content of texts. It is worth bearing in mind that the customs and conceptions related to reading and writing vary as one moves from one tradition to another (Howe 1993). To choose an example from contemporary Oaxaca, the Cuicatec verb "to read" is the same as "to learn," probably because reading is linked to the school system. Another example is the Cree word "to write," which comes from a root that means "to go into debt," because they first encountered writing through the record keeping of traders with the Hudson Bay Company (Laughlin 1988a:133). It follows from this point that the shape of script should be put into the context of reading and writing practices. Byron Hamann and I have proposed a comparable if still tentative model of reading for Mesoamerican texts based largely on colonial dictionaries and ethnographic evidence from contemporary indigenous groups.

In colonial and later sources on Mesoamerican languages, the word for "to read" is most often translated as the same as or related to either the verb "to count" or the verb "to see" (see Monaghan and Hamann 1998). The connection between counting and reading in Mesoamerican texts seems transparent: they contain a great deal of material that requires one to count and recount. Codices such as the Dresden or Vaticanus (of Maya and Nahuatl provenance, respectively) contain calendrical records of days and years. The famous *tonalpohualli*, literally, "the count of the days," were divinatory records, telling the fate and fortune of those born at particular times. Many of the Mixtec codices are essentially long family records in which one might count the generations from founding ancestors to current rulers. Typically, the range of meaning contained in the idea of counting includes not only numeration but also the idea of presenting an accounting, a summary, or a final tally (e.g., Barrera Vásquez 1980:949). As in many other places, Mesoamerican writing functioned within a tradition of recitational literacy in which what was read was to be proclaimed aloud. To proclaim something as important as what was written in a codex, one needed to be skilled in the verbal arts, and the evidence suggests that these texts would be chanted or sung (e.g., M. King 1990, 1994; Monaghan 1990; Thompson 1972).

The connection between seeing and reading is equally transparent. Given the highly artistic nature of Mesoamerican texts, the visual dimension of reading would be particularly salient. Yet, the act of seeing in

Mesoamerica extends beyond optical reception in that it is something more than looking (Monaghan and Hamman 1998). In the ethnographic literature, we often find that the ability to see is considered a mark of great wisdom. In Zinacantan, a Tzotzil Maya community, Evon Vogt (1976:188) tells us that visions equal knowing. Often the person of knowledge is the priest/curer/shaman, as Alan Sandstrom (1991:233) tells us for the Nahuas of Veracruz. He or she is *tlamatiquetl*, "a person of knowledge," or in the role of diviner, *tlachixquetl*, "one who waits, sees, expects something." Among the Q'eqchi', the shaman is simply the *aj ilonel*, "the seer" (Wilson 1995:81).

The ability to see is a special gift. In the *Popol Vuh*, early humans are described as having the ability to see right into heaven. The gods then caused their vision to become less penetrating, clouded, as if they looked through "smoke on a mirror." The Lacandon say that humans lost their ability to see the gods when a man tried to hit one of them with his machete (Boremanse 1993:332–333). Similarly, the Huastec affirm that humans lost the blessing of powerful vision when they mocked the gods. The gods then retaliated by shaking maize pollen in their eyes so that people could no longer see them (Alcorn 1984:62). However, shamans have the gift of being able to see the gods, as do the Zinacantan shamans, who can view the gods in their mountain abode (Vogt 1976:27). Likewise, the call to become a curer in Tlaxcala comes to some people after they develop extraordinary visual and auditory abilities (Nutini and Nutini 1987:335). Among the Tepehua, the diviner's abilities come from having looked at lightning, which gives him a "superior vision" (Williams García 1970:3–13; see also Galinier [1990:197], who notes that the Otomi shaman has "a special vision, a clear vision," and also Lipp 1991:153, for the Mixe). The ancient Maya believed that elite vision could positively affect and change the world and was part of how hierarchy was constituted (Houston and Taube 2000); Hamann makes the additional point that elite vision enabled its bearers to see larger points and general patterns (Hamann 2004).

Although the ability to see is a gift and in the past was hierarchically distributed, it has to be cultivated. One needs to observe special taboos, such as sexual abstinence, and perform rigorous spiritual exercises. Indeed, periods of sexual abstinence for Mazatec persons of knowledge can last for up to fifty-two days at a stretch. Eckart Boege (1988:173) remarks that it would not be difficult for someone to remain largely celibate if he or she strictly adhered to the prohibitions. Throughout Mesoamerica, vision can be amplified by certain instruments. In fact, many of the things we label as divinatory items are spoken of in indigenous discourse not so much as magical objects as devices that enhance the vision of the practitioner; accordingly, many have a strong optical dimension to them. The most obvious example is crystals, used by specialists in all of Mesoamerica. Among the Nahua of Veracruz, crystals are called "mirrors" (Sandstrom 1991:235–236). In the Yucatán, they are "light stones." The Totonac call crystals *pu-lakawa*, which has been translated as "that which allows one to see" (Ichon 1973:257–258). The Totonac curer holds the crystal up to the light and then interprets the patterns he or she sees in the refraction. Using such an instrument, the curer can see individual gods, as well as persons who caused an illness if it is a case of witchcraft (see also Hanks [1990:246–252], who describes a similar use of crystals among the Yucatec Maya in a divination genre known as "illumination").

Another set of instruments for amplifying visions is the hallucinogens that persons of knowledge sometimes ingest. For example, a Chatino shaman described the experience and purpose of taking the hallucinogenic "holy fruit" in the following terms:

> La Santa is like the scribe of Holy Father Son, its messenger; it is as if it were the secretary of the municipality.... [After one ingests the seeds,] you begin to see, but one sees more than before; one is really *tai* [awakened, knowledgeable, wise, a seer]. The light of the Holy Fruit illuminates everything....One sees everything more clearly. Afterward you begin to see your fate. [Cited in Bartolomé and Bárabas 1982:132]

It is important to note that such vision allows the curer to see both into the future (e.g., whether the patient will recover) and into the past (where and how the illness was caused; Ichon 1973:257–258). Indeed, the Mazatec curer is able to go back and forth in time under the influence of mushrooms. This ability allows the curer to warn patients of danger, as well as to discover the causes of illnesses afflicting patients (Boege 1988:204–205).

In addition to crystals and hallucinogens, other objects that can be used to amplify vision include mirrors, bowls of water, and candles. What is interesting about this point for the practice of reading is that the original source of the *Popol Vuh* is referred to as an *ilbal*, which Dennis Tedlock translates as "place or instrument of seeing" (1985:23), the same term that is often used for crystals, mirrors, and even telescopes among the modern K'iche'. Similarly, the Aztecs equated divinatory chants, books, and mirrors (Taube 1983:120). Although Tedlock infers from this set of relationships that the original *Popol Vuh* was a book of prophecy, we could also see in it a more general sense of what books might be, grounded in a dominant Mesoamerican metaphor of reading as seeing, irrespective of whether the text in question had a prophetic function. Indeed, among the contemporary Mazatec, the term for book, *xon*, is used to refer to any visionary power object received during a mushroom ceremony (Edward Abse, personal communication 1998).

The evidence for the connection between books and instruments for seeing is not simply etymological. Recall that Mazatec curers must be celibate for long periods before using divinatory paraphernalia. The missionary-linguist Eunice Pike noticed that adult Mazatec converts would often go to great lengths to avoid reading scripture when she first began to work in the area. Her puzzlement increased when a young lady, who often read the Bible with Pike as a girl, suddenly refused to do so after her marriage. Investigating, Pike discovered that the Mazatec felt that anyone who read scripture must purify him- or herself and refrain from engaging in any acts that might be a source of pollution (Pike 1960).

The notion that reading is an act of seeing—and that one "sees" in dreams, visions, and altered states of consciousness—raises an interesting question about some of the Mesoamerican books that have come down to us. Implicit in most analyses of manuscripts is that they document or reflect a tradition. But Hamann and I wondered whether it could sometimes be the other way around (Monaghan and Hamann 2000). Relevant here is an observation made by Frank Lipp in his work among the Mixe. Although Mixe shamans are well versed in their craft, precise directions for prayers and ritual performances, the numerical sequences that must be followed, and the design plan and paraphernalia necessary for each specific ritual are written down in notebooks. These instructions are written in Spanish script, supplemented by mnemonic symbols and diagrams of ritual sequences. The notebooks are then passed down within families, but in time a curer may write additional rituals secured from other specialists by exchange and purchase (Lipp 1991:113–114). In another place, Lipp (1991:149–152) tells us that rituals, prayers, and other elements of the cult may be learned through dreams, while fasting, and under the influence of hallucinogenic mushrooms; presumably, this information, too, would be set down in the notebooks. The point here is that the information portrayed in the ancient books may not only reflect a tradition but also make concrete a body of emerging knowledge, situated within the larger patterns that an elite vision is able to perceive. According to an ethnographer of contemporary Mazatec religious specialists, the books of knowledge they consult are not always complete and beyond modification. Rather, they are built up from or amended by the accumulation of human encounters with the divine during the mushroom rituals. These experiences can then be consulted by those who come after, who in turn may add to the book's contents (Edward Abse, personal communication 1998).

In consequence, the Mesoamerican book might best be understood as an ongoing project, a continuing story or an emerging history, not a finished text. There are manuscripts in the surviving Mesoamerican corpus that contain blank pages at the end, sometimes with the boustrophedonic guidelines painted on, as if waiting to be filled in (Monaghan and Hamann 2000).

MESOAMERICAN WRITING IN THE SIXTEENTH CENTURY

Spaniards sometimes questioned the usefulness of Mesoamerican texts because of the difficulty they had understanding these and because of doubts about their general reliability. Mesoamerican books were also burned in the course of Inquisition investigations and other efforts to stamp out idolatry. When these facts are cited in the literature, scholars are left with the impression of something just short of an official policy to eliminate native writing. However, Spaniards were not uniformly hostile to native writing. Despite some official skepticism, Mesoamerican people never stopped submitting pre-Columbian-style texts as evidence in lawsuits and property claims, and the courts continued to accept them and use them in making decisions. A treasure trove of indigenous manuscripts, which towns and villages submitted to buttress their land claims beginning in the 1920s, centuries after they were produced, exists in Mexico's Agrarian Reform archives (e.g., Memoria de Linderos 1997). In some ways, the truth value of such texts increased over time (Boone 2000:246; Smith and Parmenter 1991). When they were presented generations after they were painted, their antiquity lent them a degree of historical accuracy that could not be duplicated by other sources (this also helps to explain why so many of them are altered—there will be more to say about this below).

At the same time, the accounts of Spanish officials complaining about the reliability of Mesoamerican texts can easily be balanced by Spanish complaints about the reliability of alphabetic texts presented in court. Clearly, some genres of writing did better than others. Historical texts were widely produced during the colonial period. Elizabeth Boone suggests that this was because of their local importance (see below) and because the pictorial format structured the telling of the story (Boone 2000:247–248). Also, alongside the celebrated cases in which Spanish friars burned manuscripts, there were friars who lamented this destruction; there is ample evidence that Spanish clerics consulted Mesoamerican writings to compile official reports and histories. This fact indicates that at least some were able to distinguish between Mesoamerican writing in general and specifically idolatrous texts. Finally, it is unclear how widespread book burning actually was. The best-documented cases are those that ensued after friars uncovered "heretical" practices among supposedly sincere converts, suggesting that as long as people adhered to Christian teachings and produced works that did not offend Christian sensibilities, the existence of native books and manuscripts was not considered to be a matter of grave concern.

Although there may not have been an official policy to extirpate native scripts, colonial developments had a massive impact on Mesoamerican writing. One way Mesoamerican texts changed was through an effort on the part of those producing them to enhance comprehension by the colonizers. Writers were motivated to do this because they needed documents to use in legal proceedings. In pre-Columbian times, documents may have been used to resolve disputes. But with the establishment of a central authority, an expanding civil and religious bureaucracy that inserted itself in matters beyond the concerns of officials in pre-Columbian empires (let alone small kingdoms), and an imposed peace that made the courts the venue for what had been interpolity disputes, the production of documentary evidence acquired a new and powerful stimulus. We have no real idea about the size of the Mesoamerican corpus before the Spanish arrived. It could be that only a handful of manuscripts might be in the possession of any royal house, and there is no evidence for extensive libraries. It may be that the number of texts produced after the conquest was not that different from the quantity created before the Spanish arrived, but at the least, the Spanish court system provided an incentive for the production of documents.

The kinds of cases brought before the Spanish courts that involved Mesoamerican people spanned the gamut of possible civil and criminal matters. However, disputes over property in particular stimulated the production of supporting texts following pre-Columbian conventions. In the sixteenth century, property disputes might occur between competing royal claimants over succession; competing groups over rights to land; nobles and commoners over tribute obligations; and Spaniards and indigenous people over tribute and land rights; and among all these groups over payment for services. There were also documents generated with respect to the entailment of estates and the confirmation of land boundaries. One of the things that emerged from all of these disputes was a set of texts that Barbara Mundy has characterized as "little histories" (2001:122). In the Mixteca, the majority of these documents are called *lienzos* (literally, "canvases"), since they are painted on cloth and are designed to be viewed flat, although there are some that retain a codex-style screenfold format, like the Codex Muro, of which more will be said below. This genre of document characteristically combined a map with some information on the indigenous rulers of the area. Unlike pre-Columbian manuscripts, the purpose of these documents was not so much to show the connections between a particular family or group and important historical and cosmic events and significant polities (Pohl 2003); rather, they emphasized local boundaries, settlements and specific events related to prominent royal lineages (Mundy 2001). Mesoamerica had a cartographic tradition before the Spanish arrived, but many scholars feel that the *lienzo* is a hybrid, combining Meso-american graphic techniques with some European mapmaking conventions. Usually, the symbols for toponyms were written around the four sides of the *lienzo* (often with east at the top); the middle was filled in with the glyphs for towns, palaces, and hamlets (which were often associated with a church), the roads linking them, major rivers, mountain chains, and perhaps other features of the landscape. At the center would be placed the head town, again symbolized by a church or palace. Included on the *lienzo* in many cases would be a ruling couple and often a genealogy depicting married pairs, sometimes going back many generations to the origins of the dynasty. In all cases, the focus of the document was local. Authors were not concerned with how they fit into a larger Spanish territorial entity, their relationship with large cities and capitals, or even with how local rivers and mountains were connected to larger geographic and environmental features (Mundy 1996:105).

The reason that so many of these documents are a combination of map and genealogy is that property rights were tied up with dynastic succession. The Spanish introduced the notion of the entailed estate almost from the beginning of the colony, and it was very important in the Mixteca. Even as late as the nineteenth century, Mixtec noble families were very much aware of their ancient pedigrees and based their claims to property on descent. Later on, many *lienzos* ended up in the hands of commoners, who used them to justify claims to community property. From the Mixteca alone, dozens of *lienzos* remain. Many are in museums, but others are still owned by Mixtec towns, jealously guarded by town officials (e.g., Parmenter 1982). Although the production of *lienzos* was stimulated by the colonial legal system, the evidence we have indicates that they had tremendous local significance. It may be that they were regularly displayed, and throughout the colonial period, towns that possessed a *lienzo* were very proud of it, as they still are today. The people of Santa María Yucuhiti have a late colonial *lienzo* that they periodically unfold to discuss its meaning. *Lienzos*, irrespective of their value in court, continue to be one of the ways indigenous people represent themselves to themselves. In a *lienzo*, people can see where they come from, who their ancestors are, where their home is, the extent of their territory, and how they relate to other groups (see also Boone 2000; Mundy 1996:72, 111).

A *lienzo* or other postcolonial pictorial may contain scenes that look like ones found in the pre-Columbian codices, yet we also see in them many things that do not appear in the pre-Columbian manuscripts. For example, roads once symbolized by parallel lines containing human footprints now include those of hoofed animals, probably cattle or horses. Also appearing on *lienzos* are churches, individuals on horseback, figures dressed in European clothing, and other novelties. Postconquest documents depict indigenous people's everyday experience of the colonial state. Weapons, armor, and men on horseback often appear in accounts of battles between Spaniards and indigenous people. Other objects—such as tables that officials sit at, monks writing with quill pens, individuals seated on a kind of throne—are somewhat less obvious, but they represent key manifestations of colonial control (Monaghan 2004). In a recent paper, Elizabeth Boone (n.d.) outlines the influences that European illusionistic painting and drawing had on colonial Mexican pictography, such as when native manuscript painters began to adopt European conventions for depicting three-dimensional space. Although the discontinuities between pre-Columbian and postconquest pictorial manuscripts can serve as an analytic focus, one of the attributes that makes the pre-Columbian texts so valuable for those interested in the Mesoamerican past is that they often depict, along with the comings and goings of gods, heroes, and ancestors, the kinds of things an average person might see in his or her surroundings: items of material culture, geography, flora and fauna, and different kinds of social actors. It would be strange indeed, then, if things introduced by the Spaniards did not make their way into the postcolonial native texts. To put this another way, although it is easy to distinguish between precolonial and postcolonial pictorial documents, there are also substantial continuities between them. In most Mixtec documents of the sixteenth century, the semantically complex graphs, for the most part toponyms, show little change. Some are fully comprehensible, but only if they are read in the Mixtec language. Mixtec is a tonal language, and the writing system makes use of tone puns to convey information that is abstract or otherwise difficult to represent. To use a well-known case provided by Alfonso Caso, the words "large" and "break" are distinguished in Mixtec only by tone, so Mixtec scribes developed a convention in which they would show a man bending or breaking something to indicate its large size (Caso 1949; Smith

1983:241). Similarly, terms for body parts are extensively used as locatives in Mixtec, and a hill that appears to be standing on two feet means "at the foot of the hill." Even what is, for experts used to looking at the pre-Columbian manuscripts, the jarring introduction of perspective in colonial indigenous texts can be seen as a feature that enriches the pictorial tradition (Gruzinski 1992:160).

But certainly the content of the manuscripts was edited for Spanish eyes. To choose one example, the complex, branching genealogies that existed in pre-Columbian manuscripts gave way in the colonial period to straightforward if implausible ones in which a ruling couple produces a male descendant, who marries and produces a male descendant, and so on, down through many generations (see Hamann 1998). In part, this simplification was done to clarify the identity of the legitimate heir by not introducing the possible confusions from collateral lines. Yet, it also may have been done to obscure family relationships. Because the colonial genealogies focus only on the marriage of a couple and on a single descendant, there is no direct indication that the marriages portrayed might be between the kinds of close relatives that would give the Spanish cause to regard the marriages as incestuous (Mixtec dynasties, like those in Egypt and Hawaii, sometimes contracted marriage between brothers and sisters; see Christensen 1998).

REGISTERS IN THE *LIENZOS*

A curious feature of many of the postcolonial *lienzos* and codices is that they are heavily annotated in alphabetic script, often in Spanish but also in Mixtec, Nahuatl (a lingua franca in pre-Columbian and early colonial times), and in a few cases, Chocho. They were also cut up, divided, erased, and supplemented with additional pictorial elements. It is fair to say that for most scholars the essence of these documents is their pre-Columbian content; the annotations are a symptom of the retrenchment and eventual loss of the use of the indigenous script for communication. Moreover, the annotations and other alterations can sometimes hinder our understanding the original text. There are manuscripts in which the annotations obliterate the original signs and images, and still others to which the annotations were added decades or even centuries after the manuscripts were produced. The relationship of such annotations to the original text is tenuous, with many cases occurring in which the annotation has almost nothing to do with the pre-Columbian-style text. But there is good reason not to disregard these markings. As Mary Elizabeth Smith has shown, the layering of these annotations over time can provide insight into changes in indigenous society during the colonial period, such as shifting practices of assigning names (Smith 2005). Perhaps a more suitable way to look at this issue would be to think of the Mixtec and alphabetic text as functioning together, although their respective roles changed over time. In other words, instead of viewing the annotations Mixtec people were making to their books and *lienzos* as a sometimes helpful, sometimes unhelpful addition to a Mixtec text, these should be viewed as separate registers that contribute to the meaning of the manuscript. And rather than see the annotations as tokens of cultural deterioration or loss, their combination of scripts in fact bears witness to substantial continuities with established traditions.

For the sixteenth century, the Mixtec pictographic register was key to understanding the *lienzo*. The alphabetic register usually provided a translation of the Mixtec text and occasionally supplemented it. Much depended on whether the scribe who produced the pictorial was also the one who added the alphabetic text and, if not, whether the person adding the alphabetic register was Spanish or indigenous. In most cases in the sixteenth century, it seems that the alphabetic register was put there for the uninformed reader. The Lienzo of Ocotepec, for example, features a sign for Yucutiaca, "Hill of the Grasshopper." Underneath in European script is written "Chapultepec," or "Hill of the Grasshopper" in Nahuatl. Additional information conveyed in alphabetic script includes the names of individuals in the genealogies, the names of towns and subsequent owners of the manuscript, and important dates such as when the annotations were made or when the documents were submitted in a court case. Again, the alphabetic register does not do much more than provide a gloss or translation of the Mixtec signs. When trying to do more, it creates a context for an uninformed reader. Barbara Mundy provides an example from the map of Tamazcatepec, on which the author wrote, "I put the houses where the macehualtin [commoners] live, twenty-two of them," next to a drawing of the houses (Mundy 1996:171). The alphabetic text does not supplant the pictorial register. The alphabetic register was often awkwardly inserted between, under, and above figures, sometimes with lines attached to the sign to let the reader know what it is referencing. Longer texts were placed in empty areas in the composition. Alphabetic writing never acquires the display quality of the indigenous text but rather stands in sharp contrast to the often brilliantly colored pictorial register; the letters are small and, though not illegible, rarely approach calligraphic quality.

THE DILEMMA FOR NATIVE READERS

A document like a *lienzo* presents a snapshot of a dynamic setting. The genealogies they contain record a line of succession only up to a given moment in time. Not only are subsequent generations omitted, but so, too, are the individuals in preceding generations who might be important to the claims of later nobles—quite simply, they were not significant at the time the *lienzo* was prepared. As a map, the *lienzo* similarly freezes the dynamism of changing land use, political boundaries, and human settlements. The result is that as time passes, the *lienzo* becomes increasingly anachronistic. This was not much of a problem in the sixteenth century since indigenous scribes could provide ruling families and town leaders with a new and updated document. An excellent illustration of this practice comes from the Codex Selden. Scribes covered the earlier text with a thick coat of gesso and then painted on it a new text that was relevant to the situation in the mid-sixteenth century.

Some time in the 1590s or early 1600s, Mixtecs lost the ability to write in their own system. A number of things came to a sudden halt at the end of the sixteenth century, not just the scribal tradition. These losses can be attributed to devastating plagues that culminated in a shocking demographic collapse. Mesoamerican populations were first exposed to smallpox in 1519 by an infected soldier in Cortés' party. Over the next eighty years, Mesoamerican people suffered through repeated epidemics of typhus, diphtheria, whooping cough, chicken pox, measles, and influenza. These strongly infectious diseases devastated the New World populations who had not been exposed to them, but they had a lesser effect on Old World populations with acquired resistance. Although the precise numbers are a matter of scholarly debate, it is estimated that there were eighteen to thirty million people living in Mexico when Cortés arrived in 1519 and by 1610 there were about one million. Large areas were completely depopulated, thriving towns disappeared, and the Spanish began to import African slaves to replace native populations. The population of Mexico did not reach twenty-five million again until the 1950 census. Given that those trained in the production of native script were in all likelihood only a small subset of the total population, it is easy to see how a disease could eliminate all the writers in a given area. In point of fact, even alphabetic texts produced by Mesoamerican people were reduced by the end of the sixteenth century. Litigation, a tremendous stimulus to the production of texts, almost completely stopped, resuming only after the population began to recover. The immediate survivors of the plagues had little to fight over.

Nonetheless, history continues, new knowledge emerges, and stories unfold for those individuals and communities that endure. By all indications, survivors were very concerned with recording and seeing this done through manuscripts painted in the indigenous graphic system. The problem after the 1590s was how to do so in the absence of trained scribes. There appear to have been two solutions. One was to try to revive the old system by producing new pictorial manuscripts. The examples of this approach are sometimes copies of sixteenth-century texts, whereas in other cases they are whole new compositions, but lacking the conventions that characterize Mixtec writing (see Boone 2000:248). In the second half of the seventeenth century, in an area just to the north and east of Mexico City, a fairly widespread tradition of pictorial, *lienzo*-like composition emerged and lasted about fifty years. Known as Techialoyan, some fifty-five examples are extant, almost all of them primordial titles dealing with the rights of small communities to land (e.g., Noguez 1999). They thus contain scenes from the history of the town, focusing on events such as its founding, the conversion of its inhabitants to Christianity, and other events that legitimated the collective claim to property. Although not identifiable as part of a single stylistic tradition, pictorial documents continued to be produced in the Mixteca right up to the nineteenth century. Unfortunately, these have sometimes been dismissed as fakes rather than seen as part of an effort—underpinned by a set of practices associated with reading and a tradition that valued the pictorial as a source of truth—to maintain or revive a graphic tradition developed by Mesoamerican people.

The other ways Mixtec people continued to record the changes going on around them was through the alphabetic register. This approach is best illustrated with the use of a concrete case, that of the colonial-period Codex Muro (fig. 9.1). Of all the Mixtec manuscripts, it appears to be the most inelegant in its composition. Strange bits of costume were added to the people in the genealogy, crude figures were drawn in a seemingly random way, and every page was scribbled on. In short, to an outsider's gaze it looks a complete mess. Thanks to the work of Manuel Hermann Lejarazu (2003) and Mary Elizabeth Smith (2005), we now have a better understanding of the kinds of additions that were made and the sequence in which they were added. The earliest appear to date from the late sixteenth century, and the last were added in the late eighteenth century (Hermann Lejarazu 2003:163) or perhaps even as late as the nineteenth century (Smith 2005:389). In the script alone, Hermann Lejarazu (2003:161–229) has identified ten, perhaps eleven, different hands. The original genealogy was added to on at least two and perhaps three occasions (Hermann Lejarazu 2003:56–58; Smith 2005:384). The names of individuals in the genealogy were inserted, as were the hometowns of many of the women. At some point, feather headdresses and other feathered elements were added to some of the figures, perhaps to make them seem more archaic or

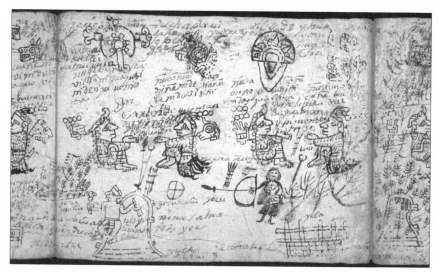

FIGURE 9.1

Codex Muro, page 7, ca. 1570–1684 CE. Museo Nacional de Antropología, Mexico City.
Supplied by Miguel Gasca, Instituto Nacional de Antropología e Historia, Mexico.

pre-Christian. The final pairs of figures are accompanied by seventeenth-century dates. On top of all of this, the boundaries of several different towns were added to certain pages in the codex as if the towns themselves were being inserted. Santiago Amatitlán was placed on pages three to five, Adeques on pages nine to eleven, the *cacicazgo* (noble estate) of Cantaros (which was a regional map touching on fourteen towns) on pages five to eight, and finally, a list of the boundaries of San Miguel Adeques (which represents the fissioning of Adeques into two parts) on pages nine to eleven; Santa Catarina and San Miguel were placed on the last pages of the codex during the colonial period (Hermann Lejarazu 2003).

What we have is a document on which members of the nobility first supplemented the original information with further genealogical details about their lines and perhaps recorded the boundaries of a regional *cacicazgo*. But also recorded are the boundaries of several different towns that were, presumably, added not by noble rulers, or *caciques*, but by townspeople themselves. It is almost as if the manuscript circulated throughout the region and people then took turns writing on it. In each case, the guiding purpose behind all these annotations was to add new knowledge to the codex—the names of new descendants of the original founding pair of *caciques*, areas of conflict between towns along primordial boundaries, and the appearance of new settlements and social divisions. Note that when people wrote on the manuscript, they did so on only specific parts, as if what they were doing was adding to the story without cancelling out the larger narrative or denying its foundational and enduring truths. The script may have changed from pre-Columbian-style glyphs to alphabetic writing, but the nature of the codex gives the text a seamlessness that is not otherwise apparent.

In the case of the Muro, the accumulation of annotations has made it almost unreadable. It is difficult to see, as the alphabetic register expanded, what use the document could have had in legal proceedings, since it is not at all clear what is going on even to the experts who have studied the manuscript, let alone to untrained court personnel. Mary Elizabeth Smith concludes that the Codex Muro was at all times "a local document" (2005: 401), suggesting that its significance lies primarily in what it meant to the people of the region, not its use as evidence in court cases, something that Hermann Lejarazu (personal communication 2007) also observes. To put this in a way that is consistent with the analysis of Mesoamerican reading practices, the people of the region were using the document as "an instrument for seeing" emerging knowledge. But what were they trying to use the codex to see?

It is a truism that there were momentous changes taking place among the indigenous inhabitants of colonial-period Mexico. In the context of the massive population decline, we often find that the connections between seventeenth-century *cacique* families claiming ownership of entailed estates and their ancestors in the sixteenth century are not at all clear. Part of this lack of clarity has to do with gaps in the documents, but it has long been suspected that cadet lineages and other distant relations stepped into these *cacicazgos* after entire royal lineages had succumbed to the plagues. This process may be recorded in the Codex Muro, in which the individuals added in the late sixteenth and early seventeenth centuries as direct descendants of the founding *caciques* break with earlier patterns: they are individuals from towns not previously mentioned or are named in other sources as members of the secondary nobility and not as kings and queens (Hermann Lejarazu 2003:259–260; Smith 2005:399). It is interesting in the Muro that not only the genealogies were extended but also names were written over earlier glosses added to the genealogy, perhaps the names of different individuals to make an eighteenth-century *cacique* look like the direct descendent of people in the sixteenth century (Hermann Lejarazu 2003:280). This kind of fiddling with genealogies is not unique—we see that figures have been erased during other times of the colonial period as well—nor is it new, since Hamann (1998) has shown that the unbroken sequence of successions shown in many manuscripts is statistically improbable over the number of generations depicted. Like a map, a genealogy freezes a dynamic situation, and it, too, must be expanded to stay current.

In addition to having to deal with breaks in succession, as the colonial period wore on, the indigenous nobility faced constant challenges from below as subjects sought to curtail their power. We know a lot about this because commoners regularly used the colonial court system to contest *caciques'* claims to land and tribute. *Caciques*, who controlled local government at the beginning of the colonial period, were increasingly marginalized. As the colonial period wore on, it became less and less common for *caciques* to hold political office. Sometimes towns took advantage of weak *caciques* who were unable to administer their far-flung holdings. In these cases, townspeople denied *caciques'* rights and privileges altogether. In later years, towns became so hostile that the *caciques* were unable to manage their estates and were forced to relinquish their holdings.

Once freed from *cacique* control, newly independent towns ironically began to fission as subordinate settlements struggled to become independent of their head towns. The precise reasons for this process are complex and the pace varied over time, but for our purposes, it is simply necessary to note that it was widespread, continuous, and often successful (it is an oft remarked fact that Oaxaca, with only about 4 percent of the Mexican population, has a quarter of its municipalities). The important point here is that as the institution that dominated the Mixteca from pre-Columbian times until well into the colonial period—the noble house—began to disappear, genealogy could no longer be the guarantor of land. So the question becomes, what replaced genealogy as an ideological argument for rights to property? What institution emerged to replace the noble estate? Looking at the historical record, one sees that there were a number of possibilities. Deeded private titles or viceregal grants were common and were used to establish numerous ranches, haciendas, plantations, and common-use lands. But many groups in the Mixteca were able, at least initially, to reconstitute themselves as landholding communities.

The example of the Muro shows us that Mixtec people continued to record the changes going on around them in a *lienzo* or codex format by expanding the alphabetic register on the document. Serge Gruzinski has observed that by the late sixteenth century, the alphabetic text becomes "the primary vector of information" (1992:161) and the pictorial content was relegated to the role of illustration. Thus, as people lost the ability to write Mixtec and read specific graphs, alphabetic writing went from being an explanatory comment or caption added to the text to something that determined the meaning of the document. By the eighteenth century, the alphabetic register in the Muro redefined the pictorial graphs and now informs us that it was concerned with commoner land rights. Similarly, the Codex Tulane, originally produced as a genealogy and history of the rulers of Acatlán, Puebla, becomes, according to the alphabetic register added around 1800, a document concerned with the land claims of the small town of San Juan Numi, some 100 km away from Acatlán (Smith and Parmenter 1991).

Although it was true that the alphabetic text carried a greater communicative load, the pictorial content did not simply decay to the level of mere illustration in the postconquest *lienzos* and codices. No matter what the alphabetic register said, people needed to take note of the pictorial register. It is interesting that when forced to confront the somewhat obvious gap between the listing of Mixtec rulers, their marriages, and their offspring on a codex or *lienzo* or other such document, as well as the use of the document as a guarantee of town boundaries, townspeople will sometimes say in court cases that the *caciques* functioned in the past as communal authorities. Such is the case in a 1945 letter from the *comisariado* (agrarian representative) of Yucuquimi to the Chief of the Agrarian Department, in which he explained that although the documents that support the land claims of the town from 1709 and 1756 indicate that the land was the property of *caciques*, these individuals served "as indigenous communal representatives, according to the customs of that time."[1] In the past, *caciques* represented their noble houses, and although they sometimes did aid communities with claims, a *cacique* could not possibly be equated with a more contemporary town mayor or communal overseer. In any event, the pictorial register communicates a history in which the past is distinct from the present to anyone viewing the document.

What changed, then, was the relationship between the alphabetic and pictorial registers. Although the alphabetic register did come to define the meaning of the document for the people reading it after the sixteenth century, it did this because people deployed the alphabetic register to keep their story going. In other words, if these documents are treated as indigenous histories of the social changes taking place around them, then the pictorial is something other than simple illustration. If we view the pages with the town boundaries written on them in the Codex Muro in this light, then their significance lies in their use by local people to make the transformation from noble house to community visible, at least to themselves. From the sixteenth to the seventeenth centuries and perhaps into the eighteenth century, these manuscripts remained part of a noble identity, documenting the ancient pedigree of those who possessed it and the noble houses' rights to their estates. But by taking possession of this codex, a document chronicling the rulers of a sixteenth-century kingdom, and then adding their town boundaries to parts of it, the people of Adeques and the other towns at that time did not so much seek to obliterate the Muro's existence as a royal title covering numerous dependencies in a large area as seek to use it to tell the story of an emerging social order in which possession of land would be guaranteed not by genealogical ties but by the moral ties of community. The region would go from being one of entailed estates to one where independent towns held sway. The alphabetic register enabled people to write themselves into the image so that they could "see" what they had become and, in a sense, place themselves in this heroic history. For good reason, when Arnulfo Pérez and Saturnino Rojas, communal representatives of Cuanachinicha, Guerrero, wrote to the Chief of the Agrarian Department on October 10, 1951, asking that he return the town titles sent to him to verify their land claims, they explained that the documents are "the holy price paid by the many sacrifices by our ancestors and the life and honest work of the present generation."[2]

The significance of the Muro for people in the towns where they resided for so many years lies both in the discursive power it bestowed upon them by its great antiquity and in its indigeneity. Therefore, it could be the vehicle through which people reinscribed themselves as independent communities controlling their own land and destiny. Although no one was producing Mixtec writing anymore, the texts themselves remained vitally relevant to the way indigenous people saw their history unfolding, understood the changes that were taking place around them, and linked themselves to the essential truths first enunciated in the pictographic register.

Notes

1. Registro Agrario Nacional, Oaxaca City, Yucuquimi, 276.1/202.

2. The Spanish reads: "precio sagrada de tanto sufrimieno [*sic*] de nuestros mayores y vida y trabajo honrado de la actual generación." Registro Agrario Nacional, Mexico City, Cuanachinicha 76.1/467.

10

Trends and Transitions in the History of Written Numerals

Stephen Chrisomalis

Scripts and numerical notations are parallel graphic systems that use discrete symbols to represent aspects of culturally conceived realities. They are used in many of the same contexts and very often in the same documents. Virtually every numerical notation system is used alongside one or more scripts. Conversely, the vast majority of scripts are accompanied by one or more numerical notation systems—few scripts require that numerals always be written using phonetic signs. Like scripts, numerical notation systems undergo both paleographic and broader structural changes and may be replaced by competitors.

The history of numeration has traditionally been conceptualized strictly as part of the history of mathematics (e.g., Cajori 1928; Guitel 1975; Menninger 1969 [1958]). This approach has furthered the notion that numerical systems are purely aids to arithmetical computation and, as such, have a progressive evolutionary history that can be explained through the increasing application of reason (Dehaene 1997; Ifrah 1998; Zhang and Norman 1995). Yet, the functions of written numerals are diverse and rarely directly arithmetical. They are domain-specific but nonetheless general-function communicative systems, and their history, like that of scripts, is "disobedient" rather than simple or lawlike (cf. Pettersson 1994). Like writing systems, they are amenable to historical, epigraphic, and archaeological analysis and can be incorporated into broader social and historical approaches within the historical sciences (Crump 1990; Schmandt-Besserat 1992; Steensberg 1989). Yet, in epigraphy and paleography, letter-forms attract considerable attention, whereas numerals remain understudied. This neglect is in no small part due to the unwarranted division of labor between scholars of literacy and numeracy.

Numerical notation systems, like scripts, regularly transform as a result of social and paleographic pressures, to some extent in ways peculiar to the phenomenon. Nowhere is this clearer than in paths of diffusion and adoption—the Latin alphabet descends from Greek, Phoenician, and ultimately Egyptian antecedents, but the Hindu-Arabic numerals (or, as I call them hereafter to avoid confusion, Western numerals)[1] were borrowed through the intermediary of the Islamic world ultimately from an Indian ancestor. The transformation, transmission, adoption, and replacement of numerical notation systems deserve careful attention to clarify the points of both similarity and contrast between these two parallel means of representation. I begin with a discussion of some general principles, then proceed with some extended examples primarily drawn from the Roman and Western numerals, not because they are more important than other systems but because their histories are so much more thoroughly understood.

WHAT IS NUMERICAL NOTATION?

Numerical notation systems are structured but primarily nonphonetic systems of graphic signs for representing numbers. Like scripts, they consist of sets of conventionalized graphemes, but instead of representing sounds, words, or general ideas, they represent numbers. Since 3500 BCE, well over one hundred numerical notation systems have been developed, only a small number of which remain in regular, active use today.

Numerical notation systems are distinguishable from simple tallying systems that use the principle of one-to-one correspondence to notate numbers. As early as the Upper Paleolithic (ca. 40,000–10,000 years ago), prehistoric hunter-foragers notated bone and stone artifacts with sequential tally-marks, producing information storage systems that may have related to hunting, seasonal cycles, or ritual activities (Absolon 1957; d'Errico and Cacho 1994; Marshack 1972). Tallying is thus a very early form of representation, of greater antiquity than either written language or written numeration. A wide range of small-scale and large-scale societies use tallying activities as a means of keeping a cumulative and ongoing record of some quantity, whether counting days since the last full moon or recounting votes in a hotly contested election (Lagercrantz 1968, 1970). Tally systems are sometimes structured through the use of different marks,

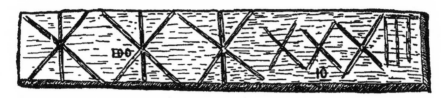

FIGURE 10.1

Samoyed "tally-stick" bearing numerical notation (Montefiore 1895:403).

but they always use one sign for each object, enabling an ongoing and open-ended count to be taken (e.g., IIIN IIN II or HH HH III for 13).

Numerical notation, in contrast, uses the principle of the numerical base (usually but not always decimal) and powers of that base to structure numeral-phrases and is thus conceptually different from tallying. One cannot simply count the marks used, but must understand the different values of various marks and how they combine into meaningful strings. Whereas tallies are notated sequentially as necessary and can be expanded upon as needed, numeral-phrases once written cannot normally be modified in this way—for instance, one cannot simply adjust the Roman numeral LXXVIII by adding signs to the end. Whereas tallies are produced as acts of computation, numerical notation is more broadly representational. It is thus essential not to define tallies in terms of medium. Inka khipu knot-records, once derided for their status as "not-writing," frequently exhibit a decimal, positional numerical notation (Urton 2005). Figure 10.1 depicts a Samoyed "tally-stick" that in reality contains a decimal numeral-phrase for 333 structurally identical to the Roman numeral CCCXXXIII (Montefiore 1895:403). There is a substantial cognitive and functional contrast between sequential markings producing a cumulative record with one mark for each item and base-structured, single-episode numerical notations.

All numerical notation systems follow one of five basic structures to express numbers, depending on how they group numeral-signs within each power of the base (intraexponential notation) and how the different powers of the base are combined (interexponential notation) (Chrisomalis 2004, 2010). Cumulative-additive systems like the Roman or Egyptian hieroglyphic numerals concatenate several numeral-signs together within each power, and then the reader takes the sum of each power. Ciphered-additive systems like the Greek alphabetic numerals use only one sign for each power of the base but are likewise simply the sum of their constituent numeral-signs. Cumulative-positional systems like the Babylonian numerals or Inka khipu concatenate like signs within each power of the base, but each

Principle	Example System	Numeral-phrase for 8357
Cumulative-Additive	Mycenaean (Linear B)	◇-◇-◇-◇ ○○○ ══ ▯▯▯▯ ◇-◇-◇-◇ ══ ▯▯▯ 1000s 100s 10s 1s
Ciphered-Additive	Georgian alphabetic	Ⴞ Ⴍ Ⴆ Ⴟ 8000 300 50 7
Cumulative-Positional	Babylonian	ΤΤ ⟨ΗΗ ⟨ΤΗΗ 2(x3600) 19(x60) 17 (x1)
Ciphered-Positional	Tibetan	⟨ᢌᡕᠵ 8 3 5 7
Multiplicative-Additive	Malayalam	൮ആഩ ൰ഌ ൵ഩ 8 1000 3 100 5 10 7

FIGURE 10.2

Typology of numerical notation systems.

power's signs are multiplied by a place-value indicated by the signs' position within the phrase. Ciphered-positional systems like the modern Arabic and Western numerals have only one sign for each power of the base and also use the principle of place-value. Finally, multiplicative-additive systems use two signs within each power, a unit-sign and a power-sign, and the sum of the products of the various powers gives the total value of the phrase. Examples of these five basic principles are given in figure 10.2. There are several additional complexities in the typology of numerical systems, but all systems ever attested to have been used follow these principles in general outline.

Numerical notation arose very early in the history of representational systems wherever writing emerged independently—at least five and possibly as many as seven times in the development of ancient civilizations. That this has occurred several times independently suggests that there is something fundamental about numbers that recommends itself to the human mind for written representation. That it only occurs in particular types of social context (ancient state societies) suggests, nonetheless, that numerical notation is an emergent phenomenon with functional and social prerequisites.

It has frequently been suggested that administrative and bureaucratic functions were among the first and most important reasons for the rise of writing—hence explaining why numerical notation, with its obvious utility in bookkeeping, would emerge as a precursor to writing (Postgate et al. 1995; Schmandt-Besserat 1992). Yet, this argument is weakened by the fact that the functions of the earliest numerals are as diverse as the functions for early writing—calendrical and onomastic in lowland Mesoamerica, divinatory in China, display and elite iconography in Egypt, accounting records in Mesopotamia (Baines 2004a; Chrisomalis 2009). Although it is possible that numerals served unattested administrative functions in each of these societies prior to the advent of writing, there is no direct evidence to suggest that this was the case. In fact, of the numerous Upper Paleolithic artifacts to which a tallying function has been attributed, none have been interpreted as economic documents, whereas many have been "read" as calendrical "texts" or general mnemonic devices. It is plausible that such notational "tallying" artifacts were conceptually prior to and functionally prerequisite to the development of writing in several different regions and that the first scripts were "word signs bundled with systems of numeration that probably had a different and far more ancient origin" (Houston 2004c:237). This process is still imperfectly understood and requires further evidentiary substantiation, however, and the speculations of Schmandt-Besserat (1992) on the numerical origins of writing have received considerable criticism. Moreover, although much attention has been paid to the Mesopotamian case—where an early administrative function for writing and numeration is incontestable—the development of numerical notation in other regions has been insufficiently studied.

Turning from the diachronic or evolutionary aspects of the relationship to synchronic ones, Houston (2000:148) notes that in both the Classic Maya hieroglyphic and Mesopotamian cuneiform inscriptions, writing and numbering were conceptualized as two distinct activities. Yet, in a wide variety of languages, including many Mayan languages, the verbs "to count" and "to read" are identical, suggesting that the conceptual link between the two activities may sometimes be close (Brown 1991; Monaghan, chapter 9, this volume). Literate individuals are not necessarily aware of the historical separation of the two representational systems, and a conceptual distinction between the two domains may not have much practical effect. Although Throop (2004) argues that the Oriental connotations of the Western numerals initially hindered their aesthetic and conceptual integration into early modern typographic practices, this is hardly the case with the Western numerals today. Numerals are ubiquitous in virtually any sort of text, and the choice to employ lexical number words or nonlexical numerical notation is not a simple one, as anyone who has ever had to edit a text to conform to a style manual knows. And, of course, numerals also play a major role in the graphic and organizational arrangement of texts, from the mighty chapter heading to the humble footnote.[2]

One of the more significant recent developments in the typology of scripts is Houston's (2004b) distinction between "open" and "closed" writing systems, the former serving the needs of diverse languages and cultures, the latter serving one culture, usually in a much more linguistically specific manner. This conceptualization avoids tired debates over evolutionary sequences of pictography leading to phonography, at the same time acknowledging that the utility of representational systems lies in their ability to serve various communicative strategies (Houston 2004b:279). Yet, when applied to numerical notation systems, the open versus closed distinction needs some refinement.

Numerical notation systems share with open writing systems the characteristic of using phonography to a limited degree in comparison with closed writing systems. Open writing systems such as those of central Mexico are nonetheless embedded in cultural codes and worldviews that prevent those unfamiliar with them from readily interpreting them. Modern open pictographic systems such as the ISO 3864 standard for safety symbols (toxic, biohazard, radioactive, and so on) or the Western symbolic system for musical notation are, likewise, conventionalized but opaque to the non-initiated. Deciphering such systems in the absence of cultural context would be extraordinarily difficult. Yet, in contrast to open systems but in common with closed systems, numerical notation systems require limited knowledge of culturally specific conventions or practices underlying particular representations. They express an abstraction (number) that is nonetheless discrete and cross-culturally universal (but see Everett 2005; Hurford 1987). Although one needs to understand the language in which a text is written in order to understand its meaning, one can pronounce a text in a language one cannot understand, as long as the correspondence between graphemes and phonemes is known. These differences are expressed in figure 10.3.

For this reason, it is significantly easier to interpret unknown numerical notation systems than it is to interpret open writing systems such as the central Mexican scripts. It is no coincidence that the first parts of most undeciphered scripts to be understood are the numeral-signs. Numerical notation systems are frequently highly iconic and, moreover, are frequently structured in a way that allows ready interpretation. For instance, when strokes are found in groupings of one to nine but never greater, one can reasonably conclude that the system has a decimal base. This is true even of systems whose signs are not highly iconic strokes or dots. One might well be able to decipher a numbered list in Western numerals even without a substantial knowledge of the meanings of the particular numerical symbols, simply because they are arranged sequentially and because the same signs

Representational system	Cultural conventionality	Phonography
Numerical notation	Limited	Limited
'Closed' writing systems	Limited	High
'Open' writing systems	High	Limited

FIGURE 10.3

Numerals and "open" and "closed" scripts.

(e.g., the "1" in "10...19" and "100...199") are repeated in more leftward positions. In contrast, the central Mexican scripts make sense only in terms of conventional meanings that, although translinguistic, are not fully transcultural, because they depend on the existence of a shared, learned cultural code (one that remains imperfectly known, although its numerals are readily comprehensible). They cannot be "deciphered" in the same manner as numerical notation.

This is not to say that there are no difficulties in interpreting numerical notation systems. The tremendous controversies concerning the status of the Inka khipu (Urton 2005) and the polyvalence of the proto-cuneiform tablets (Damerow 1996; Nissen et al. 1993) demonstrate that knowing how to read numbers does not necessarily tell us very much about how these systems were used. Even in the hypothetical case of a numbered list, one would need to know the convention that numbers are used to ordinate items in a sequence. Yet, there is a substantial difference between the openness of numerical notation and the openness of open writing systems, and that difference lies at the level of conventionality. Regardless of cultural context, numerical notation systems represent the same basic domain of number and can be translated cross-linguistically and cross-culturally on that basis.

Despite this very significant difference, the integration of numerals within written texts occurs in a wide variety of ways, and it would be an error to separate numeral-signs too radically from other conventional representations, phonetic or otherwise. In morphosyllabic scripts such as the Egyptian and Maya hieroglyphs or Chinese writing, numeral-signs occupy a structured role within the numerical notation system but also can act as phonetic (usually syllabic) signs within the script. For instance, the Classic Maya grapheme for 4 (●●●●), with the phonetic value *ka'an* or *chan*, can also be used homonymically as a rebus meaning "sky" (Macri and Looper 2003:261–263). Likewise, Chinese numerals are used ubiquitously as paronomastic graphs for their homonyms. This is not radically different from modern homonymic formations in English such as *K-9* for "canine" or, if one prefers the Roman numerals, the name of the band *Boyz II Men*. As Steinke (chapter 6, this volume) notes in the case of Bronze Age China, rebus-like transformations such as these do not imply an evolutionary typological change, even where widespread; they can be both playful and practical without being teleological.

The integration of numeral and script can alternatively be graphemic rather than phonetic. Bodel (2001:25) draws attention to an inscription describing the life and offices of one MaXXimus, in which XX is a visual pun meant to be read graphically but also to convey the numerical value of twenty. The modern hacker argot pronounced /li:t/, written as "leet," "l33t," or "1337," uses graphic similarities between letters and numerals, punctuation, or auxiliary characters to create a hierarchy of increasingly arcane graphic registers whose command marks their users as being "leet," or elite (Perea et al. 2008).[3] Leet graphical formations have moved into the mainstream, as in the title of the popular television show *Numb3rs*, and are also ubiquitous in junk emails, where they serve the practical function of eluding junk mail or spam filters. I know of no integration of writing and numeration more complex and fascinating than the (non-leet) graphic, phonetic, and semantic intricacies of the title of David Fincher's 1995 movie, *Se7en*.

Written numerals are partly independent from scripts but integrate with them in many respects and always have done so. Because numerical notation systems differ structurally from scripts, it is worth treating their typology separately from that of scripts. Moreover, because they are translinguistic, they can diffuse in different ways than scripts, particularly in relation to economic and political changes. Yet, the evidence for the conceptual integration of the two representations is so overwhelming as to demand that numerals be considered as a form of writing rather than as a form of written mathematics.

TRANSFORMATION AND INNOVATION

Because numerical notation is radically translinguistic and radically open, its diachronic patterns of transformation and intercultural transmission and adoption differ significantly from the ways in which both open and closed writing systems change and diffuse. These differences can best be understood by examining some instances of transformations in numerical systems in response to changing social context. Radical transformations in numerical notation systems—even when they are borrowed by highly different societies—are relatively rare, yet less drastic alterations are much more common.

Over the past 5,500 years, a numerical notation system using one of the five basic principles described above is known to have given rise to one that used a different principle only twenty-three times (Chrisomalis 2010: 381–383). Nevertheless, there is a general but multilinear trend observable: positional systems rarely if ever give rise to additive descendants, and ciphered systems rarely give rise to cumulative descendants. Why this should be is complex and beyond the scope of this chapter. Numerical notation systems are generally highly resistant to change and in some cases persisted for several millennia with virtually no structural or paleographic transformation. The Egyptian hieroglyphic numerals of the predynastic period (Dreyer 1998) would have been comprehensible to any Roman-period user of the hieroglyphs 3,500 years later.

Yet, numerical systems, like scripts, do undergo transformations of various sorts. Some of these reflect largely unintentional and unexplainable paleographic drift of the kind that Salomon (chapter 5, this volume) suggests is ubiquitous in scripts. Many graphemic changes, however, are best understood as the product of intentional action, for example, to distinguish a sign from graphically similar numerical or phonetic signs—the use of 7 with a horizontal stroke across the diagonal to distinguish it from 1 or the use of a 0 with a diagonal bar to distinguish it from the letter *O*. Other paleographic changes served the exact opposite function, however, acting to obscure rather than clarify. Figure 10.4 shows some highly unusual fifteenth- and sixteenth-century numerical expressions identified by Jenkinson (1926) from British archives. These are in fact Roman numerals—the bottom right one is 47, and the other three are 147—highly modified and extremely arcane, even to trained paleographers. Similarly, the *siyaq* signs used in Ottoman and later Persian accounting are reductions of the corresponding Arabic numeral-words, stripped of their phonetic association and thereby made opaque (Bagheri 1998).

The process of "cursivization" in graphemic systems is only beginning to be theorized by scholars but generally involves alterations to sign-forms that facilitate rapid writing, often on perishable media and using writing tools that encourage flowing and ligatured words and phrases. Numerical notation is no exception to this general tendency, as shown in several examples in figure 10.5. The Brāhmī numeral-signs for 1 through 3, originally horizontal unit-strokes, became ligatured over time into the distant lineal ancestors of the signs 1, 2, and 3. The Aramaic system has a special sign for 20, which in the eighth through sixth centuries BCE was composed of two

FIGURE 10.4

Roman numerals from the fifteenth and sixteenth centuries in British archives (Jenkinson 1926:273, Figure 10).

parallel horizontal strokes for 10, each with a rightward tail. Over a period of centuries, the top and bottom strokes became ligatured at the right side by means of this tail, resulting in a single sign for 20 that was then used in Aramaic and all its descendant notations in the Near East and Central Asia.[4]

Cursivization is not necessarily a matter of minor transformations, however, but can act as a precursor to dramatic, systemwide, structural changes to the basic principles of numerical notation. The well-known Egyptian hieroglyphic numerals, best known through their use in monumental inscriptions, are cumulative-additive, but the cursive hieratic numerals are ciphered-additive. Möller (1909–1927) and Goedicke (1988) describe in great detail the paleographic reduction of sets of cumulative hieroglyphic signs to single graphemes over several centuries throughout the Old Kingdom. In most cases it would be virtually impossible to reconstruct the original cumulative grouping of hieroglyphic signs from its Middle Kingdom or New Kingdom hieratic descendant. Yet, cursivization does not inherently require structural changes in numerical systems; as Baines

Aramaic (8th–6th c. BCE)	⟶ (10) + ⟶ (10) → ⇒ (20) → ⟍⟋
Hieratic (25th–12th c. BCE)	⦙⦙⦙ (6) → 𖤐 → 𖤐 → 𝑙
Demotic–Greek (6th c. BCE)	⋜ (6) → Greek alphabetic Ϝ
Roman (5th–6th c. CE)	vi (6) → Ϙ or Ϲ

FIGURE 10.5

Cursivization and alphabetization.

(chapter 2, this volume) notes, alongside the hieroglyphic and hieratic scripts were the cursive hieroglyphs, used more formally than hieratic but on media and in contexts where the more regular and linear hieroglyphs were not demanded by the principles of decorum governing that genre. Indeed, the cursive hieroglyphic numerals are cumulative, not ciphered, and can be linked readily to the ordinary (monumental) figures. A somewhat similar instance of cursivization in numerical notation systems is that of the poorly known Pahlavi numerals used for writing Middle Persian in the first millennium CE. Their origins lay in the gradual reduction of the cumulative-additive signs of the earlier Sasanian script into single ciphered figures, particularly for the tens. I thus disagree with Salomon (chapter 5, this volume), who makes a strong distinction between gradual paleographic change and abrupt or radical structural transformations. At least for numerical notation, if not for scripts, one can lead to the other.

Numerals and phonetic scripts are further interlinked through the existence of alphabetic numerical systems, which assign numerical values to the set of graphemes of a script in a specified order.[5] The earliest and best-known case is that of the Greek alphabetic (Ionian) numerals. The Greek alphabet had developed distinctly from its Phoenician ancestor since at least the eighth century BCE and possibly earlier, with a specified and largely Semitic-derived ordering of the letters, as attested in abecedaries (McCarter 1975; Swiggers 1996). Yet, this order was not numerical—at the very most, the signs were assigned ordinal numerical values in order, starting with A = 1, but without any further structure. In the first quarter of the sixth century BCE, Ionian traders along the western coast of Asia Minor assigned numerical values to the letters in a very different manner, with signs for 1–9, 10–90, and 100–900 in an ordinary ciphered-additive structure (Jeffery 1990; Johnston 1979). This notation derived from the demotic ciphered-additive numerical tradition employed widely in Egypt at that time, a system that would certainly have been known to the

Ionians through their emporion (trading port) at Naukratis in the western Nile delta (Chrisomalis 2003). The demotic numerals (like their hieratic ancestor) were decimal and ciphered-additive, but they were also abstract and were not otherwise signs used in phonetic Egyptian writing. The Ionians therefore integrated the Semitic principle of alphabetical ordering with the Egyptian principle of ciphered numbering, thereby obviating the need for learners to master dozens of additional number signs and providing a new function for alphabetic order. Gamkrelidze (1994) and Psychoyos (2005), in turn, have discussed the effect that alphabetic numeration has had on various scripts. Because alphabetic numeral signs in a decimal system require twenty-seven signs to write numbers as high as 999 and thirty-six signs to write numbers as high as 9,999, letter-forms that otherwise served no or limited phonetic functions were often preserved in alphabets in order to fill out the complement of signs adequately.

A slightly different example of the "alphabetization" of numerical systems comes from the Roman numerals, which originated as inverted or halved variants of the Etruscan numerals, which themselves were probably related to older and as yet unattested tallying marks (Keyser 1988).[6] The changes made to the Etruscan signs may well reflect the growing Roman desire to express its political and cultural independence among the polities of the Italian peninsula (Bodel, chapter 3, this volume). Once developed, the Roman numerals underwent further change throughout the late Republican and Imperial periods, taking the form of the alphabetic signs that they most closely resembled. For instance, L = 50 began as ↓ and later ⊥ before assuming its final form in the Augustan period (Gordon and Gordon 1957:181); similarly, D = 500 was originally Ð before being reinterpreted as a letter, possibly under the acrophonic folk etymology *demimille*. C = 100 was originally Ɔ in Etruscan numerals before being flipped along the vertical axis, so the graphic form preceded its association with *centum*. M = 1,000 remained vanishingly rare and was nonstandard prior to the late medieval era, but eventually it too underwent the process of alphabetic reinterpretation (Gordon 1983:45).

By late antiquity in Spain and North Africa, the Roman numerals were sometimes written cursively to distinguish the numerical signs from the corresponding letters (Mallon 1948; Salama 1999). The late antique Roman numerals, especially in the Eastern Empire and in Spain, utilized a special sign for 6, a cursive reduction of VI into a single unit that is not readily decomposed into its constituent elements.[7] Although originating in the cursive tradition of Roman writing on papyrus in Egypt, the use of cursive Roman numerals eventually became ensconced in the monumental writing

FIGURE 10.6

Latin inscription with cursive Roman numeral for 556 (end of line 5) (Mallon 1948:Plate I).

tradition of early medieval Spain. Figure 10.6 shows an inscription found in Extremadura, Spain, that dates to 518 CE. At the end of line 5, the number 556 is written with a cursive D, a cursive L, and the sign for 6 and is thus hardly recognizable as a Roman numeral at all; the numerical D and L contrast with the alphabetic signs elsewhere in the inscription (Mallon 1948:Plate I).

Thus, the writing of 6 as six unit-strokes in the Egyptian hieroglyphs was cursively reduced to a single ciphered abstract symbol in hieratic and demotic numeration, which then became an alphabetic sign in Greek. The Greek alphabet gave rise to the Etruscan and Roman alphabets, and the originally abstract numerals of these scripts became reconstrued as letter-forms over time, first in a lapidary script but later in cursive script on papyrus. Finally, this cursivized script tradition led to the transformation of VI (6) once again into a single cursive cipher, which then re-entered the monumental tradition to distinguish letter-forms from numerals. This complex series of paleographic changes is rendered sensible only through knowledge of the design principles of both monumental and cursive texts, the social contexts of cultural transmission, and the interactions between written language and written number.

A situationally specific source of paleographic change in the Western numerals involved a set of rotations resulting from the fact that the numerical signs were used on medieval counting-boards. In the late tenth century

CE, Gerbert of Aurillac (later Pope Sylvester II) advocated the use of Western numerals in Europe on the "abacus with apices" after he was exposed in Toledo to Arabic arithmetic using positional numerals (Burnett 2002:241; Lemay 1977). The apices were small round tokens on which a Western numeral was written, used on a board (abacus) by moving the tokens around to perform arithmetic. In the twelfth and thirteenth centuries, the users of this system, known as abacists, engaged in a lengthy intellectual and social debate with algorithmists, advocates of pen-and-paper arithmetic using Arabic-derived computational techniques (Evans 1977; Gibson and Newton 1995; Lemay 1977).[8] Although the algorithmists eventually "won" this debate in the sense that pen-and-paper arithmetic became the standard means of using Western numerals to compute, several of the signs underwent rotational paleographic change because the apices, as tokens, could be rotated in any orientation (Beaujouan 1947). The numeral-forms became "fixed" orientationally only after the broader debate over computational technique had been settled. This unusual case highlights the importance of technology and media in transforming representational systems.

Aside from paleographic changes, various major and minor structural changes occur within numerical notation systems. One of the key constraints governing numerals is the conciseness of numeral-phrases. Changes to systemic structure that result in shorter numeral-phrases are far more common than ones resulting in longer numeral-phrases. Ciphered systems are more concise than cumulative ones for most numbers (e.g., 322 instead of CCCXXII), but not universally so (2,000 versus MM). One structural change that can increase conciseness considerably in a cumulative system is the use of subtractive notation (e.g., MCMXCIX instead of MDCCCCLXXXXVIIII for 1999). This form of notation originated in late Republican Rome but was never the rule in classical inscriptions, most often used when space was a consideration in writing an inscription (Gordon and Gordon 1957:176–181). To this day, however, because of aesthetic considerations related to symmetry, 4 is written as IIII on Roman-numeral clock faces, although 9 is always IX (Hering 1939:319). A similar notation was used in some Mesopotamian numeral-phrases, whereby 19 was written as 20 – 1 using a subtractive logogram, LAL, as early as 2650 BCE in the archaic Sumerian tablets from Fara, a practice that continued at least to the end of the Old Babylonian period a millennium later (Jestin 1937:Plate LXXXIV; Thureau-Dangin 1939:106).

Other transformations in numerical systems relate to increasing the maximum number expressible in a system without the need to develop a wealth of new symbols. The most common way of doing so was to introduce a multiplier-sign for a particular power of the base, turning a purely cumulative or ciphered system into a partly multiplicative-additive one for the higher exponents of the base. For instance, decimal ciphered-additive systems like the Greek alphabetic numerals require nine signs for each power of ten, and in alphabetic systems in which the set of characters is inherently limited by the sign-count of the script, writing high numbers requires the adoption of such techniques. The original Greek alphabetic system only expressed the numbers 1 through 999 using the twenty-four Greek letters plus three episemons (archaic or unused letters from the alphabet's Phoenician heritage). During the fifth century BCE, however, a *hasta* (a small diagonal line usually to the left and below a numeral) could be added to indicate that the numeral's value should be multiplied by 1,000 (Threatte 1980:115). Cumulative systems also sometimes employ the multiplicative principle for high powers. The Roman numerals of the Republican period had distinct signs for each power of ten up to 100,000 (and each half-power of ten up to 50,000). Starting in the first century BCE, a horizontal bar (*vinculum*) added above a numeral indicated that its value should be multiplied by 1,000, and shortly thereafter, enclosing a numeral in a box on both sides and on the top indicated multiplication by 100,000 (Cagnat 1964:31–32; Gordon 1983). Ciphered-positional systems like the Western numerals are, of course, infinitely extendable without the need to develop new signs.

However, even though these changes are understandable in terms of the structures of the systems being modified and the motivations of writers in using them, they are never predictable and usually complex. Every transformation of a numerical system comes with some sort of cognitive cost. For instance, the use of subtraction, though increasing conciseness, may decrease the legibility of the resulting numeral phrase; 444 as CDXLIV is not as intuitive as CCCCXXXXIIII. The addition of new techniques such as multiplicative signs similarly makes the resultant numeral trickier to learn and read. Moreover, the assumption that increased conciseness is always valued, even if it is generally so, is untested and in some cases untrue. The *Columna rostrata* erected in Rome in 260 BCE in honor of the consul Gaius Duilius to celebrate his naval victory over Carthage, and later restored in the early Imperial period, contained at least twenty-two Roman numeral-signs for 100,000 to indicate an amount of more than two million *aes* of loot taken (Menninger 1969 [1958]:43–44). As can be seen in figure 10.7, the intent can only have been to impress viewers with the size of the booty—a sort of conspicuous calculation. Numerals do not serve only to compute or

FIGURE 10.7

Columna rostrata *with repeated Roman numeral signs for 100,000 (Sandys 1919:96).*

even simply to communicate numbers according to rational criteria; aspects of aesthetics and display play major roles in the choice of a particular numerical representation.

REPLACEMENT OF NUMERICAL SYSTEMS

The outright or partial replacement of numerical notation systems has been relatively common—at least, substantially more common than the development of new, structurally radically distinct numerical notation systems out of older ones. Of well over one hundred numerical notation systems ever used, only a few (Western, Arabic, Chinese, Devanāgarī, and a few other South Asian systems) are used frequently today, and several others (such as Roman numerals or Hebrew alphabetic numerals) are used only vestigially. As with the transformation of systems, positional systems are not replaced by additive systems, and ciphered systems are not replaced by cumulative systems, except in extremely rare cases (Chrisomalis 2004). The overlap of patterns of transformation and replacement produces a substantial trend towards ciphered and positional systems over time.

When one asks adults in Western societies, "Why don't we use Roman numerals any longer?" among those who have any answer whatsoever, most invoke computational efficiency, answering something like, "Have you ever tried to multiply with those things?" or a similar answer based on the perceived cumbersomeness of the system. Most North American children learn Roman numerals relatively early in their mathematical education, when they are confronted with artificial arithmetical problems such as DCLXV ÷ XXV, which they are then expected to solve (presumably, in these cases, simply by translating them into Western numerals first, doing the arithmetic, and then translating back to Roman numerals). The assumption that there is a direct functional explanation for the retention, alteration, or abandonment of numerical notation systems is very widespread in the scholarly literature on numeration (Dehaene 1997; Ifrah 1998; Nickerson 1988; Zhang and Norman 1995). This notion reflects a pervasive unilinear evolutionary bias on the part of such authors. If the history of scripts remains stuck in a quagmire of unilinear evolutionism, then the history of numerical notation is up to its neck and sinking fast.

Of course, the Romans did not do written arithmetic as modern North Americans do, nor in fact did they do much written arithmetic at all. Instead, they relied on a variety of techniques, of which the pebble-board abacus was the most common, along with finger arithmetic and mental computation (Keyser 1988; Taisbak 1965; but see Maher and Makowski 2001). There exist no known Roman texts with anything like our pen-and-paper arithmetic, nor, indeed, anything else involving the direct manipulation of written numeral-signs. This is true of most numerical notation systems that have ever been used. It is highly ethnocentric to assume that the functions for which we currently use numerals are the primary criteria on which we should judge the efficiency of all numerical notations. The only legitimate way to use the concept of efficiency of a numerical system is to ask for what purposes it was used and in what contexts. The notion that the Roman numerals were an inherently inferior numerical notation system is soundly refuted by their survival, essentially unchanged, for more than two millennia of constant use and an enormous variety of functions. The fact that they were never used for arithmetic further supports the conclusion that unilinear progressivism has no place in the history of numeration. Yet, the Roman numerals were replaced, as were many other systems worldwide—a fact that demands an explanation.

Despite the debate between the abacists and algorithmists described earlier, most scribes, merchants, and even many theologians and mathematicians in western Europe continued to use Roman numerals for most everyday functions for centuries after the introduction of Western numerals. In certain contexts, the use of the new notation was forbidden, as in the edict of 1299 of the Arte del Cambio (moneychangers' guild) of Florence (Struik 1968). The late sixteenth-century English Lord High Treasurer William Cecil (Lord Burghley) would frequently transcribe Hindu-Arabic into Roman numerals to work with them, being rather uncomfortable with the former (Stone 1949:31). In some extreme cases, as in the tally-records kept by the English Parliament until 1724 (their burning in 1834 caused the destruction of the parliament building) or the Roman numerals used by Swiss peasants in the early twentieth century, their replacement by Western numerals was very long in coming (Baxter 1989:82; Gmür 1917).

Our knowledge of the chronology of the replacement of Roman numerals can hardly be better—a wide variety of multiyear records simply switch from one to the other system at a given date, and the dates in books' front matter provide a reliable framework for evaluating the decline of Roman numerals over several centuries. By and large, books began to be paginated and dated using Western numerals between 1475 and 1550, in the first decades after the invention of movable-type printing. In Portuguese manuscripts and printed books, this transition largely occurred between 1490 and 1510 (Barrados de Carvalho 1957:125), yet for general use, it did not take place until at least a century later (de Oliveira Marques 1996). Wardley and White's (2003) study of probate inventories similarly indicates that the transition for many scribes occurred as late as 1600–1630 in most of England. Although no study has been undertaken of the dating of gravestones, this would provide additional information on the transition. Despite this descriptive work, no systematic study has yet attempted to explain the process by which Western numerals replaced Roman numerals, leaving us the unenviable choice between an explanation based solely on a comparison of the two systems' structures and no explanation at all.

The introduction of Western numerals brought about effects other than the narrow choice of one or the other system. Around 1130, the mathematician Ocreatus described a system using the Roman numeral-phrases for 1 through 9 (I, II, ... IX) in various positions, as well as a zero-sign (O or t), which he called *teca* or *tsiphra*, to indicate an empty position (Murray 1978:167; Smith and Karpinski 1911:55). Positions were separated by a dot to avoid confusion. Thus, 1,089 was expressed as I.O.VIII.IX. This case, as well as the use of hybrid numerals such as "xxx3" and "xl7" in Durandus of

Saint-Pourçain's *Commentary on the Sentences of Peter Lombard* (1336), do not seem to reflect a real misunderstanding of the system and were probably playful in origin (Preston 1994). Certainly playful are the hybrid notations used for a time by the late eighteenth-century French horologer Jean-Antoine Lépine, who created several timepieces whose hours were marked with odd mixtures of Roman and Western numerals—for instance, V3 for 8 or X2 for 12 (Chapiro 1988). Being neither errors nor systematically new notations, such sporadic modifications emphasize that questions of efficiency and function are not always the right ones to ask when considering the shape of script.

Despite these developments, by around 1600 the Roman numerals were less common than Western numerals throughout western Europe and became increasingly uncommon in the four succeeding centuries. The precise explanation of this change is, however, far less clear. If Roman numerals were so inefficient for the functions for which they were used, why would they have been retained for so many centuries? And if they were not, why would they be replaced at all? The ascendance of Western numerals in the sixteenth and seventeenth centuries relates directly to a set of interrelated sociohistorical factors, not primarily structural considerations. These factors may include the following:

(a) The development of printed books and the consequent spread of literacy to previously nonliterate social classes and regions. This change had the effect of producing new readers who were not bound by custom to the Roman numerals. The first book paginated using Western numerals was Chrysostomus' *Homiliae*, printed in Rome in 1470 (McPharlin 1942:20–21). The transition occurred quite rapidly in printed Bibles in Protestant regions (Williams 1997) starting in the mid-sixteenth century and was slightly slower in Catholic ones.

(b) The expansion of the practice of dating coins by calendar year in western European mints. This practice, which became widespread in the late fifteenth century, could not have been initiated effectively by using Roman numerals, given the length of Roman numeral-phrases for the numbers 1400 to 1500. J. Williams (1995) argues persuasively that the difficulty in working with fractional values using Roman numerals made it highly useful for coin minters to adopt Western numerals, because of the complexity of the calculations involved. The first English coins dated using Western numerals were those of "Henric 8" (Henry VIII), dating to 1526–1544 (Wardley and White 2003:15–16).

(c) The rise of mercantilism and early capitalism, starting in Italy in the late thirteenth century and developing (albeit at different rates) through the sixteenth and seventeenth centuries. One of the definite advantages of pen-and-paper arithmetic is that it preserves the intermediate steps of calculations, and this advantage cannot have been lost on guildmasters, merchants, and bookkeepers (Crosby 1997).

(d) The rise of mathematics education outside theological instruction, first through series of printed books such as Robert Record's *The grounde of artes* (1543), as well as through formal tutoring. Although the earliest such programs of instruction taught both counting-board and written computation, the use of written numerals rapidly superseded the former.

The Roman numerals, of course, are retained today for two general purposes. First, when writing numbers meant to convey a sense of age or an air of prestige—as when numbering monarchs, popes, or Super Bowls—Roman numerals are generally preferred. Burge (1994) has shown that Cornish church sundials dating from 1670 to 1850 systematically used Roman numerals even though they were no longer current in ordinary texts. Even today, diplomas and cornerstones on prestigious buildings tend to contain Roman numeral dates. Note, however, that in the Henric 8 coin just mentioned, the Western numerals were deployed for this prestigious purpose. There has been a complete status inversion—once esteemed for their novelty, Western numerals are now perceived as mundane, and the Roman numerals are now praised for their antiquity.

Second, and more importantly, a secondary numerical notation system is highly useful when one wishes to distinguish two separate enumerated lists or to enumerate subsections of a list. Thus, it remains commonplace that the prefatory material of a book is paginated in Roman numerals to distinguish it from the body of the book and that acts of plays are notated in Roman numerals and scenes are enumerated using Western numerals. Although academics for more than a century have decried the use of Roman numerals (e.g., Cohen 2007; Yerkes 1904) on the basis that they are cumbersome and lead to errors, there seems little likelihood that any such inconvenience will override the tremendous utility of having a second set of numerals available when needed.

Far from being an exceptional circumstance, the use of multiple numerical notation systems simultaneously is well attested cross-culturally. The Greek acrophonic and alphabetic numerals coexisted for several centuries in Athens (ca. 400–50 BCE) and for shorter periods of time elsewhere in the Hellenistic world. Both systems were used on a variety of media and text genres but were used exclusively in texts written in the Greek alphabet—in fact, both used Greek letters, albeit in radically different ways, to represent numbers. Although originally the acrophonic numerals were primarily an Athenian system and the alphabetic numerals were primarily Ionian, this regional/ethnic distinction had lost any significance by 400 BCE (Johnston 1979; Threatte 1980). Conversely, the Egyptian hieroglyphic and hieratic scripts each used structurally quite dissimilar numerical notation systems, which appeared on radically different media and text genres, even though an individual scribe learned both scripts and both numerical systems.

Perhaps the best example of what Berggren called "a promiscuous blend of systems" (2002:358) was found in medieval Spain, where no fewer than six numerical notation systems were used simultaneously. The Roman numerals were, of course, employed in various administrative and literary contexts just as in the rest of western Europe. In Arabic-influenced and Arabic-speaking areas, the Arabic *abjad* (consonantal) numerals, the Arabic positional numerals, and the western Arabic Maghribi variant (essentially identical to Western numerals) were all employed. The Fez numerals (*al-qalam al-fāsī*) were a semi-alphabetic system developed by the Mozarabs (Arab Christians) of Toledo in the twelfth century; they were used cryptographically and in legal documents (Guergour 1997). Finally, a set of unusual Arabico-Hispanic variants of the Roman numerals were sometimes employed (Labarta and Barceló 1988).

Transitional periods during which one numerical notation is phased out and another adopted are sometimes characterized by hybrid notations, usually short-lived and not extremely widespread. These systems can nonetheless shed light on the process by which new notations are borrowed and accepted by individual users in particular social contexts. When the ciphered-additive Brāhmī numeration transformed into a ciphered-positional system with a zero-sign between the sixth and ninth centuries CE, several copperplate inscriptions contained numerals that fused the characteristics of both systems; for instance, "100 3 7" rather than "137" or "100 30 7" (Acharya 1993; Mukherjee 1993; cf. Salomon 1998:62–63). Perhaps some writers were only partly familiar with the new system, or perhaps the hybrid notation was used to clarify for readers as yet unfamiliar with positional numbering.

The complexity of these situations is not unusual. The social analysis of biscriptal individuals and groups may serve as a partial guideline to explaining the retention of secondary or archaic numerical notations (C. King 1994; Scribner and Cole 1981; Sebba 2009). However, because numerical notation systems are relatively easy to learn and because, thanks to their nonphonetic nature, they are not attached to a particular set of number words in a particular language, retaining multiple such systems is far more common than the use of multiple scripts. As with most technical innovations, including scripts and numerical notations, a situation in which two systems are used simultaneously can lead to the outright replacement of one of the systems or more often to the gradual assumption by one system of more and more functions. These processes can only be understood socially, in terms of the relationships between the various users of the two systems, rather than strictly in terms of the structures of the systems themselves. The replacement of the Roman numerals in early modern Europe demonstrates just how complex this process can be. But is it a special case, or part of a larger pattern?

MODERN TRANSFORMATIONS AND EXTINCTIONS

Between 3500 BCE and 1400 CE, the number of numerical notations in use worldwide at any given time increased gradually; between 1450 and 1750, however, nearly half of the world's numerical notation systems ceased to be regularly used for most purposes (Chrisomalis 2010:423).[9] Some of these episodes of replacement, such as the extinction of the Maya bar-and-dot numerals and the general abandonment of the Inka khipu, were directly related to the Spanish conquests and subsequent suppression of local representational systems. Yet, they also include instances such as the replacement of Church Slavonic, Georgian, and Armenian alphabetic numerals by the Western numerals in circumstances in which the local polities remained independent and, more interestingly, the local scripts continued to flourish. A perspective that treats the replacement of numerical notation systems solely in terms of military conquest is therefore insufficient.

A better understanding of these changes can be acquired using world-systems theory. The increasing ubiquity of Western numerals was intertwined with western European economic and political hegemony starting in the fifteenth century (Wallerstein 1974). In the framework used by the evolutionary theorists Boyd and Richerson (1985), a frequency-dependent bias in cultural transmission occurs when individuals are more likely to accept a cultural variant that is already used by many individuals, whereas a prestige bias occurs when a variant is accepted thanks to the high status of its current users. Because numerical systems, like scripts, are primarily communication systems, it may be expected that both of these biases play a major role in their adoption, regardless of the perceived efficiencies and inefficiencies of such systems. All other factors being equal, it is to the advantage of a script adopter (or numeral adopter) to communicate with as many and as prestigious individuals as possible. In the modern world system, those individuals are the wealthier members of core societies, particularly those who interact in the spheres of international economics and intellectual activities.

Yet, because scripts are well suited to represent specific languages and poorly suited to represent other ones whereas numerical notation is translinguistic, replacing a numerical notation system is far simpler than replacing a script. Even where there are discordances between the verbal numerals of a language and its number symbols, this poses no great difficulty. German speakers have no difficulty reading 347 as *dreihundertsieben-undvierzig* and not *dreihundertvierzigundsieben*, despite the lexical inversion of the tens and units. Moreover, changes in number word systems are directly connected to economic and institutional changes, such as the introduction of new currencies and new metrological standards (Crump 1978). The Western numerals thus enjoyed a considerable advantage over local numerals that had virtually nothing to do with their efficiency for representation or computation, or indeed any structural feature whatsoever. Scripts have no such correlative features that would encourage a shift (aside from language death). The greater propensity for numerical systems to be transmitted and adopted, eventually replacing older local systems, is best explained by their translinguistic nature and usefulness in commerce. Of course, communicating with the core of the world system was not the only motive prompting the replacement or retention of numerical notation systems (or scripts). In fact, the replacement of the traditional numerical notations of eastern Europe, the Caucasus, and the Middle East was only partial and remains so, because of the retention of these systems in limited contexts, particularly religious ones (Gamkrelidze 1994).

By the nineteenth and twentieth centuries, a number of previously nonliterate, non-Western societies developed scripts, having newly become aware of one or more existing scripts or feeling for the first time an imperative to emulate existing scripts. These developments were the latest in a long history of peripheral peoples emulating imperial powers—for example, the development of the runic script on the basis of a Roman (or possibly North Italic) antecedent (Williams 2004). Many of these scripts never developed distinct numerical notations, instead using Western numerals—the well-known script developed by the Vai of Liberia is one such example. The Cherokee script developed by Sequoyah (George Gist) in the early nineteenth century has enjoyed considerable success and today is taught at various levels of education (Holmes and Smith 1977; Walker and Sarbaugh 1993). Yet, although Sequoyah developed a set of numerals to accompany his script, the Cherokee tribal council rejected them in favor of the

Western numerals. The numerals are unknown today except as a curiosity, but one can purchase a Cherokee numeral clock should one so desire.

Nevertheless, many colonially inscribed societies, such as the Pahawh Hmong of Laos (Smalley et al. 1990), the Mende of Sierra Leone (Tuchscherer 1996), and the Varang Kshiti of Bihar, India (Pinnow 1972), did create numerical notations to accompany their indigenously developed scripts. These systems (like the Cherokee numerals) are structurally distinct from any of their possible cultural influences (the positional Arabic, Western, or Indian numerals). Interestingly, several of these "descendants" of positional systems are additive and thus constitute exceptions to the general historical trend towards positionality. It remains to be seen whether these systems will be successful; all of them (as well as the corresponding scripts) are at risk of obsolescence in competition with more widely used and state-supported representational systems.

By no means are newly developed numerical notation systems limited to indigenous or colonial contexts. Hexadecimal (base-16) positional numerals, which are ubiquitous in computing and electronics functions, use the letters A through F to represent 10 through 15, respectively (yet another instance of the interaction of phonetic scripts and numerical notation). This system was developed for computing purposes and promoted widely through the conversion tables published by Carl-Erik Fröberg (1952) to facilitate human interaction with binary computers.[10] Hexadeci-mal notation represents a sensible compromise between the constraints of electronic technology, in which circuits are necessarily binary, and the cognitive limitations of the mind, which cannot easily manipulate long strings of binary numbers. Mathematical reformers have proposed a wide range of alternative numeration systems to Western numerals, most famously duo-decimal (base-12; Andrews 1935) but also binary-decimal (Harris 1905) and base-32 (Yajnik 1998). Because these reformers focus on simplifying arithmetic, they fall prey to the functionalist fallacy that numerals exist primarily to facilitate computation. It is thus unsurprising that these efforts have met with little success. More fanciful but no less interesting are the numerical notations invented by the science fiction writer Frederik Pohl (1966) and the strikingly bizarre notation developed by the industrial engineer Luigi Serafini in his surrealist alien encyclopedia, the *Codex Seraphinianus* (1981), written in an artificial and intentionally undecipherable script. Yet, the numerals of the codex can be securely "deciphered," even though their structure is bizarrely unlike any existing numerical system, by both tracing the progression of the pagination and examining the resulting patterns of signs. I do not regard this decipherability to be solely a result of authorial intent, but rather a consequence of the structured, ordered, and decontextualized nature of numerical systems in comparison with scripts.

It is possible that the recent florescence of new, local, and special-purpose numerical notations in Western and non-Western contexts alike—despite the increasing prevalence of Western numerals for most ordinary functions—reflects the values of an era obsessed with quantification. Yet, it is equally possible that short-lived offshoots of well-known numerical notation systems have been invented more frequently in the past than traditionally believed and that because of the vagaries of preservation, many notations have simply not survived to be studied. The Armenian variant numerals developed in the seventh century by the astronomer-mathematician Anania Shirakatsi (Shaw 1938–1939) and the unusual hybrid decimal positional system used in a few cuneiform inscriptions from Mari in the eighteenth century BCE (Durand 1987) are short-lived and sporadic notations for which only a smattering of evidence has survived to attest to their inventors' numerical creativity. Radical transformations of numerical notations may be relatively easy to conceive and develop but unlikely to be adopted widely; it is in adoption rather than invention that new systems survive or fail. This constraint might also have implications for the patterns observed in the history of scripts.

The fact that positional and ciphered systems (and particularly ciphered-positional systems, which combine these two characteristics) have been overwhelmingly successful in comparison with cumulative and additive systems (and to a lesser extent, multiplicative systems) is an important trend in the history of numerical notation. Yet, to portray this success as inevitable or as a linear and predictable outcome of a single process—the march towards efficiency—would be a gross mischaracterization. Instead, numerical systems change because of a complex combination of cognitive, sociopolitical, and cultural factors, no one of which determines the eventual outcome. These historically situated outcomes in turn constrain (but do not determine) the range of variability of future developments. The process of innovation in new numerical notation systems continues; we have clearly not reached, nor is there any reason to believe we will ever reach, the "end of history" of numeration.

Notes

1. There is a risk to be balanced in the use of the term "Western" in that it potentially obscures the system's history, but just as we do not call our alphabet the "Phoenicio-Graeco-Roman" script for the very good reason that these scripts each have their own history, the Indian and Arabic numerical traditions

can be obscured entirely by conflating them under the term "Hindu-Arabic."

2. Bodel's (chapter 3, this volume) term "paragram" is an extremely useful tool for conceptualizing issues of arrangement, auxiliary nonsemantic marking, and issues of display within numerical systems, just as it is for scripts. Numerals are not paragrams but in fact utilize a wide repertoire of paragrammatic representations in their own right, such as the use of commas to separate powers of large numbers (1,000,000). The subject of numerical paragrams is so vast that it requires separate treatment in a future publication.

3. For instance, the word "banned" is frequently transliterated "B&," using the logogram phonetically, but to add a further layer of obscurity, it can be written as "B7" because the ampersand key is shift-7 on most keyboards.

4. The use of the sign for 20 that is graphemically "10 + 10" parallels and may have originated from the fact that in most Semitic languages (including Aramaic), the numeral word for "twenty" is etymologically the dual form of "ten" (e.g., Hebrew *eser* "ten," *esrim* "twenty").

5. The Greek, Hebrew, Arabic, and Slavonic numerals are the best known of such systems but certainly not the only ones.

6. The once widely accepted "lost-letter" theory of Mommsen (1965 [1909]), which asserts that the higher Roman power-signs were borrowed from Greek letters that were not used in the Latin alphabet, has now been superseded by Keyser's work. Of course, it too relies on a link between phonetic and numerical systems.

7. Ironically, this sign resembles closely the Greek alphabetic sign "stigma," which also carries the numerical value 6; however, it appears that this graphic and semantic similarity is purely coincidental!

8. The abacists were not users of either the common medieval counting-board or the older Greco-Roman abacus, which used groups of pebbles or beads in rows. The debate between the two groups was not primarily about which numerical system to use but on what media and through what computational technique Western numerals were best employed.

9. No study that examines patterns in the rate of development and extinction of scripts in a parallel fashion exists, although one would be highly desirable and possible using the data provided in Daniels and Bright 1996.

10. In fact, in a curious example of the interdependent interaction of numerals, the alphabet, notational media, and technological limitations, in a parallel and short-lived notation developed in 1952 for use in the ILLIAC computer, the numbers 10 through 15 were expressed as K, S, N, J, F, and L, respectively (Robertson 1980). This seemingly random collection of letters was chosen to minimize the effort needed to modify a Teletype machine for data entry.

References

'Abd al-Tawwāb, Ramaḍān

1967   *Laḥn al-'āmma wa-l-taṭawwur al-lughawī*. Cairo: Dār al-Ma'ārif.

Absolon, Karel

1957   Dokumente und Beweise der Fähigkeiten des fossilen Menschen zu zählen im mährischen Paläolithikum. *Artibus Asiae* 20:123–150.

Acharya, Subrata Kumar

1993   The Transition from the Numerical to the Decimal System in the Inscriptions of Orissa. *Journal of the Epigraphical Society of India* 19:52–62.

Adams, James N.

2003   *Bilingualism and the Latin Language*. New York: Cambridge University Press.

al-. Names beginning with *al-* are alphabetized under the letter following the hyphen.

Alcorn, Janis

1984   *Huastec Mayan Ethnobotany*. Austin: University of Texas Press.

Aldred, Cyril

1971   *Jewels of the Pharaohs: Egyptian Jewellery of the Dynastic Period*. London: Thames and Hudson.

Allen, James P.

2005   *The Ancient Egyptian Pyramid Texts*. Writings from the Ancient World 23. Atlanta, GA: Society of Biblical Literature.

2009   Old and New in the Middle Kingdom. In *Archaism and Innovation: Studies in the Culture of Middle Kingdom Egypt*, edited by David P. Silverman, William Kelly Simpson, and Josef Wegner, pp. 263–275. New Haven, CT: Department of Near Eastern Languages and Civilizations, Yale University; Philadelphia: University of Pennsylvania Museum of Archaeology and Anthropology.

Alster, Bendt

2005   *Wisdom of Ancient Sumer*. Bethesda, MD: CDL.

REFERENCES

Amenta, Alessia

2002　　The Egyptian Tomb as a House of Life for the Afterlife? In *Egyptological Essays on State and Society*, edited by Rosanna Pirelli, pp. 13–26. Serie Egittologica 2. Naples: Universitàt degli Studi di Napoli "L'Orientale," Dipartimento di Studi e Richerche su Africa e Paesi Arabi.

Amino, Yoshihiko

1993　　*Nihonron no shiza: Rettō no shakai to kokka.* Shōgakkan raiburarī. Tokyo: Shōgakkan.

n.d.　　*Rethinking Japanese History.* Translated by Alan Christy. Ann Arbor: Center for Japanese Studies, University of Michigan. Forthcoming.

Ampolo, Carmine

1997　　L'interpretazione storica della più antica iscriziones del Lazio (dalla necropolis di Osteria dell'Osa, tomba 482). In *Le necropolis arcaiche de Veio: Giornata di studio in memoria di Massimo Pallottino*, edited by Gilda Bartoloni, pp. 211–217. Rome: Università degli studi di Roma "La Sapienza."

Andrews, Carol

1994　　*Amulets of Ancient Egypt.* London: British Museum Press.

Andrews, Frank Emerson

1935　　*New Numbers: How Acceptance of a Duodecimal (12) Base Would Simplify Mathematics.* New York: Harcourt and Brace.

Ariga, Chieko

1989　　The Playful Gloss: Rubi in Japanese Literature. *Monumenta Nipponica* 44(3):309–336.

Arnold, Dieter

1992　　*The Pyramid Complex of Senwosret I. The South Cemeteries of Lisht, Metropolitan Museum of Art.* Egyptian Expedition 3. New York: Metropolitan Museum of Art.

Arnold, Dorothea

1991　　Amenemhat I and the Early Twelfth Dynasty at Thebes. *Metropolitan Museum Journal* 26:5–48.

Arnold, Felix

1990　　*The Control Notes and Team Marks: The South Cemeteries of Lisht III.* Egyptian Expedition 23. New York: Metropolitan Museum of Art.

al-'Askarī, Abū Hilāl al-

1982　　*al- Awā'il*, vol. II. Edited by Walīd Qassāb and Muḥammad al-Maṣrī. Riyāḍ: Dār al-'Ulūm.

Assmann, Jan

1994　　Ancient Egypt and the Materiality of the Sign. In *Materialities of Communication*, edited by Hans Ulrich Gumbrecht and K. Ludwig Pfeiffer, pp. 5–31. Stanford, CA: Stanford University Press.

Ayoub, Georgine
2007   Laḥn. In *Encyclopedia of Arabic Language and Linguistics*, vol. 2. Edited by Kees Versteegh, pp. 628–634. Leiden: E. J. Brill.

Backhouse, A. E.
1993   *The Japanese Language: An Introduction*. Melbourne: Oxford University Press.

Bagheri, Mohammad
1998   Siyaqat Accounting: Its Origin, History, and Principles. *Acta Orientalia Academia Scientiarum Hungaricae* 51:297–301. Budapest: Akadémiai Kiadó.

Bagley, Robert
2004   Anyang Writing and the Origin of Chinese Writing. In *The First Writing: Script Invention as History and Process*, edited by Stephen D. Houston, pp. 190–249. Cambridge: Cambridge University Press.

Baines, John
2004a   The Earliest Egyptian Writing: Development, Context, Purpose. In *The First Writing: Script Invention as History and Process*, edited by Stephen D. Houston, pp. 150–189. Cambridge: Cambridge University Press.

2004b   Modelling Sources, Processes, and Locations of Early Mortuary Texts. In *D'un monde à l'autre: Textes des Pyramides et Textes des Sarcophages*, edited by Susanne Bickel and Bernard Mathieu, pp. 15–41. Bibliothèque d'Etude 139. Cairo: Institut Français d'Archéologie Orientale.

2007   *Visual and Written Culture in Ancient Egypt*. Oxford: Oxford University Press.

2008   Writing and Its Multiple Disappearances. In *The Disappearance of Writing Systems: Perspectives on Literacy and Communication*, edited by John Baines, John Bennet, and Stephen Houston, pp. 347–362. London: Equinox.

Baines, John, John Bennet, and Stephen Houston, eds.
2008   *The Disappearance of Writing Systems: Perspectives on Literacy and Communication*. London: Equinox.

Barnes, Gina
2007   *State Formation in Japan: Emergence of a 4th-Century Ruling Elite*. London: Routledge.

Barradas de Carvalho, Joaquim
1957   Sur l'introduction et la diffusion des chiffres arabes au Portugal. *Bulletin des études portugaises* 20:110–151.

Barrera Vásquez, Alfredo
1980   *Diccionario Maya Cordemex*. Mérida, Mexico: Ediciones Cordemex.

Bartolomé, Miguel A., and Alicia M. Bárabas
1982   *Tierra de la palabra: História y etnografía de los Chatinos de Oaxaca*. Colección Científica 108. Mexico City: Instituto Nacional de Antropología e Historia.

Basso, Keith
1989   The Ethnography of Writing. In *Explorations in the Ethnography of Speaking*, edited by R. Bauman and J. Sherzer, pp. 425–432. Cambridge: Cambridge University Press.

REFERENCES

Bauer, Thomas
1998   *Liebe und Liebesdichtung in der arabischen West des 9 und 10. Jahrhunderts.*
        Wiesbaden: Harrassowitz.

Baxter, W. T.
1989   Early Accounting: The Tally and Checkerboard. *The Accounting Historians
        Journal* 16:43–83.

Beaujouan, Guy
1947   Étude paléographique sur la "rotation" des chiffres et l'emploi des apices du
        Xᵉ au XIIᵉ siècle. *Revue d'histoire des sciences* 1:301–313.

Beekman, Christopher S.
1992   A Case of Regional Specialization in a Quarry from the Río Santa Amelia
        Region, Guatemala. *Mexicon* XIV:98–102.

Beliaev, Dimitri, and Raphael Tunesi
2005   A Possible Full Form of the <yu> Syllable. *Mesoweb*: Electronic document,
        http://www.mesoweb.com/articles/syllable/yu.pdf.

Benelli, Enrico
2008   L'aspetto grafico. In *Una nuova iscrizione da Magliano Sabina. Scrittura e cultra
        nella valle del Tevere*, edited by Paola Santoro, pp. 23–27. Pisa, Italy: Fabrizio
        Serra.

Berger-el Naggar, Catherine
2004   Des Textes des Pyramides sur papyrus dans les archives du temple funéraire
        de Pépy Ier. In *D'un monde à l'autre: Textes des Pyramides et Textes des
        Sarcophages*, edited by Susanne Bickel and Bernard Mathieu, pp. 85–90.
        Bibliothèque d'Etude 139. Cairo: Institut Français d'Archéologie Orientale.

**Berger-el Naggar, Catherine, Jean Leclant, Bernard Mathieu, and
Isabelle Pierre-Croisiau**
2001   *Les textes de la pyramide de Pépy Ier*. Mission Archéologique Française de
        Saqqâra: Mémoires de l'Institut Français d'Archéologique Orientale 118.
        Cairo: Institut Français d'Archéologie Orientale.

Berggren, J. Lennart
2002   Medieval Arithmetic: Arabic Texts and European Motivations. In *Word,
        Image, Number: Communication in the Middle Ages*, edited by John J. Contreni
        and Santa Casciani, pp. 351–365. Florence: Edizioni del Galluzzo.

Berlin, Heinrich
1958   El glifo "emblema" en las inscripciones mayas. *Journal de la Société des
        Américanistes* 47:111–119.

1977   *Signos y significados en las inscripciones mayas*. Guatemala City: Instituto de
        Antropología e Historia.

Berry, Mary Elizabeth
2006   *Japan in Print: Information and Nation in the Early Modern Period*. Berkeley:
        University of California Press.

Beyer, Hermann

1932   *The Stylistic History of the Maya Hieroglyphs.* Middle American Research Series 4, pp. 71–102. New Orleans: Tulane University.

1934   La historia de la escritura maya. *Investigación y progreso* VIII:300–305.

1937   *Studies on the Inscriptions of Chichen Itza.* Contributions to American Archaeology 21. Washington, DC: Carnegie Institution of Washington.

Bisson de la Roque, Fernand

1937   *Tôd (1934 à 1936).* Fouilles de l'Institut Français d'Archéologie Orientale 17. Cairo: Institut Français d'Archéologie Orientale.

Bloch, Raymond

1960   L'origine du culte des Dioscures à Rome. *Revue de philologie, de literature et d'historie anciennes* 34:182–193.

Bodel, John

2001   *Epigraphic Evidence: Ancient History from Inscriptions.* London: Routledge.

Boege, Eckart

1988   *Los Mazatecos ante la Nación.* Mexico City: Siglo XXI.

Bohas, Georges, Jean-Patrick Guillaume, and Djamel Kouloughli

1990   *The Arabic Linguistic Tradition.* London: Routledge.

Boltz, William

1994   *The Origin and Early Development of the Chinese Writing System.* New Haven, CT: American Oriental Society.

2001   *Monosyllabicity and the Origin of the Chinese Script.* Preprint 143. Berlin: Max Planck Institute for the History of Science.

Bonebakker, Seeger A.

2000   Tawriya. In *The Encyclopedia of Islam*, vol. 10, rev. ed., edited by P. J. Bearman, T. Bianquis, C. E. Bosworth, and W. P. Heinrichs, pp. 395–396. Leiden: E. J. Brill.

Bonfante, Giuliano, and Larissa Bonfante

1983   *The Etruscan Language: An Introduction.* New York: New York University Press.

Bonfante, Larissa

1996   The Scripts of Italy. In *The World's Writing Systems*, edited by Peter T. Daniels and William Bright, pp. 297–311. New York: Oxford University Press.

Boodberg, Peter A.

1937   Some Proleptical Remarks on the Evolution of Archaic Chinese. *Harvard Journal of Asiatic Studies* 2:329–372.

1940   'Ideography' or Iconolatry? *T'oung Pao* 35:266–288.

Boone, Elizabeth

2000   *Stories in Red and Black: Pictorial Histories of the Aztecs and Mixtecs.* Austin: University of Texas Press.

2007   *Cycles of Time and Meaning in the Mexican Books of Fate.* Austin: University of Texas Press.

n.d.   Ruptures and Unions: Graphic Complexity and Hybridity in Sixteenth-
         Century Mexico. In *Scripts, Signs, and Notational Systems in Pre-Columbian
         America*, edited by Elizabeth Boone and Gary Urton. Washington, DC:
         Dumbarton Oaks Research Library and Collection.

Boot, Eric
2006   What Happened on the Date 7 Manik' 5 Wo? An Analysis of Text and Image
         on Kerr Nos. 07171, 7447, and 8457. *Wayeb Notes* 21. Electronic document,
         http://www.wayeb.org/notes/wayeb_notes0021.pdf.

Boremanse, Dider
1993   The Faith of the Real People: The Lacandon of the Chiapas Rain Forest. In
         South and Meso-American Native Spirituality, edited by Gary Gossen and Miguel
         Leon-Portilla, pp. 324–351. New York: Crossroads Press.

Bottéro, Françoise
2004   Writing on Shell and Bone in Shang China. In *The First Writing: Script
         Invention as History and Process*, edited by Stephen D. Houston, pp. 250–261.
         Cambridge: Cambridge University Press.

Boyd, Robert, and Peter J. Richerson
1985   *Culture and the Evolutionary Process*. Chicago: University of Chicago Press.

Brewer, Stewart
1998   The Ergative Pre-consonant U Glyph in Classic Maya Inscriptions.
         Manuscript on file, Department of History and Political Science, Bethany
         College, Lindsborg, Kansas.

Brown, Cecil H.
1991   Hieroglyphic Literacy in Ancient Mayaland: Inferences from Linguistic
         Data. *Current Anthropology* 32:489–496.

Brunton, Guy
1928   *Qau and Badari II*. British School of Archaeology in Egypt, Twenty-ninth
         Year, 1923. London: British School of Archaeology in Egypt.

Burge, Len
1994   Numerals on Cornish Church Sundials. *Cornish Archaeology* 33:206–222.

Burnett, Charles
2002   Indian Numerals in the Mediterranean Basin in the Twelfth Century, with
         Special Reference to the "Eastern Forms." In *From China to Paris: 2000 Years'
         Transmission of Mathematical Ideas*, edited by Yvonne Dold-Samplonius, Joseph
         W. Dauben, Menso Folkerts, and Benno van Dalaen, pp. 237–288. Stuttgart:
         Franz Steiner.

Cagnat, René
1964   *Cours d'épigraphie latine*. 4th ed. Rome: L'Erma di Bretschneider.

Cajori, Florian
1928   *A History of Mathematical Notations*. 2 vols. Lasalle, IL: Open Court.

Calvin, Inga

2006   Between Text and Image: An Analysis of Pseudo-Glyphs on Late Classic Maya Pottery from Guatemala. Ph.D. diss., University of Colorado, Boulder.

Camodeca, Giuseppe

1999   *Tabulae Pompeianae Sulpiciorum.* 2 vols. Rome: Quasar.

Carnarvon, Earl of, and Howard Carter

1912   *Five Years' Explorations at Thebes: A Record of Work Done 1907–1911.* London: Oxford University Press.

Carter, Nicholas P.

2010   Paleographic Trends and Linguistic Processes in Classic Ch'olti'an. M.A. thesis, Brown University.

Caso, Alfonso

1949   El Mapa de Teozacoalco. *Cuadernos Americanos* 8:145–181.

Chapiro, Antoine

1988   *Jean-Antoine Lépine, Horloger (1720–1814).* Paris: Les Éditions de l'Amateur.

Charpin, Dominique

2004   Histoire politique du Proche-Orient amorrite (2002–1595). In *Mesopotamien: Die altbabylonische Zeit: Annäherungen 4,* edited by Pascal Attinger, Walther Sallaberger, and Markus Wäfler, pp. 23–480. Orbis Biblicus et Orientalis 160/4. Fribourg, Switzerland: Academic Press.

Chow, Kai-wing

2004   *Publishing, Culture, and Power in Early Modern China.* Stanford, CA: Stanford University Press.

Chrisomalis, Stephen

2003   The Egyptian Origin of the Greek Alphabetic Numerals. *Antiquity* 77:485–496.

2004   A Cognitive Typology for Numerical Notation. *Cambridge Archaeological Journal* 14:37–52.

2009   The Origins and Co-evolution of Literacy and Numeracy. In *The Cambridge Handbook of Literacy,* edited by David R. Olson and Nancy Torrance, pp. 59–74. Cambridge: Cambridge University Press.

2010   *Numerical Notation: A Comparative History.* New York: Cambridge University Press.

Christensen, Alexander

1998   Ethnohistoric Evidence for Inbreeding Among the Prehispanic Mixtec Ruling Caste. *Human Biology* 70:363–377.

CIL

1986   *Corpus Inscriptionum Latinarum. Inscriptiones Latinae Antiquissimae ad C. Caesaris Mortem.* Pars Posterior, editio altera, fasciculus IV, cura Atilii Degrassi, addenda tertia auxit et edenda curavit Ioannes Krummrey. I. Textus. Berlin and New York: De Gruyter.

REFERENCES

CIS. See Commission du Corpus inscriptionum semiticarum

Civil, Miguel, and Robert D. Biggs

1966   Notes sur textes sumériens archaïques. *Revues d'Assyriologie et d'Archéologie Orientale* 60:1–16.

Clanchy, Michael T.

1979   *From Memory to Written Record: England 1066–1307.* Oxford: Basil Blackwell.

Coe, Michael D.

1977   Supernatural Patrons of Maya Scribes and Artists. In *Social Process in Maya Prehistory: Studies in Honour of Sir Eric Thompson*, edited by Norman Hammond, pp. 327–347. New York: Academic Press.

Coe, Michael D., and Justin Kerr

1998   *The Art of the Maya Scribe.* New York: Harry Abrams.

Cohen, M. R.

2007   The Role of Drug Packaging and Labeling in Medication Errors. In *Medication Errors*, edited by M. R. Cohen, pp. 111–152. Washington, DC: American Pharmacists Association.

Cohen, Mark E.

1993   *The Cultic Calendars of the Ancient Near East.* Bethesda, MD: CDL.

Cohodas, Marvin

1989   Transformations: Relationships between Image and Text in the Ceramic Paintings of the Metropolitan Master. In *Word and Image in Maya Culture: Explorations in Language, Writing, and Representation*, edited by William F. Hanks and Don S. Rice, pp. 198–231. Salt Lake City: University of Utah Press.

Coleman, Judith

1996   *Public Reading and Reading Public in Late Medieval England and France.* Cambridge: Cambridge University Press.

Collier, Mark

2009   Lots I and II from Lahun. In *Archaism and Innovation: Studies in the Culture of Middle Kingdom Egypt*, edited by David P. Silverman, William Kelly Simpson, and Josef Wegner, pp. 205–259. New Haven, CT: Department of Near Eastern Languages and Civilizations, Yale University; Philadelphia: University of Pennsylvania Museum of Archaeology and Anthropology.

Collier, Mark, and Stephen Quirke

2002   *The UCL Lahun Papyri: Letters.* BAR International Series 1083. Oxford: Archaeopress.

2004   *The UCL Lahun Papyri: Religious, Literary, Legal, Mathematical and Medical.* BAR International Series 1209. Oxford: Archaeopress.

2006   *The UCL Lahun Papryi: Accounts.* BAR International Series 1471. Oxford: Archaeopress.

Collins, James

1995   Literacy and Literacies. *Annual Review of Anthropology* 24:75–93.

Collins, James, and Richard K. Blot

2003   *Literacy and Literacies: Texts, Power, and Identity.* Cambridge: Cambridge University Press.

Colonna, Giovanni

2004   Intervento, Oriente e Occidente: Metodi e discipline a confronto: Riflessioni sulla cronologia dell'età Ferro italiana. Atti dell'Incontro di Studio. In *Mediterranea: Quaderni annuali dell'Istituto di studi sulle civilta italiche e del mediterraneo antico del Consiglio nazionale delle ricerche 1,* edited by Gilda Bartoloni and Filippo Delpino. Pisa, Italy: Istituti Editoriali e Poligrafici Internazionali.

Commission du Corpus inscriptionum semiticarum

1881   *Corpus Inscriptionum Semiticarum,* vol. 2. Paris: Academie des inscriptions et belles-lettres.

Commons, Anne

1998   Kokuji. Unpublished manuscript, Department of East Asian Studies, University of Alberta.

Conlan, Thomas D.

2009   Traces of the Past: Documents, Literacy and Liturgy in Medieval Japan. In *Currents in Medieval Japanese History: Essays in Honor of Jeffrey P. Mass,* edited by Gordon Berger, Andrew Edmund Goble, Lorraine F. Harrington, G. Cameron Hurst III, Thomas D. Conlan, and Karl F. Friday, pp. 19–50. Los Angeles: University of Southern California East Asian Studies Center / Figueroa Press.

Conway, Robert S.

1933   *The Venetic Inscriptions.* Vol. 1 of *The Prae-Italic Dialects of Italy.* Cambridge, MA: Harvard University Press.

Corriente, Federico

1971   On the Functional Yield of Some Synthetic Devices in Arabic and Semitic Morphology. *Journal of Qur'ānic Studies* 62:20–50.

Coulmas, Florian

1989   *The Writing Systems of the World.* Cambridge, MA: Basil Blackwell.

1996   Typology of Writing Systems. In *Schrift und Schriftlichkeit (Writing and Its Use),* vol. 1, edited by Hartmut Günther and Otto Ludwig, pp. 1380–1387. Berlin and New York: De Gruyter.

2003   *Writing Systems: An Introduction to Their Linguistic Analysis.* Cambridge: Cambridge University Press.

Cristofani, Mauro

1978   L'alfabeto etrusco. In *Popoli e civiltà dell'Italia antica,* vol. 6, edited by Aldo L. Prosdocimi, pp. 401–428. Rome: Biblioteca di Storia Patria.

Crosby, Alfred W.

1997   *The Measure of Reality: Quantification in Western Society, 1250–1600.* Cambridge: Cambridge University Press.

REFERENCES

Crump, Thomas

1978   Money and Number: The Trojan Horse of Language. *Man*, n.s., 13:503–518.

1990   *The Anthropology of Numbers.* Cambridge: Cambridge University Press.

Cuneiform Digital Library Initiative. http://cdli.ucla.edu.

Damerow, Peter

1996   *Abstraction and Representation: Essays on the Cultural Evolution of Thinking.* Dordrecht: Kluwer.

Daniels, Peter T.

1990   Fundamentals of Grammatology. *Journal of the American Oriental Society* 110:727–730.

1996   The Study of Writing Systems. In *The World's Writing Systems*, edited by Peter T. Daniels and William Bright, pp. 3–17. New York: Oxford University Press.

2006   On *Beyond Alphabets. Written Language and Literacy* 9:7–24.

Daniels, Peter T., and William Bright, eds.

1996   *The World's Writing Systems.* New York: Oxford University Press.

Darnell, John Coleman, F. W. Dobbs-Allsopp, Marilyn J. Lundberg, P. Kyle McCarter, and Bruce Zuckerman, with the assistance of Colleen Manassa

2005   Two Early Alphabetic Inscriptions from the Wadi el-Ḥôl: New Evidence for the Origin of the Alphabet from the Western Desert of Egypt. *The Annual of the American Schools of Oriental Research* 59:63–123.

Davids, Achmat

1991   The Afrikaans of the Cape Muslims from 1815 to 1915: A Socio-linguistic Study. M.A. thesis, University of Natal, Durban.

Davies, Nina M.

1958   *Picture Writing in Ancient Egypt.* London: Oxford University Press for Griffith Institute, Oxford.

Deetz, James

1996   *In Small Things Forgotten.* 2nd ed. New York: Anchor Books / Doubleday.

DeFrancis, John

2002   The Ideographic Myth. In *Difficult Characters: Interdisciplinary Studies of Chinese and Japanese Writing*, edited by Mary S. Erbaugh, pp. 1–20. Columbus: National East Asian Language Resource Center, The Ohio State University.

Degrassi, Atilio

1947   *Inscriptiones Italiae*, vol. XIII: *Fasti et Elogia, Fasciculus I—Fasti Consulares et Triumphasles.* Rome: Libreria dello Stato.

1963   *Inscriptiones Italiae*, vol. XIII: *Fasti et Elogia, Fasciculus II—Fasti Anni Numani et Iuliani. Tabulae et Indices.* Rome: Libreria dello Stato.

Dehaene, Stanislas

1997   *The Number Sense: How the Mind Creates Mathematics.* New York: Oxford University Press.

de Maaijer, Remco, and Bram Jagersma

1997–1998   Review of *The Sumerian Dictionary of the University Museum of the University
            of Pennsylvania*, vol. 1 A, parts I and II. *Archiv für Orientforschung*
            44/45:277–288.

de Oliveira Marques, A. H.

1996   L'introduction des chiffres arabes dans les documents médiévaux portugais.
            In *Graphische Symbole in mittelalterlichen Urkunden*, edited by P. Rück, pp.
            503–508. Sigmaringen, Germany: Jan Thorbecke.

Déroche, François

1992   *The Abbasid Tradition: Qur'ans of the 8th to the 10th centuries AD*. London: Nour
            Foundation.

2000   *Manuel de codicologie des manuscrits en écriture arabe*. Paris: Bibliothèque
            Nationale de France.

2004   *Le livre manuscript arabe: Préludes à une histoire*. Paris: Bibliothèque Nationale
            de France.

d'Errico, Francesco, and Carmen Cacho

1994   Notation versus Decoration in the Upper Paleolithic: A Case-Study from
            Tossal de la Roca, Alicante, Spain. *Journal of Archaeological Science* 21:185–200.

Dévényi, Kinga

2007   I'rāb. In *Encyclopedia of Arabic Language and Linguistics*, vol. 2, edited by Kees
            Versteegh, pp. 401–406. Leiden: E. J. Brill.

Diem, Werner

1976a   Die Hauptentwicklungsstadien der arabischen Orthographie. In *Akten des VII
            Kongresses für Arabistik und Islamwissenschaft*, edited by Albert Dietrich, pp.
            101–107. Göttingen, Germany: Vandenhoeck & Ruprecht.

1976b   Some Glimpses at the Rise and Early Development of the Arabic
            Orthography. *Orientalia* 45:251–261.

1979   Untersuchungen zur frühen Geschichte der arabischen Orthographie i: Die
            Schreibung der Vokale. *Orientalia* 48:207–257.

Dietrich, Manfred, and Oswald Loretz

1988   *Der Keilalphabete: Die phönizisch-kanaanäischen und altarabischen Alphabete in
            Ugarit*. Münster: Ugarit-Verlag.

Doyle, James A.

2009   A Paleographic Approach to Political Change Using Classic Maya Day Sign
            Variants. Paper presented at the 14th European Maya Conference, Cracow,
            Poland.

Dreyer, Günter

1998   *Umm el-Qaab I: Das prädynastische Königsgrab U-j und seine frühen Schriftzeugnisse*.
            Deutsches Archäologisches Institut, Abteilung Kairo, Archäologische
            Veröffentlichungen 86. Mainz, Germany: Phillipp von Zabern.

Dubiel, Ulrike

2008   *Amulette, Siegel, und Perlen: Studien zu Typologie und Tragsitte im Alten und Mittleren Reich.* Orbis Biblicus et Orientalis 229. Fribourg, Switzerland: Academic Press; Göttingen, Germany: Vandenhoeck & Ruprecht.

Dunham, Dows

1937   *Naga-ed Dêr Stelae of the First Intermediate Period.* London: Oxford University Press, Humphrey Milford, for the Museum of Fine Arts Boston.

Durand, Jean-Marie

1987   Questions de chiffres. Mari: *Annales de Recherches Interdisciplinaires* 5:605–610.

Duri, A. A., H. L. Gottschalk, and G. S. Colin

1965   Dīwān. In *The Encyclopedia of Islam*, vol. 2, rev. ed., edited by B. Lewis, C. Pellat, and J. Schacht, pp. 323–332. Leiden: E. J. Brill.

Edel, Elmar

1955–1964   *Altägyptische Grammatik.* Analecta Orientalia 34, 39. Rome: Pontificum Institutum Biblicum.

Eichler, Eckhard

1991   Untersuchungen zu den Königsbriefen des Alten Reiches. *Studien zur Altägyptischen Kultur* 18:141–171.

Electronic Text Corpus of Sumerian Literature. http://etcsl.orinst.ox.ac.uk/.

Englund, Robert K.

1998   Texts from the Late Uruk Period. In *Mesopotamien: Späturuk-Zeit und Frühdynastische Zeit: Annäherungen 1*, edited by Pascal Attinger and Markus Wäfler, pp. 15–223. Orbis Biblicus et Orientalis 160/1. Fribourg, Switzerland: Universitätsverlag.

Erman, Adolf

1919   *Reden, Rufe und Lieder auf Gräberbildern des Alten Reiches.* Abhandlungen der Preussichen Akademie der Wissenschaften, Philosophisch-historische Klasse 1918:15. Berlin: Akademie der Wissenschaften.

Evans, Gillian R.

1977   From Abacus to Algorism: Theory and Practice in Medieval Arithmetic. *The British Journal for the History of Science* 10:114–131.

Everett, Daniel L.

2005   Cultural Constraints on Grammar and Cognition in Pirahã. *Current Anthropology* 46:621–646.

Fecht, Gerhard

1982   Prosodie. In *Lexikon der Ägyptologie*, vol. 4, edited by Wolfgang Helck and Wolfhart Westendorf, columns 1127–1154. Wiesbaden: Harrassowitz.

Février, James Germain

1984   *Histoire de l'écriture.* Paris: Payot.

Fields, Virginia M., and Dorie Reents-Budet

2005   *Lords of Creation: The Origins of Sacred Maya Kingship.* London: Scala.

Finnegan, Ruth
1988 *Literacy and Orality: Studies in the Technology of Communication.* Oxford: Basil Blackwell.

al-Fīrūzābādī, M. b. Yaʻqūb
1988 *al-Muthallath al-mukhtalif al-maʻnā.* Edited by ʻAbd al-Jalīl al-Tamīmī. Sabhā, Libya: Manshūrāt Jāmiʻat Sabhā.

Fischer, Henry George
1973a An Eleventh Dynasty Couple Holding the Sign of Life. *Zeitschrift für Ägyptische Sprache und Altertumskunde* 100:16–28.
1973b Redundant Determinatives in the Old Kingdom. *Metropolitan Museum Journal* 8:7–25.
1977 *The Orientation of Hieroglyphs I, Reversals.* Egyptian Studies 2. New York: Metropolitan Museum of Art.
1986 *L'écriture et l'art de l'Egypte ancienne: Quatre leçons sur la paléographie et l'épigraphie pharaoniques.* Collège de France, Essais et Conférences. Paris: Presses Universitaires de France.

Fleisch, Henri
1971 Iʻrāb. In *The Encyclopedia of Islam*, vol. 3, rev. ed., edited by B. Lewis, V. L. Ménage, C. Pellat, and J. Schacht, pp. 1248–1250. Leiden: E. J. Brill.

Formigli, Edilberto
1992 Indagini archeometriche sull'autenticità della Fibula Prenestina. *Mitteilungen des Deutschen Archäologischen Instituts Römische Abteilung* 99:329–343.

Foxvog, Daniel A.
1996 Ur III Economic Texts at Berkeley. *Acta Sumerologica* 18:47–92.

Franke, Detlef
1987 Zwischen Herakleopolis und Theben: Neues zu den Gräbern von Assiut. *Studien zur Altägyptischen Kultur* 16:121–160.
1991 The Career of Khnumhotep III of Beni Hasan and the So-called "Decline of the Nomarchs." In *Middle Kingdom Studies*, edited by Stephen Quirke, pp. 51–67. New Malden, UK: SIA.
1995 The Middle Kingdom in Egypt. In *Civilizations of the Ancient Near East*, vol. 2, edited by Jack M. Sasson, John Baines, Gary Beckman, and Karen S. Rubinsohn, pp. 735–748. New York: Charles Scribners.

Fröberg, Carl-Erik
1952 *Hexadecimal Conversion Tables.* Lund: Gleerup.

Fröhlich, Judith
2007 *Rulers, Peasants and the Use of the Written Word in Medieval Japan: Ategawa no sho, 1004–1304.* Bern: Peter Lang.

Fück, Joachim
1955 *ʻArabīya; Recherches sur l'histoire de la langue et du style arabe.* Translated by Claude Denizeau. Paris: M. Didier.

Fujimoto, Yukio

1988   Kodai Chōsen no gengo to moji bunka. In *Nihon no kodai 14: Kotoba to moji*, edited by Kishi Toshio, pp. 175–240. Tokyo: Chūō Kōronsha.

Gacek, Adam

2001   *The Arabic Manuscript Tradition: A Glossary of Technical Terms and Bibliography*. Leiden: E. J. Brill.

2008   *The Arabic Manuscript Tradition: A Glossary of Technical Terms and Bibliography, Supplement*. Leiden: E. J. Brill.

Gager, John

1992   *Curse Tablets and Binding Spells in the Ancient World*. Oxford: Oxford University Press.

Galambos, Imre

2005   A Corpus-Based Approach to Palaeography: The Case of the Houma Covenant Texts. *Asiatische Studien* LIX(1):115–130.

Galenson, David

2005   *Old Masters and Young Geniuses: The Two Life Cycles of Artistic Creativity*. Princeton, NJ: Princeton University Press.

Galinier, Jacques

1990   *La mitad del mundo*. Mexico City: Instituto Nacional de Antropología e Historia / Instituto Nacional Indigenista.

Gamkrelidze, Thomas V.

1994   *Alphabetic Writing and the Old Georgian Script*. Delmar, NY: Caravan Books.

Gansu sheng kaogu yanjiusuo, Gansu sheng bowuguan, Zhongguo wenwu yanjiusuo, and Zhongguo shehui kexue yuan lishi yanjiusuo

1994   *Juyan xin jian*. Beijing: Zhonghua shuju.

Gardiner, Alan H.

1909   *Die Erzählung des Sinuhe und die Hirtengeschichte*. Hieratische Papyrus aus den Königlichen Museen zu Berlin 5, Literarische Texte des Mittleren Reiches 2. Leipzig: J. C. Hinrichs.

1916   The Egyptian Origin of the Semitic Alphabet. *Journal of Egyptian Archaeology* 3:1–16 and plates I–V.

1955a   *The Ramesseum Papyri*. Oxford: Oxford University Press for Griffith Insitute, Oxford.

1955b   A Unique Funerary Liturgy. *Journal of Egyptian Archaeology* 41:9–17.

1957   *Egyptian Grammar: Being an Introduction to the Study of Hieroglyphs*. 3rd ed. London: Oxford University Press for Griffith Insitute, Oxford.

Gardiner, Alan H., T. E. Peet, and Jaroslav Cerný

1952–1955   *The Inscriptions of Sinai*. London: Egypt Exploration Society.

Gates, William E.

1978 [1931]   *An Outline Dictionary of Maya Glyphs: With a Concordance and Analysis of Their Relationships*. New York: Dover; Baltimore, MD: The Johns Hopkins Press.

Gelb, Ignace J.

1963   *A Study of Writing.* Rev. ed. Chicago: University of Chicago Press.

Genette, Gérard

1997   *Paratexts: Thresholds of Interpretation.* Translated by Jane E. Lewin. Cambridge: Cambridge University Press.

Gibson, Craig A., and Francis Newton

1995   Pandulf of Capua's *De calculatione:* An Illustrated Abacus Treatise and Some Evidence for the Hindu-Arabic Numerals in Eleventh-Century South Italy. *Medieval Studies* 57:293–335.

Glass, Andrew

2000   A Preliminary Study of Kharoṣṭhī Manuscript Paleography. M.A. thesis, University of Washington.

Gmür, Max

1917   *Schweizerische Bauernmarken und Holzurkunden.* Bern: Stämpfli.

Goedicke, Hans

1970   *Die privaten Rechtsinschriften aus dem Alten Reich.* Beihefte zur Wiener Zeitschrift für die Kunde des Morgenlands 5. Vienna: Notring.

1988   *Old Hieratic Paleography.* Baltimore, MD: Halgo.

Goldwasser, Orly

2006   Canaanites Reading Hieroglyphs: Horus Is Hathor?—The Invention of the Alphabet in Sinai. *Ägypten und Levante* 16:121–160.

Gonzales-Quijano, Ives

1999   The Birth of a Media Ecosystem: Lebanon in the Internet Age. In *New Media in the Muslim World: The Emerging Public Sphere,* edited by Dale F. Eickleman and Jon W. Anderson, pp. 60–79. Bloomington: Indiana University Press.

Gordon, Arthur E.

1973   *The Letter Names of the Latin Alphabet.* University of California Publications. Classical Studies 9. Berkeley: University of California Press.

1983   *Illustrated Introduction to Latin Epigraphy.* Berkeley: University of California Press.

Gordon, Joyce S., and Arthur E. Gordon

1957   *Contributions to the Palaeography of Latin Inscriptions.* Berkeley: University of California Press.

Gottlieb, Nanette

1995   *Kanji Politics: Language Policy and Japanese Script.* London: Kegan Paul International.

Grafton, Anthony

1997   *The Footnote: A Curious History.* Cambridge, MA: Harvard University Press.

Gragg, Gene B.

1996   Mesopotamian Cuneiform: Other Languages. In *The World's Writing Systems,* edited by Peter T. Daniels and William Bright, pp. 58–72. New York: Oxford University Press.

Graham, Ian, and Eric von Euw

1992   *Corpus of Maya Hieroglyphic Inscriptions*, vol. 4, part 3: Uxmal, Xcalumkin. Cambridge, MA: Peabody Museum of Archaeology and Ethnology, Harvard University.

Green, M. W.

1981   The Construction and Implementation of the Cuneiform Writing System. *Visible Language* 15:345–372.

Griffith, F. Ll.

1896   *Beni Hasan III*. Archaeological Survey of Egypt 5. London: Egypt Exploration Fund.

1898a   *A Collection of Hieroglyphs: A Contribution to the History of Egyptian Writing*. Archaeological Survey of Egypt 6. London: Egypt Exploration Fund.

1898b   *The Petrie Papyri: Hieratic Papyri from Kahun and Gurob*. London: Bernard Quaritch.

Grohmann, Adolf

1971   *Arabische Paläographie II: Das Schriftwesen und die Lapidarschrift*. Vienna: The Austrian Academy of Sciences and Hermann Böhlau.

Grube, Nikolai

1990   *Die Entwicklung der Mayaschrift: Grundlagen zur Erforschung des Wandels der Mayaschrift von der Protoklasik bis zur spanischen Eroberung*. Berlin: Karl-Friedrich von Flemming.

1994   Observations on the History of Maya Hieroglyphic Writing. In *Seventh Palenque Round Table, 1989*, edited by Virginia M. Fields, pp. 177–186. Palenque Round Table Series, vol. 9. San Francisco: Pre-Columbian Art Research Institute.

1998   Speaking Through Stones: A Quotative Particle in Maya Hieroglyphic Inscriptions. In *50 años de estudios americanistas en la Universidad de Bonn: Nuevas Contribuciones a la arqueología, etnohistoria, etnolingüística y etnografía de las Américas*, edited by Sabine Dedenbach-Salazar Sáenz, Carmen Arellano Hoffmann, Eva Köning, and Heiko Prümers, pp. 543–558. Markt Schwaben, Germany: Verlag Anton Saurwein.

Gruendler, Beatrice

1993   *The Development of the Arabic Scripts: From the Nabatean Era to the First Islamic Century according to Dated Texts*. Atlanta, GA: Scholars Press.

2004   Sheets. In *Encyclopedia of the Qur'ān*, vol. IV, edited by J. D. McAuliffe, W. al-Kadi, C. Gilliot, A. Rippin, and W. Graham, pp. 587–589. Leiden: E. J. Brill.

2006a   Arabic Language. In *Medieval Islamic Civilization: An Encyclopedia*, vol. 1, edited by Josef W. Meri, pp. 56–59. London: Routledge.

2006b   Arabic Alphabet: Origin. In *Encyclopedia of Arabic Language and Linguistics*, vol. I, edited by Kees Versteegh, pp. 148–165. Leiden: E. J. Brill.

2009a   *Tawqī'* (Apostille): Royal Brevity in the Pre-modern Islamic Appeals Court. In *The Weaving of Words: Approaches to Classical Arabic Prose*, edited by Lale

Behzadi and Vahid Behmardi, pp. 101–129. Beirut and Wiesbaden, Germany: Ergon.

2009b   Books, Notes, and Words: The Beginnings of Arabic-Islamic Book Culture. *Convivencia Conference*, CSIC Madrid. Electronic document, http://www.yale.edu/nelc/documents/Gruendler_Communicative_Choices.pdf.

2009c   Abū Aḥmad al-'Askarī. In *Encyclopedia of Islam*, 3rd. ed., vol. 3, edited by Gudrun Krämer, Denis Matringe, John Nawas, and Everett Rowson. Leiden: Brill Online. Electronic document, http://www.brillonline.nl/subscriber/entry?entry=ei3_SIM-22689.

Gruzinski, Serge

1992   *Painting the Conquest: The Mexican Indians and the European Renaissance*. Paris: Flammarion.

Guarducci, Margareta

1981   La cosidetta Fibula Praenestina: Antiquari, eruditi, e falsari nella Roma dell'ottocento. *Memorie dell'Academia nazionale dei Lincei*, 8th ser., 24(4):413–574.

1984–1986   La cosidetta Fibula Praenestina: Elementi nuovi. *Memorie dell'Academia nazionale dei Lincei*, 8th ser., 28(1):125–177.

Guergour, Youcef

1997   Les différents systèmes de numérotation au Maghreb à l'époque ottomane: L'exemple des chiffres rumi. In *Sciences, Technology and Industry in the Ottoman World*, edited by E. Ihsanoglu, A. Djebbar, and F. Günergun, pp. 67–74. Proceedings of the XXth International Congress of History of Science, vol. 6. Burlington, VT: Ashgate / Variorum.

Guitel, Geneviève

1975   *Histoire comparée des numérations écrites*. Paris: Flammarion.

Hamann, Byron

1998   First-Born Son of a First-Born Son? Discontinuous Succession in the Codex Selden. *Indiana Journal of Hispanic Literature* 13:53–58.

2004   Seeing and Mixtec Screenfolds. *Visible Language* 38:68–122.

Hamilton, Gordon J.

2006   *The Origins of the West Semitic Alphabet in Egyptian Scripts*. Catholic Biblical Quarterly, Monograph Series 40. Washington, DC: Catholic Biblical Association of America.

Hanks, William

1990   *Referential Practice*. Chicago: University of Chicago Press.

Haring, Ben

2010   Nineteenth Dynasty Stelae and the Merits of Hieroglyphic Palaeography. *Bibliotheca Orientalis* 67:22–34.

al-Ḥarīrī, al-Qāsim ibn 'Alī

1969   *Sharḥ Maqāmāt al-Ḥarīrī li-l-Sharīsī*, vol. 3. Edited by Muhammad Abū l-Faḍl Ibrāhīm. Cairo: al-Mu'assasa al-'Arabiyya al-Ḥadītha il-Tab' wa-l-Tawsī'.

Harper, Donald

1999   Warring States Natural Philosophy and Occult Thought. In *The Cambridge History of China: From the Origins of Civilization to 221 BC*, edited by Michael Loewe and Edward L. Shaughnessy, pp. 813–884. Cambridge: Cambridge University Press.

Harris, R. A.

1905   Numerals for Simplifying Addition. *American Mathematical Monthly* 12:64–67.

Hartmann, Markus

2005   *Die frühlateinischen Inschriften und ihre Datierung.* Bremen, Germany: Hempen.

Healey, John

1990   The Nabatean Contribution to the Development of Arabic Script. *Aram* 2:93–98.

Helck, Wolfgang

1974   *Altägyptische Aktenkunde des 3 und 2. Jahrtausends v. Chr.* Münchner Ägyptologische Studien 31. Munich and Berlin: Deutscher Kunstverlag.

Hering, D. W.

1939   Numerals on Clock and Watch Dials. *Scientific Monthly* 49:311–323.

Hermann Lejarazu, Manuel

2003   *Códice Muro.* Oaxaca, Mexico: Gobierno del Estado de Oaxaca / Biblioteca Nacional de Anthropología e Historia.

Herring, Adam

2005   *Art and Writing in the Maya Cities, A.D. 600–800.* Cambridge: Cambridge University Press.

Holmes, Ruth Bradley, and Betty Sharp Smith

1977   *Beginning Cherokee.* 2nd ed. Norman: University of Oklahoma Press.

Hopkins, Simon

1984   *Studies in the Grammar of Early Arabic: Based upon Papyri Datable before A.H. 300/A.D. 912.* Oxford: Oxford University Press.

Horváth, Zoltán

2007   Remarks on the Temple of Heqet and a Sarcastic Letter from el-Lahun. In *Life and Afterlife in Ancient Egypt during the Middle Kingdom and Second Intermediate Period*, edited by Silke Grallert and Wolfram Grajetzki, pp. 81–90. Egyptology 7. London: Golden House Publications.

Hōshōkai henshūbu, ed.

1916   *Gotai jirui.* Tokyo: Saitō shobō.

Houston, Stephen D.

1994   Literacy Among the Precolumbian Maya: A Comparative Perspective. In *Writing Without Words: Alternative Literacies in Mesoamerica and the Andes*, edited by Elizabeth Boone and Walter Mignolo, pp. 27–49. Durham, NC: Duke University Press.

2000   Into the Minds of Ancients: Advances in Maya Glyph Studies. *Journal of World Prehistory* 14:121–201.

2004a   Overture to *The First Writing.* In *The First Writing: Script Invention as History and Process,* edited by Stephen D. Houston, pp. 3–15. Cambridge: Cambridge University Press.

2004b   Writing in Early Mesoamerica. In *The First Writing: Script Invention as History and Process,* edited by Stephen D. Houston, pp. 274–312. Cambridge: Cambridge University Press.

2004c   The Archaeology of Communication Technologies. *Annual Review of Anthropology* 33:223–250.

2004d   Final Thoughts on First Writing. In *The First Writing: Script Invention as History and Process,* edited by Stephen D. Houson, pp. 349–353. Cambridge: Cambridge University Press.

2008   The Small Deaths of Maya Writing. In *The Disappearance of Writing Systems: Perspectives on Literacy and Communication,* edited by John Baines, John Bennet, and Stephen Houston, pp. 231–252. London: Equinox.

n.d.a   The Shape of Script: How and Why Writing Systems Change. Proposal for a School of American Research Advanced Seminar. Manuscript on file, School for Advanced Research, Santa Fe, New Mexico.

n.d.b   All Things Must Change: Maya Writing over Time and Space. In *Their Way of Writing: Scripts, Signs, and Pictographs in Pre-Columbian America,* edited by Elizabeth Boone and Gary Urton. Washington, DC: Dumbarton Oaks Research Library and Collection.

Houston, Stephen D., ed.
2004   *The First Writing: Script Invention as History and Process.* Cambridge: Cambridge University Press.

Houston, Stephen, John Baines, and Jerrold Cooper
2003   Last Writing: Script Obsolescence in Egypt, Mesopotamia, and Mesoamerica. *Comparative Studies in Society and History* 45:430–479.

Houston, Stephen D., Oswaldo Chinchilla Mazariegos, and David Stuart
2001   Introduction. In *The Decipherment of Ancient Maya Writing,* edited by Stephen D. Houston, Oswaldo Chinchilla Mazariegos, and David Stuart, pp. 3–19. Norman: University of Oklahoma Press.

Houston, Stephen D., and Michael D. Coe
2003   Has Isthmian Writing Been Deciphered? *Mexicon* 25:151–161.

Houston, Stephen, Héctor Escobedo, Richard Terry, David Webster, George Veni, and Kitty F. Emery
2000a   Among the River Kings: Archaeological Research at Piedras Negras, Guatemala, 1999. *Mexicon* 22:8–17.

Houston, Stephen, John Robertson, and David Stuart
2000b   The Language of the Classic Maya Inscriptions. *Current Anthropology* 41:321–355.

2004   Disharmony in Maya Hieroglyphic Writing: Linguistic Change and Continuity in Classic Society. In *The Linguistics of Maya Writing*, edited by Søren Wichmann, pp. 83–101. Salt Lake City: University of Utah Press.

Houston, Stephen, David Stuart, and Karl Taube
2006   *The Memory of Bones: Body, Being, and Experience among the Classic Maya.* Austin: University of Texas Press.

Houston, Stephen D., and Karl Taube
2000   An Archaeology of the Senses: Perception and Cultural Expression in Ancient Mesoamerica. *Cambridge Archaeological Journal* 10:261–294.

Howe, Nicolas
1993   The Cultural Construction of Reading in Anglo-Saxon England. In *The Ethnography of Reading*, edited by Jonathan Boyarin, pp. 58–79. Berkeley: University of California Press.

Hubei sheng bowuguan and Zhongguo shehui kexue yanjiusuo
1989   *Zeng Hou Yi mu.* Beijing: Wenwu chubanshe.

Hudson, Alan
1992   Diglossia: A Bibliographic Review. *Language in Society* 21(4):611–674.

Hurford, James R.
1987   *Language and Number.* Oxford: Basil Blackwell.

Hyman, Malcolm D.
2006   Of Glyphs and Glottography. *Language and Communication* 26:213–249.

Ibn Fāris
1963   *al-Sāḥibī fī fiqh al-lugha.* Edited by Musṭṭafā al-Shuwaymī (El-Chouémi). Beirut: Badrān.

Ibn Khallikān
1968–1972   *Wafayāt al-a'yān [Obituaries of the Nobles]*, vol. 4. Edited by Iḥsān 'Abbās. Beirut: Dār al-Thaqāfa.

Ibn Khayr al-Ishbīlī, Abū Bakr. M.
1963   *al-Fahrasa.* Edited by F. Codera and J. Ribera. Cairo: al-Khānjī.

Ibn Manẓūr
1955–1956 [1883–1891]   *Lisān al-'arab*, vol. I. Beirut: Dār Ṣādir.

Ibn al-Muqri', Ismā'īl b. Abī Bakr
1996   *'Unwān al-sharaf fī 'ilm al-fiqh wa-l-'arūḍ wa-l-ta'rīkh wa-l-naḥw wa-l-qawāfī [The Dependable Badge of Honor in the Sciences of Jurisprudence, History, Grammar, Prosody, and Rhyme Theory].* Edited by 'Abdallāh b. Ibrāhīm al-Anṣārī. Beirut: al-Maktaba al-'Aṣriyya.

Ibn Qutayba
1963   *Adab al-Kātib [The Craft of the Scribe].* Edited by M. M. 'Abdalḥamīd. Cairo: al-Maktaba al-Tijāriyya al-Kubrā.

Ibn al-Sīd al-Baṭalyawsī

1981 [1401] *al-Muthallath.* 2 vols. Edited by Ṣalāḥ Mahdī ʿAlī al-Farṭūsī. Baghdad: Dār al-Rashīd.

Ibn al-Sikkīt

1965 *Iṣlāḥ al-manṭiq.* Edited by A. M. Shākir and ʿAbdassalām Hārūn. Cairo: Dār al-Maʿārif.

Ichon, Alain

1973 *La religión de los totonacas de la sierra.* Colección SEP/INI 16. Mexico City: Instituto Nacional Indigenista.

Ifrah, Georges

1998 *The Universal History of Numbers.* Translated by David Bellos, E. F. Harding, Sophie Wood, and Ian Monk. New York: John Wiley and Sons.

Inomata, Takeshi

1995 Archaeological Investigations at the Fortified Center of Aguateca, El Petén, Guatemala: Implications for the Study of the Classic Maya. Ph.D. diss., Vanderbilt University.

2001a In the Palace of the Fallen King: The Royal Residential Complex at Aguateca, Guatemala. *Journal of Field Archaeology* 28:287–306.

2001b Power and Ideology of Artistic Creation: Elite Craft Specialists in Classic Maya Society. *Current Anthropology* 42:321–349.

Inomata, Takeshi, Daniela Triadan, Erick Ponciano, Richard E. Terry, and Markus Eberl

2002 Domestic and Political Lives of Classic Maya Elites: The Excavation of Rapidly Abandoned Structures at Aguateca, Guatemala. *Latin American Antiquity* 13:305–330.

Irvine, Judith T.

1989 When Talk Isn't Cheap: Language and Political Economy. *American Ethnologist* 16:248–262.

Irvine, Judith T., and Susan Gal

2000 Language Ideology and Linguistic Differentiation. In *Regimes of Language: Ideologies, Polities, and Identities,* edited by Paul V. Kroskrity, pp. 35–83. Santa Fe, NM: School of American Research Press.

Jakobson, Roman

1987 [1959] Linguistic Aspects of Translation. In *Language in Literature,* edited by Krystyna Pomorska and Stephen Rudy, pp. 428–435. Cambridge, MA: The Belknap Press of Harvard University Press.

Jeffery, Lilian H.

1990 *The Local Scripts of Archaic Greece: A Study of the Origin of the Greek Alphabet and Its Development from the Eighth to the Fifth Centuries B.C.* 2nd ed. Oxford: Clarendon Press / Oxford University Press.

Jenkinson, Hilary

1926   The Use of Arabic and Roman Numerals in English Archives. *The Antiquaries Journal* 6:263–275.

Jéquier, Gustave

1911   *Le Papyrus Prisse et ses variantes: papyrus de la Bibliothéque Nationale (nos 183 à 194), papyrus 10371 et 10435 du British Museum, Tablette Carnarvon au Musée du Caire, publiés en fac-similé.* Paris: Paul Geuthner.

1921   *Les frises d'objets des sarcophages du Moyen Empire.* Mémoires Publiés par les membres de l'Institut Français d'Archéologie Orientale du Caire 47. Cairo: Institut Français d'Archéologie Orientale.

Jestin, Raymond

1937   *Tablettes sumériennes de Šuruppak conservées au musée du Stamboul.* Paris: E. de Boccard.

Johnston, A. W.

1979   *Trademarks on Greek Vases.* Warminster, UK: Aris and Philips.

Justeson, John S., and Terrence Kaufman

1997   A Newly Discovered Column in the Hieroglyphic Text on La Mojarra Stela 1: A Test of the Epi-Olmec Decipherment. *Science* 277:207–210.

2008   The Epi-Olmec Tradition at Cerro de las Mesas in the Classic Period. In *Classic Period Cultural Currents in Southern and Central Veracruz*, edited by Philip J. Arnold III and Christopher Pool, pp. 161–194. Washington, DC: Dumbarton Oaks Research Library and Collection.

Kahl, Jochem

1999   *Siut–Theben: zur Wertschätzung von Traditionen im alten Ägypten.* Probleme der Ägyptologie 13. Leiden: E. J. Brill.

Kara, Gyorgy

1996   Kitan and Jurchin. In *The World's Writing Systems*, edited by Peter T. Daniels and William Bright, pp. 230–238. New York: Oxford University Press.

Kaufman, Terrence, and John Justeson

2008   The Epi-Olmec Language and Its Neighbors. In *Classic Period Cultural Currents in Southern and Central Veracruz*, edited by Philip J. Arnold III and Christopher Pool, pp. 55–83. Washington, DC: Dumbarton Oaks Research Library and Collection.

Kaye, Alan S.

1996   Adaptations of the Arabic Script. In *The World's Writing Systems*, edited by Peter T. Daniels and William Bright, pp. 743–762. New York: Oxford University Press.

Keil, Heinrich

1859   *Grammatici Latini*, vol. VII. Leipzig: B. G. Teubner.

Kelley, David

1962   Fonetismo en la escritura maya. *Estudios de Cultura Maya* 2:277–317.

1976   *Deciphering the Mayan Script.* Austin: University of Texas Press.

Kenzelmann Pfyffer, A., T. Theurillat, and S. Verdan

2005   Graffiti d'époque géométrique provenant du sanctuaire d'Apollon Daphnéphoros à Erétrie. *Zeitschrift für Papyrologie und Epigraphik* 151:51–83.

Kerr, Barbara, and Justin Kerr

1988   Some Observations on Maya Vase Painters. In *Maya Iconography*, edited by Elizabeth P. Benson and Gillett G. Griffin, pp. 236–259. Princeton, NJ: Princeton University Press.

Keyser, Paul

1988   The Origin of the Latin Numerals 1 to 1000. *American Journal of Archaeology* 92:529–546.

al-Khalīl b. Aḥmad

1980   *Kitāb al-ʿAyn.* 7 vols. Edited by Mahdī al-Makhzūmī and Ibrāhīm al-Sāmarrāʾī. Baghdad: Dār al-Rashīd li-l-Nashr.

Khan, Geoffrey

1992   *Arabic Papyri: Selected Material from the Khalili Collection.* London: Azimuth Editions; Oxford: Oxford University Press.

Kim, Mun-Kyŏng

1988   Kanji bunkaken no kundoku genshō. In *Wakan hikaku bungaku kenkyū no shomondai*, edited by the Wakan hikaku bungakkai (Association for Comparative Studies of Chinese and Japanese Literature), pp. 175–204. Wakan hikaku bungaku sōsho 8. Tokyo: Kyūko shoin.

Kim, Yŏng-uk

2005   Kanji/kanbun no Kankokuteki juyō: Shoki ritō to shakudoku kuketsu shiryō o chūshin ni. In *Nihongaku/Tonkōgaku/kanbun kundoku no shin tenkai*, edited by Ishizuka Harumichi kyōju taishoku kinenkai (Committee for the Commemoration of the Retirement of Professor Ishizuka Harumichi), pp. 575–601. Tokyo: Kyūko shoin.

King, Christopher

1994   *One Language, Two Scripts: The Hindi Movement in Nineteenth Century North India.* Bombay: Oxford University Press.

King, Mark

1990   Rethinking Codices: Poetics and Metaphor in Mixtec Writing. *Ancient Mesoamerica* 1:141–187.

1994   Hearing the Echoes of Verbal Art in Mixtec Writing. In *Writing Without Words*, edited by Elizabeth Boone and Walter D. Mignolo, pp. 102–136. Durham, NC: Duke University Press.

King, Ross

2007   Korean Kugyŏl Writing and the Problem of Vernacularization in the Sinitic Sphere. Paper presented at the Annual Meeting of the Association for Asian Studies, Boston.

Klein, Jacob

1990 Šulgi and Išmedagan: Originality and Dependence in Sumerian Royal Hymnology. In *Bar-Ilan Studies in Assyriology Dedicated to Pinhas Artzi,* edited by Jacob Klein and Aaron Skaist, pp. 63–136. Ramat Gan, Israel: Bar-Ilan University Press.

Knight, Stan

1998 *Historical Scripts: From Classical Times to the Renaissance.* New Castle, DE: Oak Knoll Press.

Knorosov, Yuri V.

1958 The Problem of the Study of the Maya Hiergolyphic Writing. *American Antiquity* 23:248–291.

Kobayashi, Y.

1983 Jikun shiryō to shite no Heijō-kyū mokkan: Kojiki no yōjihō to hikaku o hōhō to shite. *Mokkan kenkyū* 5:87–100.

1988 Hyōki no oki no tenkai to buntai no sōzō. In *Nihon no kodai 14: Kotoba to moji,* edited by Kishi Toshio, pp. 265–324. Tokyo: Chūō kōronsha.

1998 *Zusetsu Nihon no kanji.* Tokyo: Taishūkan.

Koch, Roland

1990 *Die Erzählung des Sinuhe.* Bibliotheca Aegyptiaca 17. Brussels: Fondation Egyptologique Reine Elisabeth.

Kornicki, Peter F.

1998 *The Book in Japan: A Cultural History from the Beginnings to the Nineteenth Century.* Leiden: E. J. Brill.

Kraus, Fritz Rudolf

1973 *Vom mesopotamischen Menschen der altbabylonischen Zeit und seiner Welt: Eine Reihe Vorlesungen.* Mededelingen der Koninklijke Nederlandse Akademie van Wetenschappen, afd. Letterkunde. Nieuwe Reeks 36. Amsterdam: North-Holland Publishing Company.

Krebernik, Manfred

1998 Die Texte aus Fara und Tell Abu Salabih. In *Mesopotamien: Späturuk-Zeit und Frühdynastische Zeit: Annäherungen 1,* edited by Pascal Attinger and Markus Wäfler, pp. 237–427. Orbis Biblius et Orientalis 160/1. Fribourg, Switzerland: Universitätsverlag.

Krecher, Joachim

1987 DU = ku.(r) "eintreten", "hineinbringen." *Zeitschrift für Assyriologie* 77:7–21.

Kris, Ernst, and Otto Kurz

1979 *Legend, Myth, and Magic in the Image of the Artist: A Historical Experiment.* New Haven, CT: Yale University Press.

Kroskrity, Paul V.

2000 Regimenting Languages: Language Ideological Perspectives. In *Regimes of*

Language: Ideologies, Polities, and Identities, edited by Paul V. Kroskrity, pp. 1–34. Santa Fe, NM: School of American Research Press.

Kurozumi, Makoto
2000   Kangaku: Writing and Institutional Authority. In *Inventing the Classics: Modernity, National Identity, and Japanese Literature,* edited by Haruo Shirane and Tomi Suzuki, pp. 201–209. Stanford, CA: Stanford University Press.

Kychanov, E. I.
1996   Tangut. In *The World's Writing Systems,* edited by Peter T. Daniels and William Bright, pp. 228–229. New York: Oxford University Press.

Labarta, Ana, and Carmen Barceló
1988   *Números y cifras en los documentos Arábigohispanos.* Córdoba, Spain: Universidad de Córdoba.

Lacadena García-Gallo, Alfonso
1995   Evolución formal de las grafias escriturias mayas: Implicaciones históricas y culturales. Ph.D. diss., Universidad Complutense de Madrid.
2000   Los escribas del Códice de Madrid: Metodología paleográfica. *Revista Española de Antropología Americana* 30:27–85.

Lacau, Pierre
1904   *Sarcophages antérieurs au Nouvel Empire.* Catalogue Général des Antiquités Egyptiennes du Musée du Caire. Cairo: Institut Français d'Archéologie Orientale.

Lacau, Pierre, and Henri Chevrier
1956–1969   *Une chapelle de Sésostris Ier à Karnak.* Service des Antiquités de l'Egypte. Cairo: Institut Français d'Archéologie Orientale.

Lagercrantz, Sture
1968   African Tally-Strings. *Anthropos* 63:115–128.
1970   Tallying by Means of Lines, Stones, and Sticks. *Paideuma* 16:52–62.

Langdon, Merle
2005   A New Greek Abecedarium. *Kadmos* 44:175–182.

Lange, H. O., and Heinrich Schäfer
1902–1925   *Grab- und Denksteine des Mittleren Reiches.* 4 vols. Catalogue Général des Antiquités Egyptiennes du Musée du Caire. Cairo: Institut Français d'Archéologie Orientale.

Lange, Kurt, and Max Hirmer
1968   *Egypt: Architecture, Sculpture, and Painting.* 4th ed. London: Phaidon.

Language Log
2007   The Prehistory of Emoticons. Electronic document, http://itre.cis.upenn.edu/~myl/languagelog/archives/004935.html, accessed September 29, 2010.

Laughlin, Robert
1988a   What Is a Tzotzil? *RES* 15:133–155.

1988b   *The Great Tzotzil Dictionary of Santo Domingo Zinacantán*, vol. I. Smithsonian Contributions to Anthropology 31. Washington, DC: Smithsonian Institution Press.

Lave, Jean, and Etienne Wenger
1991   *Situated Learning: Legitimate Peripheral Participation*. Cambridge: Cambridge University Press.

Ledderose, Lothar
2000   *Ten Thousand Things: Module and Mass Production in Chinese Art*. Princeton, NJ: Princeton University Press.

Ledyard, G. K.
1966   The Korean Language Reform of 1446: The Origin, Background, and Early History of the Korean Alphabet. Ph.D. diss., University of California, Berkeley.

1997   The International Linguistic Background of the Correct Sounds for the Instruction of the People. In *The Korean Alphabet: Its History and Structure*, edited by Young-Key Kim-Renaud, pp. 31–87. Honolulu: University of Hawai'i Press.

1998   *The Korean Language Reform of 1446*. Kungnip kugŏ yon'guwŏn ch'ongsŏ 2. Seoul: Sin'gu munhwasa.

Lee, Iksop, and S. Robert Ramsey
2000   *The Korean Language*. Albany: State University of New York Press.

Lee, Ki-Moon
1997   The Inventory of the Korean Alphabet. In *The Korean Alphabet: Its History and Structure*, edited by Young-Key Kim-Renaud, pp. 11–30. Honolulu: University of Hawai'i Press.

Lemay, Richard
1977   The Hispanic Origin of Our Present Numeral Forms. *Viator* 8:435–462.

Leprohon, Ronald J.
2009   The Stela of Sehetipibre (CG 20538): Borrowings and Innovation. In *Archaism and Innovation: Studies in the Culture of Middle Kingdom Egypt*, edited by David P. Silverman, William Kelly Simpson, and Josef Wegner, pp. 277–292. New Haven, CT: Department of Near Eastern Languages and Civilizations, Yale University; Philadelphia: University of Pennsylvania Museum of Archaeology and Anthropology.

Lepsius, Richard
1867   *Aelteste Text des Todenbuchs, nach Sarkophagen des altaegyptischen Reichs im Berliner Museum*. Berlin: Wilhelm Hertz.

Lewis, Mark Edward
1999   *Writing and Authority in Early China*. Albany: State University of New York Press.

Lichtheim, Miriam

1973   *Ancient Egyptian Literature: A Book of Readings I, The Old and Middle Kingdoms.*
Berkeley: University of California Press.

1988   *Ancient Egyptian Autobiographies Chiefly of the Middle Kingdom: A Study and an Anthology.* Orbis Biblicus et Orientalis 84. Fribourg, Switzerland: Universitätsverlag; Göttingen, Germany: Vandenhoeck & Ruprecht.

Lipiński, Edward

2001   *Semitic Languages: Outline of a Comparative Grammar.* Leuven, Belgium: Peeters.

Lipp, Frank J.

1991   *Mixe of Oaxaca: Religion, Ritual, and Healing.* Austin: University of Texas Press.

Loprieno, Antonio

1995   *Ancient Egyptian: A Linguistic Introduction.* Cambridge: Cambridge University Press.

Ludwig, Marie-Christine

1990   *Untersuchungen zu den Hymnen des Išme-Dagan von Isin.* SANTAG. Arbeiten und Untersuchungen zur Keilschriftkunde 2. Wiesbaden, Germany: Harrassowitz.

Luft, Ulrich

1992   *Das Archiv von Illahun.* Hieratische Papyri aus den Staatlichen Museen zu Berlin—Preussicher Kulturbesitz 1. Berlin: Akademie.

2006   *Urkunden zur Chronologie der späten 12. Dynastie: Briefe aus Illahun.* Österreichische Akademie der Wissenschaften, Denkschriften der Gesamtakademie 34; Contributions to the Chronology of the Eastern Mediterrean 7. Vienna: Verlag der Österreichischen Akademie der Wissenschaften.

Lurie, David B.

2006   Language, Writing, and Disciplinarity in the Critique of the "Ideographic Myth": Some Proleptical Remarks. *Language and Communication* 26:250–269.

2007   The Subterranean Archives of Early Japan: Recently Discovered Sources for the Study of Writing and Literacy. In *Books in Numbers,* edited by Wilt Idema, pp. 91–112. Hong Kong: Chinese University Press.

2011   *Realms of Literacy: Early Japan and the History of Writing.* Cambridge, MA: Harvard University Asia Center.

Macri, Martha J., and Matthew G. Looper

2003   *The New Catalog of Maya Hieroglyphs,* vol. 1: *The Classic Period Inscriptions.* Norman: University of Oklahoma Press.

Macri, Martha J., and Laura M. Stark

1993   *A Sign Catalog of the La Mojarra Script.* Pre-Columbian Art Research Institute Monograph 5. San Francisco: Pre-Columbian Art Research Institute.

Macri, Martha J., and Gabrielle Vail

2009   *The New Catalog of Maya Hieroglyphs,* vol. 2: *Codical Texts.* Norman: University of Oklahoma Press.

REFERENCES

Maeda, Ai

2004 From Communal Performance to Solitary Reading: The Rise of the Modern Japanese Reader. Translated by James Fujii. In *Text and the City: Essays on Japanese Modernity*, edited by James Fujii, pp. 223–254. Durham, NC: Duke University Press.

Mahadevan, Iravatham

2003 *Early Tamil Epigraphy: From the Earliest Times to the Sixth Century A.D.* Harvard Oriental Series 62. Madras, India: Cre-A; Cambridge, MA: The Department of Sanskrit and Indian Studies, Harvard University.

Maher, David W., and John F. Makowski

2001 Literary Evidence for Roman Arithmetic with Fractions. *Classical Philology* 96(4):376–399.

Mallon, Jean

1948 Pour une nouvelle critique des chiffres dans les inscriptions latines gravées sur pierre. *Emerita* 16:14–45.

Marchand, Sylvie, and Georges Soukiassian

2010 *Balat VIII: Un habitat de la XIIIe dynastie—2e période intermédiaire à Ayn Asil.* Fouilles de l'IFAO 59. Cairo: Institut Français d'Archéologie Orientale.

Marchant, Anne Jones

1990 Old Babylonian Tablets from Larsa in the Lowie Museum of Anthropology. Ph.D. diss., University of California, Berkeley.

Marcillet-Jaubert, Jean

1959 Review of *Contributions to the Palaeography of Latin Inscriptions*, by Joyce S. Gordon and Arthur E. Gordon. *Gnomon* 31:137–141.

Marcus, Joyce

1992 *Mesoamerican Writing Systems: Propaganda, Myth, and History in Four Ancient Civilizations.* Princeton, NJ: Princeton University Press.

Marshack, Alexander

1972 *The Roots of Civilization.* New York: McGraw Hill.

Martin, Geoffrey Thorndike

1971 *Egyptian Administrative and Private-Name Seals, Principally of the Middle Kingdom and Second Intermediate Period.* Oxford: Griffith Institute.

Martin, Simon, and Nikolai Grube

1995 Maya Superstates. *Archaeology* 48(6):41–46.

2008 *Chronicle of the Maya Kings and Queens: Deciphering the Dynasties of the Ancient Maya.* 2nd ed. London: Thames and Hudson.

McCarter, P. Kyle

1975 *The Antiquity of the Greek Alphabet and the Early Phoenician Scripts.* Missoula, MT: Scholars Press.

McDonald, Angela

2007   A Metaphor for Troubled Times: The Evolution of the Seth Deity Determinative in the First Intermediate Period. *Zeitschrift fur Ägyptische Sprache und Alterumskunde* 134:26–39.

McPharlin, Paul

1942   *Roman Numerals, Typographic Bases and Pointing Hands: Some Notes on Their Origin, History, and Contemporary Use.* New York: The Typophiles.

Memoria de Linderos: Gráfica Agraria de Oaxaca

1997   *Documentos del Archivo Historico de la Secretaría de la Reforma Agraria en Oaxaca.* Oaxaca, Mexico: Instituto de Artes Gráficas de Oaxaca.

Menninger, Karl

1969 [1958]   *Number Words and Number Symbols.* Translated by Paul Broneer. Göttingen: Vandenhoeck; Cambridge, MA: MIT Press.

Michalowski, Piotr

1995   Sumerian Literature: An Overview. In *Civilizations of the Ancient Near East,* edited by Jack M. Sasson, pp. 2279–2291. New York: Charles Scribner's Sons.

Miller, Mary E.

1986   *The Murals of Bonampak.* Princeton, NJ: Princeton University Press.

Miller, Mary, and Simon Martin

2004   *Courtly Art of the Ancient Maya.* San Francisco: Fine Arts Museum of San Francisco.

Miller, Roy A.

1967   *The Japanese Language.* Chicago: University of Chicago Press.

Miyake, Marc Hideo

2003   *Old Japanese: A Phonetic Reconstruction.* London: Routledge.

Möller, Georg

1909–1927   *Hieratische Paläographie: Die Aegyptische Buchschrift in ihrer Entwicklung von der fünften Dynastie bis zur römischen Kaiserzeit I–III.* Leipzig: J. C. Hinrichs.

Moltke, Erik

1985   *Runes and Their Origin: Denmark and Elsewhere.* Copenhagen: National Museum of Denmark.

Mommsen, Theodor

1873   *Corpus Inscriptionum Latinarum Volumen III. Inscriptiones Asiae, provinciarum Europae Graecarum, Illyrici Latini, Pars II. Inscriptionum Illyrici partes VI. VII. Res gestae divi Augusti. Edictum Diocletiani de pretiis rerum. Privilegia militum veteranorumque. Instrumenta Dacica.* Berlin: De Gruyter.

1965 [1909]   *Philologische Schriften.* Vol. 7 of *Gesammelte Schriften.* Berlin: Weidmann.

Monaghan, John

1990   Performance and the Structure of the Mixtec Codices. *Ancient Mesoamerica* 1:133–140.

2004   Shamanism, Colonialism and the Mesa in Mesoamerican Religious Discourse. In *Mesas and Cosmologies in Mesoamerica*, edited by Douglas Sharon, pp. 141–148. Museum Papers No. 42. San Diego, CA: San Diego Museum of Man.

2008   Revelatory Scripts, the Unlettered Genius, and the Appearance and Disappearance of Writing. In *The Disappearance of Writing Systems: Perspectives on Literacy and Communication*, edited by John Baines, John Bennett, and Stephen Houston, pp. 323–334. London: Equinox.

Monaghan, John, and Byron Hamann

1998   Reading as a Social Practice and Cultural Construction. *Indiana Journal of Hispanic Literatures* 13:131–140.

2000   La construcción cultural de la lectura en Mesoamérica. In *Códices y documentos sobre México, Tercer Simposio Internacional*, edited by Constanza Vega, pp. 485–492. Mexico City: Instituto Nacional de Antropología e Historia.

Montefiore, Arthur

1895   Notes on the Samoyads [*sic*] of the Great Tundra. *Journal of the Anthropological Institute of Great Britain and Ireland* 24:388–410.

Montgomery, John E.

1995   Sculptors of the Realm: Classic Maya Artists' Signature and Sculptural Style During the Reign of Piedras Negras Ruler 7. M.A. thesis, University of New Mexico, Albuquerque.

Mora-Marín, David

2009   A Test and Falsification of the "Classic Ch'olti'an" Hypothesis: A Study of Three Proto-Ch'olan Markers. *International Journal of American Linguistics* 75(2):115–157.

Morandi, Alessandro

1982   *Epigrafia Italica*. Rome: L'Erma de Bretschneider.

Morison, Stanley

1972   *Politics and Script: Aspects of Authority and Freedom in the Development of Graeco-Latin Script from the Sixth Century B.C. to the Twentieth Century A.D.* Oxford: Clarendon Press.

Morley, Sylvanus G.

1938   *Inscriptions of Petén*, vol. I. Carnegie Institution of Washington Publication 437. Washington, DC: Carnegie Institution of Washington.

1975 [1915] *An Introduction to the Study of the Maya Hieroglyphs*. New York: Dover; Washington, DC: Government Printing Office.

Morritt, Robert D.

2010   *Stones That Speak*. Newcastle upon Tyne, UK: Cambridge Scholars.

Mountford, John

1996   A Functional Classification. In *The World's Writing Systems*, edited by Peter T. Daniels and William Bright, pp. 627–632. New York: Oxford University Press.

Mukherjee, B. N.

1993   The Early Use of Decimal Notation in Indian Epigraphs. *Journal of the Epigraphical Society of India* 19:80–83.

Müller, Walter W.

1994–1996   Die altsüdarabische Schrift. In *Schrift und Schriftlichkeit: Writing and Its Use*, vol. 1, edited by H. Günther and O. Ludwig, pp. 307–312. Berlin and New York: De Gruyter.

Müller-Wollermann, Renate

2005   Die Felsinschriften des Alten Reiches aus Elkab. In *Texte und Denkmäler des ägyptischen Alten Reiches*, edited by Stephan Johannes Seidlmayer, pp. 263–274. Berlin-Brandenburgische Akademie der Wissenschaften, Thesaurus Linguae Aegyptiae 3. Berlin: Achet Verlag, Dr. Norbert Dürring.

Mundy, Barbara

1996   *The Mapping of New Spain: Indigenous Cartography and the Maps of the Relaciónes Geográficas.* Chicago: University of Chicago Press.

2001   Lienzos. In *The Oxford Encyclopedia of Mesoamerican Cultures*, vol. 2, edited by Davíd Carrasco, pp. 120–123. Oxford: Oxford University Press.

Murray, Alexander

1978   *Reason and Society in the Middle Ages.* Oxford: Clarendon Press.

Naim, C. Mohammed

1971   Arabic Orthography in Some Non-Semitic Languages. In *Islam and Its Cultural Divergence: Studies in Honor of Gustave E. von Grunebaum*, edited by Girdhari I. Tikku, pp. 113–144. Urbana: University of Illinois Press.

Nakamura, Tamotsu

1988   Kanji bunkaken no tenkai. In *Kanji kōza 1: Kanji to wa*, edited by Satō Kiyoji, pp. 117–134. Tokyo: Meiji shoin.

Nehmé, Laïla

2010   A Glimpse of the Development of the Nabatean Script into Arabic based on Old and New Epigraphic Material. In *The Development of Arabic as a Written Language*, edited by Michael C.A. Macdonald, pp. 47–88. Oxford: Archaeopress.

Newberry, Percy E.

1893   *Beni Hasan I.* Archaeological Survey of Egypt. London: Egypt Exploration Fund.

Nickerson, Raymond S.

1988   Counting, Computing, and the Representation of Numbers. *Human Factors* 30:181–199.

Nissen, Hans J., Peter Damerow, and Robert K. Englund

1993   *Archaic Bookkeeping.* Translated by Paul Larsen. Chicago: University of Chicago Press.

REFERENCES

Noguez, Xavier

1999   *Códice Techialoyan de San Pedro Tototepec (Estado de México).* Toluca, Mexico: Colegio Mexiquense.

Nutini, Hugo, and J. Forbes de Nutini

1987   Nahualismo, control de los elementos y hechicería en Tlaxaca Rural. In *La heterodoxia recuperada en torno a Angel Palerm,* edited by Susana Glantz, pp. 321–346. Mexico City: Fondo de Cultura Económica.

O'Connor, David

1969   Abydos and the University Museum: 1898–1969. *Expedition* 12(1):28–39.

Okumura, Etsuzō

1978a   Kana monjo no seiritsu izen. In *Ronshū Nihon bungaku Nihongo,* vol. 1, edited by Hamada Keisuke, pp. 225–248. Tokyo: Kadokawa shoten.

1978b   Kana monjo no seiritsu izen, zoku. *Man'yō* 99:37–58.

1985   Wago, kundokugo, hon'yakugo. *Man'yō* 121:30–41.

1988   Kurashi no kotoba, tegami no kotoba. In *Nihon no kodai 14: Kotoba to moji,* edited by Kishi Toshio, pp. 325–372. Tokyo: Chūō kōronsha.

1999   Kotoba ga erabu mono, kotoba o erabu mono. *Kokugo to kokubungaku* 76(5):25–35.

Oliver, Revilo P.

1949   The Claudian Letter Ⱶ. *American Journal of Archaeology* 53:248–257.

1951   The First Medicean MS of Tacitus and the Titulature of Ancient Books. *Transactions of the American Philological Association* 82:232–261.

Osing, Jürgen, and Gloria Rosati

1998   *Papiri geroglifica e ieratici da Tebtynis.* Florence: Istituto papirologico G. Vitelli.

Owens, Jonathan

2006   *A Linguistic History of Arabic.* Oxford: Oxford University Press.

Ōya, Tōru

1909   *Kanazukai oyobi kanajitai enkaku shiryō.* Tokyo: Kokutei kyōkasho kyōdō hanbaijo.

Pantalacci, Laure

1998   La documentation épistolaire du palais des gouverneurs à Balat—'Ayn Aṣīl. *Bulletin de l'Institut Français d'Archéologie Orientale* 98:303–315.

Parkinson, Richard B.

1991a   *The Tale of the Eloquent Peasant.* Oxford: Griffith Institute.

1991b   *Voices from Ancient Egypt: An Anthology of Middle Kingdom Writings.* London: British Museum Press.

1996   Individual and Society in Middle Kingdom Literature. In *Ancient Egyptian Literature: History and Forms,* edited by Antonio Loprieno, pp. 137–155. Probleme der Ägyptologie 10. Leiden: E. J. Brill.

1999   *Cracking Codes: The Rosetta Stone and Decipherment.* London: British Museum Press.

2002   *Poetry and Culture in Middle Kingdom Egypt.* London: Continuum.

2009   *Reading Ancient Egyptian Poetry: Among Other Histories.* Chichester, UK: Wiley-Blackwell.

Parmenter, Ross

1982   *Four Lienzos of the Coixtlahuaca Valley.* Studies in Precolumbian Art and Archaeology 26. Washington, DC: Dumbarton Oaks.

Pellat, Charles

1986   *Laḥn al-'āmma.* In *The Encyclopedia of Islam,* vol. 5, rev. ed., edited by C. E. Bosworth, E. van Donzel, B. Lewis, and C. Pellat, pp. 605–610. Leiden: E. J. Brill.

Perea, M., J. A. Duñabeitia, and M. Carreiras

2008   R34D1NG W0RD5 W1TH NUMB3R5. *Journal of Experimental Psychology, Human Perception and Performance* 34(1):237–241.

Peruzzi, Emilio

1980   *Mycenaeans in Early Latium.* Rome: Edizioni dell'Ateneo and Bizzarri.

1992   Cultura greca a Gabii nel secolo VIII. *Parola del Passato* 47:459–468.

Pétrosyan, Yuri A.

1994   *De Baghdad à Ispahan: Manuscrits islamiques de la Filiale de Saint-Petersbourg de l'Institut d'Etudes Orientales, Académie des Sciences de Russie.* Lugano, Switzerland: Fondation ARCH; Paris: Editions des Musées de la Ville de Paris; and Milan: Electa.

Pettersson, John Sören

1994   Evolutionary Accounts of Writing and the Disobedient History of Scripts. *Language and Communication* 14:129–153.

Piggott, Joan R.

1997   *The Emergence of Japanese Kinship.* Stanford, CA: Stanford University Press.

Pike, Eunice

1960   Mazatec Sexual Impurity and the Bible. *Practical Anthropology* 7:49–53.

Pilgrim, Cornelius von

1996   *Elephantine XVIII: Untersuchungen in der Stadt des Mittleren Reiches und der Zweiten Zwischenzeit.* Archäologische Veröffentlichungen des Deutschen Archäologischen Instituts, Abteilung Kairo 91. Mainz, Germany: Philipp von Zabern.

Pinnow, Heinz-Jürgen

1972   Schrift und Sprache in den Werken Lako Bodras im Gebiet der Ho von Singbhum (Bihar). *Anthropos* 67:822–857.

Poccetti, Paolo

2008   Il vaso iscritto dall necropolis de Magliano Sabina. In *Una nova iscrizione da Magliano Sabina. Scrittura e cultura nella valle del Tevere,* edited by Paola Santoro, pp. 29–42. Pisa, Italy: Fabrizio Serra.

Pohl, Frederik

1966   *Digits and Dastards.* London: Dobson.

Pohl, John

2003   Creation Stories, Hero Cults, and Alliance Building: Confederacies of Central Mexico. In *The Postclassic Mesoamerican World,* edited by Michael E. Smith and Frances F. Berdan, pp. 61–66. Salt Lake City: University of Utah Press.

Poinikastas: Epigraphic Sources for Early Greek Writing

2010   http://poinikastas.csad.ox.ac.uk.

Posener-Kriéger, Paule, and Jean Louis de Cenival

1968   *The Abu Sir Papyri.* Hieratic Papyri in the British Museum, 5th series. London: British Museum.

Postgate, Nicholas, Tao Wang, and Toby Wilkinson

1995   The Evidence for Early Writing: Utilitarian or Ceremonial? *Antiquity* 69:459–480.

Preston, Jean F.

1994   Playing with Numbers: Some Mixed Counting Methods Found in French Medieval Manuscripts at Princeton. In *Medieval Codicology, Iconography, Literature, and Translation: Studies for Keith Val Sinclair,* edited by Peter R. Monks and D. D. R. Owen, pp. 74–78. Leiden: E. J. Brill.

Prosdocimi, Aldo

1984   *Le tavole iguvine.* Florence: L. S. Olschki.

Proskouriakoff, Tatiana

1950   *A Study of Classic Maya Sculpture.* Carnegie Institution of Washington Publication 593. Washington, DC: Carnegie Institution of Washington.

1960   Historical Implications of a Pattern of Dates at Piedras Negras, Guatemala. *American Antiquity* 25:454–475.

1961   Portraits of Women in Maya Art. In *Essays in Pre-Columbian Art and Archaeology,* edited by Samuel K. Lothrop, D. Z. Stone, G. F. Ekholm, J. B. Bird, and
G. R. Willey, pp. 81–90. Cambridge, MA: Harvard University Press.

1963   Historical Data in the Inscriptions of Yaxchilán. *Estudios de Cultura Maya* 3:149–167.

PSI. See **Società italiana per la ricerca dei papiri greci e latini in Egitto**

Psychoyos, Dimitris K.

2005   The Forgotten Art of Isopsephy and the Magic Number KZ. *Semiotica* 154:157–224.

Puin, Gerd-Rüdiger

1970   *Der Dīwān von 'Umar ibn al-Ḥaṭṭāb: Ein Beitrag zur frühislamischen Verwaltungsgeschichte.* Bonn: Rheinische Friedrich-Wilhelms-Universität.

Pulleyblank, Edwin G.
1995   *Outline of Classical Chinese Grammar.* Vancouver: University of British
         Columbia Press.

Qiu Xigui
2000   *Chinese Writing.* Translated by Gilbert L. Mattos and Jerry Norman. Berkeley,
         CA: Society for the Study of Early China.

Quack, Joachim Friedrich
2006   Zur Lesung und Deutung des Dramatischen Ramesseumspapyrus. *Zeitschrift*
         für Ägyptische Sprache und Alterumskunde 133:72–89.

Quirke, Stephen
2004   *Egyptian Literature 1800 BC: Questions and Readings.* Egyptology 2. London:
         Golden House Publications.

2007   The Hyksos in Egypt 1600 BCE: New Rules without an Administration. In
         Regime Change in the Ancient Near East and Egypt, from Sargon of Agade to Saddam
         Hussein, edited by Harriet Crawford, pp. 123–139. Proceedings from the
         British Academy 136. Oxford: Oxford University Press; London: British
         Academy.

Quṭrub, Muḥammad b. al-Mustanīr
AH 1315 (1897)   *Muthallathāt Abī ʿAlī Muḥammad b. al-Mustanīr al-maʿrūf bi-Quṭrub.*
         Commentary in prose of the versified *Muthallathāt,* by Sadīd al-Dīn ʿAbd al-
         Wahhāb al-Bahnasī (d. 1286). Cairo: al-Maṭbaʿa al-Ḥamīdiyya al-Miṣriyya.

18th century *Sharḥ qaṣīdat Muthallathāt Quṭrub.* MS Yale Landberg 489, folio 1b
         (Nemoy no. 189). Super-commentary in prose by Ibrāhīm b. Hibatallāh al-
         Maḥallī al-Lakhmī (d. 1321) of the Muthallathāt versification by Sadīd al-Dīn
         ʿAbd al-Wahhāb al-Bahnasī (d. ca. 1286), partially parallel with MS Garret
         Houtsma 288, 24 fols. n.d. (Hitti no. 246).

1908   *Sharḥ Muthallathāt Quṭrub,* edited by C. L. Cheikho. *Mashriq:*516–522.

1914   Sharḥ Muthallathāt Quṭrub fī l-rajaz. In *al-Bulgha fī shudhūr al-lugha: Dix*
         anciens traités de philologie arabe, edited by Auguste Haffner and Louis
         Cheikho, pp. 168–174. Beirut: Imprimerie Catholique.

Rao Zongyi and Zeng Xiantong
1985   *Suixian Zeng Hou Yi mu zhong qing mingci yanjiu.* Hong Kong: Zhongwen
         daxue chubanshe.

Rawson, Jessica
1987   *Chinese Bronzes: Art and Ritual.* London: British Museum Publications.

Record, Robert
1543   *The Ground of Artes.* London: R. Wolfe.

Reisner, George Andrew
1955   Clay Sealings of Dynasty XIII from Uronarti Fort. *Kush* 3:26–69.

Richards, Fiona V.
2001   *The Anra Scarab: An Archaeological and Historical Approach.* BAR International
         Series 919. Oxford: Archaeopress.

Richards, Janet E.

2005   *Society and Death in Ancient Egypt: Mortuary Landscapes of the Middle Kingdom.* Cambridge: Cambridge University Press.

Ricketson, Oliver, Jr.

1937   *Uaxactun, Guatemala: Group E—1926–1931*, part I: *The Excavations.* Carnegie Institution of Washington Publication 477. Washington, DC: Carnegie Institution of Washington.

Ritner, Robert Kriech

1993   *The Mechanics of Ancient Egyptian Magical Practice.* Studies in Ancient Oriental Civilization 54. Chicago: The Oriental Institute of the University of Chicago.

Rix, Helmut

2005   Alphabete im vorrömischen Kampanien. In *Otium: Festschrift für Volker Michael Strocka*, edited by Thomas Ganschow and Matthias Steinhart, pp. 323–330. Remshalden-Grumbach, Germany: Bernhard Albert Greiner.

Robertson, James E.

1980   The ORDVAC and the ILLIAC. In *A History of Computing in the Twentieth Century*, edited by N. Metropolis, J. Howlett, and Giancarlo Rota, pp. 347–364. New York: Academic Press.

Robertson, John S., Stephen Houston, Alfonso Lacadena, Daniel Law, David Stuart, and Marc Zender

n.d.   A Return to Classical Ch'olti' as the Language of the Mayan Hieroglyphic Script. Manuscript on file, Department of Anthropology, Brown University, Providence, Rhode Island.

Robertson, Merle G.

1977   Painting Practices and Their Change through Time of the Palenque Stucco Sculptors. In *Social Process in Maya Prehistory: Studies in Honour of Sir Eric Thompson*, edited by Norman Hammond, pp. 297–326. London: Academic Press.

Robicsek, Francis, and Donald M. Hales

1981   *The Maya Book of the Dead: The Ceramic Codex; The Corpus of Codex Style Ceramics of the Late Classic Period.* Charlottesville: University of Virginia Art Museum.

Robins, Gay, ed.

1990   *Beyond the Pyramids: Egyptian Regional Art from the Museo Egizio, Turin.* Atlanta, GA: Emory University Museum of Art and Archaeology.

Robson, Eleanor

2003   Tables and Tabular Formatting in Sumer, Babylonia, and Assyria, 2500–50 BCE. In *The History of Mathematical Table-Making, from Sumer to Spreadsheets*, edited by M. Campbell-Kelly, M. Croarken, R. G. Flood, and Eleanor Robson, pp. 18–47. Oxford: Oxford University Press.

2004   Accounting for Change: The Development of Tabular Book-Keeping in Early Mesopotamia. In *Creating Economic Order: Record-Keeping,*

Standardization, and the Development of Accounting in the Ancient Near East, edited by Michael Hudson and Cornelia Wunsch, pp. 107–144. International Scholars Conference on Ancient Near Eastern Economies 4. Bethesda, MD: CDL Press.

2007   Digital Corpus of Cuneiform Mathematical Texts. *Open Richly Annotated Cuneiform Corpus.* Electronic document, http://oracc.museum/upenn.edu/dccmt.

2008   *Mathematics in Ancient Iraq: A Social History.* Princeton, NJ: Princeton University Press.

Romano, James F.

1979   *The Luxor Museum of Ancient Egyptian Art: Catalogue.* Cairo: American Research Center in Egypt.

Rosenthal, Franz

1971   *Significant Uses of Arabic Writing.* Leiden: E. J. Brill.

Rothe, Russell D., William K. Miller, and George Rapp, Jr.

2008   *Pharaonic Inscriptions from the Southeastern Desert of Egypt.* Winona Lake, IN: Eisenbrauns.

Rubinger, Richard

2007   *Popular Literacy in Early Modern Japan.* Honolulu: University of Hawai'i Press.

Rubio, Gonzalo

2006   Writing in Another Tongue: Alloglottography in the Ancient Near East. In *Margins of Writing, Origins of Cultures,* edited by Seth L. Sanders, pp. 33–66. Chicago: The Oriental Institute of the University of Chicago.

Ruíz, María Elena

1985   Observaciones sobre canteras in el Petén, Guatemala. *Estudios de Cultura Maya* 16:19–53.

al-Ṣafadī, Khalīl b. Aybak

1962–1997   *al-Wāfī bīl-Wafayāt,* vol. 5, edited by H. Ritter. Wiesbaden, Germany: Steiner.

Sakaki, Atsuko

2000   Kajin no kigū: The Meiji Political Novel and the Boundaries of Literature. *Monumenta Nipponica* 55:83–108.

Salama, Pierre

1999   Anomalies paléographiques des chiffres sur les inscriptions africaines de l'antiquité tardive. *Antiquité Tardive* 7:231–254.

Sallaberger, Walther

1993   *Der kultische Kalender der Urr III-Zeit.* Untersuchungen zur Assyriologie und vorderasiatischen Archäologie. Ergänzungsbände zur Zeitschrift für Assyriologie und vorderasiatische Archäologie 7. Berlin: De Gruyter.

1999a   Ur III-Zeit. In *Mesopotamien: Akkade-Zeit und Ur III-Zeit, Annäherungen 3,* edited by Pascal Attinger and Markus Wäfler, pp. 121–390. Orbis Biblicus et Orientalis 160/3. Fribourg, Switzerland: Universitätsverlag.

1999b   *"Wenn Du mein Bruder bist, ..." Interaktion und Textgestaltung in altbabylonischen Alltagsbriefen.* Cuneiform Monographs 16. Groningen, Netherlands: Styx Publications.

2004   Das Ende des Sumerischen: Tod und Nachleben einer altmesopotamischen Sprache. In *Sprachtod und Sprachgeburt,* edited by Peter Schrijver and Peter-Arnold Mumm, pp. 108–140. Bremen, Germany: Hempen.

Salomon, Richard

1995   On the Origin of the Early Indian Scripts. *Journal of the American Oriental Society* 115:271–279.

1996   Brāhmī and Kharoṣṭhī. In *The World's Writing Systems,* edited by Peter T. Daniels and William Bright, pp. 373–383. New York: Oxford University Press.

1998   *Indian Epigraphy: A Guide to the Study of Inscriptions in Sanskrit, Prakrit, and Other Indo-Aryan Languages.* New York: Oxford University Press.

2000   Typological Observations on the Indic Script Group and Its Relationship to Other Alphasyllabaries. *Studies in the Linguistic Sciences* 30:87–103.

2003   Writing Systems of the Indo-Aryan Languages. In *The Indo-Aryan Languages,* edited by George Cardona and Dhanesh Jain, pp. 67–103. Routledge Language Family Series. London: Routledge.

2004   Review of Mahadevan 2003. *Journal of the American Oriental Society* 124:565–569.

al-Samʿānī, ʿAbd al-Karīm b. Muḥammad

1952   *Adab al-imlāʾ wa-l-istimlāʾ [Die Methodik des Diktatkollegs].* Edited by Max Weisweiler. Leiden: E. J. Brill.

Sandstrom, Alan

1991   *Corn Is Our Blood.* Norman: University of Oklahoma Press.

Sandys, Sir John Edward

1919   *Latin Epigraphy.* Cambridge: Cambridge University Press.

Sanni, Amidu

2008   Beyond Fück and Ullmann: The Discourse on *laḥn* in Arabic Philological and Literary Traditions. In *XXX. Deutscher Orientalistentag, Freiburg, 24–28 September 2007. Ausgewählte Vorträge,* edited by Rainer Brunner, Jens Peter Laut, and Maurus Reinkowski. Electronic document, http://webdoc.urz.uni-halle.de/dot2007/publikation.php.

Santoro, Paola, ed.

2008   *Una nuova iscrizione de Magliano Sabrina: Scrittura e cultura nella valle del Tevere.* Pisa, Italy: Fabrizio Serra.

Sasahara, Hiroyuki

2006   Kokuji no hassei. In *Moji to kodai Nihon 5: Moji hyōgen no kakutoku,* edited by Hirakawa Minami, pp. 284–298. Tokyo: Yoshikawa kōbunkan.

Sass, Benjamin

1988   *The Genesis of the Alphabet and Its Development in the Second Millennium B.C.* Wiesbaden, Germany: Harrassowitz.

Sasse, Hans-Jürgen

1981   Die Semitischen Sprachen. In *Die Sprachen Afrikas*, edited by B. Heine, T. C. Schadeberg, and E. Wolff, pp. 224–238. Hamburg: Buske.

Satterthwaite, Linton, Jr.

1938   Maya Dating by Hieroglyphic Styles. *American Anthropologist* 40:416–428.

1965   Maya Practice Stone-Carving at Piedras Negras. *Expedition* 7:9–18.

Saturno, William A., David Stuart, and Boris Beltrán

2006   Early Maya Writing at San Bartolo, Guatemala. *Science* 311:1281–1283.

Schäfer, Heinrich

1986 [1974] *Principles of Egyptian Art*. Rev. ed. Edited by Emma Brunner-Traut, translated and edited by John Baines. Oxford: Griffith Institute.

Schallenberg, Gino

2006   Voices of the "Periphery": Reactions on New Bulletins Posted on Arabic Websites. Paper presented at the 23rd Congress of the Union Européenne des Arabisants et Islamisants (UEAI), Sassari, Sardinia, Italy.

Schele, Linda

1982   *Maya Glyphs: The Verbs*. Austin: University of Texas Press.

Schmandt-Besserat, Denise

1992   *Before Writing*. Austin: University of Texas Press.

Schneider, Nikolaus

1935   *Die Keilschriftzeichen der Wirtschaftsurkunden von Ur III*. Rome: Päpstliches Bibelinstitut.

Schneider, Thomas

2008   Neues zum Verständnis des Dramatischen Ramesseumspapyrus: Vorschläge zur Übersetzung der Szenen 1–23. In *Mythos und Ritual: Festschrift für Jan Assmann zum 70. Geburtstag*, edited by Benedikt Rothöhler and Alexander Manisali, pp. 231–255. Religionswissenschaft: Forschung und Wissenschaft 5. Münster, Germany: LIT.

Schoeler, Gregor

2002   *Écrire et transmettre dans les débuts de l'islam*. Paris: Presses Universitaires de France.

2006   *The Oral and the Written in Early Islam*. Translated by Uwe Vagelpohl and edited by James Montgomery. London: Routledge.

Scribner, Sylvia, and Michael Cole

1981   *The Psychology of Literacy*. Cambridge, MA: Harvard University Press.

Sebba, Mark

2009   Sociolinguistic approaches to writing systems research. *Writing Systems Research* 1(1):35–49.

Seeley, Christopher

1991   *A History of Writing in Japan*. Leiden: E. J. Brill.

Seidlmayer, Stephan Johannes

1987   Wirstschaftliche und gesellschafliche Entwicklung im Übergang vom Alten zum Mittleren Reich: Ein Beitrag zur Archäologie der Gräberfelder der Region Qau-Matmar in der Ersten Zwischenzeit. In *Problems and Priorities in Egyptian Archaeology*, edited by W. Vivian Davies, Jan Assmann, and Günter Burkard, pp. 175–217. London: KPI.

2000   The First Intermediate Period (c. 2160–2055 BC). In *The Oxford History of Ancient Egypt*, edited by Ian Shaw, pp. 118–147. Oxford: Oxford University Press.

2005   Bemerkungen zu den Felsinschriften des Alten Reiches auf Elephantine. In *Texte und Denkmäler des ägyptischen Alten Reiches*, edited by Stephan Johannes Seidlmayer, pp. 297–308. Berlin-Brandenburgische Akademie der Wissenschaften, Thesaurus Linguae Aegyptie 3. Berlin: Achet Verlag, Dr. Norbert Dürring.

Serafini, Luigi

1981   *Codex Seraphinianus.* Milan: Franco Maria Ricci.

Sethe, Kurt

1928   *Dramatische Texte zu altägyptischen Mysterienspielen.* Untersuchungen zur Geschichte und Altertumskunde Ägyptens 10. Leipzig: J. C. Hinrichs.

Sezgin, Fuat

1982   *Lexikographie.* Vol. 8 of *Geschichte des arabischen Schrifttums.* Leiden: E. J. Brill.

Shanghai bowuguan

1959   *Yu ding Ke ding.* Shanghai: Shanghai bowuguan.

Shaw, Allen A.

1938–1939   An Overlooked Numeral System of Antiquity. *National Mathematics Magazine* 13:368–372.

Shedid, Abdel-Ghaffar

1994   *Die Felsgräber von Beni Hassan in Mittelägypten.* Zaberns Bildbände zur Archäologie 16. Mainz, Germany: Philipp von Zabern.

Shinkawa, Tokio

2002   *Kanji bunka no naritachi to tenkai.* Nihonshi riburetto 9. Tokyo: Yamakawa shuppansha.

Shirakawa Shizuka

2004   Kinbun tsūshaku 11: No. 59 [1965]. In *Shirakawa Shizuka chosakushū bekkan: Kinbun tsūshaku,* vol. 1, part 2, edited by Shizuka Shirakawa, pp. 591–619. Tokyo: Heibonsha.

Shirane, Haruo

2005   *Classical Japanese: A Grammar.* New York: Columbia University Press.

Sigrist, Marcel

1984   *Neo-Sumerian Account Texts in the Horn Archaeological Museum.* Berrien Springs, MI: Andrews University Press.

Silverman, David P.

2000   The Threat-Formula and Biographical Text in the Tomb of Hezi at Saqqara. *Journal of the American Research Center in Egypt* 37:1–13.

Silverman, David P., William Kelly Simpson, and Josef Wegner, eds.

2009   *Archaism and Innovation: Studies in the Culture of Middle Kingdom Egypt.* New Haven, CT: Department of Near Eastern Languages and Civilizations, Yale University; Philadelphia: University of Pennsylvania Museum of Archaeology and Anthropology.

Silverstein, Michael

1979   Language Structure and Linguistic Ideology. In *The Elements: A Parasession on Linguistic Units and Levels,* edited by Paul R. Clyne, William F. Hanks, and Carol L. Hofbauer, pp. 193–247. Chicago: Chicago Linguistic Society.

Simpson, William Kelly

1963   *Papyrus Reisner I: The Records of a Building Project in the Reign of Sesostris I, Transcription and Commentary.* Boston: Museum of Fine Arts.

1986   *Papyrus Reisner IV: Personal Accounts of the Early Twelfth Dynasty, Transcription and Commentary, with Indices to Papyri Reisner I–IV and Palaeography to Papyrus Reisner IV.* Sections F, G prepared by Peter der Manuelian. Boston: Museum of Fine Arts.

1991   Mentuhotep, Vizier of Sesostris I, Patron of Art and Architecture. *Mitteilungen des Deutschen Archäologischen Instituts Abteilung Kairo* 47:331–340.

2009   Rulers and Administrators—Dynasty 12: The Rule of the House of Itj-towy with Some Personal Reminiscences. In *Archaism and Innovation: Studies in the Culture of Middle Kingdom Egypt,* edited by David P. Silverman, William Kelly Simpson, and Josef Wegner, pp. 295–304. New Haven, CT: Department of Near Eastern Languages and Civilizations, Yale University; Philadelphia: University of Pennsylvania Museum of Archaeology and Anthropology.

Skjærvø, P. Oktor

1996   Aramaic Scripts for Iranian Languages. In *The World's Writing Systems,* edited by Peter T. Daniels and William Bright, pp. 515–535. New York: Oxford University Press.

Smalley, William A., Chia Koua Vang, and Gnia Yee Yang

1990   *Mother of Writing: The Origin and Development of a Hmong Messianic Script.* Chicago: University of Chicago Press.

Smith, David Eugene, and L. C. Karpinski

1911   *The Hindu-Arabic Numerals.* Boston: Ginn.

Smith, Mary Elizabeth

1973   *Picture Writing from Ancient Southern Mexico.* Norman: University of Oklahoma Press.

1983   The Mixtec Writing System. In *The Cloud People: Divergent Evolution of the Zapotec and Mixtec Civilizations,* edited by Kent V. Flannery and Joyce Marcus, pp. 238–244. New York: Academic Press.

2005   The Codex Muro as a Land Document. In *Painted Books and Indigenous Knowledge in Mesoamerica: Manuscript Studies in Honor of Mary Elizabeth Smith*, edited by Elizabeth Boone, pp. 383–414. Middle American Research Institute Publication 69. New Orleans: Middle American Research Institute, Tulane University.

Smith, Mary Elizabeth, and Ross Parmenter
1991   *The Codex Tulane*. New Orleans: Middle American Research Institute, Tulane University.

Smith, Stuart Tyson
1990   Administration at the Egyptian Middle Kingdom Frontier: Sealings from Uronarti and Askut. In *Aegean Seals, Sealings and Administration: Proceedings of the NEH-Dickson Conference of the Program in Aegean Scripts and Prehistory of the Department of Classics, University of Texas at Austin, January 11–13, 1989*, edited by Thomas G. Palaima, pp. 197–219. Aegaeum 5. Liège, Belgium: Université de Liège.

2001   Sealing, Literacy and Administration in the Middle Kingdom. *Cahiers de Recherche de l'Institut de Papyrologie et Egyptologie de Lille* 22:171–194.

Smither, Paul C.
1945   The Semnah Despatches. *Journal of Egyptian Archaeology* 31:3–10.

Società italiana per la ricerca dei papiri greci e latini in Egitto
1912   *Papiri greci e latini*. Florence: Tipografia E. Ariani.

Sollberger, Edmond
1966   *Business and Administrative Correspondence under the Kings of Ur*. Texts from Cuneiform Sources 1. Locust Valley, NY: Augustin Publishers.

Staehelin, Elisabeth
1990   Zu den Farben der Hieroglyphen. In *Zwei ramessidische Königsgräber: Ramses IV. und Ramses VII.*, edited by Erik Hornung, pp. 101–119. Theben 11. Mainz, Germany: Philipp von Zabern.

Starcky, Jean
1966   Pétra et la Nabatène. In *Dictionnaire de la Bible: Supplément VII*, edited by L. Pirot, Robert A. Pirot, Henry Cazelles, and André Feuillet, pp. 886–1017. Paris: Letouzey et Ané.

Steensberg, Axel
1989   *Hard Grains, Irrigation, Numerals and Script in the Rise of Civilizations*. Copenhagen: Royal Danish Academy of Sciences and Letters.

Steiner, Richard C.
2011   *Early Northwest Semitic Serpent Spells in the Pyramid Texts*. Harvard Semitic Studies 61. Winona Lake, IN: Eisenbrauns.

Steinkeller, Piotr
2003   An Ur III Manuscript of the Sumerian King List. In *Literatur, Politik und Recht in Mesopotamien: Festschrift für Claus Wilcke*, edited by Walther

Sallaberger, Konrad Volk, and Annette Zgoll, pp. 267–292. Orientalia Biblica et Christiana 14. Wiesbaden, Germany: Harrassowitz.

Stone, Lawrence

1949   Elizabethan Overseas Trade. *The Economic History Review*, n.s., 2:30–58.

Street, Brian V.

1984   *Literacy in Theory and Practice.* Cambridge: Cambridge University Press.

Street, Brian V., ed.

1993   *Cross-Cultural Approaches to Literacy.* Cambridge: Cambridge University Press.

Strohmaier, Gotthard

2003   *Hellas im Islam: Interdisziplinäre Studien zur Ikonographie, Wissenschaft und Religionsgeschichte.* Wiesbaden, Germany: Harrassowitz.

Strudwick, Nigel

2005   *Texts from the Pyramid Age.* Writings from the Ancient World 16. Atlanta, GA: Society of Biblical Literature.

Struik, Dirk J.

1968   The Prohibition of the Use of Arabic Numerals in Florence. *Archives Internationales d'Histoire des Sciences* 21:291–294.

Stuart, David

1989   The Maya Artist: An Iconographic and Epigraphic Analysis. B.A. thesis, Princeton University.

1990   *A New Carved Panel from the Palenque Area.* Research Reports on Ancient Maya Writing 32. Washington, DC: Center for Maya Research.

2002   Spreading Wings: A Possible Origin of the k'i Syllable. *Mesoweb.* Electronic document, http://www.mesoweb.com/stuart/notes/Wings.pdf.

2005   *The Inscriptions from Temple XIX at Palenque.* San Francisco: Pre-Columbian Art Research Institute.

Stuart, David, and Ian Graham

2003   *Corpus of Maya Hieroglyphic Inscriptions*, vol. 9, part 1: *Piedras Negras.* Cambridge, MA: Peabody Museum of Archaeology and Ethnology, Harvard University.

Stuart, David, and Stephen Houston

1994   *Classic Maya Place Names.* Studies in Pre-Columbian Art and Archaeology 33. Washington, DC: Dumbarton Oaks.

Suleiman, Yasir

2007   'Arabiyya. *In Encyclopedia of Arabic Language and Linguistics*, vol. 1, edited by Kees Versteegh, pp. 173–178. Leiden: E. J. Brill.

al-Ṣūlī, Abū Bakr

1341   *Adab al-kuttāb [The Craft of Scribes].* Edited by M. Bahja al-Atharī. Baghdad: al-Maktaba al-'Arabiyya.

Swiggers, Pierre

1996   Transmission of the Phoenician Script to the West. In *The World's Writing Systems*, edited by Peter T. Daniels and William Bright, pp. 261–270. New York: Oxford University Press.

Taisbak, C. M.
1965   Roman Numerals and the Abacus. *Classica et Medievalia* 26:147–160.

Tambiah, Stanley J.
1968   The Magical Power of Words. *Man* 3:175–208.

Tate, Carolyn E.
1992   *Yaxchilan: The Design of a Maya Ceremonial City.* Austin: University of Texas Press.

Taube, Karl
1983   The Teotihuacan Spider Woman. *Journal of Latin American Lore* 9:107–189.
1988   A Prehispanic Maya Katun Wheel. *Journal of Anthropological Research* 44:183–203.

al-Tawḥīdī, Abū Ḥayyān
1953   *al-Imtāʻ wa-l-muʼānasa.* 2nd ed. Edited by Aḥmad Amīn and Aḥmad al-Zayn. Beirut: al-Maktaba al-ʻAṣriyya.

Tedlock, Dennis
1985   *Popol Vuh: The Definitive Edition of the Mayan Book of the Dawn of Life and the Glories of Gods and Kings.* New York: Simon and Schuster.

Terrace, Edward L. B.
1968   *Egyptian Paintings of the Middle Kingdom.* London: George Allen and Unwin.

Thompson, J. Eric S.
1962   *A Catalog of Maya Hieroglyphs.* Norman: University of Oklahoma Press.
1970   *Maya History and Religion.* Norman: University of Oklahoma Press.
1972   *A Commentary on the Dresden Codex.* Philadelphia: American Philosophical Society.

Threatte, Leslie
1980   *Phonology.* Vol. 1 of *The Grammar of Attic Inscriptions.* Berlin: De Gruyter.

Throop, Liz
2004   Thinking on Paper: Hindu-Arabic Numerals in European Typography. *Visible Language* 38:290–303.

Thureau-Dangin, François
1939   Sketch of a History of the Sexagesimal System. Translated by S. Gandz. *Osiris* 7:95–141.

Trigger, Bruce G.
2003   *Understanding Early Civilizations: A Comparative Study.* Cambridge: Cambridge University Press.

Tsujimura, Natsuko
1996   *An Introduction to Japanese Linguistics.* Cambridge, MA: Blackwell.

Tsukishima, Hiroshi
1965   *Heian jidai no kanbun kundokugo ni tsukite no kenkyū.* Rev. ed. Tokyo: Tōkyō daigaku shuppankai.
1969   *Heian jidaigo shinron.* Tokyo: Tōkyō daigaku shuppankai.
1981   *Kana.* Nihongo no sekai 5. Tokyo: Chūō kōronsha.

Tuchscherer, Konrad T.

1996   The Kikakui (Mende) Syllabary and Number Writing System. Ph.D. diss., London School of Oriental and African Studies.

Twine, Nanette Gottleib

1991   *Language and the Modern State: The Reform of Written Japanese.* London: Routledge.

Ueda, Akiko

2008   Sound, Scripts, and Styles: *Kanbun kundokutai* and the National Language Reforms of 1880s Japan. *Review of Japanese Culture and Society* 20:133–156.

Ullman, Berthold L.

1932   *Ancient Writing and Its Influence.* New York: Longmans, Green and Co.

Ullmann, Manfred

1979   *Wa-khayru l-ḥadīthi mā kāna laḥnan. Beiträge zur Lexikographie des Klassischen Arabisch Nr. 1.* Munich, Germany: Bayerische Akademie der Wissenschaften.

Umehara Sueji

1934   *Hakutsuru kikkinshū.* Hyōgo, Japan: Hakutsuru Bijutsukan.

Urton, Gary

2005   Khipu Archives: Duplicate Accounts and Identity Labels in the Inka Knotted String Records. *Latin American Antiquity* 16:147–167.

Vachek, Josef

1989   Some Remarks on the Stylistics of Written Language. In *Written Language Revisited,* selected and edited by Philip A. Leulsdorff, pp. 43–52. Amsterdam: Benjamins.

Valbelle, Dominique, and Charles Bonnet

1996   *Le sanctuaire d'Hathor, maîtresse de la turquoise: Sérabit el-Khadim au Moyen Empire.* Paris and Aosta, Italy: Picard.

Vanhove, Martine

1993   *La langue maltaise.* Wiesbaden, Germany: Harrassowitz.

van Stone, Mark

2000   *Identifying Individual Hands in the Monuments of K'inich Ahkal Mo' Naab of Palenque.* Report submitted to FAMSI. Electronic document, http://www.famsi.org/reports/99027/index.html 8.

Veldhuis, Niek C.

1997   Elementary Education at Nippur: The Lists of Trees and Wooden Objects. Ph.D. diss., University of Groningen. Electronic document, http://irs.ub.rug.nl/ppn/30177613X.

2005   Review of Markus Hilgert, *Cuneiform Texts from the Ur III Period in the Oriental Institute,* vol. 2: *Drehem Administrative Documents from the Reign of Amar-Suena. Orientalia* 74:116–119.

2006   How Did They Learn Cuneiform? "Tribute/Word List C" as an Elementary Exercise. In *Approaches to Sumerian Literature: Studies in Honour of Stip (H. L. J. Vanstiphout),* edited by Piotr Michalowski and Niek Veldhuis, pp. 181–200. Leiden: E. J. Brill / STYX.

2008a   Kurigalzu's Statue Inscription. *Journal of Cuneiform Studies* 60:25–51.

2008b   Orthography and Politics: Adda, "Carcass" and Kur₉ "To Enter." In *On the Third Dynasty of Ur: Studies in Honor of Marcel Sigrist*, edited by Piotr Michalowski, pp. 223–229. *Journal of Cuneiform Studies* 1, suppl. no. 1.

2008c   Old Babylonian Documents in the Hearst Museum of Anthropology, Berkeley. *Revue d'assyriologie et d'archéologie orientale* 102:49–70.

Venuti, Lawrence

2004   *The Translation Studies Reader.* 2nd ed. New York: Routledge.

Versteegh, Kees

1997a   *The Arabic Linguistic Tradition.* London: Routledge.

1997b   *The Arabic Language.* Edinburgh: Edinburgh University Press.

Vetter, Emil

1953   *Handbuch der italischen Dialekte.* Heidelberg, Germany: Carl Winter Univeritätsverlag.

Vogelsang, Friedrich, and Alan H. Gardiner

1908   *Die Klagen des Bauern.* Hieratische Papyrus aus den Königlichen Museen zu Berlin 4, Literarische Texte des Mittleren Reiches 1. Leipzig: J. C. Hinrichs.

Vogt, Evon

1976   *Tortillas for the Gods: A Symbolic Analysis of Zinacanteco Rituals.* Cambridge, MA: Harvard University Press.

Vovin, Alexander

2003   *A Reference Grammar of Classical Japanese Prose.* London: RoutledgeCurzon.

Wachter, Rudolf

1986   Die etruskische und venetische Silbenpunktierung. *Museum Helveticum* 43:111–126.

2005   Annex zur Fragment 3 der Graffiti von Eretria. *Zeitschrift für Papyrologie und Epigraphik* 151:84–86.

Waley, Arthur

1938   *The Analects of Confucius.* London: George Allen and Unwin.

Walker, Willard, and James Sarbaugh

1993   The Early History of the Cherokee Syllabary. *Ethnohistory* 40:70–94.

Wallace, Rex

2004   Sabellian Languages. In *The Cambridge Encyclopedia of the World's Ancient Languages*, edited by Roger D. Woodward, pp. 812–839. Cambridge: Cambridge University Press.

Wallerstein, Immanuel

1974   *Capitalist Agriculture and the Origins of European World-Economy in the Sixteenth Century.* Vol. 1 of *The Modern World-System.* New York: Academic Press.

Ward, William A., and Olga Tufnell

1978   *Studies on Scarab Seals I–II.* Warminster, UK: Aris & Phillips.

Wardley, Peter, and Pauline White

2003   The Arithmeticke Project: A Collaborative Research Study of the Diffusion of Hindu-Arabic Numerals. *Family and Community History* 6:5–18.

Wegner, Josef

2004   Social and Historical Implications of Sealings of the King's Daughter Reniseneb and Other Women at the Town of Wah-Sut. In *Scarabs of the Second Millenium BC from Egypt, Nuba, Crete and the Levant: Chronological and Historical Implications, Papers of a Symposium, Vienna, 10th–13th of January 2002*, edited by Manfred Bieatk and Ernst Czerny, pp. 221–240. Contributions to the Chronology of the Eastern Mediterranean 8. Vienna: Verlag der Österreichischen Akademie der Wissenschaften.

2007   *The Mortuary Temple of Senwosret III at Abydos*. Publications of the Pennsylvania-Yale Expedition to Egypt. New Haven, CT: Peabody Museum of Natural History.

Wenger, Etienne

1998   *Communities of Practice: Learning as a Social System*. Electronic document, http://www.co-i-l.com/coil/knowledge-garden/cop/lss.shtml.

1999   *Communities of Practice: Learning, Meaning, and Identity*. Cambridge: Cambridge University Press.

Whatmough, Joshua

1933   *The Prae-Italic Dialects of Italy*, vol. II: *The Raetic, Lepontic, Gallic, East-Italic, Messapic, and Sicel Inscriptions*. Cambridge, MA: Harvard University Press.

Wichmann, Søren

2006   Mayan Historical Linguistics and Epigraphy: A New Synthesis. *Annual Review of Anthropology* 35:279–294.

Widmer, Ghislaine

n.d.   Les inscriptions démotiques sur os de Tebtynis. In *Varia scripta*, edited by Paolo Gallazzi. Cairo: Institut Français d'Archéologie Orientale.

Wild, Stefan

1965   *Das Kitāb al-'Ayn und die arabische Lexikographie*. Wiesbaden, Germany: Harrassowitz.

Wilkinson, Alix

1971   *Ancient Egyptian Jewellry*. London: Methuen.

Willems, Harco

1988   *Chests of Life: A Study of the Typology and Conceptual Development of Middle Kingdom Standard Class Coffins*. Mededelingen en Verhandelingen van het Voorasiatisch-Egyptisch Genootschap "Ex Oriente Lux" 25. Leiden: Ex Oriente Lux.

2008   *Les Textes des Sarcophages et la démocratie: Eléments d'une histoire culturelle du Moyen Empire égyptien*. Paris: Cybele.

REFERENCES

Williams, Henrik

2004   Reasons for Runes. In *The First Writing: Script Invention as History and Process*, edited by Stephen D. Houston, pp. 262–273. Cambridge: Cambridge University Press.

Williams, Jack

1995   Mathematics and the Alloying of Coinage, 1202–1700. *Annals of Science* 52:213–263.

1997   Numerals and Numbering in Early Printed English Bibles and Associated Literature. *Journal of the Printing Historical Society* 26:5–13.

Williams García, Roberto

1970   *El mito en una comunidad indígena: Pisa Flores, Veracruz.* Cuernavaca, Mexico: Centro Internacional de Documentación.

Wilson, Richard

1995   *Maya Resurgence in Guatemala.* Norman: University of Oklahoma Press.

Winfield Capitaine, Fernando

1988   *La Estela 1 de La Mojarra, Veracruz, México.* Research Reports on Ancient Maya Writing 16. Washington, DC: Center for Maya Research.

Wingo, E. Otha

1972   *Latin Punctuation in the Classical Age.* The Hague: Mouton.

Winter, Erich

1967   Der Entwurf für eine Türinschrift auf einem ägyptischen Papyrus. *Nachrichten der Akademie der Wissenschaften in Göttingen I, philologisch-historische Klasse* 3:59–80.

Wittgenstein, Ludwig

1958   *Philosophical Investigations: The English Text of the Third Edition.* Translated by G. E. M. Anscombe. New York: Macmillan Publishing.

Wixted, John Timothy

1998   *Kanbun:* Histories of Japanese Literature, and Japanologists. *Sino-Japanese Studies* 10:23–31.

2006   *A Handbook to Classical Japanese.* Ithaca, NY: East Asia Program, Cornell University.

Wollheim, Richard

1974   *On Art and Mind: Essays and Lectures.* Cambridge, MA: Harvard University Press.

Wünsch, Richard

1897   Defixionum Tabellae Atticae. *Inscriptiones Graecae 3.3*, appendix. Berlin: De Gruyter.

Yajnik, Kirit S.

1998   A 32-Base Numeral System. *Current Science* 74:283.

Yamada, Yoshio
1935   *Kanbun kundoku ni yorite tsutaeraretaru gohō*. Tokyo: Hōbunkan.

Yerkes, Robert M.
1904   The Use of Roman Numerals. *Science*, n.s., 20:309–310.

Yetts, W. Perceval
1929   *The George Eumorfopoulos Collection Catalogue of the Chinese and Corean Bronzes, Sculpture, Jades, Jewellery, and Miscellaneous Objects*, vol. 1: *Bronzes: Ritual and Other Vessels, Weapons Etc.* London: E. Benn.

Yi, Sŏng-si
2005   Kodai Chōsen no moji bunka: Miete kita moji no kakehashi. In *Kodai Nihon moji no kita michi: Kodai Chūgoku/Chōsen kara rettō e*, edited by Hirakawa Minami, pp. 32–65. Tokyo: Taishūkan shoten.

Yoshida, Kanehiko, Hiroshi Tsukishima, Ishizuka Harumichi, and Masayuki Tsukimoto
2001   *Kuntengo jiten*. Tokyo: Tōkyōdō shuppan.

al-Zajjājī
1973 [1393]   *al-Īḍāḥ fī ' ilal al-naḥw*. Edited by Māzin Mubārak. Beirut: Dār al-Nafā'is.
1995   *al-Īḍāḥ fī ' ilal al-naḥw [The Explanation of Linguistic Causes]*. Translated by Kees Versteegh. Amsterdam and Philadelphia: John Benjamins.

Zayyāt, Ḥabīb
1992   *al-Wirāqa wa-ṣinā'at al-kitāba wa-mu'jam al-sufun [Book Production and the Writer's Craft and The Dictionary of Ships]*. Beirut: Dār al-Ḥamrā'.

Zender, Marc
1999   Diacritical Marks and Underspelling in the Classic Maya Script: Implications for Decipherment. M.A. thesis, University of Calgary.
2006   Review of *The New Catalog of Maya Hieroglyphs*, vol 1: *The Classic Period Inscriptions*, by Martha J. Macri and Matthew G. Looper. *Ethnohistory* 53:439–441.

Zhang, Jiajie, and Donald A. Norman
1995   A Representational Analysis of Numeration Systems. *Cognition* 57:271–295.

Zhongguo shehui kexue yanjiusuo
1984–1994   *Yin Zhou jinwen jicheng*. Beijing: Zhonghua shuju.

Zimmermann, Günter
1956   *Die Hieroglyphen der Maya-Handschriften*. Abhandlungen aus dem Gebiet der Auslandskunde Band 62-Reihe B. Hamburg, Germany: Universität Hamburg.

al-Zubaydī, M. b. al-Ḥasan
1981   *Laḥn al-'āmma*. Edited by 'Abd al-'Azīz Maṭar. Cairo: Dār al-Ma'ārif.
1984   *Ṭabaqāt al-naḥwiyyīn wa-l-lughawiyyīn*. Edited by M. Abū l-Faḍl Ibrāhīm. Cairo: Dār al-Ma'ārif.

Index

relation to language, 135–137; and *kundoku* method, 169–172; and literacy, 185n22; and logographs, 177–178, 184n18; Middle, 182n10; and monosyllabicity, 136–138, 157n2, 157n5, 162; and phonographs (*kana*), 182n7, 184n18; Qiu Xigui's study of, xix–xx, 135–136, 138–143; Standard, 141–142, 166; on wood tablet, 152. *See also* Japanese writing; logographics; specific dynasties

Chinese Writing (Qiu Xigui), 135–136, 138–143
Chrisomalis, Stephen, xvii, xxi
Christian Latin texts, 91
Christianity, 91, 209, 216, 222
Chrysostomus, Johannes, 247
Church Slavonic numerals, 250
Claudius (Roman emperor), 75–76, 91n3
Codex Dresden, 211
Codex Madrid, 201
Codex Muro, 217, 222–227
Codex Selden, 221
Codex Seraphinianus (Serafini), 252
Codex Tulane, 226
Codex Vaticanus, 211
codices, 188, 190–192, 201, 210–211, 216–217, 219, 222–227, 252. *See also* specific names
codicological conventions, 103–105
Coe, Michael, 196, 200
Coffin Texts, 60–61
coffins, 50, 59–61
coins, 160, 247–248
colonialism, xxi, 192, 217–219, 224–225, 252. *See also* Spanish colonialism
Columna rostrata, 243–244
Commentary on the Sentences of Peter Lombard (Durandus), 247
computation, 231, 242, 245, 248, 252, 254n8, 254n10
Confucian texts, 169, 176, 183n12
connected text. *See* sentences
consonants: and Arabic script, 93–98, 102, 106, 112, 117; and Chinese script, 162–163; and Egyptian script, 127–128; and Greek alphabet, 126–127, 129; and Indic script, 122, 130–131, 132n2, 133n7; and Japanese writing, 182n9; and Semitic script, 129; and stroke reduction/reordering, 122–124. *See also* abjad (consonant-based alphabet); Aramaic
copyists, 17, 104, 112–113, 161, 222. *See also* scribes
Cortés, Hernán, 221
cosmology, 181, 185n23
Coulmas, Florian, 96, 112
counting-boards. *See* abacus
cryptographic writing, 37

Cuanachinicha, Guerrero, Mexico, 227
cultural: attitudes toward writing, 180; change, 196; conventions, 234–235; influences, xxi, 35, 76, 120, 129, 131, 240, 252; materials, xviii; production, xv; systems, xv; texts, 61–62; transmission, xiv, 241, 250; values, 50
cuneiform writing system, xvii, 12, 133n9, 181; as administrative tool, 22–23; developments/changes in, 3–8, 22; and numerals, 233, 253; orthographic changes in, 8–11; teaching of, 17, 22; and Ur III dynasty, 8–11
curers, 212–214
cursive writing, xxi–xxii, 11–12, 22; aesthetic qualities of, 32; in ancient Egypt, 28–29, 35, 50–59; changes in, 50, 103–104; and Chinese/Japanese scripts, 165–167, 174, 177, 184n19; Demotic, 62–63; and hieroglyphs, 31–32, 43, 45, 48–49, 55–56, 58–62, 239; and Maya script, 191–192; and numerals, 240–241; Roman, 77
cursivization, xviii–xix, 166, 177, 237–239

Daniels, Peter, 94, 119
dedicatory texts, 79–80, 82–85, 92n4, 243–244
DeFrancis, John, 180
Delta, Egypt, 61
demographic collapse, xv, 221, 224
Demotic cursive script, 62–63
demotic numeration, 239–241
Devanāgarī (India): numerals, 244; script, 125, 132n2
diacritics, 98–102, 106–107, 111–112, 123, 129, 176, 181, 182n9
dictionaries, 113, 171, 211
Diem, Werner, 99
diglossia, xiv, xx, 71, 110
Diringer, David, 119
display writing, xviii, xx–xxi, 27–28, 31, 39, 43, 50, 143, 145, 156, 202, 207, 220, 233
divination: items for, 20, 212–214; practitioners of, 212–214; texts of, 7, 13, 15, 210–211, 213, 233
Dos Pilas site (Maya), 195
Dravidian language, 101, 130
"Duenos" vase, 78–79, 83, 85
Durandus of Saint-Pourçain, 246–247
Durrat al-ghawāṣṣ fī awhām al-khawāṣṣ (al-Ḥarīrī), 111
Dutch language/people, 102

East Asia, 180–181, 185n23
economics, xxi, 236, 250–251
economy, principle of, 121–123, 195
effigies, 40, 42

lexical lists/texts, 5, 20
Liberia, 251
Lienzo of Ocotepec (Mexico), 220
lienzos (Mixteca histories), 216–221, 225–226
limestone, 28–29, 35, 47–48, 82–83
linear alphabet, 127–128
linear writing, 11, 19–20, 28
linguistics, xviii–xix, 8, 11, 39, 58, 71, 76, 95, 100, 103, 106, 110, 113, 126, 136, 175, 184n19
Lipiński, Edward, 112
Lipp, Frank, 214
literacy: in Egypt, 43, 59, 62; ideological model of, xiv; in Japan, 161, 172, 175, 177, 181, 183n14, 185n22; in Mexico, 209, 211; spread of, 247
literary texts: of ancient Egypt, 35, 50–51, 57–59; Arabic, 105–106, 114; Old Babylonian, 13–15, 17; and Roman numerals, 249; vernacular (Japanese), 161, 167
litteratura, 71
logographics, 8, 30; and Arabic script, 94, 97; in Chinese script, 137; and cuneiform writing, 3, 6–7; in Egyptian script, 127–128; evolution of, 141; and Japanese writing, xx, 112, 163, 169, 172–175, 177–181, 184n18, 185n23, 185n24; and Maya script, 188, 193; and Sumerian/Akkadian writing, 6–7
logograms, 6–7, 67
Looper, Matthew G., 190
Lukalla, 10–11
Lurie, David, xiv, xvii, xx

Macri, Martha J., 190
magical spells, texts for, 27, 51–53, 56–57, 160, 201
Magliano Sabina, Italy, 78
Mahadevan system, 131
Malayalam, India, 130
Maltese language, 102
Man 'yōshū, 173, 182n7
Mandaic script, 96–97
Mandarin, 180
maps, 195, 217, 220–221, 223
Marcus, Joyce, 198
Mari (of Old Babylonia), 11, 15, 23n4
Marquis of Xing, 147
Marquis Yi tomb/artifacts, 143, 145, 151, 155–156
Marsiliana d'Albegna (Etruria), 71–72
Martin, Simon, 194
mathematics, 13, 15, 229, 245–246, 248, 252
Mawangdui manuscript, 137–138
Maya: languages, 193–194, 233; people, 213
Maya script, xvii, 103; background of, 187–189;

changes in, 196–207; of Classic period, 190–194, 196; codices of, 188, 190–192, 201; earliest examples of, 197–198; of Early Classic period, 198–199, 203, 205–207; execution of, 196–200; as expressive practice, 187, 199; glyph blocks of, 31, 197, 199; glyphs of, xx, 187–191, 193–204, 207–208, 208n1, 208n2; iconic origin of, 203–204; of Late Classic period, xx, 194–196, 198–199, 201, 203–207; of Late Postclassic period, 190; and motivation, 196, 202–207; and numerals, 233, 235, 250; Postclassic, 191–192, 196–197, 199, 201; and pottery, 192, 196–197, 200; Preclassic, xx, 189, 198, 202, 205–206; prior studies of, xx, 189–196; on stela, 193; of Terminal Classic period, 191–193, 196, 199, 205–206; transmission of, 196, 200–202, 205, 207
Mayapan, Mexico, 199
Mazatec people (Mexico), 212–214
McCarter, Kyle, xvii–xix
McLuhan, Marshall, 106
medical texts, 13, 15, 27, 52–53, 56
medieval era, 120, 131, 240–241, 249, 254n8
Mediterranean world, 39, 70
Memphis/Memphite area (Egypt), 29–30, 34, 40, 46, 61
Menard, Pierre, 170
Mende script/numerals (Sierra Leone), 252
Mentuhotep (Egyptian vizier), 46
Meroitic alphabet, 30
Mesoamerica, 198; affected by diseases, 221; and diviners/curers/shaman, 212–214; languages of, 211; and numerals, 233; and scripts with sacred meaning, xiv; study of, xx–xxi. *See also* Mixtec language
Mesoamerican texts, xix, xx–xxi; and act of seeing, 211–214, 224; and books of ritual knowledge, 214–215; and *caciques*, 223–226; destroyed by the Spanish, 215–216; and land/property disputes, 215–216, 225–227; native readers of, 220–227; pictorial format of, 210, 215, 217–219, 222; and reading practices, 211, 213, 224; and Spanish colonialism, 209–211. *See also* Mixtec scripts/texts; pre-Columbian writing/texts
Mesopotamia, 11, 21, 96, 233, 242
metatextual signs/information, 67, 87
metrological systems, 4
Mexican scripts, xxi, 234–235. *See also* Mesoamerican texts; Mixtec script/texts; specific cities
Mexico City, Mexico, 222
Middle Ages, 87
middle class, 35, 37, 110

Middle East, 251
Middle Persian, 103, 239
Miller, R. A., 183n15
Minoan palace (Crete), 78
Minturnae, Italy, 92n4
Mixtec language, 209–210, 218–219
Mixtec script/texts, xvii, xxi; specific codices; and alphabetic registers, 220, 222, 224–227; and demographic collapse, 221; dominated by the noble house, 225; European influence on, 218–219; as genealogies, 211, 217–219; and land/property disputes, 222, 225–226; *lienzos*, 216–221, 225–226; pictorial format of, 218–223, 225–227; and reading practices, 222; tones marked in, 209, 218–219; visual-arts qualities of, 210. *See also* Mesoamerican texts
Möller, Georg, 238
Mommsen, Theodor, 88
Monaghan, John, xvii, xxi
monosyllabicity, 131, 136–138, 157n2, 157n5, 162
monumental forms of writing, 28, 83, 142–143, 188–189, 192–193, 238, 240–241. *See also* hieroglyphs
monuments: of ancient Egypt, 25, 27, 31–35, 37, 39, 43, 44, 59, 61–62, 238; of ancient Italy, 83, 85, 88–89; of Mexico, 192
Monumentum Ancyranum, 88–89
Morley, Sylvanus G., 191–192
morphemes, 6, 66, 112, 138, 157n2, 157n5, 162–164
morphology, 5–6, 95, 108–109, 111–112, 123, 126, 179
mortuary: chapels, 48; complexes, 40, 56–57; compositions, 61; paraphernalia, 59; temples, 35, 50, 56–57
Mozarabs (Arab Christians), 249
Mufaḍḍaliyyāt (al-Muffaḍḍal), 106
muhmal (undotted) signs, 98–99
mummies, 77
Mundy, Barbara, 216, 220
murals, 202
musical notation, 234
Muslims, 102, 108
Mustanīr, Muḥammad b. al-. *See* Quṭrub
Muthallath (Quṭrub), 115

Nabatean script, 94, 97–100
Nagʿ el-Deir, Egypt, 50
Nahuas of Veracruz, Mexico, 212–213
Nahuatl language/texts, 209, 211, 219–220
Nara, Japan, 161, 165, 174, 184n18
narrative texts, 17
National Museum of China, 148–149

Near East, 36, 238
Nihon shoki, 173
Nile River, 27
Ninurta temple, 20
Nippur (Egypt), 20
Nissen, Hans, 4
North Abydos, Egypt, 48
North Africa, 240
notebooks, 105–106, 214–215
Nubia, Egypt, 51
numerical notation systems, xvii, xxi; acrophonic, 248–249; and aesthetics, 242–244; alphabetization of, 240; and colonial contexts, 252; as communication, 229, 250; and decimals, 231, 234, 240, 243, 252–253; extinction of, 250–253; five basic structures/principals of, 231–232, 237–238; history/definition of, 229–236; modern transformations of, 250–253; and paragrams, 254n2; and phonetics, 237, 252, 254n6; ready interpretation of, 234–235, 249; replacement of, 244–251; transformation/innovation of, 236–244; translinguistic nature of, 236, 251; and typology, 232–234; used simultaneously, 248–250; and world-systems theory, 250–251; and writing systems, 232–236, 239, 241; written cursively, 240–241
Nūr-Suen, 10

Oaxaca, Mexico, 210–211, 225
Object Verb (OV), 170–171
Ocreatus (mathematician), 246
official documents, 82, 142–143, 152, 156
Old Assyrian letters/texts, 7–8
Old Babylonian period, xvii, 23n4; scribes trained during, 15–18; and Sumerian scribal language, 6, 242; texts of, 5, 7, 9, 13–15; two-dimensional tables of, 19–20; writing during, 11–22
Old Canaanite alphabet/script, 94–96, 99
Old Ethiopic script, 96
ondoku reading method, 173
Ong, Walter, 106
onomastic system/practice, 76, 233
oracle bones (Shang), 135, 139–140, 142, 157n9
oral: communication, 67; interpretation, 170; intonation, 67; performance, xix, 161; transmission, xiii, 103, 105–107, 110, 117, 170, 179
order/orientation, of script, 68–69, 77–84, 86, 91
Origin and Early Development of the Chinese Writing System, The (Boltz), 135–139
Oriya script (India), 125

Oscan texts (Italy), 70, 77, 83, 86
Osiris (Egyptian god), 46
Osteria dell Osa (Gabii), Italy, 78
Ottoman period, 102, 111, 237

Pahawh Hmong script/numerals (Laos), 252
Pahlavi script (Iran), 123–124, 239
painted inscriptions, 188, 190, 193, 196,
    198–200, 202, 207, 216–217, 221
Palace Tablet (Palenque, Mexico), 193
Palenque, Mexico, 193, 196, 198
Palestine, 37, 39
Palestrina, Italy, 91n2, 92n4
papyrus, 8, 27–28, 32–34, 50–58, 77, 86,
    103–104, 108, 240–241
paragrams, xviii, 68–69, 84–85, 88, 90–91, 254n2
paratexts, 65, 68
Parkinson, Richard, 37, 58
Pashto language, 102
Pepy I, King, 56–57
Pérez, Arnulfo, 227
Persians/Persian language, 102–103, 113, 181,
    237
personal digital assistants (PDAs), 121
personal names, 110, 164
Phaistos disk, 78, 85
philology, 108, 112
philosophical texts, 173
Phoenicians, 69, 71, 91n2, 94, 97, 126–128,
    230, 239
phonemes (diacritical marks), 66, 85, 109–110,
    126–127, 130, 133n7, 204, 234
phonetics, 239; and Arabic script, 93, 100; and
    Chinese script, 128, 136–137, 139–140,
    157n7; and Egyptian script, 240; and Indic
    scripts, 130–131; and Japanese writing,
    169, 184n18; and Maya script, 187, 193,
    235; and numerals, 237, 252, 254n6; and
    Roman script, 69–76, 87
phonographs/phonography: and Chinese
    script, 163–164, 182n7; and Japanese writ-
    ing, xx, 163–169, 172–181, 182n6, 182n9,
    184n18, 184n19, 184n20, 185n24; and
    numerals, 234–235
phonology, 117n5, 126, 130, 179, 182n9
pictograms, 4, 67
pictographic writing, 78, 95, 136, 139–140, 234
pictorial elements, xviii; animals, 40–49, 58; on
    coffins, 59–60; deities, 40, 42; and hiero-
    glyphs, 31–34, 39–41, 46, 48, 58–59;
    human figures, 28, 31, 40, 43, 45–47; lay-
    out of, 31; in Mesoamerican texts, xxi, 210,
    215, 217–223; of mortuary paraphernalia,
    59; and script forms, 29. See also
    Mesoamerican texts; Mixtec script/texts

Piedras Negras, Guatemala, 191, 201–203
Pike, Eunice, 214
Pillow Book, 174
plagues, 221, 224
Plautus (Italian comedy writer), 77
poetry: Arabic, 101, 105–106, 110, 113–115,
    118n7; Chinese-style, 171, 173; vernacular
    (Japanese), 165, 173–175, 177–178, 182n7
Pohl, Frederik, 252
politics, xvii–xviii, 10–11, 21–22, 34, 194, 207,
    221, 236, 240, 250
Pompeii, 77, 86
Popol Vuh, 212–213
popular scripts/texts, 142–143, 161–162, 178
Portuguese manuscript, 246
pottery, 28, 77–79, 85, 92n4, 192–193, 196–197,
    200
Praeneste, Italy, 73
Prakrit dialect, 130, 133n8
Pratica di Mare, Italy, 79–80
pre-Columbian writing/texts, 210, 215–219,
    224. See also Mesoamerican texts
prestige, xiv, xviii; of Arabic language, xix, 108;
    of Arabic texts, 110, 117; bias, 250; in
    color, 44; of Egyptian texts, 25, 28, 58–59;
    of Maya language, 194, 208n2; of Sumerian
    language, 12
printed forms, of writing, xx; commercial, 162;
    and movable-type, 167–168, 246; wood-
    block, 161–162, 176–177
proper names, 19, 110–111, 164–165
Proskouriakoff, Tatiana, 192
Proto-Canaanite script, 127
Proto-Sinaitic script, 95, 127
publishing, 162
Publius Valerius dedication statue, 82–83
punctuation, xviii, 66–67, 69, 78, 81, 84–91, 98,
    176, 181, 236
Punic script, 96–97
Puteoli, Italy, 91n2
Puzriš-Dagan site, 9–11
Pyramid Texts, 27, 33, 56–57
Pyrgi, Italy, 91n2

Q'eqchi people (Mexico), 212
Qiu Xigui, 135–136, 138–143, 145, 156, 157n7,
    157n8, 157n9, 158n13
Quintilian (professor of Latin rhetoric), 76,
    87–88
Quixote (Menard), 170
Qur'ān, 98–100, 103–105
Quṭrub, 113–116, 118n6

Rajaz poems. See poetry
Ramesseum papyri, 51–53, 55–57

School for Advanced Research Advanced Seminar Series

PUBLISHED BY SAR PRESS

CHACO & HOHOKAM: PREHISTORIC REGIONAL SYSTEMS IN THE AMERICAN SOUTHWEST
  Patricia L. Crown & W. James Judge, eds.

RECAPTURING ANTHROPOLOGY: WORKING IN THE PRESENT
  Richard G. Fox, ed.

WAR IN THE TRIBAL ZONE: EXPANDING STATES AND INDIGENOUS WARFARE
  R. Brian Ferguson &
  Neil L. Whitehead, eds.

IDEOLOGY AND PRE-COLUMBIAN CIVILIZATIONS
  Arthur A. Demarest &
  Geoffrey W. Conrad, eds.

DREAMING: ANTHROPOLOGICAL AND PSYCHOLOGICAL INTERPRETATIONS
  Barbara Tedlock, ed.

HISTORICAL ECOLOGY: CULTURAL KNOWLEDGE AND CHANGING LANDSCAPES
  Carole L. Crumley, ed.

THEMES IN SOUTHWEST PREHISTORY
  George J. Gumerman, ed.

MEMORY, HISTORY, AND OPPOSITION UNDER STATE SOCIALISM
  Rubie S. Watson, ed.

OTHER INTENTIONS: CULTURAL CONTEXTS AND THE ATTRIBUTION OF INNER STATES
  Lawrence Rosen, ed.

LAST HUNTERS–FIRST FARMERS: NEW PERSPECTIVES ON THE PREHISTORIC TRANSITION TO AGRICULTURE
  T. Douglas Price &
  Anne Birgitte Gebauer, eds.

MAKING ALTERNATIVE HISTORIES: THE PRACTICE OF ARCHAEOLOGY AND HISTORY IN NON-WESTERN SETTINGS
  Peter R. Schmidt & Thomas C. Patterson, eds.

CYBORGS & CITADELS: ANTHROPOLOGICAL INTERVENTIONS IN EMERGING SCIENCES AND TECHNOLOGIES
  Gary Lee Downey & Joseph Dumit, eds.

SENSES OF PLACE
  Steven Feld & Keith H. Basso, eds.

THE ORIGINS OF LANGUAGE: WHAT NONHUMAN PRIMATES CAN TELL US
  Barbara J. King, ed.

CRITICAL ANTHROPOLOGY NOW: UNEXPECTED CONTEXTS, SHIFTING CONSTITUENCIES, CHANGING AGENDAS
  George E. Marcus, ed.

ARCHAIC STATES
  Gary M. Feinman & Joyce Marcus, eds.

REGIMES OF LANGUAGE: IDEOLOGIES, POLITIES, AND IDENTITIES
  Paul V. Kroskrity, ed.

BIOLOGY, BRAINS, AND BEHAVIOR: THE EVOLUTION OF HUMAN DEVELOPMENT
  Sue Taylor Parker, Jonas Langer, &
  Michael L. McKinney, eds.

WOMEN & MEN IN THE PREHISPANIC SOUTHWEST: LABOR, POWER, & PRESTIGE
  Patricia L. Crown, ed.

HISTORY IN PERSON: ENDURING STRUGGLES, CONTENTIOUS PRACTICE, INTIMATE IDENTITIES
  Dorothy Holland & Jean Lave, eds.

THE EMPIRE OF THINGS: REGIMES OF VALUE AND MATERIAL CULTURE
  Fred R. Myers, ed.

CATASTROPHE & CULTURE: THE ANTHROPOLOGY OF DISASTER
  Susanna M. Hoffman &
  Anthony Oliver-Smith, eds.

URUK MESOPOTAMIA & ITS NEIGHBORS: CROSS-CULTURAL INTERACTIONS IN THE ERA OF STATE FORMATION
  Mitchell S. Rothman, ed.

REMAKING LIFE & DEATH: TOWARD AN ANTHROPOLOGY OF THE BIOSCIENCES
  Sarah Franklin & Margaret Lock, eds.

TIKAL: DYNASTIES, FOREIGNERS, & AFFAIRS OF STATE: ADVANCING MAYA ARCHAEOLOGY
  Jeremy A. Sabloff, ed.

GRAY AREAS: ETHNOGRAPHIC ENCOUNTERS
WITH NURSING HOME CULTURE
Philip B. Stafford, ed.

PLURALIZING ETHNOGRAPHY: COMPARISON
AND REPRESENTATION IN MAYA CULTURES,
HISTORIES, AND IDENTITIES
John M. Watanabe & Edward F. Fischer, eds.

AMERICAN ARRIVALS: ANTHROPOLOGY
ENGAGES THE NEW IMMIGRATION
Nancy Foner, ed.

VIOLENCE
Neil L. Whitehead, ed.

LAW & EMPIRE IN THE PACIFIC:
FIJI AND HAWAI'I
Sally Engle Merry & Donald Brenneis, eds.

ANTHROPOLOGY IN THE MARGINS
OF THE STATE
Veena Das & Deborah Poole, eds.

THE ARCHAEOLOGY OF COLONIAL
ENCOUNTERS: COMPARATIVE PERSPECTIVES
Gil J. Stein, ed.

GLOBALIZATION, WATER, & HEALTH:
RESOURCE MANAGEMENT IN TIMES OF
SCARCITY
Linda Whiteford & Scott Whiteford, eds.

A CATALYST FOR IDEAS: ANTHROPOLOGICAL
ARCHAEOLOGY AND THE LEGACY OF
DOUGLAS W. SCHWARTZ
Vernon L. Scarborough, ed.

THE ARCHAEOLOGY OF CHACO CANYON: AN
ELEVENTH-CENTURY PUEBLO REGIONAL
CENTER
Stephen H. Lekson, ed.

COMMUNITY BUILDING IN THE TWENTY-
FIRST CENTURY
Stanley E. Hyland, ed.

AFRO-ATLANTIC DIALOGUES:
ANTHROPOLOGY IN THE DIASPORA
Kevin A. Yelvington, ed.

COPÁN: THE HISTORY OF AN ANCIENT MAYA
KINGDOM
E. Wyllys Andrews & William L. Fash, eds.

THE EVOLUTION OF HUMAN LIFE HISTORY
Kristen Hawkes & Richard R. Paine, eds.

THE SEDUCTIONS OF COMMUNITY:
EMANCIPATIONS, OPPRESSIONS, QUANDARIES
Gerald W. Creed, ed.

THE GENDER OF GLOBALIZATION: WOMEN
NAVIGATING CULTURAL AND ECONOMIC
MARGINALITIES
Nandini Gunewardena & Ann Kingsolver, eds.

NEW LANDSCAPES OF INEQUALITY:
NEOLIBERALISM AND THE EROSION OF
DEMOCRACY IN AMERICA
*Jane L. Collins, Micaela di Leonardo,
& Brett Williams, eds.*

IMPERIAL FORMATIONS
*Ann Laura Stoler, Carole McGranahan,
& Peter C. Perdue, eds.*

OPENING ARCHAEOLOGY: REPATRIATION'S
IMPACT ON CONTEMPORARY RESEARCH AND
PRACTICE
Thomas W. Killion, ed.

SMALL WORLDS: METHOD, MEANING, &
NARRATIVE IN MICROHISTORY
*James F. Brooks, Christopher R. N. DeCorse,
& John Walton, eds.*

MEMORY WORK: ARCHAEOLOGIES OF
MATERIAL PRACTICES
Barbara J. Mills & William H. Walker, eds.

FIGURING THE FUTURE: GLOBALIZATION
AND THE TEMPORALITIES OF CHILDREN AND
YOUTH
Jennifer Cole & Deborah Durham, eds.

TIMELY ASSETS: THE POLITICS OF
RESOURCES AND THEIR TEMPORALITIES
*Elizabeth Emma Ferry &
Mandana E. Limbert, eds.*

DEMOCRACY: ANTHROPOLOGICAL
APPROACHES
Julia Paley, ed.

CONFRONTING CANCER: METAPHORS,
INEQUALITY, AND ADVOCACY
Juliet McMullin & Diane Weiner, eds.

PUBLISHED BY CAMBRIDGE UNIVERSITY PRESS

THE ANASAZI IN A CHANGING ENVIRONMENT
George J. Gumerman, ed.

REGIONAL PERSPECTIVES ON THE OLMEC
Robert J. Sharer & David C. Grove, eds.

THE CHEMISTRY OF PREHISTORIC HUMAN
BONE
T. Douglas Price, ed.

THE EMERGENCE OF MODERN HUMANS:
BIOCULTURAL ADAPTATIONS IN THE LATER
PLEISTOCENE
Erik Trinkaus, ed.

THE ANTHROPOLOGY OF WAR
Jonathan Haas, ed.

THE EVOLUTION OF POLITICAL SYSTEMS
Steadman Upham, ed.

CLASSIC MAYA POLITICAL HISTORY:
HIEROGLYPHIC AND ARCHAEOLOGICAL
EVIDENCE
T. Patrick Culbert, ed.

TURKO-PERSIA IN HISTORICAL PERSPECTIVE
Robert L. Canfield, ed.

CHIEFDOMS: POWER, ECONOMY, AND
IDEOLOGY
Timothy Earle, ed.

RECONSTRUCTING PREHISTORIC PUEBLO
SOCIETIES
William A. Longacre, ed.

PUBLISHED BY UNIVERSITY OF NEW MEXICO PRESS

NEW PERSPECTIVES ON THE PUEBLOS
Alfonso Ortiz, ed.

THE CLASSIC MAYA COLLAPSE
T. Patrick Culbert, ed.

SIXTEENTH-CENTURY MEXICO:
THE WORK OF SAHAGUN
Munro S. Edmonson, ed.

ANCIENT CIVILIZATION AND TRADE
Jeremy A. Sabloff &
C. C. Lamberg-Karlovsky, eds.

PHOTOGRAPHY IN ARCHAEOLOGICAL
RESEARCH
Elmer Harp, Jr., ed.

THE VALLEY OF MEXICO: STUDIES IN
PRE-HISPANIC ECOLOGY AND SOCIETY
Eric R. Wolf, ed.

EXPLANATION OF PREHISTORIC CHANGE
James N. Hill, ed.

MEANING IN ANTHROPOLOGY
Keith H. Basso & Henry A. Selby, eds.

EXPLORATIONS IN ETHNOARCHAEOLOGY
Richard A. Gould, ed.

SOUTHWESTERN INDIAN RITUAL DRAMA
Charlotte J. Frisbie, ed.

SIMULATIONS IN ARCHAEOLOGY
Jeremy A. Sabloff, ed.

SHIPWRECK ANTHROPOLOGY
Richard A. Gould, ed.

LATE LOWLAND MAYA CIVILIZATION:
CLASSIC TO POSTCLASSIC
Jeremy A. Sabloff & E. Wyllys Andrews V, eds.

PUBLISHED BY UNIVERSITY OF
CALIFORNIA PRESS

WRITING CULTURE: THE POETICS
AND POLITICS OF ETHNOGRAPHY
James Clifford &
George E. Marcus, eds.

PUBLISHED BY UNIVERSITY OF
ARIZONA PRESS

THE COLLAPSE OF ANCIENT STATES AND
CIVILIZATIONS
Norman Yoffee &
George L. Cowgill, eds.

Participants in the School for Advanced Research advanced seminar "The Shape of Script: How and Why Writing Systems Change" chaired by Stephen D. Houston, April 15–19, 2007. *Standing, from left*: Beatrice Gruendler, Stephen D. Houston, P. Kyle McCarter Jr., John Monaghan, David Lurie, Stephen Chrisomalis, Niek Veldhuis, John Baines, Richard Salomon; *kneeling, from left*: Kyle Steinke, John Bodel. Photograph by Katrina Lasko.